Christian Parenting

Christian Parenting

Wisdom and Perspectives from American History

David P. Setran

WILLIAM B. EERDMANS PUBLISHING COMPANY

GRAND RAPIDS, MICHIGAN

Wm. B. Eerdmans Publishing Co.
4035 Park East Court SE, Grand Rapids, Michigan 49546
www.eerdmans.com

Book design by Jamie McKee

Printed in the United States of America

28 27 26 25 24 23 22   1 2 3 4 5 6 7

ISBN 978-0-8028-7476-4

Library of Congress Cataloging-in-Publication Data

Names: Setran, David P., author.
Title: Christian parenting : wisdom and perspectives from American history /
    David P. Setran.
Description: Grand Rapids : William B. Eerdmans Publishing Company, 2022. |
    Includes bibliographical references and index. | Summary: "A survey of the
    varying ways in which American Protestants envisioned the task of childrearing
    during the colonial and Victorian eras, accompanied by reflections on what this
    historical legacy might mean for our understanding and practice of contempo-
    rary Christian parenting"—Provided by publisher.
Identifiers: LCCN 2022001189 | ISBN 9780802874764
Subjects: LCSH: Parenting—Religious aspects—Protestant churches—History. |
    Child rearing—Religious aspects—Protestant churches—History. | Parenting—
    United States—History. | Child rearing—United States—History.
Classification: LCC BV4529 .S428 2022 | DDC 248.8/45—dc23/eng/20220128
LC record available at https://lccn.loc.gov/2022001189

Unless otherwise indicated, Scripture quotations are from
the English Standard Version.

*To Holly, my partner in this
delightful journey of Christian parenting*

CONTENTS

Acknowledgments

Writing a book is itself a kind of parental process, and I am grateful for those who helped nourish and sustain my work from its infancy. My interest in the history of American Christian parenting was birthed around the PhD seminar tables at Indiana University. I am particularly indebted to my dissertation advisor, B. Edward McClellan, who encouraged me to look more deeply into the family's historical role in the moral and religious education of American children. His love for the topic was contagious, and his own work in the history of character education laid a strong foundation on which to build. His kindness and encouragement urged me forward in ways I can never repay.

My colleagues at Wheaton College over the years have provided unwavering support and friendship during the long days of teaching, meetings, research, and writing. It was Lyle Dorsett who, through his mentoring and modeling, helped me see that I could blend historical research with the disciplines of spiritual formation and ministry. My fellow department members over the past several years—Laura Barwegen, Dan Haase, Jim Wilhoit, Barrett McRay, Tom Schwanda, Scottie May, and Mimi Larson—have stimulated my thinking and supported my efforts in more ways than I can recount. Tom gave me many good directions to pursue as I looked at Puritan sources, and Scottie and Mimi offered countless resources and their own passion and expertise in children's spirituality. My colleague Tim Larsen also provided generous encouragement and a historian's keen wisdom along the way. I have had a number of TAs who have provided both help and insight on this project. I am especially grateful to Ashley Condra and Nathan Snyder, both of whom found critical resources and worked tirelessly to make them accessible to me. I can't name all the others at Wheaton who strengthened my work through their conversations, prayers, and friendship, but I have found in the writing process how important it is to be part of such an excellent community of scholars.

I also want to express my gratitude to the many institutions that supported my efforts along the way. Wheaton College provided released time to work on the book through the gracious provision of the Price-LeBar endowed chair. Staff members at a host of libraries provided invaluable support in helping me locate hard-to-find resources. I am especially grateful to the staff members at the American Antiquarian Society, the Presbyterian Historical Society, the Methodist Center for Archives and History, the American Baptist Historical Society, and the Congregational Library and Archives for their enthusiastic service and assistance. I am also so thankful to all of the Eerdmans staff members and especially to David Bratt, who championed this work from the beginning and skillfully answered my many questions along the way.

As with just about everything in my life, my greatest debt of gratitude goes to my family. As I have realized countless times throughout the writing process, my own spiritual formation is deeply connected to the nurturing influence of Christian parenting. I am so grateful to my own parents, Ray and Evey Setran, who shaped me in powerful ways through their love for God's word, their belief in the power of prayer, their commitment to the local church, and their loving nurture. I am who I am today in large part because of their parental faithfulness. This is the legacy that I have attempted to continue in my own parenting. In fact, I wrote this book because I hoped I could learn from those in the past how better to fulfill my own role as a parent. It is my greatest privilege to be the father of Parker, Anna Joy, Owen, and Emily, and it is my whole desire that they know and love the Lord Jesus and make him known in their own spheres of influence. I am so grateful to them for looking past my flaws and reflecting God's goodness in my life in so many tangible ways. And finally, no words can express my love and admiration for my wife, Holly, my partner in this crazy and delightful journey of Christian parenting. Her capacity to care, serve, teach, pray, and nurture has generated a home environment that glorifies Christ and attracts our children to his gracious and loving arms. Proverbs 31:28 (NIV) says it best: "Her children arise and call her blessed; / her husband also, and he praises her."

In Search of
the "Good" Christian Parent

Train up a child in the way he should go;
even when he is old he will not depart from it.

—Proverbs 22:6

What does it mean to be a "good" Christian parent? The biblical call to "train up a child" has encouraged Christian parents throughout the centuries to be intentional about the work they do in raising up their children in the faith. The words of Deuteronomy 6 implored early Israelite parents to teach God's commands "diligently" to their children by talking about them at all times, "when you sit in your house, and when you walk by the way, and when you lie down, and when you rise" (v. 7). Psalm 78 served as a bracing reminder for parents to teach God's commands to their children (v. 5) and to "tell to the coming generation / the glorious deeds of the Lord, and his might, / and the wonders that he has done" (v. 4). The high calling of godly parenting was not only to benefit one's own children but also to ensure the continuity of the faith, "that the next generation might know them, / the children yet unborn, / and arise and tell them to their children" (v. 6). In such ways, Scripture links the future faithfulness and obedience of God's people to parents' mission to bring up their children "in the discipline and instruction of the Lord" (Eph. 6:4).

The biblical witness also points to the tragic and often long-lasting consequences of parental shortcomings. On an individual level, Isaac and Rebekah's competing allegiances to their two sons led to betrayals of trust and to ongoing sibling rivalries and hostilities between Jacob and Esau (Gen. 25). Jacob's parental favoritism toward Joseph set the stage for sibling envy and a murderous plot (Gen. 37). Scripture speaks of Eli's unwillingness to restrain his wicked sons and how this led to the defiling of God's offering and eventual judgment on his family (1 Sam. 2–4). Likewise, David's failure to admonish his sons Amnon and Adonijah (2 Sam. 13:21; 1 Kings 1:6) caused ongoing suffering within his family and among the people of Israel. On a more corporate level, the years after Joshua's death seemed to reveal a lack of parental intentionality in fulfilling the call of Psalm 78. After that generation died, the text indicates, "there arose another generation after them who did not know the LORD or the work that he had done for Israel" (Judg. 2:10). These scriptural commands and examples point to a reality that most people intuitively recognize: parents matter.

Contemporary research actually confirms the importance of Christian parenting. A number of recent studies demonstrate that parents play the most significant role in shaping the spiritual commitments of their children, an influence that often lasts throughout the life span.[1] In his research on both teenagers and emerging adults, Christian Smith found that, despite stereotypes about the decline of parental influence in these years, parents had the greatest impact on the shape of their children's growing faith.[2] Perhaps not surprisingly, therefore, sociologist Vern Bengtson demonstrated that there are statistically significant similarities between parents and their young adult children in such areas as religious affiliation (remaining within a particular tradition), religious intensity (how religious one claims to be), religious participation (religious service attendance), views of the Bible (biblical literalism), and the perceived importance of religion in civic life.[3] As Christian Smith and Amy Adamczyk summarize,

> All research in the United States today shows clearly that parents are by far the most important factor influencing their children's religion, not only as youth but also after they leave home. Not clergy, religious schools, youth ministers, neighborhoods, Sunday school, mission trips, service projects, summer camp, peers, or the media. Parents. That is who matters here and now. Parents define for their children the role that religious faith and practice ought to play in life, whether important or not, which most children roughly adopt. Parents set a "glass ceiling" of religious commitment above which their children rarely rise. Parental religious investment and involvement is in almost

all cases the necessary and even sometimes sufficient condition for children's religious investment and involvement.[4]

While other factors—church, friends, mentors, schools, technology, and various life experiences—are obviously also critical, such studies point to the unique power and importance of Christian parents in the ongoing spiritual formation of their children.[5]

Despite widespread consensus regarding the importance of parenting, there is less agreement on what it means to be a "good" Christian parent. Leaders, authors, and parents themselves debate whether infants should be put on strict feeding and sleeping schedules or given more freedom in these areas. They question the relative merits of "attachment" parenting, including issues related to co-sleeping and more extended breastfeeding. They debate the competing methods of the hovering "helicopter" parent and the hands-off "free-range" parent. They argue over whether Christian parents should seek moment-in-time conversion experiences or simply raise children up in the faith without the need for a "new heart." They deliberate over disciplinary techniques: spanking, grounding, "time out," and many others. They discuss how they should teach their children, how they should pray, how they should conduct family devotions, and how they should (or should not) observe the Sabbath. They weigh the importance of home-based spiritual formation against the contributions of church-related programs. In these areas and many others, parents and faith leaders wrestle with how to interpret general biblical principles and give them concrete application in the Christian home.

While Christian parenting advice books abound, few have looked to the wisdom and perspectives of the past to inform the ways contemporary parents think about Christian nurture in the home. American Protestant authors have grappled with parenting concerns since colonial times and have attempted to provide hopeful pathways to parents in the midst of significant cultural and theological challenges. This book explores the advice given to American Protestant parents between the early 1600s and the late 1800s about how to raise up their children in the faith, looking also at the legacy of these proposals in the twentieth century and into contemporary times. It looks at the changing principles and "best practices" that key northern Protestant leaders recommended for parents as they sought to promote home-based Christian education and formation for their children.[6] By looking at the advice given to parents in these formative years, I hope to demonstrate the unique ways in which Christian leaders sought to answer the question, "What does it mean to be a 'good' Christian parent?"

More specifically, the book traces such advice across two key time periods that reflected different visions of effective Christian parenting. Between the early 1600s and mid-1700s, colonial Protestants in New England (the Puritans and their close allies) set forth a vision of parenting that sought to impart biblical and theological wisdom, to foster obedience and reverence, to invite children into worship, and to seek children's salvation. They viewed "good" parents as evangelists (seeking to lead their children toward conversion), priests (seeking to guide their children into the presence of God through worship and prayer), prophets (seeking to teach their children the doctrines of the Christian faith in formal and informal ways), and kings (seeking to restrain their children's waywardness through the exercise of proper authority and discipline). Within these areas of proclamation, worship, teaching, and discipline, parents—especially fathers—were encouraged to guide their children into spiritual maturity and submission to God's larger plans for their lives. Urging parents to foster daily practices of Christian education and worship, pastors wanted colonial households to imitate the functions of local congregations, becoming "little churches" in their children's lives.

In the second time period, roughly from the 1830s to the 1880s, a new Victorian-era vision of Christian parenting emerged that was linked more to the environmental "impressions" and relationships formed within the home. The rise of the Protestant "domestic ideal" in this era set up the home as a sacred space in which a nurturing physical and relational environment would help children develop in faith from the earliest years. Authors saw "good" Christian parents as architects (seeking to provide ideal Christian environments for children within their homes), mothers (seeking to form children spiritually through nurturing relationships with pure and loving mothers more than with fathers), and memory-makers (seeking to foster warm and intimate relationships with family members to promote a "cheerful" faith). Within these areas, nineteenth-century Protestant authors tended to highlight the sacred home as a physical and relational space that would promote Christian nurture in the midst of everyday life. They saw the Spirit at work, not as much through distinct and formal family worship and instruction as through the informal inter-actions between parents (especially mothers) and children and the impres-sions of a loving home environment.

The shift across these two time periods represented a sea change in the very definition of what it meant to be a Christian parent. The colonial approach to parenting was more formal, hierarchical, paternal, doctri-nal, practice-driven, and geared toward conversion. The approach of the Victorian era was more informal, democratic, maternal, environmental, relationship-driven, and geared toward gradual nurture. Of course, both visions existed in both time periods. Key colonial leaders still stressed the importance of parents' loving and caring relationships with their children. Victorian authors, likewise, recognized the importance of family Chris-tian practices. Furthermore, many of a more conservative stripe (those historian Philip Greven has described as "evangelical" in temperament) kept various aspects of the colonial vision alive throughout the nine-teenth century.[7] Yet the tide was clearly shifting among advice writers of all Protestant persuasions, setting the stage for a different tone and style of parenting that has deeply shaped the ways we think about Christian child-rearing in the present day.

Why should those living in the era of Instagram and iPhones care about the history of Christian parenting advice? First, while contemporary parents face a host of novel challenges, a focus on the past raises a number of important and perennial issues related to Christian formation in the home. For example, it provides perspective on the changing parental roles and responsibilities of mothers and fathers, looking specifically at the broad and elevated spiritual leadership of fathers in colonial child-rearing and the rising spiritual dominance of mothers in nineteenth-century households. It calls attention to changing views of children, looking at the shifts from the colonial focus on child sinfulness to a wider diversity of views that emphasized children's malleability and even angelic inno-cence. It traces changing conceptions of child discipline from the more hierarchical and formal rhetoric of "subduing," "restraint," and "correction" in the colonial era to the Victorian use of "wounded love" and emotional and physical withdrawal in order to internalize the child's sense of guilt. It brings into view a number of means and methods of teaching faith to children, highlighting the centrality of catechism training in the seven-teenth and eighteenth centuries and the shift to more impression- and story-based approaches after the 1820s. It looks at changing fears among Christian parents, ranging from children's internal sin and threats of hell to external fears related to the potentially corrupting influences of the culture. It also highlights the changing relative weight given to such practices as family devotions, prayer, modeling, conversion experiences, church involvement, Sabbath-keeping, home decorating, family rituals, and fun family activities and play. Since many of these issues continue to be of concern among Christian parents, this historical analysis will hopefully bring necessary perspective to contemporary child-rearing patterns and practices.

Second, while the study of the past cannot tell us exactly what we should do in the present, it does provide resources to help contemporary Christian parents reconsider their responsibilities, purposes, and practices. History helps us understand the roots of our present parenting ideas and practices. It reveals the sources of our contemporary approaches, helping us recognize how and why we have come to think and act as we do (and therefore how Christian families have come to operate as they do). We are influenced deeply by those who have gone before us and by our cultural, philosophical, and theological traditions. Only when we acknowledge these influences and recognize these historical threads can we begin to properly discern and evaluate our own thoughts and practices in the present.

Third, history can help contemporary parents become more self-critical. We are inevitably shaped by the "take for granted" parenting practices of our time. We are, in fact, often oblivious to our underlying assumptions and presuppositions because they are simply "normal" to us, the very air we breathe. One of the chief ways that we develop an awareness of our own subconscious perspectives is by coming face-to-face with alternative options. When we visit another country, for example, we begin to "see" our own cultural values to a much greater extent. Similarly, exposure to historical parenting approaches can help us recognize that our own views are not simply "normal" but are particular viewpoints shaped by our own cultural and theological contexts. As we are confronted with the "strangeness" of the past—the different beliefs, values, practices, attitudes, and questions of previous eras—our own viewpoints and practices become more visible. We become more self-conscious of our perspectives so that we are able to evaluate them against competing options. As Rowan

Williams has suggested, "History will not tell us what to do, but will at least start us on the road to action of a different and more self-aware kind, action that is moral in a way it can't be if we have no points of reference beyond what we have come to take for granted."[8]

Fourth, looking to the past can broaden and enlighten our perspectives in important ways. History expands our range of available sources of new ideas, giving voices to those in the past who can speak in new ways to current issues. Importantly, the study of the past may not only give us new answers to our present questions but may actually force us to ask new questions rising from unique historical circumstances. In fact, one of history's greatest contributions is to raise questions we would never have thought to ask. We are subject to certain blind spots because of the times we live in, and C. S. Lewis has noted that such blindness is increased if we read only contemporary perspectives. "The only palliative," he suggests, "is to keep the clean sea breeze of the centuries blowing through our minds, and this can be done only by reading old books." Lewis goes on to say that people from the past were no "cleverer" than they are now. They made mistakes as well. The reason they are helpful to us is that they did not make the same mistakes and can therefore open our eyes to our characteristic errors and omissions.[9] It is my hope that each of the chapters ahead will provide perspectives on parenting issues that can both open our eyes to our blind spots and give us new strategies and questions to consider.

Fifth, looking at historic parenting wisdom can actually provide us with insight into the changing nature of American Protestant faith over the past centuries. Christian parenting theory, for example, tells us a good deal about American Protestants' changing views of God. Since God is often referred to in parental terms in Scripture, changing parenting styles and approaches to teaching and discipline implicitly reflect changing beliefs about God's parental role. In Scripture, God is referred to as "Father" (Deut. 32:6; Matt. 6:9). He adopts children into his family (Eph. 1:5; Gal. 4:5; John 1:12), and his children cry out "Abba," an Aramaic word for "father" that expressed an intimate parent-child relationship (Rom. 8:15). God compares himself to a father who gives good gifts to his children (Matt. 7:9–11), including an "inheritance" to his heirs (Rom. 8:17; Eph. 1:11). He describes his love as that of a father's love (1 John 3:1; Luke 15:24–32), and his fatherly sacrifice of his own Son displays the extent of that love (Rom. 8:32). Scripture also compares God's discipline to that of an earthly father. Proverbs 3:12 (NIV) notes that "the Lord disciplines those he loves, / as a father the son he delights in." Hebrews 12 suggests that when God disciplines his people, he is "treating [them] as his children. For what children are not disciplined by their father?" (v. 7 NIV). Similarly, God's compassion is expressed in parent-child terms, not only visually in the parable of the prodigal son (Luke 15:11–32), but also more directly in the Psalms: "As a father has compassion on his children, / so the Lord has compassion on those who fear him" (103:13 NIV). Since these comparisons are quite direct, a historical look at parenting advice can provide a window into the changing ways that American Protestants have thought about the character of God. Is God more authoritarian or permissive? More distant or imminent? More a disciplinarian or doting parent? Authors' recommendations to parents often tell us much about Protestants' shifting perspectives on the very nature of God's parental character.

In addition, a study of Christian parenting advice reveals a great deal about Protestants' changing views of human nature, especially the nature of children. Parenting advice always presupposes a particular view of the child—a theological anthropology—that provides both the rationale and the motivation for specific approaches to child-rearing. In looking at the history of Christian parenting in these years, this theme emerges very clearly. Beliefs as to whether children were "dead" in their sins, completely pliable, or innocent and angelic deeply influenced whether parents thought that they needed a radical conversion, more gradual nurture, or safety and protection. Even before the internet and social media, such beliefs also helped determine whether children's chief threats were internal (the sin nature within) or external (the surrounding culture) and whether parents thought children needed to be protected from the adult world or immersed within it. Some of these concerns were even reflected in the ages that parents thought were most important in terms of faith formation, leading to different emphases on either early childhood or later "youth." All of this demonstrates that childhood itself is not just a biological but also a social and theological concept. Different perceptions of children's needs, concerns, and contributions often emerge from deep-seated beliefs about human nature, and Christian parenting advice is often a reflection of these disparate views. Changing beliefs about parenting tell us much about American Protestants' changing opinions on these important issues, and they also reveal a good deal about Christians' hopes and dreams about the future of the faith. As Don S. Browning and Bonnie J. Miller-McLemore have noted, "One learns something unique about religion—something special and profound—when one views it from the perspective of what it says about children."[10]

This study attempts to fill a gap in historical writing about Christian parenting. Since the 1960s and 1970s, historians have provided detailed and wide-ranging insights into historical views of children, family structures and relationships, child-rearing practices, and the contributions of educational leaders, institutions, and methodologies.[11] Such historical works are extremely helpful, but they rarely address issues of family religion. Those works that do look at such issues tend to focus on single time periods (thus minimizing the appreciation of historical change) or look at Christian nurture as one very small component of a broader childhood education.[12] Historians of Christian education, likewise, tend to give only cursory attention to Christian formation within the home, focusing more distinctly on church and school settings.[13] As many would consider the home to be the most critical venue for Christian formation and discipleship in a child's life, this is obviously a significant shortcoming.

Historians of Christianity, on the other hand, rarely address children and the family except in the most general ways. In part, this neglect may relate to the fact that children are often "invisible" in the larger events of religious history.[14] For both theologians and church historians, children are often dismissed as unimportant historical actors, fading to the background in works that address adult concerns. Such neglect may also relate to the larger tendency of religious historians to focus on theological, political, or institutional concerns, neglecting the penetration of Christianity into the affairs of everyday life. As historian Colleen McDannell suggests, however, in addition to "denominational religion" and "civil religion," Americans have participated in a "domestic religion" that has allowed the more abstract principles of the faith to find a "real presence in everyday life."[15] The historical neglect of such domestic religion is actually quite shocking when one considers the profound impact that family relationships and household practices have on the shape of one's beliefs, behaviors, and conceptions of the "good life." While the daily routines of Christian parenting often seem trivial—even "uninteresting"—such expressions of faith have much to do with the way that Christianity has been lived out and passed on in American history.[16] As an important aspect of practical piety, domestic religion deserves more focused attention.

Two books have explored approaches to Protestant parenting in more depth, and my work here builds on these important studies. Philip Greven's *The Protestant Temperament: Patterns of Child-Rearing, Religious Experience, and the Self in Early America* (1977) provides a fascinating look at three religious "temperaments" in early America—the evangelical, the moderate, and the genteel—and traces the perspectives of each in relation to child-rearing. Greven is less concerned about chronological change in this work, and he doesn't concentrate on the specific faith-building practices of the Christian home, but his work provides a rich portrait of the ways that faith and child-rearing theories intertwined in different family "types" during these eras. Margaret Bendroth's more recent work, *Growing Up Protestant: Parents, Children, and Mainline Churches* (2002), provides a clear and thorough portrait of changing approaches to mainline Protestant parenting in the nineteenth and twentieth centuries, tracing the key themes in home-based Christian nurture across these two centuries.[17] Her work does not include the colonial era and focuses more on the twentieth century, but her text, sensitive to both the history of the family and the history of American religion, serves as a model for historians interested in tracing the contours of domestic religion. Greven and Bendroth sparked my own passion to explore godly parenting in greater depth, and I see my contributions here as largely building on their groundbreaking studies.

The scope of this particular book is limited in several ways. Since I am focused on parenting advice literature, I am looking chiefly at white, northern, educated (and, in the nineteenth century, middle-class) Protestants and their perspectives on these issues.[18] Most of the written books, articles, sermons, and lectures on Christian parenting in these eras came from such individuals, and they therefore assume the class, racial, and regional biases of such sources. In addition, while some denominational distinctives will be noted throughout, the concern in this book is for central tendencies, those "consensus" parenting concerns that often cut across denominational divides. Furthermore, since this is a study of advice literature, it does not necessarily point to the actual practices and beliefs of individual parents. While the book includes concrete examples of specific parenting practices from diaries, biographies, and autobiographies, I am most concerned with the changing ways in which Protestant leaders—pastors, educators, and popular authors—thought about the ideals and practices of Christian parenting over time. We have a good sense, especially in the nineteenth century, that middle-class parents did read many of these materials, but there is no way to know how much they affirmed or rejected, much less internalized and enacted, the perspectives offered on these pages.[19] Still, the viewpoints are important and speak to the shifting cultural ideals of how Christian parents were advised to raise up their children in the faith. Whether or not people agreed with the "typical" points of view of these eras, such principles did create aspirational models and set the stage for key discussions and debates in churches and in individual households.

Such a work is also limited by my own biases. In writing a book related to Christian parenting, I have often been very conscious of how easy it is to read historical sources through the lens of my own Christian upbringing and the practices my wife and I have implemented with our four children. It is also quite tempting to address only those issues that originate in, affirm, or speak directly into contemporary issues and struggles. My hope is that this book allows these authors from the past to speak in the context of their own times and to raise and answer the questions that were of utmost importance to them.[20] I have tried to read and interpret these sources in their historical context and with a charitable spirit that is alert to the unique perspectives and challenges of these different eras. My desire, therefore, is not to identify a particular golden age of Christian parenting. There was no such time. Even throughout the periods of this study, at every stage there were Christian leaders bemoaning the state of the family, the moral deterioration of youth, and the general flaws of Christian parents. Henry Clay Trumbull, writing in 1888 to those who were complaining about the low state of family religion in his day, indicated that at every stage over the previous two hundred years there had been Christian leaders lamenting the deplorable state of Christian families and the failures of Christian parents.[21] Complaints about the decline of family religion are thus themselves a venerable historical tradition! Living through distinct time periods, leaders in each era had their characteristic insights and blind spots. As in our own time, parents and children worked within the challenges, opportunities, and mental frameworks of their own historical periods, doing the best they could with the resources and ideas at their disposal.

In the pages to come, what I set forth is not so much a comprehensive history of Protestant parenting as an exploration of the parenting "postures" that key authors identified with "good" parenting in each era. Conversations on Christian parenting over the last century have drawn on both the colonial emphases on teaching, Christian worship, and conversion and the Victorian celebration of loving nurture, warm home environments, and intimate relationships. These varied approaches, the fruit of particular cultural and theological perspectives, have shaped the ways contemporary Christian parents envision and pursue their discipling roles with their children. In the end, I propose that parents' ability to shepherd their children in the faith may depend on their ability to listen to and learn from both perspectives.

What does it mean to be a "good" Christian parent? In the history of Protestant America, the many answers to this question perhaps give us a more complete picture of the ways in which parents are to live out the high calling to "train up a child" (Prov. 22:6). It is my hope that these pages will provide wisdom and perspectives from the past to educate, to expand, to caution, and to inspire those who care about the profound and multigenerational influence of Christian parenting.

PART I

Colonial Christian Parenting:
1620–1770

CHAPTER 1

The Parent as Evangelist
Raising Up a Godly Seed

This should be their first and chief Care for their Children, that
they may be a *godly Seed to serve the Lord.*

—William Cooper, *God's Concern for a Godly Seed*[1]

When the congregants of the Brattle Street Church gathered for a day of fasting and prayer on March 5, 1723, they joined to seek "the Effusion of the Spirit of Grace" on their children.[2] Along with other days set aside for prayer for the "rising generation," this meeting was devoted to helping Christian parents make commitments to pray for their children, to raise them up in the faith, and to set up their houses to "be a *Bethel*, a *House of God*; wherein His Fear and Worship shall be maintain'd, and in which He may delight to dwell."[3] Listening to their two renowned pastors, William Cooper and Benjamin Colman, these parents would have heard a near perfect articulation of the goals of Christian parenting in colonial New England. Cooper, using Malachi 2:15 as his text, began by calling parents to "seek a Godly Seed," raising up their children to be doctrinally sound, holy, prayerful, and committed to church and Sabbath observance. Cooper noted that Satan would "*do all he can to hinder*" this work, using his "Arts and Stratagems" to "debauch, corrupt, and spoil" Christian children so that they would become his "seed" instead. Since parents were involved in warfare against the devil, he concluded that they must "be stirred up to counter-work him" through godly parenting.[4] If parents were faithful in this task, their children would grow to "propagate their Godliness" and to continue a lineage of faith across the generations.[5]

In the second sermon of the day, Colman, drawing from 1 Chronicles 29:19, called on parents to pray for their children to receive from God a *"perfect heart."*[6] Citing David's prayer for his son Solomon, Colman reminded parents that their children were eternally lost and hopeless without a "new heart" and that they must pray for God to "*sanctify* 'em to himself, and fill them with his *Holy Spirit* and keep them by his grace, and bring them to his glory."[7] Since these children belonged to God through a baptismal covenant and were only "lent" to parents for a time, fathers and mothers were charged as stewards to instruct them, to pray for them, and to seek their salvation. If they did this, Cooper and Colman suggested, parents could be confident that their children would "arise to fill your places in the House of God among us, and at the Table of Christ; be faithful to the Cause of God . . . and *be known to be the Seed which the Lord hath blessed."*[8]

The goals set forth at this day of prayer—particularly the desire for a "godly seed" with a "new heart"—nicely articulated the vision of Christian parenting among New England's key spiritual leaders in the seventeenth and eighteenth centuries. They recognized that a godly society would require not only a healthy dose of religious zeal but also a plan for long-term generational continuity. While economic trials certainly played a role in families' decisions to leave for America, pastors were quick to remind New England parents of their primary purpose. "*Why came you into this Land? was it not mainly with respect to the Rising Generation?*" asked Eleazer Mather. "And what with respect to them? was it to leave them a rich and wealthy people? was it to leave them Houses, Lands, Livings? Oh no: but to leave God in the midst of them."[9] Since New England's spiritual legacy depended on the ability of parents to raise up a "godly seed," family discipleship emerged as a central lynchpin of leaders' hopes and expectations for the future.[10]

Such a perspective reflected the urgency—and anxiety—of leaders who recognized how fleeting their godly experiment might be without intentional Christian parenting. Since they drew regular comparisons between themselves and Old Testament Israel—sharing with these biblical ancestors a common "errand into the wilderness"—biblical case studies of generational decline served as powerful warnings against parental neglect.[11] John Cotton reminded mothers and fathers to take "tender care that you look well to the Plants that spring from you, that is, to your

Children, that they do not degenerate, as the *Israelites* did."[12] According to Colman, failure in Christian parenting would mean the failure of the entire community project and the loss of God's favor. "Consider also, what will become of Religion in this Land, if our Children and young People don't prove a godly Seed," he warned. "It will fail and sink; God's truths will be lost or corrupted. The *Work of God*, in planting *New-England*, will fall to the Ground. . . . They will be a *Generation of God's Wrath*; will pull down his Judgments upon them; and drive away his Presence upon which their Prosperity depends."[13] Since families were the "nurseries of all societies," these early colonial pastors certainly understood what was at stake in Christian parenting. *"Ruine families, and ruine all,"* Eleazer Mather concluded. "So on the other hand, keep God there, and keep him every-where."[14]

While the church obviously retained a central place in New England society—both geographically and symbolically—most agreed that the dispersed homes in local communities would be the primary settings in which children would be directed toward salvation and spiritual growth. In fact, Cotton Mather went so far as to say that it was the family, not the church, that would be the primary means of salvation among children in the new world. "If *Parents* did *their* Duties as they ought," he suggested, "the *Word* publickly preached, would not be the ordinary means of *Regeneration* in the Church, but only *without* the Church, among Infidels."[15] In England, seventeenth-century Puritans highlighted the importance of household religion far more than their church-centered Anglican and Catholic counterparts.[16] In New England, this theoretical commitment became even more of a practical necessity as frontier conditions and the scarcity of local churches, ministers, and schools forced parents to assume responsibility as the primary educators of their children.[17] Pastors certainly contributed—they catechized, visited homes, led days of fasting, and promoted voluntary associations of young people. Yet parents were often reminded that this was their primary calling. As Cooper put it, "This should be the Care of *Ministers*. They should labour the Instruction and Conversion of Young Ones to God. . . . But in a very particular manner this should be the Care of *Parents for their own Children*."[18]

This commitment to family religion sparked an outpouring of advice—mostly printed sermons and lectures—for Christian parents in colonial New England. Between the early seventeenth and the mid-eighteenth centuries, authors broadly identified with the Puritan movement on both sides of the Atlantic dominated the publishing industry when it came to works on Christian parenting.[19] The works of Puritan and nonconformist British authors—widely read by New England leaders—stood alongside a growing collection of homegrown sermons and lectures from American Puritans such as the Mathers (especially Eleazer, Increase, and Cotton Mather), Isaac Ambrose, Samuel Willard, Deodat Lawson, and Benjamin Wadsworth. The works of other New England pastor-theologians in this era such as Benjamin Colman, William Cooper, John Barnard, Joseph Belcher, and Jonathan Edwards, though not technically Puritans, also had a deep influence on those concerned about raising up their children in the faith. By the mid-eighteenth century, there was an enormous literature on Christian parenting that possessed a distinctly New England flavor.

The Shape of the Colonial Family

Pastoral advice literature was directed toward parents whose households looked very different from contemporary American versions. First of all, these families were often quite large. According to most estimates, the average mother in colonial New England could expect to give birth to between seven and nine children, delivering at regular intervals every twenty to thirty months.[20] Since most continued to bear children into their forties, parents often had children in the home quite late in their lives, certainly into their sixties if they lived that long.[21] In addition, the range of ages in the home could be quite large; it was not uncommon for families to have an infant and a child preparing to marry in the household at the same time.[22] Since women in New England tended to marry in their late teens or early twenties (about five years earlier than women in England), and because they were generally healthier within more stable families, these households often included more children than their English counterparts.[23] While the desire for large families may have reflected economic realities, particularly the need for able-bodied agricultural laborers, it also pointed to the fact that colonial Christians saw children as cherished gifts to their households, to the larger community, and to God's kingdom. As Colman effused, "A Mother with a Train of Children after her is One of the most admirable and lovely Sights in the Visible Creation of God. . . .

Children are among the Choice Favours and Gifts of Providence, and we should have a high Sense of the Gracious Favour of God to us in them."[24]

While families were larger and more stable than in England, child death rates were still quite high and shaped New England families in significant ways. According to historical estimates, even relatively healthy communities like Andover and Dedham saw infant mortality rates of 10 percent during the first year of life.[25] In addition, approximately one-fourth of all children in such locations failed to make it to their tenth birthdays, while a third or more died prior to their twenty-first birthdays.[26] In other areas, such as Boston and Salem, death rates were much higher—sometimes two to three times higher—as a result of diseases such as smallpox, measles, mumps, diphtheria, whooping cough, and scarlet fever.[27] Such figures were also greatly elevated during epidemics, such as the 1677–1678 smallpox outbreak that decimated as much as one-fifth of Boston's population and the diphtheria epidemic in 1736–1737 in which 802 of the 948 deaths in New Hampshire were children under the age of ten.[28] Of his fourteen children, Samuel Sewall buried eight under the age of two. Cotton Mather lost eight of his fifteen children before the age of two, and one soon after.[29] As historian David Stannard indicates, since the average married woman gave birth to between seven and nine children, "a young couple embarking on marriage did so with the knowledge that in all probability *two or three* of the children they might have would die before the age of ten."[30] Or as Anne Bradstreet, who lost several young grandchildren, poetically mused, "O bubble blast, how long can'st last? / that always art a breaking, / No sooner blown, but dead and gone, / ev'n as a word that's speaking."[31]

These large and vulnerable New England families operated quite differently than the smaller and more isolated units that would emerge in the nineteenth century. In an era devoid of many specialized institutions, homes served multiple social roles as businesses, schools, vocational institutes, churches, houses of correction, hospitals, nursing homes, orphanages, and poorhouses.[32] Families, that is to say, were responsible for economic production, children's education, religious practices, vocational preparation, and the care of a wide range of individuals in need of physical care or reformation. While many of these functions would later be taken over by other institutions, in the colonial era they were typically consolidated within the home. Historian John Demos refers to the family in colonial New England as "a little commonwealth," a centralized and functional society that was responsible for the holistic care of its members and the larger community.[33] Within such settings, family members all worked together to contribute to these common tasks, providing many teachable moments along the way.

Because of these many functions, families in colonial New England were more "permeable" and "fluid" than those of later generations. Children, especially sons, often spent considerable time in other households. Though less common than in England, lengthy apprenticeships, in which sons were "put out" into the home of a master in order to learn a trade, were still popular. Such arrangements began no later than the age of fourteen and often a good deal earlier, continuing normally until the age of twenty-one.[34] In these arrangements, the master played a parental role, providing care, education, and religious training for the apprentice, who was "legally and culturally a 'child' of the household for the duration of their residence."[35] Recognizing the perils associated with living in a different family, pastors often warned parents to choose such homes on the basis of godly values rather than mere economic benefit.[36] "Parents care is not to be confined to the time wherein Children are under their immediate government, but is especially to be exprest towards them, when they are to be placed in other families," Watertown pastor Henry Gibbs warned. "And they are very culpable, who for the sake of some worldly interest, will betrust their Children in families where the service of God is not encouraged, nor his Worship upheld; the sad effects whereof have been often seen."[37] Children could also be sent to other homes for reasons beyond vocational training. At times this practice was associated with the death of a parent or significant financial need. It could also be utilized as a means of reforming a child's character or finding a better home for those whose parents were negligent.[38] Some colonial families sent their children away even when there was no apparent need. It is possible that this is because parents, as Edmund Morgan famously argued, did not trust themselves with their own children, fearing an overindulgence that would weaken the child's spiritual fiber.[39]

In addition to sending children out to other homes, New England households also frequently brought others in. Though the primary structure of the household was nuclear (parents and children), families often housed servants, apprentices, destitute children from other homes, and various relatives and guests. Samuel Sewall, for example, took in "several boys who came to prepare for Harvard College; three orphaned grandchildren; a distant cousin's young son . . . and a niece who came to live with the family in her youth."[40] These kinds of mixed households blurred the boundaries between the family and the community, between the private and public spheres of life. Many children grew up in multiple temporary homes with many different individuals, a reality that limited the intensity of nuclear family ties that would exist in later years. Such household structures also limited what moderns would see as the uniqueness of the parent-child bond. Children mixed freely with adults who were not their parents and were therefore privy to the wisdom (or foolishness) of a broader range of potential mentors. Parents, likewise, were often called on to raise and nurture children who were not their own, and all were considered part of the "family." As John Gillis has suggested, these colonial Christians "spiritualized the household but refused to sanctify the nuclear family as such."[41]

In many ways, this involvement of the community in family life was a natural extension of the notion of the covenant. Colonial parents were obviously devoted to their families, but their ultimate loyalty was to the larger covenantal community—the family of God. Unlike the elite Anglican families in the South, where family bonds regularly trumped greater religious allegiances, the larger New England church family in many ways took precedence over the individual family in terms of obligation.[42] The command to "honor parents," for example, extended beyond the nuclear family to include all adults and superiors in the community and the church.[43] There was also a joint commitment among congregation members to help parents raise their children in the faith. Within such a setting, family privacy was regularly trumped by the community's involvement. Government officials regularly checked up on families to ensure that parents were fulfilling their responsibilities (including the work of Christian teaching and discipline). Church and community members were encouraged to speak to parents about behavioral or character flaws they observed in each other's children. Whether seeking to help or to diagnose and confront sin, community watchfulness was a regular—and in fact celebrated—part of life.[44] As historian Mary Ryan puts it, "The objective of the covenant was to link Christians together in a circle of loyalty, harmony, and mutual care that was larger than the family. . . . The prerogatives of the individual were routinely sacrificed in order to protect the integrity of the covenanted community."[45]

This broader understanding of family also demonstrated a desire that God, rather than family members, be maintained at the center of their affections. As important as children were, it was equally true that parents were to constantly be on guard against idolizing them. Colonial pastors regularly remarked that children were blessings of God designed to afford personal joy, but they also recognized that these creaturely pleasures could easily replace the Creator God in their parents' affections. This was especially true if children proved to be godly, as parents might begin to take credit for their goodness and to hold them up as trophies rather than expressing thanks to God for them.[46] Colman warned parents that "it may be you will be too apt to *Dote* on the Creature and *Idolize* what you should only *Love*, and thank God for."[47] Distrusting earthly bonds, authors reminded parents that they were temporary exiles in the world, ardently pursuing their heavenly home while using their earthly homes as places of preparation for this ultimate reward. In other words, they did not want the transient relationships of the household to blur their eternal vision by making them too much at home in this world.[48] John Cotton noted as much in warning about those times "when we exceedingly delight our selves in Husbands, or Wives, or Children, which much benumbs and dims the light of the Spirit."[49] This fear and suspicion of strong parent-child attachments, a staple of colonial child-rearing literature, would be largely discarded by the nineteenth century.

A "New Heart" for Dead Souls

Because God's glory was the central aim of the New England family, parents were charged with fulfilling his purposes, not their own, for their children. When pastors addressed their congregations on parenting responsibilities, one of the first things they wanted parents to know was that they were the stewards, not the owners, of their children. They urged parents to remember that their children belonged to God and were only lent to them for a time so that they could be raised up for his purposes and glory. Most colonial parenting advice echoed the words of Richard Baxter: "Consider that God is the Lord and Owner of your children, both by title of creation and redemption. Therefore, in justice you must resign them to him and educate them for him. Otherwise you rob God of his own creatures and rob Christ of those for whom he died, and this is to give them to the Devil, the enemy of God and them."[50] Since God was the covenant owner of children—a fact often rehearsed in infant baptismal ceremonies—parents' authority was always derivative. Parents were to view themselves as caretakers rather than owners, raising up their children to embrace God's rightful claims on them. As one pastor articulated, "He doth . . . Put them Out to us; as *Pharaohs* Daughter did *Moses*, to the Hebrew Woman *his Mother*, saying as She Did . . . *Take this Child, and Nurse it for ME*."[51]

As stewards of God's purposes, parents were called on to attend, first and foremost, to the salvation of their children's souls. Pastors lamented that some parents were more concerned about passing on an earthly rather than a heavenly "inheritance," storing up goods for their children's earthly success while failing to lay up treasures in heaven for their offspring.[52] Others were concerned that parents cared more for children's perishable bodies than their imperishable souls, noting that such priorities revealed a troubling worldliness that elevated the temporal over the eternal.[53] As Cotton Mather urged, "The *Souls* of your *Children*, must survive their *Bodies*, and are transcendentally Better and Higher & Nobler Things than their *Bodies*. Are you sollicitous that their *Bodies* may be *Fed*? You should be more solicitous that their *Souls* may not be *Starved*, or go without the *Bread of Life*. Are you sollicitous that their *Bodies* may be *Cloath'd*? You should be more sollicitous, that their Souls may not be Naked, or go without the *Garments* of *Righteousness*."[54] While pastors in colonial New England did not neglect the importance of children's bodily care, they clearly wanted parents to prioritize the care of souls.[55]

This was so critical because children's souls were disfigured by sin. Nearly all appeals to parental discipleship in colonial New England began with a clear statement of the child's perilous spiritual condition. Pastors reminded parents that all children, from the time of conception, inherited the sin of Adam, who, as federal head of the human race, passed down this sinful stain to all future offspring. To learn the first letter of the alphabet, in fact, children regularly recited the reality of their condition from the *New England Primer*: "In Adam's Fall, We Sinned All."[56] This doctrine of original sin meant that children bore the guilt of sin from conception and also possessed sinful dispositions and inclinations to sin "as soon as they begin to act."[57] As Cotton Mather put it, children had a "Fountain of Sin" in their hearts "from whence the Vile Streams of [their] Actual Sins have issued."[58] Benjamin Wadsworth famously stated of children that "their Hearts naturally, are a meer nest, root, fountain of Sin, and wickedness; an *evil Treasure* from whence proceed *evil things*, viz. *Evil Thoughts, Murders, Adulteries* &c. Indeed, as sharers in the guilt of *Adam's* first Sin, they're *Children of Wrath by Nature*, liable to Eternal Vengeance, the Unquenchable Flames of Hell."[59] Such statements were designed to help parents see that children were born spiritually "dead," devoid of the capacity to heal their own spiritual blindness. Thomas Shepard thus indicated that the child was "empty of every inward principle of life, void of all graces, and hath no more good in him (whatsoever he think) than a dead carrion hath." "Their bodies," he concluded, "are living coffins to carry a dead soul up and down in."[60]

Pastors in colonial New England frequently reminded parents of these theological truths because they were afraid that the charm and seeming innocence of their children might blind them to the realities of the child's precarious state. Poetically, Anne Bradstreet addressed the heart of this disconnect between appearance and reality:

> Stained from birth with Adam's sinfull fact,
> Thence I began to sin as soon as act:
> A perverse will, a love to what's forbid,
> A serpent's sting in pleasing face lay hid.[61]

Bradstreet's final line articulated an important warning to parents: they should not allow the attractive appearance of young children (the "pleasing face") to obscure the reality of the soul's depraved state (the "serpent's sting"). Jonathan Edwards claimed as much when he warned parents that, "as innocent as children seem to be to us, yet if they are out of Christ, they are not so in God's sight, but are young vipers, and are infinitely more hateful than vipers."[62] If parents lacked a sense of urgency regarding their children's spiritual condition, it was only because they lacked an accurate assessment of the child's true spiritual peril.[63]

That peril was real because the child's eternal destiny was at stake.[64] Belief in hell and in the possibility of infant damnation held strong into the eighteenth century. Pastors suggested that God had chosen some children for salvation, but the inscrutable nature of God's election made it difficult to assign eternal destinies to individual children. While most simply avoided the topic, works like Michael Wigglesworth's *The Day of Doom* spoke clearly about the judgment of non-elect infants.[65] One of the most popular works outside of the Bible in seventeenth-century New England, the 224-stanza poem detailed the horrors of hell in vivid language and offered warnings to groups of people who wrongly excused themselves from God's wrath.[66] Among those groups were infants, who, though young, were still subject to judgment because of original sin. Wigglesworth allowed that children bore less accumulated sin than their elders, and yet his only consolation for this was that these young children would occupy "the easiest room in hell."[67] While Wigglesworth's poetic theology was unrepresentative, its widespread popularity likely furnished images in the colonial imagination that were difficult to shake, especially in a society with such high infant mortality rates. Nearly a century later, Jonathan Edwards could still argue that "it is most just, exceeding just, that God should take the soul of a new-born infant and cast it into eternal torments."[68] While most colonial pastors believed that God saved the majority of the dying infants and young children of godly parents, they also wanted parents to feel the weight of their children's eternal fragility.[69]

While some historians have suggested that views of children's sinfulness must have led to parental attitudes of repression, these pastors contended that the dangerous spiritual condition of children should lead parents toward compassion and an urgent longing for their salvation.[70] Increase Mather spoke in heartbreaking terms of how parents must view their unsaved children as "captives" held in bondage by Satan, crying out to their parents for release.[71] This was even more distressing because parents themselves were considered responsible for their children's miserable condition. Original sin implied that parents were genetically implicated in their children's sinful state. Parents were to blame for their child's condition, in other words, "by nature" if not "by nurture." As Wadsworth put it,

> Again, you were instrumental of bringing your Children into a State of Sin and Misery; as they came from you Sinful Parents, they were *Shapen in Iniquity and conceiv'd in Sin*. And won't you do your best, to deliver them from Sin & Misery? Will you bring them into a miry

flow, a Sea of Misery, & leave them perishing there, without using means to Save them? . . . Oh dead Affections, flinty Souls, rocky Hearts, if you can see the Souls of your poor Children, torn to pieces by Satan's malice and their own lusts; if you can see them *languishing, dying, perishing, sinking into eternal flames*, and yet not teach and instruct them, in the one only way of Salvation.[72]

In the end, such words were designed to generate heightened parental sympathy and an intensive form of child-rearing that was spiritually alert from the very beginning of life.[73] If parents had "poison'd" their children with original sin, one noted, they were under compulsion to do everything in their power to seek their children's healing.[74]

The only "cure" for their children's spiritual "disease" was the regenerating work of the Holy Spirit, a process of conversion in which the grace of Christ would provide the child with a "new heart."[75] Narratively portrayed in works such as John Bunyan's *Pilgrim's Progress*, the colonial understanding of conversion included a series of ideal stages that illustrated the "pilgrimage" of the soul's travail.[76] After hearing of God's Word, the journey of salvation commenced with a Holy Spirit-enabled recognition of depravity.[77] This awareness brought both a fear of eternal punishment and a posture of sorrow and repentance for sin. God then opened the eyes to the atoning work of Christ on the cross, generating hope in the possibility of salvation. Yet the process inevitably involved doubts, despair, and an anguished battle between God's will and self-will. Positive resolution came through an infusion of divine grace and an often-tearful surrender of the self to God, producing a growing hatred of sin and an accompanying sense of the beauty of Jesus. The ultimate aim was union with Christ, marked by a heart that was freed from its idolatrous loves and now inclined to do the will of God.[78] By the 1640s, Puritan church membership required that individuals be able to give an account (or "relation") of this process in their lives before the assembled congregation.[79]

Because of this extended and often arduous process, most colonial pastors recognized that conversion was relatively rare (though not impossible) among young children.[80] Prior to the revivals of the 1730s and 1740s, most thought that young people would more likely experience such conversion in their twenties since this was the age at which they could better understand salvation and engage in the necessary work of self-examination. In fact, the most common ages of recorded conversions in colonial New England appeared to be in the twenties and thirties, the time at which Thomas Hooker noted the "abilitie of nature comes on, insomuch that a man is able to conceive and partake of the things of grace . . . and the power of his understanding comes on whereby he is able to embrace them, therefore then is the fittest time that God should bestow his graces upon a man."[81] Such opinions seemed to be validated by the fact that most young people did not join the church as full communicants until after the age of twenty.[82] When thirty children between the ages of ten and fourteen were converted and brought into church fellowship during the revivals of the 1740s, Jonathan Edwards remarked on how earlier Puritans thought it unusual to see such young converts: "It has heretofore been looked on as a strange thing, when any seemed to be savingly wrought upon, and remarkably changed in their childhood."[83]

Yet seventeenth- and early eighteenth-century authors also had published illustrations of children who had turned to Christ at an early age. James Janeway's popular *A Token for Children* (1671) provided accounts of a number of such children in England who agonized over their eternal prospects, wept over their sins, and implored God to save them, often dying young with an eager anticipation of heaven.[84] Cotton Mather appreciated Janeway's reports so much that he generated his own imitation of this work by depicting the lives of exemplary New England children who had come to saving faith early in life.[85] Alongside those younger children converted during the revivals, Jonathan Edwards even recounted the story of Phebe Bartlett, a precocious four-year-old who experienced conversion soon after her eleven-year-old brother's awakening.[86] While most surely recognized that these children were exceptional (and many were prompted to piety by sickness and the approach of death), pastors and other leaders wanted parents to know that salvation could come at any time, thus requiring a constant vigilance in their work.[87] Cotton Mather, in fact, suggested that parents should teach their children about the necessity of conversion from the earliest years. "The People of the *Lowest Capacity*, may & should Concern themselves, about the *Grand Concern* of a *Real Conversion*," he noted. "Our *Children* themselves, tho' it be not long since they were *Weaned*, yet, supposing they can act Reasonably, they will not *Exercise themselves in things too high for them*, if they are Exercised about the *Great Matters* of their *Conversion* to God."[88]

Saving Children from False Security

Despite the fact that God had provided such clear guidance on the importance of raising up children for salvation, colonial leaders often felt that parents and children failed to engage this responsibility with sufficient urgency. While there were many reasons for this neglect, pastors tended to highlight parents' false sense of security regarding their children's spiritual condition. Specifically, they criticized parents' tendency to mistake morality for saving grace, their willingness to wait until children were older to make Christian commitments, and their belief that children would simply inherit their parents' faith. The need, most authors argued, was to expose these lies so that parents and children would be reawakened to the gravity and importance of salvation before it was too late.

One of the most common parental errors, according to colonial pastors, was to mistake children's morality for true saving grace. As parents attempted to evaluate their children's spiritual condition, many were quick to use good behavior as a means of assessing godliness. However, as Increase Mather noted, behavioral conformity could easily give a false picture of the internal work of the Holy Spirit. Many human elements might be responsible for obedience: a good education, a quiet and dutiful personality, or the constraining effects of cultural norms. By resting in the child's observable pious actions, parents were confusing God's "restraining grace" (given to the whole world as a means of limiting the effects of evil) with true "regenerating grace" (the Spirit's work in awakening the dead heart).[89] Good works were the necessary result of true salvation, but such works could also exist in the absence of grace, making outward piety an uncertain indicator of the heart's condition.[90]

In one of Satan's most cunning ploys, pastors warned, the achievement of a moral life could be the very thing that blinded parents and children to the need for a Spirit-generated "new heart." If parents rested on their children's outward obedience, Increase Mather suggested, they might build on a "false foundation" devoid of reliance on Christ's atoning sacrifice.[91] Pious behavior might even generate the pride and self-reliance that were the very marks of an unregenerate heart. While parents were often motivated to teach and pray for their obviously rebellious children, pastors feared that they might be lulled into complacency regarding those children who were dutiful and compliant. "You must get some Good Thing, above and beyond meer Morality," Cotton Mather warned. "A Fine, Civil, Hopeful *Young Man* was lost, for having no more than *That*. You may go a great way, and yet Perish, if you *Lack One Thing*; Even That Good Thing, an Heart so Renew'd, as to Prize a *Christ* above a *World*."[92] Pastors regularly urged parents to remind children of the insufficiency of their good works and the need to call on God for a renewed heart.

Another source of false security was the assumption that children's commitment to Christ could be delayed until "someday" later in life. Pastors worried that children and youth might believe (and parents might concur) that they were free to live for the pleasures of this world in their younger years, repenting and converting at a later time. In order to awaken parents to the lie behind this idea, leaders reminded them of several key realities. They spoke often of the uncertainty and potential brevity of life. Colman asked parents and children to "read the inscriptions on the gravestones and see how many under twenty and thirty to one above fifty or sixty ly interr'd there."[93] Learning their alphabet within the *New England Primer*, children recited "Time cuts down all, Both great and small" for the letter *T*, and "Youth forward slips, Death soonest nips" for the letter *Y*, both accompanied by pictures of a skeletal creature (death) with scythe and arrow (the latter pointed directly at a child). Children also recited "I in the Burying Place may see Graves shorter there than I; From death's Arrest no Age is free; Young Children too may die." A subsequent prayer, which was added to the *Primer* in 1737 and sustained a long popularity in America, reminded children of the fact that death could come at any time: "Now I lay me down to sleep, I pray the Lord my soul to keep. If I should die before I wake, I pray the Lord my soul to take."[94] By alerting parents and children of the brevity and uncertainty of life, leaders hoped to help them see that "someday" might never come.

In even more striking language, many colonial leaders reminded children that a life of childhood sinfulness was likely to invite God's wrath and lead to an early death. Cotton Mather regularly correlated the tragic deaths of children and youth in his community with God's providential punishing hand. Speaking to a group of young people, he stated, "You see such as are *Wicked Overmuch, Dy before their Time*. You see, Such as won't keep their *Tongues from Evil*, don't *see Many Days*, or *much Good in their Days*. . . . You see *Undutiful* Children Cut off by the tremendous Vengeance of God. You see Heaven Discharging its Thunderbolts on the Heads of them that will *Go on still in their Trespasses.* The Great God speaks to you in what you see."[95] While many delayed godliness so that they could enjoy their youth, colonial authors repeatedly warned that God might shut the door on those who presumed on his patience.[96] Such a sentiment was vividly portrayed in the *New England Primer*'s "Dialogue Between Christ, Youth, and the Devil," where Satan's goal was to lull young people into the false security that they could come to Christ at a later time: "Thou may'st be drunk, & swear & curse / And sinners like thee ne'er the worse, / At any time thou may'st repent, / 'Twill serve when all thy days are spent." Youth embraces this appeal and suggests to Christ, "Thou canst at last great Mercy show: / When I am Old, and Pleasure's gone." But Christ has the final word, sending the rebellious young person to hell. The conclusion states it best: "Thus end the days of wicked youth, / Who won't obey nor mind the truth. . . . They in their youth go down to hell, / Under eternal wrath to dwell, / And do not live out half their days, / For cleaving unto sinful ways."[97] Sin itself, therefore, could shorten children's lives, limiting the window in which they could respond to Christ's appeals.

Importantly, pastors also reminded parents that children's habits formed during the early years would be exceedingly difficult to relinquish later in life. Thomas Gouge used a familiar image to describe the problem: "The longer a Tree is suffer'd to grow, the deeper rooting it taketh, and the more hardly will it be pluck'd up. In like manner, the longer thou continuest in Sin, the deeper rooting will it take in thee, and with the greater Difficulty be remov'd."[98] Cotton Mather similarly suggested in vivid terms that "the Longer you continue in your Sins, the deeper and the faster will those *Weeds* of Hell be *Rooted* in your Souls: The Longer the Devil has possession of your hearts, the Strong Armed One will have so much the *Stronger hold* of you. . . . Every Day that you go on in your infidelity, you lay a New *Stone*, upon that Hideous *Wall of Separation* between God and You."[99] Bolstered by anecdotal evidence, Mather was convinced that the cumulative and desensitizing power of habitual sin changed young people's desires and dulled their ability to hear the voice of God, leaving them less capable of responding to him later in life. "Let *This* awaken you," he warned a group of young people, "That if you are not now in your *Youth* brought home unto God, it is probable that you never will be so at all."[100] "Youth" extended into the twenties for colonial Americans, but this still demonstrated that many recognized the hardening effects of age and the increasing difficulty of turning to Christ in one's later years. Despite their steadfast belief that the soul was "dead" in sin from birth, colonial pastors saw children's and youth's minds as more receptive in the earlier years than they would be later on.[101] The key, therefore, was to form godly thinking and habits in these years, allowing these patterns to solidify over time so that young people would be better able to receive and respond to the Spirit's promptings as they matured.

A final way that colonial leaders argued against delayed commitment was by emphasizing that youth was the "Spring of Life," the age at which they could devote the greatest energy and passion to God's work.[102] If children waited until later in life to enter into discipleship, they were essentially robbing God of their best and most productive years, the years of peak strength prior to being *"all clogg'd with the Infirmities of Age."*[103] Just as God's people in the Old Testament were urged to bring the *"first Fruits"* and the "young pigeons" as the best sacrifices to God, so parents were to bring their children to Christ during their time of maximum vitality and potential.[104] "O what Pity it is," Thomas Gouge suggested, "that the Devil, the World, and the Flesh, should have thy Cream and Flower. And how shameful, that God, to whom thy whole Life is due, should have only the Bran and Dregs!"[105] In order for children to be a blessing to both church and world, the key was for them to embrace "early piety," to give themselves fully to Christ when they were "the Fittest, and the Freshest for *Business*."[106]

The last form of false security pastors addressed was the belief that children would automatically "inherit" their parents' faith. Pastors celebrated the spiritual privileges bestowed on children born of godly parents, noting how they participated in God's covenantal blessings and had ready access to preaching, home instruction and worship, parental example, and parental prayers. Increase Mather's famous claim that "God hath seen good to cast the line of Election so, as that it doth . . . for the most part, run through the loins of godly Parents" was a clear expression of hope for those born into godly households.[107] However, leaders fearful of spiritual complacency also gave stiff warnings to both parents and children that these anticipated blessings were far from guarantees. While children were born into the covenant community, they would have to "own the covenant" personally as they grew. Cotton Mather was quick to warn against a false security based on a godly family tree: "You that are *Born* of *Godly*

Parents, are under as much necessity to be *New born*, as any whatsoever. When you come to an Age capable of making your choice, you must your selves Express a Disposition to choose the *God of your Parents*. . . . Thus, O Child grown up to act for thy self, Tho' *Noah*, *David*, or *Job* were thy *Father*, yet if thou dost not thy self look after a Saving *Righteousness* for thy self, thou shalt never be Saved by Theirs."[108] The faith of parents, while a tremendous help, could never ensure salvation. In fact, if children placed their hope in their family's heritage of faith, this might even blind them to their true spiritual need.

Pastors regularly reminded their congregants that Scripture itself bore witness to the fact that godly parents could have ungodly children. In spite of lineage and parental training, as Cooper put it, "there was a scoffing *Ishmael* in *Abraham's* Family; a Profane *Esau* in *Isaac's*; an Incestuous *Amnon*, and a murderous *Absalom* in *David's*; and so in others."[109] Citing the apostate children of Old Testament fathers Adam, Noah, Abraham, Samuel, Eli, Isaac, David, and Josiah, a host of leaders cautioned against viewing salvation as a spiritual birthright. Some even claimed that God allowed for godly parents to have ungodly offspring precisely so that he could demonstrate his own supremacy in election. Lest people consider the transmission of faith automatic in godly families, Cotton Mather suggested that "the Great *Sovereign* of the World, that He may Show the *Sovereignty* of His *Grace*, as He sometimes will *Convert* the Children of a *Wicked Parent*, so He sometimes will *Refuse* the Children of a *Godly* One. God will make it Evident, that it is not in the power of One man, to give *Grace* unto another; yea, that it is not in the power of *Parents* which have *Grace*, to Convey *That*, as they do *Sin*, and *Woe*, unto their own Children."[110] When God chose not to save the children of godly parents, he was showing himself to be a God who was not dependent on human genetics. In the end, leaders hoped that this reality would press parents to seek a personal experience of faith within each of their children rather than presuming on a godly heritage.

Of course, these biblical examples of failed faith transmission only reinforced what colonial pastors witnessed on a regular basis in their churches. "If a *Godly Parent*, have *many Children*, it is very *seldome* seen that *All* of them do prove *Ungodly*," Cotton Mather noted, "but it is very *often* seen, that *some* of them do so."[111] Across the early generations in New England, church leaders saw that many of the baptized children of first-generation settlers did not come to saving faith as they grew. When these second-generation children failed to demonstrate a spiritual transformation in adulthood, leaders questioned their church membership status and therefore their ability to bring their own children forward for baptism. To cast them out seemed to go against the inclusivity of the external covenant. To bring them into full membership, however, would threaten the integrity of the internal covenant of grace and the purity of churches that wished to remain populated only by converted "visible saints."[112] A position of compromise—forged by a special synod in 1662—argued that those baptized children who were not able to provide evidence of spiritual renewal in adulthood would be designated as "halfway" members. They would be able to bring their children for baptism (thus preserving the familial inclusivity of the external covenant), but they could not vote and would not be invited to participate in the Lord's Supper (thus maintaining the purity of the internal covenant of grace).[113] This "half-way covenant" provided a means by which the rising generation could remain within the protective canopy of church influence while also preserving the purity of a church membership consisting of converted Christians alone.[114]

Yet some worried that this was precisely the kind of move that would foster the ongoing false security of an "inherited faith." Jonathan Edwards, for his part, rejected the "half-way covenant" because he felt that it led to parenting that was attentive to the "external honor" of baptism but "careless about the spiritual blessing" of being a "Christian indeed."[115] The half-way covenant, he suggested, "greatly tends to establish the stupidity and irreligion of children, as well as negligence of parents. . . . And if neither of the parents appear truly pious, in the judgment of rational charity, there is not in this case any ground to expect that the children will be brought up in the nurture and admonition of the Lord, or that they will have anything worthy of the name of a Christian education, how solemnly soever the parents may promise it."[116] Edwards felt that if parents were not permitted to baptize their children without a true conversion to Christ themselves, they would be less apt to live in false security and more likely to take seriously their own spiritual life and the nurture of their children. Parents in colonial New England always had to balance the wonderful assurances of covenant blessings with the dangers of apathy, presumption, and false security.[117]

Colonial pastors did acknowledge that very young children were likely safe within their parents' faith, but they also felt it was impossible to know at what age children became responsible for their own souls.[118] This seemed to be a moving target in this era. As Catherine Brekus has suggested in her account of Sarah Osborn in the eighteenth century, parents with children who died a bit later had a more challenging time finding assurance of their salvation. Osborn's son Samuel died at the age of eleven, and while many in the seventeenth century might have placed Samuel on the safe side of the "age of accountability," the revivals of the 1730s and 1740s highlighted prominent salvation stories of youth between the ages of ten and fourteen.[119] This may have played a role in moving parents to expect religious conversion at an earlier age, likely adding to the anxiety of parents, like Osborn, whose children died without an apparent spiritual awakening.[120] Security within the womb of parental faith had an unknown expiration date, and most colonial pastors wanted to make sure that children—and their parents—did not presume on the mercy of God for too long.

For most pastors in colonial New England, the real antidote to all these forms of false security was for parents to instill a godly fear within their children.[121] In fact, parents were directed to foster spiritual anxiety so as to spark an eventual spiritual awakening. As George Marsden has noted, much Puritan upbringing was "designed to teach children to recognize how insecure their lives were."[122] This included both insecurity about continued physical life (death could come at any time) and insecurity about their eternal condition (hell was always a possibility). Anxiety was seen as a positive and healthy spiritual state, while assurance displayed an unhealthy self-confidence that might lead to spiritual apathy. This would begin to change as eighteenth-century evangelicals stressed assurance of one's conversion, but for many colonial Christians, helping their children doubt their own eternal safety was indeed a mark of parenting success.

Fear of eternal judgment was the critical spark. Janeway's popular *Token for Children* reminded children of the fate of those who spurned Christ in their youth:

> Wither do you think those Children go when they die, that will not do what they are bid but play the Truant, and lye, and speak naughty words, and break the Sabbath? . . . Why, I will tell you, they which Lie,

must to their Father the Devil into everlasting burning; they which never pray, God will pour out his wrath upon them; and when they beg and pray in Hell Fire, God will not forgive them, but there they must lie for ever. . . . O Hell is a terrible place, that's worse a thousand times than whipping.[123]

If such appeals were not enough, parents were charged to tell their rebellious children that parents would themselves approve of their eternal judgment if they resisted salvation, their parental tears serving as the "oyl to make the everlasting flames of hell burn the more vehemently upon thy Soul, throughout the dayes of Eternity."[124] Such warnings served as wake-up calls for young people to renounce their lives of sin. As Thomas Gouge put it succinctly to a group of male youth, "Must I not either turn or burn?"[125]

Children heard these messages and, in some cases, responded with deep emotion. Samuel Sewall's daughter Elizabeth repeatedly burst into tears because she feared death, certain that she was destined for hell because of her sins.[126] One pastor in Halifax, Massachusetts, recorded that a nine-year-old girl in his congregation "fell down in great distress and said, it seemed as if hell lay before her, that she was ready to fall into it: The Wrath of God was dreadful to her."[127] Janeway had indeed hoped for this result, encouraging children to "go to your Father or Mother, or some Good Body, and ask them what thou shalt do to be God's Child; and tell them that thou art afraid. . . . Get by thy self, into the Chamber . . . and fall upon thy knees, and weep and mourn, and tell Christ thou art afraid that he doth not love thee . . . ; beg of him to give thee his Grace and pardon for thy sins. . . . O give me a Christ! O let me not be undone for ever!"[128] Fear of God's wrath was, for parents, a critical evangelistic tool, motivating children to recognize their desperate need and to turn to Christ for salvation.

Christian Parenting and the Awakening of the Child's Soul

In the end, pastors in colonial New England saw the use of fear as a loving act of awakening mercy for children. Rather than viewing children as needing protection from "adult" realities, parents and pastors desired to warn them against the perils of eternal death. Such fear, of course, had the potential to create frightening images of a wrathful God in children's minds, de-emphasizing the love, compassion, and grace of the one who held children in his arms as he blessed them (Mark 10:16). While the fear of eternal punishment was no doubt effective in many cases, it may also have made it more difficult for children to desire an intimate relationship with this fearful God. But to those that argued against talking to children about such themes, Jonathan Edwards remarked, "Why should we conceal the truth from them? A child that has a dangerous wound may need the painful lance as well as grown persons. And that would be a foolish pity in such a case, that would hold back a lance and throw away the life."[129] If parents were to hide these harsh realities out of a misguided concern for children's feelings, leaders argued, they would be remarkably unloving to their spiritually vulnerable offspring, placing brief earthly comfort ahead of an eternity of suffering. Colonial pastors were less concerned about fearful emotions than they were about the false security of a fear-less spiritual complacency. "Warning" was perceived as the most loving thing they could do.

Colonial pastors therefore urged Christian parents to take part in the work of evangelism. It was parents who would help children see their depravity and their eternal peril, working to raise awareness of the need for divine grace. It was parents who would be content, not with good moral behavior, but only with a clear posture of repentance for sin and acceptance of Jesus's sacrifice. It was parents who would start the work of Christian formation early in their children's lives, recognizing that life is uncertain and that the early years are best designed to set habits of faith. It was parents who would ensure that their children did not grow complacent, lured into a false sense of security by their family background or the external covenant and its "half-way" provisions. It was parents who would be called on to raise up this godly seed so that these children would passionately pursue the Lord. Parents, in other words, were to be the heralds of salvation in their children's lives.

This was parents' purpose because this is what they perceived to be God's purpose. Paul David Tripp has helpfully distinguished "ownership" parenting from "ambassadorial" parenting. Ownership parenting, accord-ing to Tripp, sees children as the possession of their parents, giving parents the right to create a vision of what they want for their children and what they expect from them as well. Ambassadorial parenting, on the other hand, sees children as belonging to God and views the parenting task as representing his larger purposes in children's lives.[130] The colonial literature certainly highlighted parents' ambassadorial role, regularly reminding them that their children did not belong to them and highlighting the ways in which they were "on loan" from the Lord in order to fit them for the kingdom of God. They had to be vigilant against the temptation to idolize their children, instead stewarding their souls so that they would be prepared for the Holy Spirit to give them new life.

Much of the parenting advice provided by pastors in colonial New England was a direct function of their view of children. Parents were taught to see their children as lost, dead in their sins, and unable to free themselves from the tyranny of the devil. Such a view prompted compassion, a heartfelt concern over their children's precarious state. It prompted an urgency and intentionality in seeking their healing and redemption. It also prompted a belief that the greatest threat to their children was not the surrounding culture but the sin that lurked within. Parents, therefore, were not just addressing the "symptoms" of poor behavior but were instead to focus on the inner "disease" that produced those symptoms. They were called on to deal not just with individual "sins" but with the more comprehensive inward "sin" that caused outward evil. Christian parenting for colonial Christians was not a moral improvement project but a rescue mission that sought to liberate children from spiritual bondage through Christ's converting work. Behavioral conformity, as much as that was appreciated and expected, was not enough. Protection from the culture within the walls of the home was not enough. The work of parenting was to help children see their need for a "new heart." This vision of children, and the parenting goals that stemmed from it, set the framework for intense debates about the nature of "good" Protestant parenting over the next centuries.

Since colonial pastors knew that parents could not bring about their children's spiritual transformation on their own, they recommended that parents make use of the "means" God provided for his people to experience his grace. Parents would pray for their children and lead them into practices of worship within the home. They would teach their children, providing them with the biblical and doctrinal foundations that would help them understand and receive God's grace. They would exercise disciplinary authority and "government" in order to restrain their children's sin and willfulness. These parental duties—represented by many colonial authors in terms of the priestly, prophetic, and kingly offices of Christ—were considered the keys to fostering salvation in children's lives. As pastor Benjamin Wadsworth put it, "I believe the Ignorance, Wickedness (& consequent Judgments) that have prevailed, & still are prevailing among us, are not more plainly owing to any one thing, than to the neglect of Family Religion, Instruction & Government, and the reviving of these things, would yield as comfortable a prospect of our future good, as almost any one thing I can think of."[131] The following chapters will trace each of these critical parental "postures" as pathways by which parents were to raise up their children as a "godly seed" that would propagate the faith throughout the generations.

CHAPTER 2

The Parent as Priest

Leading Children into God's Presence

Oh what a sweet and comfortable thing shall this be to the soule
and conscience of such an Householder, when he hath bene so
diligent and carefull in the training and bringing up of his children
and servants in obedience and wayes of the Lord, that he may
rightly deserve to have this worthy report and commendation
given unto him, from the mouth and penne of the godly: Namely,
that he hath a Church in his house.

—John Dod and Robert Cleaver,
A Godly Forme of Household Government[1]

As colonial pastors looked to motivate mothers and fathers in the work
of Christian parenting, they often came back to the image of the
parent as a priest within the home. In part, the designation of parents as
priests was a function of the Reformation appeal to the "priesthood of all
believers," a reality that extended the priestly role of pastors to laypeople
in general and to parents specifically as ministers within their families.[2]
In addition, parents were described as priests because they were called
to embody two of the primary postures of priests in the Old Testament
Scriptures. First, observing that biblical fathers like Abraham, David,
and Job regularly gathered their families together to offer animal sacrifices to the Lord, pastors urged parents to serve as priests by gathering
their children for worship, both within the church and within the home.[3]
Second, since Old Testament priests interceded for the people, pastors
also implored parents to pray for their children, boldly approaching God's
throne with requests for their salvation, sanctification, and protection

from Satan's attacks. Whether through family worship or fervent prayer, parental priests were to usher their children into the very presence of God, thus fulfilling their obligation to "bring our Children as neer to Heaven as we can."[4]

Bringing the Child to the Church

Certainly, part of parents' priestly role was to connect children to the life of the larger church, the covenant family of God. Among the Puritans and their close colleagues, pastors spoke of the priestly importance of parents bringing their infants to the church for baptism, a ceremony that generally took place within the first two weeks of the child's life.[5] Baptism was important for several reasons. First, it was the time at which the child was given a name. Historian Daniel Scott Smith has noted that "the naming of children is never a trivial cultural act," and such was certainly the case among New England's early Christians.[6] While family names were commonly used, especially for first children, parents frequently used names as a way of pronouncing the desired character of the child.[7] Some chose to name children after distinct character traits—Roger Clap famously named some of his children Preserved, Thanks, Supply, and Hopestill—but most chose favored biblical characters, especially if they matched the names of godly ancestors.[8] In fact, scholars estimate that upwards of 80 percent of children in New England were given names from the Old and New Testaments, a practice that continued well into the eighteenth century.[9] Such names always bore the weight of the namesake's characters. Cotton Mather said that he named his daughter Hannah "with my Desires, that shee may bee a *gracious* Child, and imitate those of her Name, which are commemorated in the Oracles of God."[10] Of his daughter, Samuel Sewall noted, "I was struggling whether to call her Sarah or Mehetabel; but when I saw Sarah's standing in Scripture . . . I resolv'd on that side."[11] As John Dod and Robert Cleaver suggested, biblical names were given so that "they by hearing those names, may be excited and moved to follow the vertuous life and Christian conversation of those men and women whose names they beare."[12]

While those in colonial New England did not typically continue the practice of giving the same name to multiple siblings (a common custom in the Middle Ages), they did frequently name children after deceased siblings.[13] For example, Thomas Shepard recorded: "My wife . . . was delivered mercifully of this second son Thomas, which name I gave him because we thought the Lord gave me the first son I lost on sea in this again, and hence gave him his brother's name."[14] Giving children these "necronyms" was an attempt to ensure that certain names would live on, revealing parents' belief that God had blessed them with children to replace those who had died.[15] Many scholars have taken this practice as an indication that family heritage was valued more highly in colonial America than the unique individuality of each child. By the nineteenth century, an era in which individual identity was more generally prized, this practice of assigning necronyms largely fell out of favor.[16]

In addition to personal naming, baptism was also the time when children were named as participants in the covenant community.[17] Like Old Testament circumcision for the children of Israel, baptism linked the children of New England to God's covenantal promises, originally given to Abraham but extended through Christ to all of Abraham's future "seed."[18] Baptism did not save the child's soul and was no guarantee of future regeneration, but it was a sign and seal of the covenant blessings of God bestowed on parents and their children across the generations.[19] It was also a mark of God's commitment to these children. Cotton Mather suggested that "God by this *Baptism*, has *Pre-ingaged* these Children for Himself: He marks them for His own Propriety; He binds them closer to Himself than others; Yea, He Assures them, that if they grow up, they shall have an Opportunity under the means of Grace, to make a choice of Him for their God, and that His Holy Spirit shall Strive with them, till they impenitently & incureably Resist the Strivings."[20]

Even as they were to celebrate these covenant privileges, pastors spoke of how baptism should serve as a means of instilling within parents, children, and the larger church a sense of their ongoing responsibilities to God and to one another. For parents, baptism was to be a continual reminder that they "promised to bring them up virtuously, to lead a godly and Christian life, that they might keep God's will and commandments and walk in the same all the days of their lives."[21] For children, baptism was to serve as a perpetual sign of God's "ownership" over them and therefore of their obligations to serve him.[22] As Samuel Phillips wrote, "Your *Baptism* lays *you* under *Engagements* to be the Lord's, as your *Catechism* instructs you: The nature of Baptism is such, that *it binds* to present and perpetual Obedience: So that, for *you*, after you are come to Years of Understanding, to *delay* to seek after the God of your Fathers, is plainly to *rob God* of his Due: It is to disregard your Baptism, and put Contempt upon that; as well as to undervalue the Good Will of your Parents, in making a Dedication of you to the Lord."[23] It was at this time that members of the church also committed to care for the child and to do their part in helping parents raise up their children in the faith. In this sense, baptism revealed that parents' priestly work was never a solitary endeavor but a shared responsibility of the larger covenant community. As parents offered their children to the Lord in baptism, this ceremony served as a perpetual reminder of the joint obligations of parents, children, and the church in guiding children toward salvation.

As children grew, parents were called on to ensure that children participated in public worship on a weekly basis while developing a healthy reverence for the local church.[24] Worship services typically took place in the morning and the afternoon on the Sabbath, each service lasting about three hours.[25] With no nurseries or Sunday school classes, children were to begin attending weekly public worship as soon as they were old enough to "be kept so quiet there, as not to make a disturbance," and parents were responsible for helping their children engage as deeply as possible with these worship experiences.[26] Dod and Cleaver noted that prior to the service parents should have their children prepare their hearts by considering God's mercies and by casting away "all such cares, thoughts, and affections, as might hinder them from a diligent hearing."[27] Parents were to ensure that children were on time and that they participated with reverence and quiet attentiveness (not, as Joseph Sewall noted, being "profane and ludicrous") during the services, surely a challenge during the lengthy prayers and sermons.[28] That they did not always succeed was evidenced by the fact that members of the New Haven town meeting decided to appoint "monitors" who would "have a stick or wand wherewith to smite such as are unruly or of uncouth behavior."[29] Upon returning home after the service, parents were instructed to ask their children questions about the sermon, probing their understanding and recommending appropriate prayers and applications to carry with them throughout the week.[30]

Offering the Sacrifice: Family Worship

In addition to corporate worship, the most systematic way in which parents fulfilled their priestly role was by presiding over daily morning and evening worship with their families. It was this practice, in fact, that led many to refer to colonial households as "little churches."[31] Samuel Sewall called them "*Bethels*, Houses of GOD, Houses devoted to His more immediate Service; That they be Temples Consecrated to the Worship of GOD."[32] William Cooper, likewise, noted that "wherever the godly Seed have a *House*, God will have a *Church* in it: Their Houses will be little Churches, Places wherein God is acknowledg'd, serv'd and worshipp'd."[33] Parents, and especially fathers, were charged to serve as priests within this domestic temple, leading their children—in addition to any relatives, servants, apprentices, and guests—daily into the very presence of God.[34] Worship was always to be public (in the church) and private (in the "closet"), but it was also to be familial, joining all the members of the household together daily as a worshiping community.[35]

Befitting the designation of parents as priests, colonial authors tended to refer to home-based worship not only as "family worship" and "family prayer" but also as the "family sacrifice."[36] As Cotton Mather understood it, Old Testament sacrifices existed in two forms: "*propitiatory* sacrifices" (those pertaining to atonement for sin) and "*eucharistical* sacrifices" (those pertaining to praise and worship). Now that Christ had offered on the cross the "once for all" (Heb. 10:10) sacrifice for sin, the "new covenant" family, he argued, was called on to offer sacrifices of praise and worship in gratitude for his finished work.[37] While it appears that some (likely wealthier) families hired chaplains to perform the daily worship services in the home, the normal charge was for parents to assume priestly oversight for these daily ceremonies.[38] Reflecting this pattern, John Barnard suggested, "Every Master of a Family should take the proper Season, Evening and Morning, to offer up, with their Families, this their Sacrifice unto God, and the lifting up of their Hands should be like the continual Burnt-Offering."[39]

While the format of the "family sacrifice" varied among households, the component parts of Scripture reading, singing, and prayer were largely universal. Cotton Mather suggested that these nonnegotiable elements paralleled the sacrifices that were offered by family heads in the Old Testament. In such sacrifices, there was a lighting of the lamps, which represented the importance of Bible reading as "a lamp to my feet and a light to my path" (Ps. 119:105). For singing, Mather noted that the "Songs of Ascent" in the Psalms were meant to be sung "while the Smoke of the sacrifices was Ascending before the Lord." He went so far as to say that the Psalms, "*Graciously Sung*," were "themselves *Evangelical Sacrifices*," further commenting that "the *Angels* of God themselves, Love to be about the *Houses*, where the *Families* are often *Singing* the Praises of God."[40] Finally, there was the sacrifice itself that was "*burnt* unto the Lord," representing the family's prayers of confession, thanksgiving, and supplication that would rise to God as a sweet aroma. These three components—Scripture reading, singing, and prayer—represented the "curriculum" of family worship and the basis for a pleasing sacrifice to the Lord.[41]

Drawing from the Reformation emphasis on lay Bible reading, the oral reading of the biblical text was normally the first order of business in such family exercises. Most encouraged the practice of reading a chapter of the Bible each morning and evening, walking through the text systematically (they called this reading "in course").[42] Samuel Sewall recorded in his diary that he had, with his family, "begun in Course to read the New Testament, having ended the Revelation the night before."[43] To the degree possible, children old enough to read would follow along in their own copies of the Bible and sometimes read sections out loud. Sewall, for example, recorded on January 10 in 1689, "It falls to my Daughter Elisabeth's Share to read the 24. of Isaiah, which she doth with many Tears not being very well, and the Contents of the Chapter, and Sympathy with her draw Tears from me also."[44] Sewall often took great comfort from these family readings. Just before burying his two-year-old daughter Sarah in 1696, three of his children sequentially read Ecclesiastes 3 (speaking of "a time to be born and a time to die"), Revelation 22 on the heavenly city, and Psalm 38, which detailed David's anguish of soul. "All of this," he noted, was to his family's "mutual comfort."[45] This way of systematic reading was designed to expose children to the whole counsel of Scripture and to help them grasp the larger picture of the Bible's storyline.

In addition to providing a sense of the narrative, Bible reading was designed to offer spiritual nourishment for daily faithfulness. Most seemed to follow the advice of the Westminster Assembly, which recommended that fathers interpret the text and then lead the family to confess sins mentioned by the text, take warning from biblical words of judgment, make plans for obedience to biblical commands, draw comfort from biblical promises, and raise any questions or doubts "for resolution."[46] Yet while such father-led exposition and application remained the most popular method throughout this era, by the eighteenth century some parents began to follow up Bible reading with questions for the children, asking them to comment on what they had learned from the passage. Samuel Hopkins noted that Jonathan Edwards, in his morning and evening family worship (conducted by candlelight in the winter), would read a chapter of the Bible and ask his children follow-up questions "according to their Age and Capacity," explaining and expanding on passages as he saw fit.[47] Pastors always desired that such family reading include straightforward applications for spiritual growth.

After the reading and discussion of the text, family worship typically moved to singing, and through the early eighteenth century this usually (especially among the Puritans) consisted of the singing of psalms. Often taken from the *Bay Psalm Book*, these psalms provided a particular musical rhythm to the day. Morning songs expressed gratitude to God for the safety of the night and looked forward to the day with requests for strength and devotion.[48] Songs in the evening tended to focus on death to self and sin, repenting of daily transgressions along the way. This musical cycle of death (evening) and new life (morning) was meant to tell the gospel story daily and to remind children that their hope for daily strength and spiritual rebirth was found in God's powerful hand. Family singing was thought to be blessed because it anticipated the future reality of heaven in which all God's people would gather and lift praises to the King of kings, Cotton Mather adding that "*there is not a more Lively Resemblance of Heaven upon Earth, than a Company of Godly Christians together Singing a Psalm unto God.*"[49] This practice appeared to be quite popular. During the First Great Awakening, Benjamin Franklin noted that "one could not walk through Philadelphia in the evening without hearing psalms sung in different families of every street."[50]

While the singing of psalms continued well into the 1700s, family devotional singing expanded and diversified in the eighteenth century, primarily because of the hymn-writing contributions of Isaac Watts. Cotton Mather, who was close friends with Watts, included these hymns in many of his printed sermons on family worship and also used them in his own family devotions. When Watts sent his updated edition of *Hymns and*

Spiritual Songs to Mather in 1711, Mather made it clear that his family was to be the beneficiary. "I receive them as a Recruit and Supply sent in from Heaven for the Devotions of my Family," he suggested, adding that his household was where he "will sing them, and endeavor to bring [his] Family in Love with them."[51] It was actually in the home, rather than the church, that such hymns found their primary market in the years prior to the First Great Awakening. While local churches continued the practice of "lining out," in which a preceptor read out a translated psalm line by line while congregants echoed back the refrains, Watts's hymns became a staple of both private and family worship in local households.[52] Recognizing this potential market, Watts wrote his famous *Divine and Moral Songs for Children* in 1715. As one of the first hymnbooks to offer songs written from the perspective of children themselves, this work tailored its contents to a child's level of understanding and maturity.[53] Over sixty-eight editions were published between 1715 and 1880, and it is clear that Watts's songs created a shared religious language of praise among the children and families in this era.[54]

When reading and singing had concluded, the family went to prayer, the climax and culmination of the family sacrifice. Family prayers were either conducted spontaneously or with the help of written prayer guides and manuals. As Charles Hambrick-Stowe has pointed out, the Puritan daily rhythm of morning and evening prayers, as with their hymns, was a means of reenacting the cycle of death and resurrection, dying to sin through the cross in evening repentance and rising each morning to newness of life through recognition of his mercy.[55] The morning prayers constructed by pastors often included expressions of gratitude for salvation and for protection during sleep in addition to petitions related to daily bread, the activities of the day, family members, the poor, local leaders, and the larger world. Evening prayers provided the opportunity to give thanks and to consecrate the day's events to God. It was often a time for conscious repentance, looking back on the actions and attitudes of the heart and seeking forgiveness. Such prayers also included appeals for protection through the night and requests that God would preserve family members eternally when the "night of death" would come. Each day's prayers, therefore, reminded children of the gospel and its cadence of desperation, confession, and repentance (the nightly "death") followed by awakening to new life, gratitude, and the obedience that emerged out of such thankfulness (the morning "resurrection"). It was for colonial Christians a repetitive performance of the appeal of Psalm 92:2 "to declare your steadfast love in the morning, / and your faithfulness by night."[56]

While morning and evening prayers were offered in the context of family worship, colonial pastors also urged priestly parents to engage in mealtime prayers. As a practical means of demonstrating both reliance on God's provision and thanksgiving for his gifts, meal prayers represented the appropriate posture of created and dependent beings. While God had sanctified all food, Dod and Cleaver noted, yet "they are unholy unto us, when we do not for our part sanctifie them by faithfull prayer and thanksgiving."[57] Drawing from Scripture and the examples of early church fathers, Cotton Mather suggested that meal prayers represented the kind of reflexive thanksgiving that should characterize the recipients of God's good gifts. "We feed like *Swine*, more than like *Saints*," he noted, "if we take not our Food, with some such Action."[58] Puritans typically included two prayers within a single meal. The first, before the meal, declared dependence on God's grace in providing the resources necessary for survival. The second, coming after the meal, expressed gratitude for this sustenance and for the strength it would provide for service to community and church.[59] As the pastors of Connecticut's western district suggested, praying at meals "naturally tends to improve and confirm a spirit of dependence on God, and of thankfulness to him."[60]

For colonial authors, it was this continual rhythm of dependence and thankfulness that made it necessary for families to participate in worship every day and (at least) twice per day. Through this cyclical "pray[ing] without ceasing" (1 Thess. 5:17), they were, morning and evening, acknowledging their dependence on God for everything they needed and returning thanks to him for his care, provision, and salvation. Colonial leaders noted that families sinned daily and so required daily forgiveness. They faced daily challenges and so required daily wisdom. They had daily physical needs and so needed "daily bread." God's mercies were new every morning and so required daily thanksgiving.[61] This is why so many pastors roundly condemned those who conducted family worship only a few times per week or only on Sabbath evenings.[62] By offering prayers every morning and evening, family members expressed their desire to start and end each day with God and to allow him to speak the first and last words of every day. As Cotton Mather put it, family worship should be "the *Alpha*, and

Omega of the Day. . . . The *Key* to open our Business in the *Morning*; and the *Bar* to shut up all in the *Evening*."[63]

This was also why authors tended to condemn those parental priests who allowed the family sacrifice to be offered too late in the morning or too late at night. William Seward noted that it was important to engage family worship early in the morning "before a Throng of worldly Cares and Business crowd in upon your Mind, and while your Spirits are fresh and lively."[64] Benjamin Colman likewise noted that family prayers should be conducted when everyone was "Fresh and fasting," before work and before the first meal of the day so that God would be served before self.[65] Pastors warned families to conduct their worship in the evening at a time before family members were "benum'd with Sleep or Drowsiness," avoiding late night "visits" and, for men, late night outings to the tavern.[66] Many colonial leaders spoke about the importance of keeping consistent hours for their sleep and for family worship. Seward spoke vehemently against the practice of "sitting up late at Night," till "10 or 11 o'Clock, or even till the Hour of Midnight; and then fetching it up in profound Sleep the next Morning," because this "greatly unfits Persons for the Exercises of Piety and Devotion."[67] Since the Lord deserved the times of day when family members were at their best, early morning and early evening represented the ideal times for such exercises.

Colonial leaders did make concessions in light of the nature of childhood, regularly reminding parents not to overburden their children with arduous and lengthy devotions. "'Tis much better that your Prayers be short and fervent," Seward said, "than lengthy and dull."[68] Many authors lamented the tendency of family heads to spend too much time in expositions of biblical passages, leading children to dread these gatherings. Others spoke of long and drawn-out prayers that would tire young children (Deodat Lawson spoke of parents praying their children's hearts "into heaven" but then by drab monotony praying them "out again").[69] Family worship, in this sense, was best when it was brief but frequent, not overburdening children's young minds and bodies.[70]

To insert a bit of variety, some authors recommended that families gather collectively to participate in the practices of family worship. Cotton Mather, for example, proposed that groups of families in the same geographical location meet together periodically at a single house in order to offer up prayers, sing psalms, repeat sermons, and speak together about the things of God.[71] This was a simple way in which families, in "conference," could *"bear one another's burdens*, in whatever Distresses the Providence of God, may bring upon any of your *Families*."[72] In addition, as "Reforming Societies," these corporate family sacrifices could provide important opportunities to be "watchful over one another," giving admonitions regarding the "Infirmities" visible in one another.[73] Such a model was in keeping with the Puritan emphasis on communal "watchfulness," the collective attempt to help one another live in obedience to the truths of Scripture.[74]

While every day was to be a day of family worship, the Sabbath expanded these prayerful activities. Pastors in colonial New England developed a vision for the Sabbath far removed from the joviality characterizing medieval and early modern England. They replaced the drinking, feasting, and sports with rest and worship, enforcing such a lifestyle through legislation.[75] Sabbath observance often began at sunset on Saturday evening as household members were charged to halt work and come together for family worship, catechism training, psalm or hymn singing, and prayer.[76] The Sabbath itself typically involved two church services, conscious rest from both work and play, and personal and familial worship and study. Therefore, the "prophaning" of the Sabbath included both "idleness" in relation to religious exercises and improper activity or play that pulled children away from worship and rest.[77] In his diary, Nathaniel Mather offered a conscience-stricken reflection on how he had been *"whitling"* on the Sabbath (hiding behind a door), noting that this was "a specimen of that atheism that I brought into the world with me!"[78] Likewise, the *New England Primer* implored children to "shun the Sin of Sabbath-breaking" because "the Devil is the Play-Mate of the Child that will Play on the Sabbath-Day."[79]

As a day to "get above the *World* and above *themselves*," the weekly Sabbath paralleled daily family worship but extended the time and diminished distractions from these exercises.[80] As Colman remarked, on the Sabbath families were to "be more inlarged in Duties of Worship, both in the Closet and in the Family. . . . As the *Sacrifices* under the *Law* were doubled on the *Sabbath-day*, so it is fitting under the *Gospel* that our Family Sacrifices of Praise and Prayer be inlarg'd and doubled on the Lord's-*day*. If on other days the *Word* of God should be read in our Houses, on *this* more. If Prayer and Praise be requisite every day, surely they are more on the holy Sabbath."[81] If families would expand worship and avoid "temporal Cares and worldly Thoughts," Cooper indicated, they would *"mount up as upon Eagles Wings,* and make their *Sallies,* at least, into the Suburbs of Heaven."[82] Much was at stake in this, according to Cotton Mather. "It has been truly and justly observed, that our whole religion fares according to our Sabbaths," he noted. "Poor Sabbaths make poor Christians."[83]

Pastors had little patience for those who claimed that they had no time for family worship. After noting that many seemed to have time for other activities—such as taking part in needless diversions at local taverns—Benjamin Wadsworth indicated that a lack of time was an excuse that revealed the true nature of the heart. "If thou dost not Pray with thy Family," he contended, "tis not really because thou hast not time for it, but rather because thou hast no heart for it."[84] Colman criticized fathers specifically for being so taken up with "worldly cares and business" that they had no time for family prayer. "I'm afraid that men's worldly cares & business do too often divert them from and hinder 'em in the greater and more needful cares for their own and their children's Souls," he lamented. "They rise early to their work and continue in their lov'd worldly business until the Evening, and then they are tir'd and weary, drowsy and unfit, as well as have no list to pray."[85] Apparently perceiving that women were more naturally given to family worship than men, Cotton Mather encouraged wives to "use all the Endeavour and Artifice that ever they can to perswade and oblige their *Husbands,* to maintain *Prayer* in their Families."[86] In the end, the pastors of colonial New England viewed family worship as a non-negotiable method by which priestly parents would keep the presence of God ever before their children's hearts and minds. As Mather concluded, "Constant FAMILY-WORSHIP, is so necessary, to keep alive a Sense of God and religion in the Minds of Men, that I see not how any Family that neglects it, can in reason be esteemed A Family of Christians, or indeed have any Religion at all."[87]

Priestly Intercession: Parental Prayer

While parents exercised their priestly duties by gathering their children together for church and for daily family worship, an equally important priestly task was the act of intercessory prayer. Colonial pastors were obviously concerned about children's spiritual condition and intentional in seeking means to foster conversion and faithful commitment to Christ. At the same time, they placed little stock in parents' ability to produce such outcomes on their own. Prayer was so important for them because they knew that salvation was a supernatural gift of God. As Increase Mather so vividly stated,

> Parents cannot give Grace to their Children. . . . Only He that has a Creating Power, can *Create the New Heart*. . . . Regeneration is in the Scripture expressed by that of taking away the *heart of stone* and giving an *heart of flesh*. . . . When a Sinner is Converted, one that had been dead and buried, is brought alive out of his Grave. . . . Who but the Omnipotent God can do so miraculous a work? Therefore if Parents would have Converting Grace for their Children, it is necessary that they should go to that God who Raiseth the Dead, and by earnest prayer seek it at his hands, who can, and who alone can do it for them.[88]

Parental prayer, the act of imploring God to work in their children's hearts by the power of the Holy Spirit, was for colonial authors the key to spiritual awakening. It was the means by which God would pour out his blessings, heal spiritual blindness, and open eyes to the beauty of Jesus. "Prayer opens the Windows of Heaven," Increase Mather said to a group of gathered parents. "Assuredly, if there be Prayers, and Tears before the Lord on this account, they will come pouring down again in showers of grace at last."[89]

While parental prayer was sometimes ritualized in public forums as "Days of Prayer for the Rising Generation," authors more typically linked priestly intercession to the biblical examples of fathers (such as Abraham, David, and Job) who daily prayed for their children's souls.[90] As head priest, the father was encouraged to offer up petitions on behalf of his children. Yet leaders also provided examples of godly mothers from Scripture and church history who did the same. Drawing parallels between prayer and childbirth, Cotton Mather asked, "And especially, *Mothers*, Do you *Travail* for your *Children* over again, with your Earnest *Prayers* for their *Salvation*, until it may be said unto you, as it was unto *Monica* the Mother of Augustine, concerning him; '*Tis impossible, that the Child should perish, after thou hast Employ'd so many Prayers and Tears for the Salvation of it."*[91] In even stronger language, Colman told mothers that they had "*Authority* to pray for 'em, and your prayers may be of equal value and *prevalence* as their Fathers." He noted that mothers had "more tender, flowing *Affections* to the fruit of [their] bodies" and that they also had "more *leisure* and opportunity for Retirement and going to God" than their husbands, who were "cumber'd with the world."[92] Both fathers and mothers, therefore, were called to this critical task of parental prayer.

Such prayer was to begin while the child was still in the womb. Isaac Ambrose indicated that parents should pray vigorously for children during pregnancy, pleading with God for their souls even before birth.[93] Since children were conceived in sin and bore Adam's stain, he noted, it was never too early to begin asking God to resurrect their dead souls. Prenatal prayers for the child also reflected the sense that God was able, in his sovereignty, to work in the child's heart at any time. Thomas Belcher, for example, implored parents to be "Ernest and Importunate" in prayer for children "from their first conception" since some, like John the Baptist, had been "Sanctified from the Womb" and "*very Early* endow'd with the Sanctifying Graces of the Spirit of God."[94] Since God could impart his Spirit at any age, parents were called on to begin their supplications for the child's new birth prior to the time of physical birth.[95]

Once the child was born, prayers became more varied. While he was certainly more intentional than most, Cotton Mather's advice regarding parental prayer for children was representative of the broader pastoral advice in colonial New England. He discussed three forms of parental prayer for children: (1) regular (ordinary) daily prayers, (2) spontaneous (extraordinary) prayers, usually triggered by a certain event, and (3) crisis prayers elicited by illness, tragedy, or outright rebellion. "Regular" prayers most often focused on the child's salvation, sanctification, and protection from Satan's devices. Recognizing the need for the Spirit's divine work in regeneration, Mather implored parents to pray ardently for each child's conversion: "*Parents*, Make such a *Prayer* for your *Children, Lord, Give unto my Child, a New Heart, and a Clean Heart, and a Soft Heart; and an Heart after thy own Heart. . . . Pray* for the *Salvation* of thy *Children*, and carry the Names of every one of them, every day before the Lord, with *Prayers*, the *Cries* whereof shall pierce the very Heavens."[96] In addition to salvation, Mather urged parents to pray "regular" prayers for their children's sanctification, asking God to make them "*Vessels* of His *Glory*" and "*Temples* of *His Spirit*" in the world.[97] Suggesting that "*Prayer* and the *Devil* can't live comfortably in the same *Family*," this call to "regular" prayer also consisted of an appeal for divine protection, that "the *Evil One* may have no possession of them."[98] All in all, Mather recognized that the parents' most important aims—the salvation, sanctification, and protection of their children—could only be achieved on their knees.

Mather's own practice of "regular" prayer, as for many others, was to pray for every child by name every day.[99] While he prayed generally for salvation, sanctification, and protection, he also constructed lists of specific blessings he desired for each child individually according to his or her needs and circumstances.[100] Furthermore, he advised parents to devote special prayer time to a single child each day.[101] In other words, while he considered parental prayer for all children a nonnegotiable daily practice, he also recommended a focused form of prayer for individual children according to that child's specific needs, temptations, and struggles.[102] Regular parental prayers thus sustained both breadth and depth on a daily basis.

Mather felt that parents should pray these "regular" prayers not only *for* their children but also *in the presence of* their children. While he praised the practice of praying for children "in the closet," Mather also commended individualized prayer "conferences" in which children observed parental prayers on their behalf.[103] In his popular 1699 treatise, *A Family Well-Ordered*, Mather described his ideals for this practice:

> But, besides your *Family Prayers*, O *Parents*, why should you not now and then, take one capable *Child* after another, alone before the Lord? Carry the *Child* with you, into your *Secret Chambers*; make the *Child* kneel down by you, while you present it unto the Lord, and Implore His Blessing upon it. Let the *Child*, hear the Groans, & see the Tears, and be a witness of the Agonies, wherewith you are *Travailing* for the Salvation of it. The *Children* will never Forget what you do; It will have a marvellous Force upon them.[104]

Mather noted elsewhere that he would periodically "*Closet*" his children, speaking with them about "the State of their Souls; their *Experiences*, their *Proficiencies*, their *Temptations*" before praying and weeping to the

Lord for Christ to be formed in them.[105] On one occasion, he took his nine-year-old daughter Katy into his study and "set before her, the sinful and woful Condition of her *Nature*"; he went on, "I charg'd her, to *pray in secret Places*, every Day, without ceasing, that God for the Sake of Jesus Christ would give her a *New Heart*, and *pardon* Her sins, and make her a *Servant* of His." He then had her kneel down beside him and "poured out my Cries unto the Lord, that Hee would lay His Hands upon her, and bless her and save her, and make her a *Temple* of His Glory. It will bee so; It will be so!"[106] This practice, which was echoed by others such as Samuel Sewall and Jonathan Edwards, was for children a visible representation of the parents' priestly intercessory work.[107]

In addition to such "regular" practices, Mather also commended spontaneous "ejaculatory" prayers by parents on behalf of their children. He wanted parents to be ever mindful of the need to pray for children in the midst of daily life experiences, lifting up short prayers to God as each one came to mind or into sight. As he noted, "Yea, When thou dost cast thine Eyes upon the Little Folks, often in a day dart up an *Ejaculatory Prayer* to Heaven for them; *Lord, Let this Child be thy Servant for ever.*"[108] This practice reflected Mather's penchant for what Richard Lovelace has termed "occasional prayers."[109] Such was Mather's desire to live a life filled with prayerful attentiveness that he would often allow life events to drive him to prayer and meditation. Just as the sight of a clock might lead him to pray for good use of his time and as the practice of washing hands might lead him to pray for clean hands and a pure heart, Mather desired the sights and sounds of his children to remind him to pray for their souls.[110] Such practices demonstrated the call to informal as well as formal parental prayer, opening up pathways for parents to "pray continually" for their offspring (1 Thess. 5:17 NIV).

Finally, Mather stressed the importance of prayer for children going through crises of various kinds, particularly physical illnesses and spiritual rebellion. Mather always viewed children's sicknesses and injuries as providential in nature. His recommended prayers, therefore, always reflected both a desire for their physical healing and a deeper desire for God's intended purposes to be accomplished through the affliction. He certainly prayed fervently for his children's recoveries, setting apart whole days for fasting and prayer when they were taken with serious—often life-threatening—illnesses such as smallpox and "convulsions." At the same time, he prayed that childhood afflictions would produce spiritual benefits both for the children and for those close to them. He prayed for illnesses to awaken a sense of life's brevity and the need for eternal perspective. When his daughter Nanny developed a high fever, for example, he prayed for a cure but also that this very *"Burning"* would "bee the Occasion of her being brought more effectually than ever, Home unto Himself, and His Christ."[111] When two of his children were scorched with gun powder, he prayed for them to become more aware of the "Danger of eternal Burnings."[112] In fact, he was not averse to saying that afflictions were beneficial simply because they encouraged more parental prayers on that child's behalf. When his daughter Katy was seriously burned falling into a fire, Mather wrote in his diary, "The *Fire*, that hath wounded the Child, hath added a strong *Fire* and *Force* to the Zeal of my *Prayer* for her. . . . If this Writing of her poor Father, ever come to bee readd by her, lett her give Thanks to God, that ever Hee cast her into a *Fire*, which thus enflamed the Supplications of her Father for her."[113] This aim of sanctification perhaps explains why Mather prayed that his children would be healed only if that would be best for their spiritual formation and God's ultimate glory. The *"Hinge of Prayer,"* he suggested, was always "That *wherein our God shall be most Glorified.*"[114]

Youthful rebellion was another situation that elicited priestly parental prayers. Mather's prayers for his own wayward son Increase (named for his father) demonstrated the passion behind these appeals. From the time he witnessed seeds of rebellion in "Cresy," he documented long periods of prayerful pleading before the Lord. He set apart frequent days of fasting and prayer—once for three full days—using "extraordinary Supplications" to ask God for a changed and renewed heart.[115] He prayed for God to "cast out the Devil, that has possession of the Child."[116] He cried to the Lord "with all possible Importunity, that the almighty Arm of Heaven may be bare, for the changing of his Heart, and the holy Spirit entirely renewing of him."[117] More than with his other children, Mather frequently called on Increase to join him for his prayers, urging him to listen to literal cries for his deliverance.[118] In all of this, he recognized that in praying for Increase's heart, he was offering "Supplications, for what nothing but an almighty Arm can accomplish."[119] Mather charged parents to "Plead, and Beg, and Mourn and Weep, and Fast before the Lord" with "Agony of Soul" for their ungodly youth, bringing them before the Lord as those in the New Testament did with their diseased and possessed children.[120] Spiritual deliverance, he believed, was the fruit of such importunate prayer.

In all such occasions, persistence was perhaps the most important quality of the priestly life of parental prayer. Mather recognized that parents might grow discouraged when seemingly unanswered prayers bore little fruit in the lives of their children. He responded by defining prayer for children as a sowing time, noting that the harvest may come much later. "If thy *Prayers* are not presently answered," he recommended, "be not thereby Disheartened: Remember the Word of the Lord, in Luk.18.1 *That men ought always to pray, and not to Faint*."[121] Believing that *"Delayes are no Denials,"* he even acknowledged that parents might not see results during their lifetime, their prayers coming to fruition only after death.[122] Praying parents, he noted, left a *"Stock of Prayers"* as a godly inheritance for their children, a gift working far beyond parents' earthly lives. In some cases, in fact, he claimed that angels would come and "bring the tidings" to them in heaven, assuring them that their child had turned to God.[123] To be a praying priest meant to be a persevering priest, one who had faith in the long-term power of intercession even in the absence of visible outcomes.

Leading Children into the Priesthood: Teaching Children to Pray

In addition to leading their families into worship and praying for their children, the final priestly task of Christian parents in the colonial era was to guide children in developing a life of personal prayer, worship, and Bible reading on their own. This was, in the eyes of many, the most critical spiritual practice because it fostered—and in many ways confirmed—their children's personal intimacy with the living God. William Cooper noted that a godly seed would be a *"praying* seed," indicating that this was one of the chief marks of God's Spirit at work in the life of the child.[124] Despite the claims of naysayers, Cotton Mather was convinced that prayer should start at the earliest age possible. "O you that are grown but big enough to go up a pair of *Stairs*," he noted, "You should get up to the *Secret Places* which the *Stairs* lead unto; and there utter the *Voice of the Dove*, unto Him who says, *Let me hear thy Voice! For Sweet is thy Voice unto me!*" "Early

Piety," he claimed, "should breathe in *Early Prayer*."[125] While some parents waited until later in life to teach such principles, Mather was convinced that teaching the life of prayer was the primary means by which a young child would develop a personal, relational faith. As he put it, the Christian parents' heart cry was to be able to see their children speaking personally to God and therefore proclaim with rejoicing, "*Behold, He Prays*."[126]

Colonial leaders called on parents to help their children establish a daily practice of "secret prayer," a time each day to spend alone before the Lord in reading Scripture and in prayer—a close equivalent to the contemporary evangelical "quiet time." William Homes suggested that parents "oblige their Children . . . to read some Portion of holy Scripture, Morning and Evening; and that they do it gravely and with Attention. . . . They should also take Care that they spend some Time, Morning and Evening, in secret Prayer."[127] Most recommended both initial strong parental guidance and a gradual movement toward child initiative. Cotton Mather urged his children on occasion to write out their prayers, bringing these missives to him so that he could "discern, what sense they have of their own Everlasting Interests."[128] He regularly gave them suggestions regarding the possible subjects of prayers, helping them write down their petitions.[129] At the same time, he hoped that such parental guidance would lead to more personal approaches by the children themselves. Most encouraged children to use their closet times to probe their own souls, search for inner sin, and then turn these reflections into "free-form" prayers for forgiveness and divine help.[130]

Above all, colonial authors thought it most important for parents to teach children that prayer was the desired end of reading, study, and meditation. As what Charles Hambrick-Stowe has called a "culminating devotional act," prayer was envisioned as the climax of other pious practices.[131] For example, these leaders were adamant about the importance of turning Scripture into prayer.[132] Cotton Mather maintained that "the Scriptures are in part given us, for this very End, that we may from thence compose our Prayers."[133] Mather believed that the Scriptures would always provide fodder for adoration (by revealing God's character), thanksgiving (by documenting God's great promises and works), confession (by demonstrating the depravity of human nature), and petition (by pointing out human need). Speaking about the importance of prayerfulness during the younger years, he provided a number of examples: "Thus, When we hear a *Sin* rebuked in the Word of God, follow it with a Prayer, *Lord, save me from that sin.* When we hear a *Grace* proposed in the Word of God, follow it with a prayer, *Lord, fill me with that Grace.* When any thing is *Promised* in that Word, Pray, and Wish, *Lord, let this be my Heritage, and the rejoicing of my heart.* And when any thing *Threatened*, then Wish, *Lord, let not those Judgments come upon me.*"[134] Mather required his own children, in fact, to take a "Text or Two" out of their morning Scripture reading and "Shape it into a *Desire*, which they shall add unto their *Usual Prayer.*"[135] The key was that children's Bible reading was to be dialogical, prompting a conversation with the very God who inspired the text. "In *Reading*, first let God speak to us," he noted. "In *Praying*, let us then speak to God."[136]

Mather also called on parents to foster within children a prayerful response to church sermons. Even a child "less than Seven years old," he suggested, could begin to convert a sermon into prayer with a parent's help.[137] In describing his own role as a father, he noted that he would, on Sabbath afternoons, "mention to them over again the main Subject of (the sermon), and ask them thereupon, *What they have now to Pray for.*"[138] He particularly encouraged parents and older children, when able, to take notes during the sermons and to develop their prayers throughout the week from these notes. By securing a "New Store of Prayers in the House of God," he claimed, they would be able to pray with "a Fluency, an Enlargement, and yet a Pertinency, even to admiration."[139]

Befitting this prayerful mindset, a number of colonial leaders recommended that parents highlight the discipline of "consideration," a time to pause and reflect on one's life in prayer. Echoing the frequent colonial call to "take heed" to one's soul, regular consideration was designed to provide space to reflect on past sins and mercies, present temptations and opportunities, and future eternal realities. Cooper, for example, provided a lengthy set of guidelines that parents could use in assisting their children in the discipline of consideration. He urged them to have their children take time daily to meditate on the current "Course and Tenor" of their lives and conversations, on their particular besetting sins, and on their past struggles and victories before going to prayer.[140] He recommended a nightly review in which a young person would look over the previous day and ask, "*What have I done? Wherein have I transgressed? What Duty hath been omitted?*"[141] "If we frequently *behold our Faces in the Glass*," Cooper noted, "we shall see the *Spots* we have need to wipe off. In this way we may grow in an acquaintance with our selves than which nothing is more necessary for us."[142] For colonial leaders, consideration was a chief means by which parents could encourage children to stop and look at their lives with intentionality. As Cotton Mather concluded,

> O that young persons were so *wise*, as to Retire and *Consider* upon the circumstances of their Souls! Retire and *look upward*; consider *who* made you, and what he has prepared for you, if you seek Him. Retire, and *look downward*; consider the Everlasting *Fire* and the Never-dying *worm*, which is reserved for the Torture of all impenitent Unbelievers. Retire, and *look backward*; consider the sin in which you were *born*, and the many Follies and Errors which you have *lived* in. Retire, and *look forward*; consider the *death*, and the *Judgment*, and the *Eternity*, into which you are hastening apace every day. Retire, and *look inward*; consider whether you have yet made your *peace* with God, and whether you are yet arriv'd unto a blessed *Union* and *Communion* with the Lord Jesus Christ.[143]

As priestly parents encouraged their children to live their lives *coram Deo* (in the presence of God), they were actually enlisting them into the priesthood of all believers, urging them to offer their own sacrifices of prayer and praise to God.

As all of this would imply, the priestly function of Christian parents in the colonial era was, in the end, a commitment by parents to offer their children up to the Lord. This was symbolized as parents brought their children forward for baptism, entrusting them to the covenant-keeping God. It was lived out on a daily basis within the home as parents established family worship that placed God, rather than themselves, at the center of the child's life. It was enacted in parental prayers for their children as parents recognized their own inability and God's sufficiency to bring transformation to their children's lives. It was definitely central to the ways in which parents were called on to help their children develop personal relationships with the Lord, decentering the parental role and assigning to God the status of "first love" in their children's hearts.

Ultimately, this call to offer up the child as a sacrifice found its most complete and challenging expression when parents lost a child in death. Parents were called on to diagnose their spiritual status by carefully examining their responses to such losses. Colman stated plainly, "If Children are the gracious Gift of God, then it is *Lawful and a Duty to Mourn under the Holy and Awful hand of God in their Death*. . . . Sorrow is Natural, and may be Gracious in such Cases; but it must be in Moderation and with Resignation."[144] Both aspects were critical. Parents were to grieve "in moderation" because excessive grief might display an inordinate love for the child, an idolatry that placed the child above God in the affections. Their "resignation" demonstrated a willingness to accept God's plan in the midst of their suffering, submitting to his hand with patient endurance because they believed that "what GOD Ordains is *Well* and *Best*."[145] It also showed that parents recognized that their children were lent to them by God and that they were willing to surrender them back to God as his possession.[146] "*I know that thou fearest God*," Cotton Mather commented, "if thou withhold not thy *Isaac*, but Submissively part with him, and yield him up, when God says, *I will have him out of thy Hands*."[147] For parental priests, such moderation and resignation may have been their most challenging task. "In the deaths of your children, endured with due submission, to the Father of Spirits," Mather stated, "you offer up some of your fattest sacrifices."[148]

Practicing the Presence

The priestly work of daily family worship and parental prayer certainly reflected the larger sense that everything within the family was to be directed toward God. The days began and ended with hearing God's Word and responding to him in prayer and praise. The gospel story was rehearsed on a regular basis through singing and prayer, reminding children of the narrative within which their own lives were to be lived and interpreted. Recognizing their own insufficiency, parents were called on to beg God for mercy and grace for their children, asking him to open their eyes and regenerate their lifeless hearts. Children themselves were urged to use their own words to come to God with their confessions, thanksgivings, requests, and reflections. Sabbath days then magnified this God-centered focus once a week, rhythmically reminding parents and children to turn their gaze away from regular activities and toward the God who was their eternal hope.

It is important to see the rhythms of these colonial households as "liturgical" in nature. The twice-a-day gatherings for family worship and the weekly Sabbath observances served an important purpose in shaping the stories and the desires of colonial children. As James K. A. Smith has suggested, the liturgies of home are powerful means by which children are inculcated into a particular story of the "good life." The practice of family worship, he notes, "'enchants' our everyday lives, reminding us that the world we inhabit is not a flattened 'nature' but rather a creation charged with the presence and power of the living Spirit."[149] The colonial household was designed to be such a place. The reading of Scripture "in course" repeated the story of the Bible over and over again, helping children see that this was the larger story within which they lived their lives. Morning and evening singing and praying helped children rehearse this story in an affective manner so that it seeped into their souls over time. As Smith notes, "Insofar as we are immersed bodily in these microperformances, we are, over time, incorporated into a Story that then becomes the script that we implicitly act out. The Story becomes the background narrative and aesthetic orientation that habitually shapes how we constitute our world. We don't memorize the Story as told to us; we imbibe the Story as we perform it in a million little gestures."[150] All of the spiritual practices above were designed to shape children's desires in the direction of the kingdom of God, replacing other potentially idolatrous loves with the worship of the one true God.

Of course, such activities could be pursued in ways that were purely formulaic. The continual reminders to parents to avoid dragging out these exercises likely expressed the complaints of children who dreaded family prayers. Yet this was more than ritual and socialization. All of this priestly work—leading in family worship, interceding for children, and teaching children to grow in their personal life of prayer—demonstrated that colonial parents felt a keen responsibility to help their children come into experiential contact with the living God. Parents were creating a prayerful home culture in which children would pray with their families twice per day, would be taught to pray on their own from an early age, and would be prayed for by their parents. The description of prayer as the culminating "end" of Bible reading, church attendance, and self-reflection promoted a dialogical process that encouraged regular communion with the living God.[151]

For all of its potential monotony, the colonial approach to family worship and prayer serves as a striking counterpoint to what sociologist Christian Smith calls the "moralistic therapeutic deism" of our contemporary era. Smith's description of the "default" religion of American youth (including Christian youth) details a faith that is defined by an ability to be good, nice, and fair. This faith speaks of a God who wants children to be happy and who remains distant unless called on to solve problems as a "combination Divine Butler and Cosmic Therapist."[152] While there are obviously many reinforcing sources of such a faith, Smith recognizes that children absorb this from their culture, from their churches, and, perhaps most prominently, from their parents. Within the colonial paradigm, parents were called to strive for far more than culturally defined "goodness." They sought the regenerating power of the Holy Spirit in their children's lives. Parents were after more than the child's happiness. Even in the midst of trial, they prayerfully sought God's larger purposes and their children's sanctification. Parents were after more than a problem-solving God. They sought a prayerful connection with Christ that highlighted confession, thanksgiving, and adoration in addition to petitions for help. Parents were not simply trying to help introduce their children to Christianity so as to improve their daily lives. They were not simply life coaches. They were priests, intermediaries between their children and God who were seeking to foster a growing dialogue between the two.

The daily family worship recommended by colonial pastors, though not always dutifully engaged, would serve as the regular heartbeat of family religion for many American Protestants, at least through the nineteenth century. Yet while worship would connect children to God and give them an overarching storyline of the biblical text, pastors argued that parents must also instruct children in the key doctrines of the Christian faith so that they would resist false teachings and understand the very basis of their sin, salvation, and the Christian life. These priests, in other words, also had a prophetic role to play in their children's lives.

CHAPTER 3

The Parent as Prophet

Feeding on God's Truth

A Religious Education is a great mercy, yea, and to many of the
Elect it is the great means of their Conversion.

—Increase Mather,
Some Important Truths Concerning Conversion[1]

If colonial homes were to be "little churches," leading their families into
daily prayer and worship, they were also to be "schools," settings in
which children were instructed in the doctrines and commands of the
Christian faith. Befitting the Reformation emphasis on biblical and theological understanding for laypeople, pastors in colonial New England
focused significant attention on parental teaching within the home. In
fact, Cotton Mather noted that in the Old Testament "family sacrifice"
there was an animal "burnt unto the Lord" (family prayers), but there was
also a part that was "*Eat'n* by the Folks in the *Family*." In his eyes, this
represented the parents' role in "*feeding a Family* with the *Truths* of God."[2]
When by their "Good *Instruction*" parents set apart time to be "instilling
into them, the Knowledge of those things, *which to know is Life Eternal*,"
the household was converted into a "*School of Godliness*."[3] In the absence
of other educational institutions—there were few schools and no Sunday
schools—parents in colonial New England were given primary responsibility for their children's instruction. Parents were truly priests overseeing
prayerful sacrifices, but they were also to be prophets, educating their
children in the principles of faith that would lead toward salvation.

The charge for parents to be teachers seemed quite clear to colonial authors. Scripture called parents to teach God's commands to their

children (Deut. 6; Ps. 78), to bring them up in the discipline and instruction of the Lord (Eph. 6:4), to "exhort one another every day" (Heb. 3:13), and to teach and admonish one another (Col. 3:16), all commands they felt required application within the home.[4] Since children's rational capacities were corrupted by the fall, colonial authors felt that they were unable, on their own, to perceive God's goodness and his greater plan for them.[5] They required biblical and theological truth, illumined by the Holy Spirit, in order to enlighten their young minds. Because of original sin, most colonial Protestants did not believe that education was a process of drawing out something good from within the child. Everything good had to come from the outside, from biblical and doctrinal knowledge and from the work of the Holy Spirit through that knowledge. This is why the language of Christian education embraced by colonial pastors typically spoke of "instilling," "infusing," "dispensing," and "dropping" knowledge into children who needed such educational deposits in order to be renewed and enlightened.[6] As Richard Baxter put it, "Ignorance is your disease, and knowledge must be your cure."[7]

The acquisition of Spirit-illumined knowledge was therefore envisioned as a critical pathway to true heart change and conversion for colonial children. "Though every man be not *Good*, that hath *Knowledge*, yet a man cannot be *Good* without *Knowledge*," Cotton Mather noted. "An *Ignorant Soul* will be a *Vicious one*. . . . Every *Grace* enters into the Soul through the *Understanding*."[8] The belief that grace shaped the soul through the mind was widely shared among colonial religious leaders. Taking aim at the Catholic Church, William Cooper noted that Christians must never believe that "*Ignorance* is the Mother of Devotion," a notion they said Protestants had "exploded" as "false and pernicious."[9] Instead, as Benjamin Wadsworth insisted, "They're Children of wrath by Nature; they can't escape Hell, without true Faith and Repentance; such faith they cannot have, without some doctrinal knowledge of Christ. *How shall they believe in him, of whom they have not heard?* . . . Therefore it's absolutely necessary that they be Instructed, in the Truths & Duties of the Christian Religion; they can't escape Hell nor obtain Heaven without it."[10] While knowledge could never ensure conversion—that required the supernatural work of the Spirit—it also seemed clear that salvation was impossible without it.

Reading and the Catechism

This "religious education" was initiated as parents taught their children to read. Instruction in reading was important for colonial parents primarily because it unlocked children's ability to access the Scriptures.[11] Wadsworth implored parents, "And take care in this one great point, that they be taught to *Read* as soon as ever they are capable, that they may be able to consult God's mind in his written Word."[12] Deodat Lawson similarly exhorted parents, "Teach them to READ, and as soon as you can . . . accustome them to Read the Holy Scriptures, *Which are Able to make them Wise unto Salvation*."[13] The value of such reading was actually acknowledged by the larger colonial community. In 1647, Massachusetts made legal provision for a teacher of reading and writing in towns that reached fifty families and for the addition of Latin grammar schools in communities of more than one hundred families. The rationale for these guidelines—and for reading in general—was that it was "one chief project of that old deluder, Satan, to keep men from the knowledge of the Scriptures." While Satan had previously obscured the Scriptures by keeping them in an "unknowne tongue," these leaders suggested that he now worked to prevent biblical knowledge through illiteracy.[14] Reading was thus a potent weapon to wield against the enemy.[15]

Importantly, literacy education in this era *was* Christian education. Most non-clergy families had very few books besides the Bible, and those books they did possess were typically religious in nature.[16] Learning to read, therefore, typically involved instruction via a hornbook, primer, Psalter, catechism, Bible, and other devotional works (often sequenced in that order). The hornbook, used in early childhood, often consisted of the alphabet, combinations of vowels and consonants, and the Lord's Prayer affixed to a wooden frame and covered with transparent horn (from oxen or sheep). A leather strap was often placed through the handle so that children could carry these around the house while they learned their letters. From the hornbook, most children graduated to the primer. The *New England Primer*, by far the most popular of these in the seventeenth and eighteenth centuries, typically began with the alphabet, including letters, two-letter combinations, and sometimes words from one to five syllables in length.[17] The words chosen for practice (such as "glorifying," "fornication," and "mortification") often had religious meaning that was discussed as the words were learned. Following this, short poetic rhymes, often depicting biblical scenes, were designed to help children remember their letters. All editions included catechisms for children to memorize, typically the Westminster Shorter Catechism or John Cotton's specialized *Spiritual Milk for Boston Babes* or both. Other common features included the Ten Commandments, the Lord's Prayer, the Apostles' Creed, lists of Old and New Testament books, lists of numbers, lists of proper names, and a number of prayers and poems for children on topics of death, judgment, and obedience.[18] Conservative estimates reveal that an average of twenty thousand copies of the *New England Primer* were sold annually between 1680 and 1830. If this is indeed the case, about three million copies were sold during this century and a half of widespread usage.[19]

When children were ready to read the Bible and devotional books on their own, parents were to help them make this a daily practice. Parents, Cotton Mather suggested, were to "cause (their children) to look often into their *Bibles*, and here and there Single out some special *Sentences* from those *Oracles* of Heaven for them to get into their *memories*."[20] Scripture memorization was indeed a desired common practice among colonial children. Authors hoped that children would memorize the histories, principles, promises, and commands of the Bible every day until they became themselves "*The Libraries of the Lord Jesus Christ*."[21] For his own children, Mather urged not only Bible reading but also the study of great devotional works. He gave each child a "one-shelf library" of books for their personal study and also gave them "blank books" (blank journals) within which they could document the "agreeable and valuable Things" gleaned from these texts and thus "fill the Chambers of their Souls, with precious and pleasant Riches."[22] While Mather was likely unique in his intentionality, most colonial authors spoke of the importance of children daily storing their minds with biblical and godly truth.[23]

In addition to reading Scripture and other good books, children in colonial New England were raised on the catechism. Defined by Lawson as "*an Orderly and Methodical Instructing* [of] *Persons in the Great Doctrines of Godliness, Or the Fundamental Points* of Religion *Necessary unto Salvation*," catechism training involved teaching the basic doctrines of Christianity using a method of question and answer.[24] Its origins tracing to the mid-sixteenth century, catechetical instruction became the dominant method of children's religious education between 1570 and 1640 in both England and New England. In a culture marked by a desire for rational clarity, a need to counter Catholic doctrine, and a robust fear of false individual interpretations of Scripture, the catechism was a popular tool for generating common beliefs in the early years of life.[25] It is little wonder, then, that Wadsworth could contend that when the enemies of the church wanted to stop its progress, they aimed to suppress catechizing.[26] "So you should *use diligence, care, industry*, to teach your Children," he urged parents, "you should make a *business of it*, yea and a great business too."[27]

In light of its broad importance, catechism training for children was offered in churches, schools, and the home to ensure a comprehensive approach.[28] Yet while many local pastors and teachers catechized children, most expected this training to begin in the household. In fact, following the example of such luminaries as Richard Baxter in England, church leaders often visited homes to make sure that parents were fulfilling their obligations as God-ordained catechists. In 1669, for example, the congregation of Boston's First Church voted unanimously that the church's elders should "go from hows to hows to visit the familys and see how they are instructed in the grounds of religion."[29] Beyond church leaders, many colonial governments established laws mandating that parents catechize their children. By 1642, Massachusetts had enacted legal provisions for household Christian education, requiring parents to instruct children in "reading and understanding the principles of religion." In addition to learning the "english tongue" and the "Capital lawes" of the community, this law, as expanded six years later in 1648, mandated that

> all masters of families doe once a week (at the least) catechize their children and servants in the grounds and principles of Religion, and if any be unable to doe so much: that then at the least they procure such children or apprentices to learn some short orthodox catechism without book, that they may be able to answer unto the questions that shall be propounded to them out of such catechism by their parents or masters or any of the Select men when they shall call them to a tryall of what they have learned in this kinde.[30]

Church and government officials thought such parental teaching to be so important that they put the weight of their authoritative positions behind a forced compliance.

Fathers were given primary responsibility for such catechizing, though mothers were urged to play their part as well. Anchored by higher literacy rates and generally more advanced educational training, fathers were deemed intellectually superior and better equipped to raise up their children to read and understand the Bible and the catechism. In a word-centered culture in which most Christian education was rooted in the text, fathers' educational advantages rendered them the more qualified "teachers."[31] Yet while laws and formal statements required fathers to take the lead in catechism training, mothers were also expected to join in, especially in the child's youngest years. Cotton Mather implored mothers to make their children "Expert in some *Orthodox Catechisms*" and to "have 'em Learn to *Read* and *Write*, as fast as ever they can take it."[32] In a common expression of the day, another commented that children in a godly household would "*suck in Religion from the Mothers breasts.*"[33]

This image was more than metaphorical. For Puritans in particular, the practice of nursing was also invested with spiritual significance. While it was quite common in England to hire out wet nurses to feed young infants, Puritan pastors tended to recommend that mothers nurse their own children. The biblical text, they argued, seemed to affirm the importance of this, speaking of dry breasts as a curse and celebrating when Moses's mother was given the opportunity to nurse her own child. Yet breastfeeding was also thought to be important for the child's spiritual formation. It was thought to enhance the loving connection between mothers and children. In addition, since it was thought that both diseases and undesirable character qualities might be imbibed through the nurse's milk, breastfeeding was thought to be a helpful means of ensuring a virtuous beginning for the child.[34] Pastors and other Christian leaders refuted the typical objections to this practice—fear of sapping bodily strength, concern that it would disturb the father's sleep, and, most disturbingly, the mother's overweening desire for ease, comfort, and freedom. Cotton Mather put it simply: "If God have granted her Bottles of *Milk* on her Breast, he thinks that her Children have a Claim unto them."[35]

Despite this celebration of maternal bonding, a number of factors limited the mother's role in actual Christian teaching. First, women's lives were demanding. Because of their significant labor on behalf of the family economy—preparing food, cleaning, gardening, caring for animals, washing, spinning, and assisting husbands in their trades—the days were quite full. They were also responsible for supervising the home-based labor of various servants, apprentices, relatives, and older children. As Laurel Thatcher Ulrich has argued, most colonial mothers in New England reflected the ideal set forth in Proverbs 31, serving as manufacturers, agriculturalists, traders, and supervisors. When husbands traveled, developed illnesses, or died, women, as "deputy husbands," would often take over many of their responsibilities in addition to their own.[36] All of this left little "free time" for maternal spiritual instruction.

In addition, the work of bearing and raising numerous children itself created challenges for the mother's position as a spiritual teacher. The constant cycle of pregnancy and nursing made for an exhausting schedule.[37] Since these pregnancies were often accompanied by intense sickness and fear of death, colonial mothers were frequently saddled with particularly arduous "periods of travail." The large number of children, combined with the widespread responsibilities of caring for the household, meant that women often had little time to devote to individual children. In the real world of daily domestic life, therefore, mothers often shared their caring and nurturing responsibilities with a wide array of assistants: neighbors, relatives, servants, apprentices, older siblings, and husbands. An army of helpers contributed to caring for children, feeding and clothing them, nursing them back to health in times of sickness, and teaching from the catechism. Mothers thus lived in a shared world of child-rearing responsibility that limited their exclusive teaching and nurturing role in children's lives. As Ulrich helpfully summarizes, *"Mothering in New England was extensive rather than intensive. . . .* Mothering meant generalized responsibility for an assembly of youngsters rather than concentrated devotion to a few."[38]

When it came time for fathers and mothers to engage in the work of instruction, there were a number of competing catechisms from which to choose. In 1641 the Massachusetts General Court actually pressed for the development of a common catechism "for the instruction of youth in the grounds of religion," but this search for a uniform standard never gained traction. At first the colonists depended on English imports. Many utilized either William Perkins's *Foundation of the Christian Religion* (first published in 1590) or the longer and shorter catechisms developed by the Westminster Assembly (both published in the 1640s).[39] Through the years, however, the number of catechisms proliferated, and many local pastors produced their own varieties for the children and youth of their congregations.[40] In fact, Increase Mather noted in 1679 that there were "no less than five hundred Catechisms extant" and "no particular Catechism, of which it may be said, it is best for every Family, or for every Congregation."[41] One of the most popular for children, mentioned above, was John Cotton's *Spiritual Milk for Boston Babes*.[42] Initially published in London in 1646, it remained continuously in print for over two hundred years and has been frequently referenced as "the first children's book written and published in America."[43] With only sixty-four questions and relatively brief answers, it is little wonder that *Spiritual Milk for Boston Babes* was deemed "peculiarly, The Catechism of New England."[44]

The "Blessed Echo's of Truth": The Power of the Catechism

For colonial pastors, the catechism was perceived as the best means of child instruction for a variety of reasons. First, most recognized that it would be challenging for children and youth to develop a clear theological system from the Bible alone. Josiah Smith, who was Harvard-educated but ended up ministering in South Carolina, contended that "the *whole Bible* is too large and comprehensive a System of Divinity, for the Retention of Children; they have not ripeness of judgment to search, examine, and collect points of *Faith*, from points of *Practice*. Nor can Parents, with any tolerable conveniency, do it for them. But such is the Excellency of Catechisms, that they present to our view, in a few pages, all the Rudiments and first Principles of Christianity, free from the mixtures of lesser Points."[45] Isaac Watts indicated that catechisms could be helpful specifically because of their capacity to "collect" and "methodize" biblical truths.[46] They "collected" the scattered important truths of the Bible by bringing them into a unified system of belief. They "methodized" the biblical text by placing its themes in a more understandable order so that children could see the logical connections between them. In the words of Matthew Henry, the catechism was "a map of the land of promise."[47]

While there were a number of catechetical forms, this "map" typically traced the landscape and geography of the gospel. John Cotton's *Spiritual*

Milk for Boston Babes was representative of this general movement. The catechism began with the character of God, including his attributes and his creation of the world. After describing God as creator and king, Cotton moved on to list his requirements for people, including the Ten Commandments. The purpose of this was to reveal to children God's high standards and their inability to keep God's commands, pressing them to feel the reality of sin and their rebellion against God. In this place of need, the catechism then addressed redemption through Christ's atoning work on the cross, inserting explanations of the gospel. As Increase Mather put it, the catechism was designed to help children "know how miserable they are by Nature, and how they come to be so miserable, and that there is an absolute necessity of their being born again, and that by a Saving Faith they make sure of an Interest in Christ."[48] Following redemption, catechisms would typically move on to discuss the moral law, treating the pursuit of obedience not as a legalistic mandate but as a response of gratitude for the finished work of Christ. This latter section generally included the purpose and role of the church and various social obligations to family, neighbors, and the poor. Finally, many catechisms addressed spiritual practice, including information on the sacraments and the work of prayer. By going through these various sections, children were to come away with a framework of gospel understanding and a means by which they could "locate" themselves within the larger story of God.

Pedagogically, the catechism's question and answer method was thought to be the most effective for children and youth. Cotton Mather spoke of the question and answer method as fostering the "blessed *echo's* of truth" by generating a continual call and response.[49] Questions, Isaac Watts suggested, aroused the natural curiosity of children because they would be motivated to discover the answers to the questions.[50] In addition, he noted that this means of learning was "familiar and delightful" to children because it appeared "more like Conversation and Dialogue" than a passive and private system of memorization.[51] Some noted that children and parents would be motivated to learn the catechism by healthy competition and the desire to avoid the embarrassment of public failure. As Smith suggested, catechisms provided children "an excellent way of trying their genius and natural ambition—they will strive to excel, especially if they have to answer before a public audience—they will blush to be outstript, and it should likewise spur on the parents whose credit

and reputation is equally concerned."[52] Capitalizing on this competitive-
ness, Wadsworth commended a program in which children would receive
"small rewards and Incouragements" for their catechism achievements.
Cotton Mather went even further and recommended that parents develop
a system of rewards for diligent children memorizing their catechisms
and "a fit *Penalty*" for those who did not.[53]

Though colonial directives on catechism methods varied, there was
a general structure to the way leaders advised parents to use these materials. Catechisms were, first of all, to be memorized. Prior to widespread
literacy, the catechism was learned through a dialogical process of oral
repetition between parents and their children. To display their success
in memorization, children would recite the catechisms "without book"
to various audiences, primarily parents but also siblings, peers, visiting
pastors, schoolteachers, or government officials. Memorization was so
important because authors saw the catechism as providing children with
a vocabulary that would help them interpret their own lives and the world
around them. The catechism, as Ian Green has stated, played a role similar
to that of the study of grammar, the learning of musical scales, or the memorizing of multiplication tables. It served to drill the basic building blocks
into the mind, preparing the way for more advanced understanding. By
instilling a theological language within the mind, the catechism protected
impressionable young minds from heresy, giving them the worldview to
instinctively detect false teaching wherever it might arise. Without such a
guide, John Barnard warned, "they will be in great Danger of being drawn
away by Seducers, and such as lay in wait to deceive."[54] The purpose of
catechism memorization, in the words of historian John Sommerville,
was "to make orthodoxy the child's second nature."[55]

Catechism training was not to end, however, when children were able
to recite these precepts.[56] Parents wanted children to be able to memorize
and state ("perfectly") the answers to the catechism's questions, but Cotton
Mather implied that reciting "like Parrots" was insufficient.[57] Though he
recognized that it was important to "demand from [a child] an *Echo* to
what [the parent] Enquires of him," he also wanted children to "have their
Affections and *Practices* conformed to what they understand."[58] In order to
achieve cognitive, affective, and behavioral aims, many leaders asked parents to follow up the catechism questions with probing questions of their
own. Samuel Hopkins noted that Jonathan Edwards taught his children

from the Westminster Shorter Catechism "not meerly by taking care that they learned it by Heart; but by leading them into an understanding of the Doctrines therein taught, by asking them Questions on each Answer, and explaining it to them."[59] Barnard indicated that this approach amounted to a willingness to "catechize them upon their Catechism," putting "such pertinent short Questions unto them, as, by their Answer to which, you may discover whether they understand their Catechism, and the Principles of Religion, or no."[60] If the catechism required children to say, "*God made me, He keeps me, and He can save me*," Cotton Mather noted, the parent could follow this by asking, "*Why did He make you? was it, that you might Serve Him? And, Is it your Desire, that He would make you willing and able to do so?*"[61]

Furthermore, many hoped that learning the catechism would spark religious affections and practices by leading children into a direct dialogue with God through prayer.[62] Reading about creation, for example, could lead naturally to praise for children's physical bodies and confession regarding their "corrupt Nature." Texts about Jesus could spark thanksgiving for salvation and requests that Christ's "Offices" of prophet, priest, and king be "executed" in their lives. Learning God's commandments could prompt both confession of personal sin and requests for the Spirit's strength in obedience. "There is no point wherein they can be Catechized," Cotton Mather claimed, "but they may Pray to God, for something that relates unto it, or give Thanks for Mercies therein pointed at."[63] The appeal to prayerful affections and practices was further cemented as catechisms were increasingly composed in the first and second person rather than third person prose.[64] This allowed children to use the catechism both to reflect on their own lives and to speak their prayers and praises directly to God.

This concern for the affections confirmed that Protestant pastors saw the catechism as a direct pathway to conversion. Colonial leaders recognized that knowledge alone could never awaken the soul to the beauty of Christ, but learning was viewed as an essential means of grace and a source of "preparation" for the Spirit's work. As one put it, through such learning "you make *Men* of them, and, how can you tell, but you may make *Saints* of them too. While you are *Teaching* your *Children*, and causing your *Doctrine* to Distill as the *Small Rain upon the Tender Herbs*, it may be the *Spirit* of God will fall upon them, to make them the *Children* of God."[65]

The Spirit's work, in these cases, was to take general theological truths and apply them personally to the heart. "Thou knowest not, *O Parent*, but that by this means thou mayst save thy *Child*," Daniel Lewes proclaimed, "and were it not worth the while then to make the Tryal?"[66] Many spoke of how doctrinal truths taught by parents that seemed like "Water spilt on the Ground" or "Seed sown upon a Rock" might, later in children's lives, "come into their Minds, and thro' God's Blessing, prove the means of their Conversion."[67] The knowledge imparted by the catechism, in other words, provided the kindling that the Holy Spirit might set ablaze in the child's soul either in the moment of learning or years down the road. Parents wanted their children "To grow in Knowledge, as they grow in Years," Deodat Lawson noted, "and may have ground to hope, that by the help of the *Spirit* of God they shall also grow in *Grace*."[68]

In an atypical but widely popularized case of the catechism sparking a spiritual awakening, Jonathan Edwards told the story of Phebe Bartlett, a precocious four-year-old who was stirred to spiritual contemplation through her eleven-year-old brother's conversion. Phebe often retired several times a day to her closet to pray, and one day her mother heard her crying out to God for salvation and pardon for her sins. Convicted of her sin and fearing hell, she pleaded through tears for her parents' help. Her mother urged her to be a good girl and to pray, telling her that she hoped God would offer her salvation. While this did not comfort her, Phebe soon ceased her weeping, began smiling, and reported: "the kingdom of heaven is come to me!" When her mother inquired about her change, she asserted, "There is another come to me, and there is another; there is three." What had come to her was not a vision of the trinitarian God but rather "three passages of its catechism that came to her mind," including "Thy will be done" and "Enjoy him forever." The Spirit had used the catechism to catalyze her soul's salvation, bringing the abstract doctrines to personal application in her young life.[69]

A Growing Developmental Awareness

Bartlett's case highlights the fact that some colonial parents saw their children as capable of advanced learning in their earliest years. Some scholars have suggested that colonial authors, when it came to strategies for child-rearing, lacked a developmental awareness of age-appropriate instruction. This interpretation emerges most forcefully in the well-worn historical argument that parents treated their children as "miniature adults."[70] Since Philippe Ariès's groundbreaking work on premodern European childhood, many historians have argued that childhood up through the seventeenth century was not designated as a special and distinct stage of life. Portraits revealed young children who looked very much like their parents in dress, facial expressions, wigs, and even the stiff "uprightness" of their bodies. Special children's furniture, some argue, did not really exist, save for standing stools and other devices required to help them stand upright. The scarcity of specific playthings and child-specific artifacts seemed to demonstrate a lack of attention to children's needs. Historians have even argued that the content and form of Christian teaching revealed a lack of awareness of the unique needs and capacities of children. Attendance at adult church services, the use of themes of death and hell, and the complexity of doctrinal concepts in children's catechisms, they argue, all point to the fact that parents expected an unusually advanced level of maturity from their children.[71] As Sandford Fleming summarizes, "There was an utter failure to appreciate the distinction between the child and the adult. Children were regarded simply as miniature adults, and the same means and experiences were considered as suitable for them as for those older."[72]

It is certainly true that New England children lived in a culture far less age-stratified than our own. Parents and pastors likely did assume a capacity for knowledge, abstraction, and reading ability beyond what twenty-first-century critics would consider normal childhood development. They taught their children to read "as Early as may be," and they expected children to memorize and understand material in primers and catechisms that would likely be seen as quite advanced by contemporary standards.[73] Children did begin to work alongside adults at an earlier age (often soon after age seven). Because children and youth did not have the scaffolding of age-graded compulsory education that would emerge in later centuries, and because households were farther removed from one another, they also spent more time in the presence of adults (primarily family members, relatives, and church members). In addition, there was a kind of age leveling that followed from colonial theological convictions. Children as well as adults were tainted by original sin and therefore responsible before God for their eternal state. In this sense, the prevalence of references to death and hell in books and catechisms did not demonstrate an "adult" vision of children as much as a keen desire to lead children toward salvation in an age when they were more likely to die young.[74] As David Stannard puts it, "When the Puritan parent urged on his children what we would consider a painfully early awareness of sin and death, it was because the well-being of the child and the community *required* such an early recognition of these matters."[75]

In reality, colonial authors did increasingly think in developmental categories when it came to Christian instruction. By the end of the seventeenth century, most spoke in terms of a set sequence: "infancy" (birth to age six or seven), "childhood" (age seven to age fourteen), "youth" (age fourteen to roughly age twenty-five), middle age (age twenty-five to age forty or fifty), and old age (age fifty and beyond).[76] While they were not typically exact in these designations, they did recognize the unique needs, capacities, characteristic vices, and most appropriate methodologies for each group. Josiah Smith, for example, suggested that, in the teaching of children, "nor are we to assign every age the same part, and measure, of Instruction: A Child of *Ten* Years, must be distinguished from one of *Seven*; and that from one of *five*: All, in proportion to their respective Births."[77] Most colonial authors did not spend much time discussing Christian education for "infants" (prior to age six or seven). They certainly encouraged mothers to pray with their youngest children and to share biblical truths with them. Such children were included in family worship. Yet infants were generally considered "irresponsible and unproductive," too young for any significant responsibilities. John Cotton suggested that children under the age of seven simply spent their time in "pastime and play, for their bodies are too weak to labor and minds to study are too shallow. Even the first seven years are spent in pastime and God looks not much at it."[78] Even by the early eighteenth century, his grandson Cotton Mather noted that these young children were "too Shallow, too Heedless and too Sportful" for "serious counsels, or *to know the way of the Lord*."[79]

The age of seven appeared to be a significant turning point for many children, particularly boys. It was at this stage that the boy typically changed clothing, moving from the ankle-length petticoats to the breeches and frock coats common to older boys and men.[80] In accord with much modern developmental theory, which indicates that boys begin to separate from their mothers and identify more with their fathers at this age, colonial boys began to spend more time with their fathers as they assumed gender-specific work responsibilities such as digging potatoes, raking hay, watching livestock, or fetching water or kindling.[81] While young girls did not have the same visual change to highlight a new stage of growth, most historians concur that age seven also represented a turning point for them in which they were given more responsibilities alongside their mothers. Once boys and girls reached this age of "childhood," parents saw them as ready to receive more systematic instruction in Christian doctrine.[82] By this time they seemed better capable of understanding both spiritual truths and the conditions of their own hearts, making them more receptive to religious teaching. Many fathers began meeting with their children—both boys and girls—for individual prayer and teaching between the ages of seven and nine.[83]

While they did not have access to the social scientific notions of development that would later emerge, colonial pastors were aware of the need for pacing in keeping with the child's abilities. Puritan minister Peter Bulkeley asserted, "Children whiles they are young (at which time our pious education of them must begin) are like narrow mouth'd vessells, which can receive that which is powred into them, but by drops." So the best method was to be "often speaking to them of good things, now a little, and then a little, line upon line, precept upon precept, little and often, as they are able to receive."[84] In commending the daily use of the catechism with children, Isaac Ambrose noted that the only "Caveat" was that parents should "deal with their Children, as skillful Nurses and Mothers do in feeding their Children, not to give them too much at once: over much dulls a Child's Understanding, and breeds Wearisomeness to it."[85] These authors suggested that instruction should start slowly both because of children's limited capacities and because they wanted to make learning an enjoyable process that would motivate further receptivity. Young children, Ambrose noted, should learn with "Ease & Delight."[86] Some seventeenth-century pastors developed "shorter" catechisms specifically for younger members of the community. Cotton Mather even provided a catechism that added "*little Stars*" next to select questions, indicating that these would be appropriate for "the younger of you."[87]

While such efforts attempted to modify the amount of material communicated to young children, by the eighteenth century a growing number of leaders suggested that catechisms' language should be better adapted to children's needs. Central here was the work of Isaac Watts.[88] Watts maintained that the Westminster Shorter Catechism was too challenging for most children, its language too daunting and its concepts too complex. He noted that words were merely the "Husk or Shell of this Divine Food," and that children would never access the food if the husks were too hard for them to open (25). Just as parents would not give children nuts and almonds in hopes that one day their teeth would be strong enough to open their shells, so they should not provide impenetrable words and expect that they would provide anything in the way of spiritual sustenance. "If Children are train'd up to use Words without Meanings," he argued, "they will get a Habit of dealing with Sounds instead of Ideas, and of mistaking Words for Things" (34). In addition, they would be unlikely to go back to these words later in life, instinctively reacting against "these painful Tasks of Childhood" (30). One of Watts's great concerns, in fact, was that children would begin to associate religion with something distasteful and obscure. "*Teaching*," he suggested, "is not thrusting a set of Words into the Memory, but helping the Learner to understand what is said" (23). He added, "Words written on the Memory without Ideas, or Sense in the Mind, will never incline a Child to his Duty, nor save his Soul" (16).

To counter these problems, Watts proposed that children's catechisms should use only words that the various age groups could understand, rejecting "hard scholastick Terms" in favor of simple and age-appropriate phrases (43). He recognized that this would mean a more limited use of actual scriptural language, noting that "since the Scripture was written for *Men* rather than Children, since it abounds in metaphorical Expressions and in *Eastern* Idioms of Speech, . . . I cannot think it best to confine our Instruction of Children to the very Expressions of Scripture, when we can find shorter, easier, and more familiar Forms of Speech to convey the same Doctrines and Duties to the Understanding" (42). Watts also proposed that these early catechisms emphasize practical rather than abstract notions, focusing on the commandments they must obey, vices they must avoid, and rewards and punishments related to obedience and disobedience. In this way, Watts prefigured later developmental theorists such as Jean Piaget and Lawrence Kohlberg who envisioned children's cognitive and moral development as concrete and directed more toward particular rules than principled reasoning. Watts recognized that this might skew

the earliest catechisms a bit more in the direction of behavioral conformity and appear "too Legal" to many. However, he thought this to be an
acceptable beginning that could be clarified later (41).[89]

Watts actually produced some of the first explicitly age-graded catechisms, beginning with one for those under seven or eight, continuing
with one for those ages seven to twelve, and concluding with one for
those over the age of twelve, which was essentially an adaptation of the
Westminster Shorter Catechism. The first catechism had only twenty-four
questions, while the second had about seventy or eighty questions and also
added scriptural proofs to the various answers.[90] To these Watts added a
catechism on Bible names for those under the age of seven (consisting of
the name of the person and a character trait) and a Historical Catechism
for those over the age of seven including more detailed historical figures
and events from Scripture. These kinds of innovations revealed a growing
recognition among eighteenth-century Christian leaders of the unique
educational needs and capacities of young children.

While such adaptations revealed that children in colonial New
England were not viewed as miniature adults, it does seem clear that
adult maturity was still the desired goal. Since early childhood was viewed
as a perilous time, both physically and spiritually, parents and pastors
wanted children to mature as quickly as possible. At a purely physical
level, parents wanted their children to imitate adults in their manner and
carriage. They utilized swaddling as a means of straightening their limbs,
and they used standing stools to encourage upright posture and prevent
crawling, something they associated with the animal realm.[91]

Such physical maturity was paralleled by an overarching desire for
rapid spiritual development. Colonial pastors tended to idealize children
who were "old" before their time, demonstrating a precocious wisdom and
reason that surpassed typical childhood capacity.[92] Speaking at the funeral
of famed schoolmaster Ezekiel Cheever, Cotton Mather told the gathered
audience of children, "You may *Dy* in your *Childhood*: But you should be
ambitious, that if it should be so, you may *dy an hundred years old*; have
as much *Knowledge* and *Vertue*, as many men of an *hundred years old*."[93]
This desire reflected a prioritization of certain elements linked with adult
maturity: rationality, understanding of doctrine, wisdom, and a growing
capacity for self-interrogation. Benjamin Colman, for example, noted that
"Religion is a Manly thing in Child-hood. . . . For so far forth as Religion

governs him, He neither Speaks as a Child, nor Understands as a Child, nor Thinks as a Child,—but puts away Childish things. . . . It even ravishes a Wise Man to see a Child that looks and acts and speaks with the Consideration, Gravity and Prudence of a Man."[94] The ideal for children, therefore, was not a developmentally appropriate faith as much as it was a mature faith that reflected adult norms. If children were not miniature adults, it may be more accurate to say, as does historian Steven Mintz, that children were viewed as "adults in training."[95] This view would later be challenged as some nineteenth-century Protestants embraced a more Romantic view that sought to delay maturity and to extend childhood as long as possible.

"When You Walk along the Road": Finding Teachable Moments

Despite the significant attention given to formal teaching, colonial authors were equally concerned about the informal means by which knowledge was communicated to their children. For example, they repeatedly addressed the importance of modeling and imitation in the faith-formation process. Although he obviously cared deeply for doctrinal truth, Eleazer Mather held that "Precept without Patterns will do little good; you must lead them to Christ by examples as well as Counsel; you must *set your selves first*, and speak by Lives as well as words; you must live Religion, as well as talk Religion."[96] As visible exhibitions of Christian maturity, parents were to offer themselves as patterns to be followed by their children. In this light, it was critical for parents to avoid sinful practices or anything that might contradict the formal teaching of church and home. "Never let them see you disguised with indecent Passion, or with strong Drink; never suffer them to hear you tell a Lie, or profanely Cursing and Swearing," Barnard remarked. "Nay; how can it be supposed that your Children should hearken to your Instruction, when they see you live directly contrary to it yourselves?"[97] This is perhaps why so many noted that one of parents' chief responsibilities was to care for their own souls, ensuring that they were growing in their faith as models to their impressionable children. As Jonathan Edwards suggested, revival in the community was dependent on revival in "heads of families." "If you are much in instructing and counseling children," he concluded, "it will have little effect unless example accompanies instructions."[98]

In addition to parental example, colonial authors wanted children to learn from the exemplary lives of their faithful peers. In his popular work *A Token for Children*, James Janeway set forth the lives of pious young people so that children could emulate these models. These children, many of whom experienced God's converting grace between the ages of two and nine, found a growing assurance of their salvation and demonstrated their convictions through their piety, prayers, Sabbath observance, avoidance of play, and vigorous evangelism of others around them.[99] Mature beyond their years, these children obeyed parents, grieved over their sins, and were always willing—and often excited—to die so that they could spend eternity with Christ. Janeway suggested that parents "put them . . . upon imitating these sweet children; let them read this Book over an hundred times, and observe how they are affected, and ask them what they think of these Children, and whether they would not be such?"[100] Collective biographies such as this and a similar one penned by Cotton Mather provided children with vivid, real-life examples of the kinds of qualities they were to develop.

Beyond example, colonial leaders regularly commended the use of "teachable moments" to communicate truth in the midst of daily life experiences.[101] Just as Deuteronomy 6 implied, the prophetic work of Christian parenting involved not only formal teaching but also the mundane aspects of everyday life—"when you walk along the road" (Deut. 6:7 NIV). Leaders urged parents to find connections between daily life situations and godly instruction, using unstructured time together to communicate godly truth. When traveling with children in his "Chariot," Cotton Mather attempted to engage in a "*continual Dropping*" of biblical truth.[102] When they were at their "Games and Sports," he would "by way of occasional Reflection, as plainly as 'tis possible, mind them of those pious Instructions which the Circumstances of their play may lead them to think upon." As a general rule, if he accidentally came upon one of his children, he would attempt to "lett fall some Sentence or other, that shall carry an useful Instruction with it."[103] He used the occasion of his daughter's weaning to teach his children about the "weaned soul," while at mealtimes he would tell stories with spiritual import, ensuring that "our Diet at the Table, shall be mighty handsomely and usefully carried on."[104] Wadsworth suggested to parents, "*Take occasion from the dispensations of Providence, to give good Instruction to your Children.*" On one occasion he spoke of the opportunity provided by others' financial losses to "tell your Children, of the *uncertainty* of earthly Injoyments, & that they are not to be eagerly desir'd, not at any time trusted in."[105] Of course, all of this depended on regular and prolonged contact between parents and children, something that was indeed commonplace in this era in which children lived and worked alongside their parents (or parentlike masters) throughout their childhood years.

The power of informal and experiential teaching was especially prominent during times of pain and affliction. Parents were encouraged in times of illness to remind children of the "disease" of sin that "infected" their very souls. "When any of my Children have any Illness upon them," Cotton Mather recalled, "I would make it an Occasion to putt them in mind of the Evil in Sin, and especially of such Sin, as their Illness may most naturally mind them of; I would show them the analogous Distempers of their Souls, and instruct them how to look up unto their great Savior for the Cure of those Distempers."[106] In such times, Mather saw sickness as an ideal moment to proclaim the gospel and have them consider the "sickness" of sin and the need for spiritual "healing."[107] Parents also used such occasions to prevent children from seeking their comfort and confidence in the pleasures of this world. Along these lines, Jonathan Edwards reminded his own sick daughter that "God has now given you early and seasonable warning not at all to depend on worldly prosperity. Therefore I would advise . . . if it pleases God to restore you, to lot upon no happiness here . . . and never expect to find this world any thing better than a wilderness."[108]

When other children experienced affliction or death, parents were urged to use these trials to remind their own children of the brevity of life, the fleeting nature of earthly comforts, and God's punishing hand for those who rebelled against him. Samuel Sewall, for example, spoke to his eleven-year-old son, Sam, about the death of Sam's nine-year-old cousin, Richard, from smallpox. He used this as an occasion to tell his son "what need he had to prepare for Death, and therefore to endeavor really to pray when he said over the Lord's Prayer."[109] Edwards took the children of his town to view a home fire that claimed two girls' lives in order to speak to them about life's uncertainty.[110] Wadsworth counseled parents, "When you hear of the Death of others . . . more especially the sudden Death of *Young Ones*, how suitably might you say to your Children, 'What would have become of you, if you had been thus suddenly snatch'd away? Would your Souls have gone to Heaven, or to Hell; which of them?'"[111] Every act of God's providence was, for colonial parents, a potential teachable moment.

Special events and holidays also provided opportunities to offer spiritual instruction. While Puritans rejected Christmas for its worldly associations and claimed that there were no true festivals other than the Sabbath and the Lord's Table, there were other opportunities to ritualize a heightened spiritual attentiveness. New England Puritans celebrated periodic Days of Humiliation and Days of Thanksgiving, communal events given over to corporate repentance or praise. On Days of Humiliation, parents asked children to speak of their sins and afflictions and what good use they could make of these challenges. Days of Thanksgiving were then accompanied by directed questions regarding the particular mercies of God and the obligations they felt in light of those mercies. While some historians claim that birthdays were not celebrated until the nineteenth century, some colonial parents pointed to these occasions as milestones that could be used for spiritual benefit.[112] Cotton Mather noted that "when the *Birth-dayes* of my several Children arrive," he would "make it an Opportunity, not only to discourse very proper and pungent Things unto them, relating to their eternal Interests, but also oblige them, to consider, first, *What is their main Errand into the World*; and then, *What they have done of that Errand*."[113] He suggested that these days be used to remind the celebrants of God's purposes for their lives, challenging them to reflect on how they wished to spend the rest of their days for God's glory.

Providing Children with a Vocabulary of Faith

For colonial pastors, the home was a place of learning, a classroom in which parents instructed their children in the doctrines of the faith. While the church certainly played an educational role through sermons and occasional catechizing, and while schools played a limited role for some, the home was the primary setting for Christian teaching in this era. It was in the home that children learned both the literacy skills necessary for reading the Bible and the doctrinal content necessary for understanding God, themselves, and the world around them. Parents and pastors believed that such training would prepare children for full participation in the church and protect them from false teaching and the cunning schemes of Satan. They also believed that such teaching would lead naturally to conversion by helping children understand their own sinful state, Christ's atoning work, and their need to seek a new heart from him. When Richard Baxter noted that "education is the ordinary way for the conveyance of his grace, and ought no more to be set in opposition to the Spirit than the preaching of the Word," he was affirming the fact that teaching, like preaching, was a supernatural process ordained by God to open children's eyes and bring them to a place of personal faith.[114] Grace came to the soul through the understanding. Christian parenting, therefore, had a content-rich educational mission.

This perspective raises a number of interesting issues related to the nature of instruction in Christian families. Christian Smith's recent sociological work highlights the fact that most contemporary religious parents do not attempt to provide much in the way of specific religious teaching within the home. Some of this may be a function of the fact that parents rely on other agencies—Sunday schools, youth groups, Christian clubs, and Christian schools—to provide a Christian education. With such specialized agencies taking care of instructional concerns, parents can focus on other matters. Smith also states, however, that this may be related to the fact that parents fail to see the value of such teaching. Reflecting a more pragmatic approach, many see faith as an instrumental set of moral principles to provide comfort, support, and guidance rather than as a set of beliefs to provide a Christian worldview. Parents also tend to believe that children will acquire faith chiefly through modeling—a "semivoluntary socialization" that is unconscious and largely automatic—rather than through direct teaching.[115] Perhaps this is why Smith's research on American teenagers and emerging adults revealed that most do not think that the doctrinal beliefs of the faith matter very much. What matters instead are the core principles that guide a good ethical life and set one up for success in career and relationships.[116] The discipleship of the mind means very little in such a context.

It is certainly true that traditional catechetical approaches have limitations when it comes to producing spiritual transformation in children's lives. Educational theorists have rightly challenged purely cognitive and information-driven models, calling attention to the flaws of abstract teaching that is disconnected from children's real-life experiences. A Christian *worldview* does not always lead to a Christian *way of life* because the knowledge that is gained can be forgotten, compartmentalized, and isolated from life.[117] Despite the best intentions to connect memorized information with affections and practices, knowledge can be detached from the inner needs, desires, and purposes of the child. As James K. A. Smith has suggested, viewing human beings as "brains-on-a-stick" can neglect the reality that they are also "lovers," individuals who are driven not only by knowledge but also by their ultimate desires.[118] Children can develop and profess a particular worldview, even the kind absorbed through orthodox catechetical teaching, while their loves are oriented in very different directions because of their habits and practices. Such a reality is evident in Christian Smith's findings about the faith of many emerging adults who affirm a variety of truths about Christianity but whose beliefs are "cognitive assents, not life drivers."[119]

Yet for all of its limitations, perhaps the colonial use of the catechism reveals something important about the role of instruction within the home. In their most recent research on the parental transmission of faith to children, Christian Smith and Amy Adamczyk found that parents talking to their children about faith was one of the most important factors in promoting faith transmission in children even years down the road.[120] They hypothesize that in order to solidify faith, children must learn the language of their beliefs. Since Christian vocabulary is not communicated through mainstream culture, this is more akin to learning a second language, and regular conversations with parents about faith therefore become critical means of teaching them this new "grammar." Without a deep immersion in the language of faith, it becomes very challenging for children and youth to engage (and at times stand up against) the broader cultural narratives that surround them on a daily basis. They also note that, since people "usually talk about what they care about," regular discussions with parents about religious issues show children that religion is a significant priority amidst all the other concerns of life.[121] If parents find themselves talking most consistently about other issues and address faith directly only when it is time to head to church, children can easily pick up on the relative "weight" given to these various aspects of life. The fact that colonial parents and children studied and spoke truth together meant that they likely developed a common family language that they could refer back to during good and challenging times. This practice also likely served as a helpful means for parents to reinforce their own understanding, rehearsing the foundations of the faith on a regular basis. As Smith and Adamczyk conclude, "Strong evidence also shows that parents *talking to* their children about their religion, and not simply quietly role modeling it for them, is a powerfully important practice. If there were only one practical take-away from our research, it would be this: parents need not only to 'walk the walk' but also regularly to *talk* with their children about their walk, what it means, why it matters, why they care."[122]

This also highlights the ways that children perceive Christian knowledge alongside their other learning. The fact that children are not taught the building blocks of biblical and theological knowledge even as they are developing mastery in other academic subjects may actually undermine the importance and vitality of the faith. When parents place so much weight on academic learning and homework while neglecting faith-based teaching, they may implicitly be setting up hierarchies of priorities in their children's minds that have long-term consequences. As children learn and advance in their studies, they gain a depth of understanding and nuance in academic subject areas that they never achieve in their knowledge of the Christian faith. As they look at this advanced knowledge alongside their more simplistic exposure to Christian beliefs, it is easy to see why academic learning is taken more seriously and seen as more reliable than their relatively unsophisticated theological notions. One also wonders if the lack of such teaching in the home leaves children vulnerable to "every wind of doctrine" (Eph. 4:14) from the false teachers and ideologies around them. Relying on Sunday school lessons to counteract a flood of cultural lies and half-truths may be asking for more than a once-a-week church curriculum can provide.

Perhaps it also matters that the catechism required children themselves to verbalize the key doctrines of the faith. Christian Smith has demonstrated that most teenagers are quite inarticulate when it comes to speaking about their faith traditions. While they can talk vaguely about God and his work, they are often unable to express the particularities of their beliefs. While some may not consider this a real problem, scholars such as Peter Berger and Thomas Luckmann have suggested that there is a close relationship between articulation and one's perceived reality.[123] For a truth to seem real and to grow in importance, it must be spoken and expressed. If this is true, it is important for children not only to hear but also to speak the vocabulary of the larger faith community. Children will likely be quite fluent in the language of popular culture that bombards them on a daily basis through various entertainment and social media outlets. They will speak often about these things, making them appear meaningful and "real" in their own eyes. The relative lack of a spoken biblical and doctrinal vocabulary, a language quite different from that of the cultural mainstream, will leave them woefully lacking when it comes to constructing alternative identities as citizens of the kingdom of God.

While formal catechizing was one means of fostering such a vocabulary, also critical was the colonial role attributed to "teachable moments" in children's lives. By connecting divine truth to the mundane events of life (eating, celebrating, playing games, traveling, etc.) and to the various "providential occurrences" of blessings, losses, and afflictions, parents helped their children see that the Christian faith was involved in every aspect of their lives. While it is easy to compartmentalize religious conversations from the everyday activities of life, integrated conversations help children see that matters of faith cross categories into lived reality.[124] Many contemporary works on Christian parenting similarly note that parental teaching should include both formal and informal modes of instruction. Formal times of family worship and teaching can be balanced by informal experiences of eating together, driving in the car, working on projects together, and taking part in family rituals. While these can be divided between formal and informal experiences, both categories require intentionality. Informal teaching, no less than formal, requires a clear plan and attentiveness that recognizes the power of individual moments. Breaking down the boundaries between "sacred" and "secular" activities, colonial pastors desired a comprehensive education that connected to the fullness of life.

The importance attributed to "teachable moments" likely makes contemporary Christians painfully aware of the challenges of finding spaces for such interactions. The proliferation of youth activities, coupled with parents' own career, church, and social involvements, often means less time together in the shared space of the home. Shared meals, formerly locations for prayer, conversation, and instruction, are now the exception rather than the rule. Isolated entertainment options within the home—phones, computers, TVs, and video game systems—threaten to diminish interactions even when parents and children do share the same physical space. In addition, many of the situations that might have sparked teachable moments in the colonial home are now hidden from view. Children would often work alongside parents and see the way they engaged their vocations as Christian adults. They would see the ways parents reacted to downturns. They would watch parents give of their scarce resources for the work of ministry. They would witness sickness and death, whether that was the animal on the farm, another member of the church community, or, frequently, their own parents or siblings in their home. And, of course, they would see their parents pray and grapple with biblical and theological issues during family prayers and catechism teaching. As many of these realities have been progressively hidden from view—parents going off to work, death moved away to hospitals, giving done online, and religious practices apportioned to an isolated "quiet time"—children have lost some of the natural locations in which informal teaching could take place. The loss of what Kenda Creasy Dean has called "sacred eavesdropping" has, in the long run, made informal Christian teaching a more challenging process.[125]

For a number of reasons, the heavily teaching-focused work of Christian parenting would fall on hard times by the mid-nineteenth century. As Sunday schools rose to prominence, as fathers were increasingly absent from the home, and as authors placed more stock in environmental factors such as parental impressions and family relationships, both the perceived need and the desire for strong doctrinal teaching began to wane among many Protestant groups. Yet for a time the home as classroom turned parents into teachers and gave families a common vocabulary of faith with which to engage the world.

Nevertheless, evangelism, worship, and teaching were not enough. As colonial pastors indicated, parents' responsibilities with their children related not only to the practices they engaged in and the words they spoke but also to the very roles they played as leaders in the household. To uphold divine "order" and to help their children develop postures of reverence and obedience that would carry over into their spiritual lives, parents—and especially fathers—were called on to preserve authority and discipline as governors and "kings" of their families. As will be evident in the next chapter, parents' rule and children's submission would pave the way to a family structure that would both strengthen the social fabric and lead children to submit to God as the ultimate King of their lives.

CHAPTER 4

The Parent as King

Marking the Boundaries of Authority

Every Christian family is a little church, and the heads of it are its authoritative teachers and governors.

—Jonathan Edwards, "Revival of Religion in New England"[1]

When Jonathan Edwards stood before his Northampton congregation to deliver a "Farewell Address" in 1750, it was perhaps not surprising that the very first of his concluding "words of advice" related to the "maintaining of family order."[2] Edwards regularly commented on the wayward practices of his congregation's youth. He often chastised youth for skipping out on family worship.[3] He was grieved at the sinful conduct of young people on Sabbath evenings, noting that their "going to the tavern and into frolics" had turned a holy day into a "play day, a day of drinking and company-keeping."[4] Edwards also pointed to a growing laxity in matters of sexual purity. In addition to "acts of lasciviousness," he claimed that young people were engaging in activities that would "naturally tend to stir up lust," such as "lying in beds together."[5] This warning reflected the increasingly common practice of "bundling," in which courting couples were given permission to sleep together fully clothed with only a "bundling board" between them.[6] Several years before his address, Edwards had publicly condemned a number of young men (all were in their twenties and most were still living at home) who had been circulating popular medical texts, joking about their sexual content, and harassing local young women. In this "young folks' Bible case," so named because the young men referred to the medical text as their "Bible," Edwards was disturbed not only by the incident itself but also by the defiance of the young men and the resistance and apathy of their parents.[7] His strong pastoral response to youthful immorality was one of the things that he later noted had offended many parents and made him "so obnoxious" to his congregants.[8]

Edwards's last words to his congregation, therefore, were quite fitting. Warning against the sin of the biblical Eli, who had failed to restrain his wicked sons, he instructed parents to discipline their children so as to avoid a generational "curse." He encouraged children to "obey their parents, and yield to their instructions, and submit to their orders," since "nothing has a greater tendency to bring a curse on persons, in this world, and on all their temporal concerns, than an undutiful, unsubmissive, disorderly behavior in children towards their parents."[9] While he acknowledged the importance of order in the church, he stated: "the due regulation of your families is of no less, and in some respects, of much greater importance."[10] To parents he stated clearly that if they would not have all their "instructions and counsels ineffectual, there must be government as well as instructions, which must be maintained with an even hand, and steady resolution; as a guard to the religion and morals of the family, and the support of its good order."[11] The lack of such "order," in Edwards's eyes, was one of the key sources of New England's religious decline and one of the chief obstacles to the ongoing work of revival in that region.

Fathers, Mothers, and Parental "Government"

Edwards's address reflected a key theme of Protestant parenting in colonial New England. In addition to priestly family worship and prophetic instruction, one of the most important components of Christian parenting was kingly "government," the exercising of authority and discipline in order to maintain proper "order" within the home.[12] While the prophetic work of instruction was absolutely essential in shaping children's minds, Boston pastor John Norton was quick to point out that "Doctrine and Example alone are insufficient; Discipline is an essential part of the nurture of the Lord."[13] In fact, several authors noted that without proper authority children would be unlikely to submit themselves to be taught or to join with the family in regular worship activities. "If we do not maintain the *Vigour* of Family-Government to the utmost," Deodat Lawson noted, "Religious

Duties, are so much against the *Grain* of Natural Corruption, that we shall not be able to Comply with our own Resolutions to Serve the Lord: because this *Child . . .* will *Neglect, Dispute* against, and at last *Despise* to be *Counselled, Catechized,* and *Instructed,* much more to be *Rebuked* or *Corrected,* for the greatest miscarriages."[14] It was the parents' authority, in other words, that would allow all the other Christian parenting practices to proceed unhindered.

Such "order" was viewed as God's created design for the family. Referring frequently to "the Light and Law of Nature," colonial leaders spoke of the inherent order God structured into the creation, an order that defined the responsibilities of both parents and children.[15] Creation's order was fundamentally hierarchical at both the macro level (plants and animals subordinate to humans and humans subordinate to God) and within the small-scale human relationships of state, church, and family. Thus, governing authorities were to rule over their subjects, pastors and elders over their congregations, and, within the family unit, husbands over wives, parents over children, and masters over servants.[16] Each of the members of these pairs possessed obligations to one another. Those with God-given authority were charged with caring responsibility and wise leadership, while the subordinate members of each pair were called to reverence, obedience, and willing submission.[17] Many of the sermons and pamphlets detailing these issues laid out the specific and reciprocal duties of husbands and wives, parents and children, and masters and servants, clarifying the unique roles each would play in the social order. In keeping with this divine pattern, colonial authors celebrated families that were "well-ordered."[18]

Parental authority was given to both fathers and mothers. Men and women in colonial New England actually lived in a world that was less gender segregated than their nineteenth-century counterparts. Husbands and wives often worked in close proximity in and around the household. Men were more actively involved in both spiritual and mundane child-rearing tasks, while women were more actively involved in economically productive labor for the family. In addition, the emphases placed on conversion and piety in this era were less conscious of gender distinctions, viewing both men's and women's spiritual status equally within the categories of "saved" and "unsaved." Because of this, both parents assumed a sense of shared collaboration in the raising of children. Puritans John Dod and Robert Cleaver could affirm that when it came to family relationships, mothers and fathers were both the "governours" of their children.

Yet Dod and Cleaver also noted that the father was the "chief governour" while the mother was his "fellow-helper."[19] In their writings on parenting, colonial pastors drew on a strong Reformation heritage of patriarchal authority.[20] Most child-rearing literature in this era was directed to fathers (or generic "parents"), and many sermons and lectures had to go out of their way to remind mothers that they too had a role to play in the Christian nurture of children.[21] While infants and toddlers were primarily under the mother's care and supervision, as the children began to exhibit reason and understanding, fathers often assumed more leadership in the spiritual formation of both boys and girls. Fathers, as Christian heads of their homes, were called on to ensure their children's church attendance, to enforce Sabbath observance, to lead family worship, to share in the care for children in times of sickness, to help their children in making marriage and vocational decisions, and to offer appropriate discipline.[22] If the parents gave contrary commands to a child in a matter not prescribed by Scripture, the child was advised to obey the father over the mother.[23] Fathers were also generally given rights to child custody when husbands and wives separated. This patriarchal mode of authority continued as the dominant paradigm through much of the eighteenth century.[24]

The authority of fathers was linked to a number of mutually reinforcing factors. Most importantly, pastors viewed Scripture as granting divine authority to fathers in domestic spiritual leadership. As one prominent spokesperson noted,

The Owner of each Family is the sole Governor of it, both by the Law of God recorded in the holy Scriptures, and by the Law of Nature. The Affairs of a Family cannot be managed as they ought to be, where the Master of it does not keep his own Place, and hold the Reins of Government in his own Hand: When the Wife, e.g., endeavors to usurp the Command of the Family, Matters are speedily brought into great Disorder and Confusion: And if any other of the Family proves disobedient, it is like a Rebellion in the State; it cannot be safe, till the disobedient Member be either removed out of it, or bro't to Subjection. The Government of a Family is not only monarchial, but in some Sort arbitrary also; the Will of the Master, under God and civil Magistrate, is the Rule of his Administration: His Commands ought not to be disputed by any of his Subjects.[25]

In the very common comparison between the household and the state, fathers took their places as "governors" and "rulers" who claimed God-given positional authority and required absolute obedience. Yet because they were under the rule of God and were supposed to reflect his character, this patriarchal authority was always to be exercised with benevolent care.

In addition to this divine sanction, some of the father's authority was connected to his overarching power as the landowning patriarch. As owner of most family property, the father was also responsible for designating "portions" of land as inheritance to his children. Because the father could control the timing of this gift and in many cases held the title to the land until his death, sons were beholden to obey and to remain in the father's good graces. The power to give or withhold land provided the father with significant control in his sons' lives, largely determining their ability to marry and gain financial independence.[26] When the father became priest of the home, the combination of economic and spiritual "headship" both consolidated and solidified his authority.[27]

This authoritative position was paralleled by a sense that fathers—as men—possessed the unique character and temperament necessary for spiritual authority. A "good man" in the seventeenth and early eighteenth centuries was one who learned to curb passionate emotions by developing reason, moderation, and a focus on the attentive care of his family.[28] Since children and youth were thought to be ruled by their passions, fathers were considered to be more capable of providing the stable, rational education that was needed as they matured. They were also thought to be more capable of exercising the discipline and restraint that mothers were either unable or unwilling to provide.[29] John Robinson, one of the earliest Pilgrims, suggested that as children grew beyond infancy, fathers were "more behoveful for their forming in virtue and good manners, by their greater wisdom and authority; and ofttimes also, by correcting the fruits of their mothers' indulgence, by their severity."[30]

Despite their equality before God, women in the colonial era were given a subordinate role within this chain of parental authority. Many assumed that women were more unstable, irrational, sensual, indulgent, and emotional.[31] There were, of course, advantages to such qualities.

Women's heightened emotions and affections, as Benjamin Colman suggested, allowed the grace of God to find easier entrance into their hearts. In addition, he claimed that the trials of birth and the fear of death that accompanied pregnancy tended to make women more prayerful and alert to their eternal condition (*"so more especially to Your* Multiplied Sorrows, *the Curse pronounc'd upon our first Mother Eve, turn'd into the greatest Blessing to Your Souls"*).[32] Some of these variables, leaders surmised, helped explain the disproportionate number of women in the pews of New England churches.[33] Yet while they were capable of great spiritual appetite, many felt that women were equally susceptible to emotional outbursts, seductive schemes, weakness of will, heresy, indulgence, and even spiritual degeneracy. As Catherine Brekus has suggested, women, because of their vulnerability, were simultaneously open to the wooing of Christ and the alluring appeals of Satan. As "archetypal saints and archetypal sinners," they were therefore capable of both great piety and great evil.[34] Eve's susceptibility to Satan's temptations in the Garden of Eden provided a biblical illustration of this weakness, and both Anne Hutchinson's antinomian controversy and the later witch trials seemed to cement in colonial minds the correlation between the female gender and spiritual vulnerability.[35]

Such female characteristics were thought to be potentially dangerous in Christian parenting, inhibiting the proper authority necessary for restraining children and youth. In particular, many felt that female indulgence would result in mothers spoiling children and letting their waywardness go unchecked.[36] Their affection, in other words, was thought at times to cloud their judgment and their ability to administer proper discipline and justice. Dod and Cleaver suggested that mothers were more likely than fathers to "cocker" and spoil their children, smothering them with a "cruell love" that would lead to "wantonnesse" and "ungraciousness."[37] Cotton Mather, citing the biblical proverb "A Child Left unto himself, brings his Mother to shame" (Prov. 29:15), suggested that it was mothers who were "usually most ready to let them have their *Wills*."[38] Several noted that children were more likely to demonstrate disrespect and outright defiance toward mothers, in part because mothers coddled them and allowed them to speak with insolence. In an environment where order, discipline, and obedience were elevated as signature virtues, a "mother's love" was viewed as a dangerous threat to a child's spiritual health. Mothers certainly had spiritual responsibilities to their children, but when it came to parenting, both biblical authority and inborn characteristics favored fathers over mothers as the key authority figures in the home.

How to "Honor" Parents

When it came to children's place within this hierarchy, the proper stance was simple. Children were to "honor" their parents, a command that encompassed three primary postures: reverence, obedience, and what they called "recompense."[39] Many of the guidelines regarding reverence were designed to avoid an "overfamiliarity" between children and their parents, eliminating anything that would blur the proper lines of authority within the home.[40] As Cotton Mather said, "The God of Nature hath placed a *Distance*, between *Parents* and their *Children*." In light of this, children were to maintain an "awful Apprehension of [parental] *Superiority* over [them]," viewing parents as the "very *Deputies of God*."[41] The continual reminder that parents were representatives of God bolstered this call for reverence. Thomas Cobbett, for example, urged children as follows: "present your Parents so to your minds, as bearing the Image of God's Father-hood, and that also will help on your filiall awe and Reverence to them."[42] Many were aware that this might be an easier posture for children to feel toward fathers, but both parents were included in these appeals. "God requires that *every Person* should *fear* his Parents, not only his *Father*, but also his *Mother*," Benjamin Wadsworth noted in referencing Leviticus 19:3. "Yea the *Mother* is here mention'd *first*, possibly because Persons are more apt to disregard their *Mothers*, tho' they stand in some awe of their *Fathers*. But Children should *fear both*."[43]

Such reverence was an inward heart posture, but it was manifested externally as well. English Puritan authors often recommended that children rise (and sometimes bow) when parents entered the room and remain silent when they were speaking.[44] In America, Sereno Dwight, Jonathan Edwards's great-grandson, recalled that in Edwards's household children "were uncommonly respectful to their parents. When their parents came into the room, they all rose instinctively from their seats, and never resumed them until their parents were seated; and when either parent was speaking, no matter with whom they had been conversing, they were all immediately silent and attentive."[45] Children were also to reverence parents in their speech to them, never talking "rudely or sawcily" with their mothers and fathers but rather speaking to and about them with honor and respect.[46] Children were called to reverence parents even if their mothers and fathers grew *"Old, Crazy, Infirm, Sickly"* or if they struggled with their own sins, authors regularly reminding children that respect was related to the position, rather than the character, of the parent.[47] This is perhaps why laws on the books in seventeenth-century Massachusetts and Connecticut stated that if rebellious children over the age of sixteen were found to "curse" or "smite" their parents, they would be put to death unless those parents could be proven to be "unchristianly negligent" or "extreme and cruel" in their correction.[48] As children learned such reverence, they were preparing for a life of deferential submission to all appropriate authority figures, including the "Political, Ecclesiastical, and Scholastical parents" (governors, pastors, and teachers) that helped to rule the larger community.[49]

This desire for reverence was also the driving force behind colonial authors' insistence on training children in good manners. John Cotton had a list of rules for his children that included such behaviors as bowing before superiors, avoiding interrupting others while they were speaking, resisting staring or eavesdropping, addressing elders with proper titles, allowing others to sit first at the table, and behaving well during public worship.[50] By upholding such standards, parents taught children to be deferential to superiors and benevolent to equals and inferiors, assuming a proper place within traditional hierarchies of age and station.[51] Manners were also deemed important for Christian formation. Many authors suggested that Scripture pointed to the importance of such deportment, highlighting examples of Abraham bowing, Paul addressing leaders with proper titles, and Elihu allowing others who were older to speak before he did. More importantly, many suggested that proper manners would serve as a witness to nonbelievers. William Gouge noted that good manners would "win the respect of outsiders" (1 Thess. 4:12), while those children who displayed rude manners "bring a staine upon their profession; yea they dishonor God, as if he were the Author of unmannerliness and confusion."[52] While Wadsworth was sure to note that an overconcern among the wealthy for the "various changeable ceremonious punctilio's of carriage" were unnecessary for the Christian, he also stated that manners were a critical aspect of godly virtue and therefore a clear parental priority.[53]

In addition to reverence, obedience was a nonnegotiable posture, and children were called on to view their parents' requests as laws. Children were to seek parental consent for all actions, to obey parental instructions and commands, to honor parents' wishes, and to willingly endure correction without complaint.[54] Children were to obey immediately and completely, submitting without hesitation or question. "Make them, therefore, to know, that they owe Obedience and Submission, and that you always expect to be obeyed by them, whenever you call them, whatever you order them, or deny them, that is consistent with Reason, and the will of God," John Barnard urged. "Let them know . . . that you are determined with yourselves, and resolute, that they shall obey you."[55] Obedience was needed, of course, for practical reasons. In large families, obedience helped preserve order, and the tasks required for children as they worked alongside parents in the field or in the household also made rapid compliance essential.[56] Yet this was also a matter of biblical fidelity. Colonial authors regularly related all the curses pronounced on disobedient children in the Bible, reminding them that their earthly and eternal well-being was connected to their willingness to joyfully obey parents.[57] In fact, since parents bore the mantle of God's authority, children's obedience to parents was commonly linked to their obedience to God. Since parents "represent God," Isaac Ambrose suggested, "Children must remember, that whatever they do to their Parents, they do it to God; when they please them they please God."[58]

Since obedience was very closely linked to submission, parents were often reminded that their job was to "subdue" the child's will. Most Protestant colonial leaders made it clear that the child's will should be restrained very early in life so that a stubborn willfulness did not harden into habitual rebellion over time. Henry Gibbs suggested that only a "deplorable" family would allow children to "set up their wills against the will of their Parents, and to trample on their Authority."[59] "Children should not know," John Robinson argued, "that they have a will in their own, but in their parents' keeping: neither should these words be heard from them, save by way of consent, 'I will' or 'I will not.'"[60] Most noted that this process should begin early. Samuel Hopkins noted of Jonathan Edwards that "when they first discovered any considerable degree of Will and Stubbornness, he would attend to them till he had thoroughly subdued them and brought them to submit."[61] Likewise, it was his wife's rule to "resist the first, as well as every subsequent exhibition of temper or disobedience in the child, however young, until its will was brought into submission to the will of its parents."[62] These leaders saw the subduing of the will as a critical aspect of spiritual formation, preparing the child's heart for a similar act of obedient submission to God. As children metaphorically handed over their wills to their parents early in life, they would be prepared to do the same as they yielded to God's authority. In this sense, as historian Philip Greven has suggested, obedience was a pathway to salvation, an act that required children to give up their autonomy and self-rule and surrender their wills to their heavenly Father.[63]

Finally, "recompense" referred to the child's obligation to care for parents in their old age, visiting them in times of sickness, comforting them in mourning, providing for their physical and material needs, and caring for them through death and burial. With too many examples around them of children who either neglected or took advantage of elderly parents, colonial authors wanted to communicate how critical parental care was to the heart of God. Scripture, in fact, seemed to mandate this through examples such as Joseph, David, Ruth, Solomon, and even Jesus, who cared for his mother and made provision for her before his death.[64] Recompense spoke to the need for children to repay their parents' "Kindness, Care and Cost." They were instructed to offer service to the elderly parents who "Bore you, and Bred you, and Fed you, and Endured Thousands of Sorrows for you."[65] Out of gratitude, children were to bear with their parents' infirmities, cover up any parental shame, and help relieve any distress they may encounter in their old age.[66] "You owe them all that you are, all that you have," Cotton Mather said; "you'll never come out of their *Debt*."[67]

Much was at stake in maintaining order in the household. Because the family was considered to be the fundamental building block of society and the first pattern of hierarchical order in the child's life, the lack of family government was thought to be a primary source of both individual and societal decline.[68] Cotton Mather suggested that "*Well-ordered Families* naturally produce a *Good Order* in other *Societies*. When *Families* are under an *Ill Discipline*, all other *Societies* being therefore *Ill Disciplined*, will feel that Error in the *First* Concoction."[69] These high stakes perhaps explain why single people were not allowed to live independently but were required to live within homes under family government.[70] This also explains why most colonial governments assigned individuals to ensure that family heads were fulfilling their authoritative roles. In the early years, this responsibility fell to the selectmen and other constables. By the 1670s, however, population growth and rising fears about insubordinate youth led Massachusetts leaders to institute another layer of surveillance. Tithingmen, as they were called, consisted of "sober and discreet" persons of every town who would take charge of ten to twelve families, inspecting them on a regular basis and reporting any transgressions of laws and responsibilities. Among their duties, the tithingmen were to report "omission of family government, nurture, and religious duties, and instruction of children and servants."[71] If parents failed to maintain proper order and discipline, such authorities had the power to remove children from their homes and place them in others that would more adequately provide for family government.[72] This kind of "support staff" revealed just how much the community depended on proper family order for its ongoing flourishing.[73]

When Children Go Wrong: The Struggles of Youth

These ideal responsibilities of parents and children, of course, did not always reflect the realities of colonial homes. Especially by the eighteenth century, parents seemed to be losing both the will and the ability to restrain their children, and children themselves seemed less willing to submit to parental authority. Population growth, mobility, and the rise of a more diverse population seemed to threaten traditional hierarchies. The rise of a more prominent peer culture heightened opportunities for immorality and also pulled children away from adult role models. In addition, the declining availability of arable land meant that fathers could no longer promise land to their sons in return for their obedient compliance. Many historians have noted that this began the process of weakening patriarchal authority, sending sons away from the home in search of employment, and perhaps emboldening them to cast off parental restraints.[74]

Colonial leaders were most concerned about "youth," a stage of life ranging roughly from age fourteen to the early twenties.[75] Benjamin Colman famously labeled this the "chusing time," in which a young person would select a trade, a master, an educational trajectory, and eventually a spouse.[76] From a more spiritual angle, many viewed the teenage years and early twenties as a pivotal moment in which the young person would faithfully adopt the mantle of the covenant community or stray in rebellion beyond its protective reach.[77] This period of semi-dependency was therefore a "chusing time" spiritually as well.[78]

On the positive side, many held that this stage represented the best opportunity to make an indelible mark on the growing soul. While young children were often "too Shallow, too Heedless and too Sportful" for "serious counsels," and while "Old Men" were "too much confirmed in the ways of this world, & even Sermon-proof," youth represented "they that the calls of the gospel are likely to do the most good upon."[79] Cotton Mather, in fact, suggested, "Now the Hearers of the *Glorious Gospel* have one *special season* of Life, wherein Admonitions of Religion, are likely to be most livelily and hopefully Address'd unto them. And that *special season* is, just when they are *come to Years*, even into that *Age* wherein they pass from their *Childhood* unto their *Manhood*; that *Age* wherein they have done saying their *Catechism* to the *Parents* or *Tutors*, and it is expected, that ere long they may themselves be *Teachers* of others."[80] Mather saw some of the fruit of this spiritual passion in the formation of a weekly neighborhood "Young men's Meeting" given to prayer, sermon reading, psalm singing, and mutual accountability.[81] A few decades later, it was youth within this age range that constituted some of the greatest "fruit" of the eighteenth-century revivals.

Yet the very malleability that rendered youth responsive to spiritual appeals also left them susceptible to the vices around them. While leaders did speak of young ladies who were frivolous in their vain pursuit of physical beauty and external graces, they spent most of their energy commenting on the indiscretions of male youth.[82] Cotton Mather felt that the devil saved his most virulent attacks for young men, assailing them with "greater *frequency* and *industry* than he does assault other Ages."[83] In part, this was a result of Satan's strategic desire to build his kingdom on the shoulders of future leaders, much as Nebuchadnezzar did with the young men of Israel. Yet Mather also hypothesized that the devil saw young men as easy targets, their lust for "pleasure, profit, and grandeur" and their proclivity for sexual sin, drunkenness, and church absence providing "very agreeable *Tynder*, for the sparks of [the devil's] insinuations to fall upon."[84] "*No man* is ordinarily more *unholy* or more *unlikely* to be *Holy*," he concluded, "than the *Young man*."[85]

The chief problem with male youth was that they were vulnerable to sensuality and "the passions."[86] Thomas Foxcroft noted that each age had its own particular sins. While the elderly were given to covetousness and those in middle age to ambition, sensuality was "the emphatical blemish of wanton *Youth*."[87] Barnard noted that young people were "naturally full of Warmth and Heat, and the Appetites and Passions, are prone to be very fierce and unruly, and hurry them away rashly into many Indecencies."[88] This passionate nature led to bouts of anger and also to what William Cooper identified as the typically "youthful" sins of the tongue (profane speech and slander), sins of the body (fornication and lasciviousness), prideful arrogance, drunkenness, and general *"Foolishness."*[89] Sexual sin was, not surprisingly, a key problem for "passionate" male youth, and pastors noted that young men were often pulled into "Quagmires" by the "uncleanness" of such thoughts and acts.[90] From the late seventeenth to the late eighteenth century, in fact, the proportion of premarital pregnancies in New England rose from less than 10 percent to as high as 40 percent.[91] As Anne Lombard has pointed out, colonial leaders identified excessive "passion" with children and women, thereby associating such sins with a childish and effeminate character. "Youth" was billed as the time during which budding men were called to resist passion while developing the rationality, moderation, and self-control associated with true godly masculinity.[92] Only when they gained the capacity to battle carnal passions would young males achieve the strength that was the mark of a truly *"Manly Christianity."*[93]

Rather than moving toward self-control, however, pastors saw young men giving full vent to their lusts, fostering a collective peer culture in which such vices were enflamed. Youth growing up in rural areas in the seventeenth century probably had few real opportunities to develop close friendship outside the family and other close relatives. By the early eighteenth century, however, the emergence of a growing merchant class, many hailing from England where a more vigorous youth culture existed, alarmed colonial parents worried about unholy friendships.[94] Militia training days and celebrations of Guy Fawkes Day provided opportunities for young men to congregate with little adult supervision. Along with general unruly conduct—referred to with such titles as "night-walking," "frolicking," and "carousing"—leaders warned against the male tavern culture, lamenting the tendency of alcohol to destroy rationality and moderation while fueling passionate decadence.[95] As Lombard has pointed out, while adult male fellowship was viewed in positive terms in colonial New England, youthful friendships were thought to derail young people from the path to holiness, leaving them untethered from the adult male role models capable of pointing them toward mature rationality and piety.[96]

While colonial pastors of course lamented youthful rebellion, they did see these challenges as tools that God could use to foster parents' spiritual development. Henry Gibbs told parents that, in such times, "every affliction should awaken to self-reflection and self-examination. . . . Look back and consider how you have behaved your selves in your relations. Did you not spend your childhood and Youth in vanity? Have you not been slack and remiss in performing your duty to your children? Or have you not set your hearts too much upon them, and indulged them? . . . *HUMBLE your selves under the holy hand of God thus testifying against you.*"[97] Gibbs's comments reveal a common belief among colonial pastors: children's rebellion was often God's way of punishing parents for their past and present sins. Around the time of his rebellious son's eighteenth birthday, Cotton Mather stated, "I must penitently see my own Sins chastised in what shall thus befal me, and humbly accept the Punishment of my Iniquity."[98] Such punishment was even more likely if parents had previously sinned by disobeying their own parents. Mather claimed that a wayward child was often God's just retribution for parents' former disobedience: "Have not *you* formerly Grieved the Hearts of your own *Parents*? It may be, 'tis for *This*, that your *Children* are now Grieving of yours. . . . There is no Sin, so sure of Recompense in this Life, as that of, *Willfully Grieving the Heart of a Parent.* Yea, it is a Sin, that rarely, if ever, misses of an Exemplary *Retaliation* here."[99] This was indeed a grievous punishment, leading Mather to note that "there are *Scorpions* at the End of the *Rods*, when God makes *Rods* of *Children*, to Scourge the *Parents* with them."[100]

Ultimately, child rebellion provided a powerful opportunity for parental sanctification. Isaac Ambrose asked parents with rebellious children to make sure "that the Lord may sanctify the Correction unto them." He went on, "Consider this, O ye parents, Do you observe such and such Sins in your Children? Enter into your own Hearts, examine your selves, whether they come not from you: Consider, how justly the Hand of God may be upon you: and when you are angry with your Children, have an holy Anger with your selves."[101] Cotton Mather charged "distressed" parents to utilize the affliction of rebellious children to enhance their own *"Examination, Humiliation, and Reformation."* In fact, he believed that ungodly children could serve as spiritual *"Glasses"* for their parents, helping them see their own sin and need for repentance.[102] The pain of wayward children, in other words, was a gracious gift of God for both humbling and refining godly parents. "Art thou an *Afflicted Parent*?" Mather asked. "It is the Will of an *Heavenly Father*, that it should be so; and He therein deals no more Hardly with thee, than He hath sometimes dealt with His own dearest *Children*."[103] Colonial pastors did not want parents to waste the opportunities provided by their children's defiance. While it was easy to simply blame children for their rebellion, the better path was for parents to use such occasions to examine their own hearts.

Most of all, pastors in colonial New England noted that the hard reality of youthful disobedience should challenge parents to redouble their efforts to practice proper parental authority and discipline. Such occasions, they noted, should cause them to recognize that they had failed to pray enough, teach enough, and punish enough to eradicate sinful tendencies in their children, sparking a new sense of intentionality. In this sense, youthful disobedience could serve as a helpful wake-up call to apathetic parents. Because parents were apt to wrongly interpret children's good behavior as a sign of true salvation, children's bad behavior could actually serve as a wake-up call to help parents remember their children's true spiritual condition. While children's external goodness might foster a kind of parental complacency, in other words, youthful rebellion might alert parents to the need for vigilance in parental duties. This in itself was a positive outcome that might bear fruit for generations to come.[104]

The Tools of Parental Government

When it came to dealing with the challenges of disobedient children, colonial parents had many tools at their disposal: verbal admonition, restraint, and, if all else failed, the rod. Pastors recommended that parents start with verbal warnings and admonitions. Instead of harsh words or physical punishment, most preferred to dispel youthful passion through rational and biblical persuasion. Sarah Edwards's great-grandson recalled that "she knew how to make [children] regard and obey her cheerfully, without loud angry words, much less heavy blows. She seldom punished them; and in speaking to them, used gentle and pleasant words. If any correction was necessary, she did not administer it in a passion; and when she had occasion to reprove and rebuke, she would do it in few words, without warmth and noise, and with all calmness and gentleness of mind."[105]

Parents were told to meet individually with rebellious children, pray with them, lay out scriptural arguments, and attempt to secure verbal commitments to the proper path. They were told to read scriptural commands with their children, to speak to them candidly about their destructive behaviors, and to lead them toward repentance. "When your *Children* do amiss," Cotton Mather suggested, "call them Aside; set before them the *Precepts* of God which they have broken, and the *Threatenings* of God, which they provoked. Demand of them to profess their Sorrow for their *Fault*, and Resolve that they will be no more so *Faulty*."[106] Barnard likewise recommended "a gentle Reproof and Admonition" for most children, although he recognized that some children might require "a more sharp Rebuke" in which the parents' words were "strong and forcible, and carry Weight and Authority with them." In this sense, he concluded, children would see that parents "are in Earnest, and mean to be heard."[107]

While the hope was that such verbal admonitions would be enough for most children, colonial pastors also recognized that "restraint" would be needed when children persisted in willful sin. One of the greatest threats to proper parenting, according to many, was the inability or unwillingness to exercise such restraint. This was precisely the problem of the biblical Eli, who had offered words of reproof to his sinful sons but failed to restrain them. Jonathan Edwards directly correlated the parental practice of restraint with religious revival in his region. He chastised parents who lamented the "degeneracy and deadness of the times" while neglecting to restrain their children from activities that tended to "prevent the revival of religion." "We are often speaking of the degeneracy of young people, and how it is not amongst them as it was formerly," he noted. "But when all is said of the degeneracy of young people, it is certainly true that whenever there is a general degeneracy among young people, it is owing very much to parents."[108] He saw parents avoiding restraint out of fear of their children's negative responses or because they didn't want to restrict their children from doing things that other parents were allowing. He urged parents to utilize their God-given authority, to stand up to their children, and to resolve to restrain them for their ultimate salvation and well-being.[109]

One of the chief areas of necessary restraint related to children's friendships.[110] "Enquire into their Company," Barnard suggested, "what Company they mostly frequent, and associate themselves with; that . . . they may not be the Companions of Fools, but may walk with the wise, and be like them."[111] This was not typically a command to shun all of the ungodly, lest their children eliminate all potential for evangelism. Yet Thomas Gouge indicated that while it was necessary and permissible to associate with all kinds of people, young people should never make "dead-hearted" youth their "Bosom Friends."[112] While he encouraged youth to treat the ungodly with respect and Christian love, Cotton Mather noted that the problem came when they *"Unnecessarily, Familiarly, Delightfully* Embrace the *Society* of Ungodly men."[113] "There is a Civility to be expressed in your carriage towards all men," he allowed. "But when it comes to the point of Intimacy . . . there you will do well to use more of Reservation. . . . My *Young Men*, have as little to do with them as ever you can."[114] Mather challenged parents to be watchful over their children's companions and to stand against friends that might have a negative influence: "Ah, Parents, That can see your Children, in danger by such Company, in the very Mouth of the Dragon, and yet not pull them as *Brands out of the Burning*; Shall I call you *Foolish Parents*? You are so; And you will be the *Parents of Fools*. Yea, I will call you, *Bloody Parents*. I must faithfully tell you You will have the Blood of the Souls of your Children, to answer for."[115]

Along with this, parents were called on to restrain their children from taking part in activities that might compromise their spiritual health. As Barnard put it,

> They should also restrain them, by withholding from them, as much as may be, the Opportunities of their running into bad Practices; . . . and restrain them from gading, and wandering abroad, with a lawless Liberty, at unseasonable hours; and especially from their stroleing about, and sporting themselves, on the Lord's Day Evening. . . . For such Liberties will naturally tend to corrupt them, and draw them into mischief, whereas a Restraint wherefrom will very much keep them out of Harm's way, and prevent the Occasion, and Temptation, and Opportunity, of many Sins.[116]

In some cases, this meant imposing strict curfews on their children. Edwards himself required his children to be at home after 9:00 p.m. and to go to sleep at an early hour.[117] In other cases, the need for restraint prompted pastors to encourage cooperative efforts among Christian parents. Knowing that children would often pit parents against each other, Edwards urged parents to coordinate and make joint resolutions regarding appropriate behavior so that they could "strengthen one another's hands."[118]

When all else failed, colonial authors pointed to the necessity of "the rod." Barnard was typical in encouraging a gradually escalating sequence of discipline, starting with verbal commands, attempting restraint, and eventually moving toward physical "correction." "It may be that Admonitions and Reproofs, by Words, will not be sufficient to govern the young People, (as with many Tempers they will not)," he suggested; "if so, then Parents ought to proceed from Words to Blows, and lay the Reproof home upon them that they may feel the Smart of it." It was not enough, he reasoned, in the midst of "great and atrocious sins" such as lying, stealing, Sabbath-breaking, swearing, and "contempt of parental authority" to take Eli's path and stop at the level of verbal rebuke. Some children, he noted, "are of such a Make and Temper that nothing but the Rod of Correction will cause their Folly to depart from them. . . . So that oftentimes the Correction of the Rod, and of Stripes, is absolutely necessary, in the parental Government, and may be a Means of delivering the Child from the snares of death and the path way that leadeth down to hell."[119]

For Christian parents, it was the rod that would save the child from eternal judgment. To resist the rod was to deny children the divinely ordained method of preserving their souls from the deceitfulness of sin. Pastors regularly cited biblical passages noting that parents should "withhold not correction from the child," for if they beat "him with the rod, he shall not die" (Prov. 23:13 KJV), and if they use the rod, they shall "deliver his soul from hell" (Prov. 23:14 KJV). So important was this that William Williams declared, "Such as neglect it, when there is need, are accessary to their Children's ruine."[120] Since hell was, in James Janeway's haunting phrase, "worse a thousand times than whipping," corporal punishment was a gracious means of averting a far worse fate. As Cotton Mather perhaps most memorably put it, children were "better Whipt, than Damn'd."[121]

Yet if it was better to be whipped than damned, colonial leaders almost always mentioned that it was better to be persuaded than to be whipped. Despite its biblical warrant, physical punishment was almost always described as a "last resort," something to practice only in the worst of cases and when nothing else had worked.[122] Though he commended "correction by stripes and blowes" as "appointed by God," William Gouge indicated that it was "the last remedy which a Parent can use; a remedy which may doe good when nothing else can."[123] Cotton Mather stated that he would "never dispense a *Blow*, except it be for an atrocious Crime, or for a lesser Fault Obstinately persisted in; either for an Enormity, or for an *Obstinacy*."[124] This seemed to be the common pattern. Corporal punishment was viewed as a necessary provision by God for the good of the child's soul, but it was to be used only for particularly egregious sins, for persistent and unrepentant rebellion, or for children who, because of their personalities, could not be chastened in any other way.

The recurring theme in all colonial New England parenting literature, in fact, was that discipline should be moderate, avoiding the extremes of both indulgence and severity.[125] Many leaders were quite concerned about the rise of more permissive forms of parenting. Edwards indicated as much when he criticized parents for believing that the previous generation had been too strict. "Parents say that their forefathers were too strict, that they used to lay too great restraints upon their children, that they were too severe in governing of 'em," he noted. "But if it was so, parents nowadays err much more on the other extreme: they give their children too vast liberties."[126] Historians have indeed indicated that the eighteenth century, especially within the more "moderate" and "genteel" families, witnessed the early growth of more democratic and permissive parent-child relations.[127] For colonial pastors, the "fond indulgence" that prevented parents from confronting their children was an "overfondness" that would eventually result in spiritual destruction, leading children to become "hard-hearted, stiff necked and inflexible, never having their wills subdued and brot into subjection."[128] "*There are other creatures, besides Apes,*" Cotton Mather cautioned, "*that hug their Cubs to Death.*"[129] Mather warned indulgent parents that their undisciplined children would cause them significant grief in the long run: "Ah, Thou Indulgent Parent; If thou canst not *Cross* thy *Children*, when they are disposed unto that which is for the Dishonor of God, God will make thy *Children* to become *Crosses* unto thee."[130]

Leaders saw this indulgence come to the fore when parents took their children's side against other authority figures. Within the covenant community, colonial authors claimed that all adult figures should be tasked with bringing children's flaws to parents' attention. Yet the historical record seems to indicate that parents were at times resistant to such intervention. William Seward warned parents to "beware of that fond partial Disposition in some Parents, never to believe their own Children do amiss, never to suffer any Complaints to be brought against them, tho' with ever so good Evidence, to be displeased with a *Neighbor* or *Friend* that does it, and to take their Children's Part."[131] This problem, which appeared to be on the rise in the eighteenth century, struck at the very heart of colonial authors' quest for "order." If parents placed relationships with their children over the standards of the larger covenant community, many feared that the hierarchical structure that extended reverence and obedience to all authorities in the community would be turned on its head.

Yet despite their fear of indulgence, colonial authors were equally vigorous in their rejection of undue severity in either words of admonition or physical punishment. Some contemporary writers have assumed that the desire to subdue the will must have led to harsh and repressive forms of punishment.[132] There were, to be sure, some who operated out of such a mindset. Sarah Osborn spoke of how her parents were quite severe in their discipline, chastening beyond reasonable measures.[133] Puritan John Robinson famously recommended the ready use of "the rod" by referring to the need for children to be "broken and beaten down" in order to destroy the "fruit of natural corruption" and make them more "serviceable."[134] Yet more typically, pastors chastised parents who were constantly finding faults within their children, calling attention to every mischievous action. They scolded parents who seemed to expect too much of their children, discounting their stage of development. Many also recommended that correction be balanced with praise, commending children for obedience and for even small hints of godliness. Such praise, they noted, would invite children to continue in such paths and provide them with a positive sense of parental pride, love, and affection.[135]

Colonial pastors felt that harshness would eventually show itself to be counterproductive, souring children's relationships with their parents and inciting further rebellion down the road. Wadsworth noted that severity would "exasperate children" (explicitly prohibited in Eph. 6:4), leaving them angry, resentful, deflated, and therefore more likely to enter into sinful acts and habits.[136] Gibbs similarly suggested that "to be always upbraiding of them, to exact more of them than they can comfortably perform, to treat them as slaves and brutes with the lash and goad, debases their spirits, and precipitates to indirect courses."[137] Harshness, many argued, would enflame a hatred for parents that would fuel a "Mutiny and Rebellion" and, ultimately, an ongoing resistance to the work of God in children's hearts.[138] To prevent severity, pastors made it clear that parents should never discipline in anger (or, as many put it, "in a passion").[139] William Gouge stated that correction should always be offered in a "milde moode when the affections are well ordered and not distempered with choler, rage, furie, and other like passions."[140] Many recommended that parents take time to cool off after an altercation so that they would be able to engage their children in a calm and rational manner.[141] Even when children lived in rebellion, Cotton Mather counseled parents to make sure that their anger was tempered with love and that their disciplinary "passion" was never so strong that children would think they "have no *Compassion* for them."[142]

As a further attack on severity, colonial authors emphasized both consistency and variety in their disciplinary techniques. Many noticed that parents would at times treat children harshly for certain indiscretions while allowing others to pass without notice. Gibbs chastised parents who "will at times be all in a flame for a small offence, when at other times they will let far greater offences pass without any regard."[143] This, many argued, was confusing for children who were seeking a uniform standard of conduct. Yet variety was also important. Parents, they reasoned, should vary correction on the basis of the offense, providing small admonitions for small acts of disobedience and more significant discipline for larger sins. Recognizing that some children would repent with only a glance while others would fight and battle to the end, they also implored parents to base their discipline on the personality of the child.[144] As Anne Bradstreet put it poetically, "Diverse children have their different natures; some are flesh which nothing but salt will keep from putrefaction; some again like tender fruits are best preserved with sugar: those parents are wise that can fit their nurture according to their Nature."[145]

Ultimately, the proper balance between indulgence and severity was so necessary because it echoed the parenting style of God himself.[146] God clearly held his Israelite children to high standards and disciplined them with fatherly admonitions and the chastening rod of personal and national trials. However, his parental posture was also one of mercy and compassion. "To treat our *Children* like *Slaves*, and with such Rigour, that they shall always *Tremble* and *Abhor* to come into our presence," Cotton Mather noted, "will be very unlike to our Heavenly Father. Our *Authority* should be Tempered with Kindness, and Meekness, and Loving Tenderness, that our children may *Fear* us with *Delight*, and see that we Love them, with as much *Delight*."[147] Comparing parental discipline to God's discipline, many authors spoke of the need for both "sugar" and "salt," kindness in general and firmness when needed. "Love like Sugar, sweetens Fear, and Fear like Salt, seasons Love," stated Ambrose in speaking of parental government. "There must be a loving Fear, and a fearing Love."[148] Colonial pastors wanted children to know that God understood their weaknesses, that he tempered his wrath with pity and affection. Parents were therefore to do the same, balancing the proper fear that accompanied parental authority with the loving affection that represented God's compassionate heart. By assuming the role of "king," parents were reflecting the righteous authority of the ultimate King in their children's lives.

Authority, Submission, and Salvation

In emphasizing parental authority, colonial pastors recognized an important issue at the heart of their children's spiritual formation. This "kingly" role was so critical because they saw children's central struggle as one of authority. The key issue was not behavioral conformity but rather the changing of the heart posture that produced external rebellion. Children defied their parents, most argued, because of a prideful autonomy, reflected in their desire to rule their own lives without external restrictions of any kind. They resisted parental government because they wanted to be self-governing agents who could not be told what to do by anyone outside themselves. This desire for self-rule—whether expressed in childhood disobedience or "passionate" teenage rebellion—was viewed as a dangerous poison that would render the child increasingly incapable of submitting not only to parents but also to God's ultimate authority. The desire for a well-ordered family and the call for children's reverence, obedience, and recompense were therefore safeguards for children who, left to themselves, would place themselves on the thrones of their lives. Parental authority, colonial pastors recognized, was a God-ordained means by which children would relinquish their sinful autonomy in preparation for the ultimate surrender of their wills to the God who had made them for himself. Kingly authority, in this sense, was bent on bringing children to a place where they were ready to bend their knees to the eternal King.

The colonial approach to parental authority walked a fine line, however, when it came to representing the character of God in their authority and discipline. Pastors sought to balance children's submission with a call to kindness and empathy. At the same time, they did not, at least in their published writings, tend to emphasize God's forgiveness and grace in the midst of children's sin. The call to reproof, restraint, and correction highlighted the call to repentance and holiness, but it did not typically call attention to the comfort of God's compassionate heart for sinners. By emphasizing the warnings and punishments of God in their admonitions without highlighting the open arms, running feet, and warm embrace of the prodigal son's father, they may have fostered postures of hiding and denial that made it challenging for their children to confess their sins and bring them into the light. And because parents themselves were called on to hide their flaws so as to serve as good role models, children may have felt quite alone in their sin. While parents may have modeled godly behavior, in other words, they may not have modeled where to go with their sin. Calls for grief over sin could at times overwhelm the gratitude that God's grace covered their iniquities. And in the end, children rarely heard that biblical commands were given to lead them into true flourishing, to experience the abundant life that God had for them (John 10:10). Obedience was often portrayed as a means of avoiding God's wrath rather than a response to his love (John 14:15) and a pathway to experience more of his grace (Titus 2:11–14).

In the years to come, Protestant authors writing about Christian parenting challenged many of the beliefs resting beneath colonial approaches to evangelism, worship, teaching, and discipline. Much of the colonial system rested on the power of parental words and practices that were meant to convey to children the very authority of God in their lives. As ambassadors of God's sovereign rule, parents represented his purposes in their children's lives by bringing them into contact with his presence, his truth, and his authority. As Protestants moved into the nineteenth century, however, they developed new ideas about the power of nurturing home environments and loving and supportive family relationships that stood alongside, and sometimes eclipsed, these traditional practices. Parents were increasingly described as architects of their children's experiences, shaping and forming children in ways that would help them develop in godly character. These new ideals would transform the very style of parenting in Protestant America in ways that continue to shape contemporary understandings of the Christian home.

PART II

Victorian Christian Parenting:
1830–1890

CHAPTER 5

The Parent as Architect

Crafting a Home Environment
to Shape the Child's Soul

It can also be shown by sufficient evidence, that more is done to
affect, or fix the moral and religious character of children, before
the age of language than after; that the age of impressions . . . is in
fact their golden opportunity; when more is likely to be done for
their advantage or damage, than in all the instruction and discipline of their minority afterward.

—Horace Bushnell, *Christian Nurture*[1]

Typical child-rearing patterns in the second half of the eighteenth century maintained many of the qualities of the colonial era, including
emphases on conversion, family prayer, patriarchal patterns of spiritual
leadership, catechetical teaching, and firm discipline. Even at this time,
however, changes were evident. The evangelicalism that emerged during
the ferment of the First Great Awakening in the 1730s and 1740s continued
many of these colonial impulses but also stressed a more heart-centered,
experiential, individualistic, and evangelistic faith. Much of this reflected
a limited adoption of new Enlightenment ideals within the larger context
of evangelical Calvinism.[2] At the same time, some Protestants more fully
embraced the Enlightenment rationalism of this era, leading to the growth
of a more "liberal" vision that highlighted "tolerance, reason, free will,
human goodness, and God's benevolence."[3] In a society marked by increasing religious pluralism, these competing perspectives led to a number of
high-profile skirmishes, particularly in relation to viewpoints on human
nature and the power of human reason.[4]

While some of these debates influenced perspectives on child-rearing, the most significant reorientation of Christian parenting among northern Protestants took place between the 1830s and the 1880s. In the midst of a number of social, economic, and religious changes, beliefs about children, conceptions of Christian formation in the home, and opinions on the roles of parents were revised in significant ways. Of course, such transformations were gradual and did not influence all groups in similar ways. As historian Margaret Bendroth recounts, the evangelical parenting style of the early nineteenth century still consisted of didactic teaching that highlighted original sin, the threat of hell, breaking the will, and the need for children to gain a "new heart" through conversion.[5] Yet during this time, and especially after 1850, new perspectives on Christian parenting emerged that influenced Protestants across the theological spectrum.

One of the chief changes along these lines was the growing emphasis on parent and home "impressions" as the chief sources of spiritual growth, especially in the child's earliest years. Authors, including the influential Horace Bushnell, increasingly highlighted the power of the home's environment, the parent-created culture that would shape children and their responsiveness to God. The appeal to "Christian nurture" after midcentury tended to downplay conversion, doctrinal teaching, and worship practices while calling attention to the larger rhythms of the home and the impressions surrounding the child. In the end, this approach tended to view parents—their modeling, their interactions with the young child, and their creation of a nurturing space in the home—as the determining factors in children's faith development. Leaving behind the metaphors of priest, prophet, and king, the parent emerged as the architect of children's spiritual lives, shaping and forming them through the power of godly impressions.

From Vipers to Cherubs: Changing Visions of Childhood

Margaret Bendroth has suggested that "contemporary attitudes toward children are, in many ways, social and theological products of the early nineteenth century," and that does indeed seem to be the case.[6] Within the enormous variety of viewpoints in this era, three broad perspectives emerged among Victorian-era Protestants: the child as inherently sinful, the child as plastic and malleable, and the child as pure and innocent. Many conservative Protestants still believed in original sin, the reality of hell, and at least the possibility of infant damnation, some growing even more strident about these issues as opposition emerged from more liberal camps.[7] Like their colonial forebears, many nineteenth-century Calvinists held that children were sinful from conception, the result of a corrupt nature inherited from Adam, who as "federal head" imputed this depravity to the entire human race. These standard Calvinistic notions remained popular in the earliest decades of the nineteenth century, especially among staunch Presbyterians, and of course were retained by many throughout the century.[8]

However, such Calvinism was increasingly on the defensive. From the mid-eighteenth century forward, "liberal" theologians like John Taylor and Samuel Webster had attacked Calvinists at their most vulnerable point—belief in infant damnation and the imputation of Adam's sin to infants.[9] By the 1820s and 1830s, a growing individualism, coupled with the pervasive Enlightenment language of rights and self-determination, challenged the idea that children were blameworthy for sins they had not personally committed.[10] Such arguments began in earnest in the mid-eighteenth century with leaders like Webster, who argued that since "*Sin* and *Guilt* . . . are *personal* things," infants could not be held responsible for Adam's transgressions.[11] By the nineteenth century, such arguments were becoming more mainstream. An anonymous contributor to the orthodox *Christian Disciple*, for example, argued that "common sense" demonstrated that children could not be evil from birth:

> A new born infant sinful! Common sense asks, why, what has he done? He has only drawn a few breaths, and uttered a few unmeaning cries. . . . A sinful character is that which deserves blame and punishment. . . . It seems one of the clearest truths, that we are responsible only as far as we have power to know and do our duty. . . . What blame then can lie attached to those qualities, which are implanted in the child by the Author of his being, and which he possesses before the exercise of reason and conscience? To blame and punish him for these, would be repugnant to our natural sense of justice, as to punish him for his features and the form of his limbs.[12]

Calvinists themselves were not immune to these attacks. Back in the eighteenth century, Jonathan Edwards dealt with these arguments by resurrecting the Augustinian notion of "direct participation," maintaining that all of humanity was metaphysically present with Adam in the garden and therefore guilty of personally sinning along with him. While Edwards and his followers thought that this still left infants liable to eternal judgment, by the nineteenth century far fewer were willing to support such logic.[13] Some moderate Calvinists began to argue that children were not responsible for their sin until such sin was personally chosen (until they achieved "moral agency"). Of particular importance here was Yale professor Nathaniel William Taylor. Challenging the belief that children were born with a sin nature so that both their state of being and their acts were corrupt, Taylor held that sin consisted only in voluntary sinful acts. One of his central arguments was that sin did not arise from necessity. Instead, he contended—quite controversially—that individuals had a "power to the contrary" with regard to sin. While he did maintain an emphasis on original sin by stating that children would inevitably sin as soon as they were able to choose, he assumed that infants were not culpable for sin prior to developing a sense of right and wrong.[14] Such views actually opened the door to beliefs that children, as they grew, could choose the new heart, responding to the earnest appeals of revivalists or Sunday school teachers.[15]

As these academic arguments were unfolding, a growing number of Protestants embraced a second perspective, viewing children as fully malleable and radically open to the influence of early impressions.[16] While colonial authors recognized a malleability in the child's mind, by the mid-nineteenth century many had adopted John Locke's vision that both the mind and the soul of the child existed as a *tabula rasa* (blank slate), equally capable of movement toward good or evil.[17] Borrowing from Scottish common sense philosophy, Catherine Beecher perhaps summed this up most clearly. Noting that she had come to the conviction that the doctrine of "any infant depravity" was "not taught either by reason or in the Bible," she suggested that all of a child's growth and development was a function of training and instruction. "The question is," she asked, "are young children so made that the cause or reason of their sinning is that their minds are depraved in *constitution*, or do they sin for want of proper development, training, and advantages?"[18] For Beecher, as for many others, the answer was clear. Moving away from envisioning children as depraved beings whose sinful natures required a spiritual awakening, growing numbers of Protestants saw children through a more optimistic lens, open to and largely shaped by the environments around them.[19]

While many held to views of children as either controlled by original sin or fully malleable, a third Romantic option also grew in prominence throughout the nineteenth century. Romanticism posited that children were innocent and pure from birth. Those in this camp sought to depict children as sent from heaven and still bearing the residual glory of God's presence. Drawing on philosopher Jean-Jacques Rousseau, educator Johann Heinrich Pestalozzi, and poets such as William Wordsworth, William Blake, and Samuel Taylor Coleridge, Romantics saw children as good and "natural," requiring sheltering and protection from the evils of the corrupt adult world. Lydia Child noted in her popular *Mother's Book* (1831) that children "come to us from heaven, with their little souls full of innocence and peace; and, as far as possible, a mother's influence should not interfere with the influence of angels."[20] Speaking of the child as a little "cherub," Child reflected the belief that parents' chief role was to preserve and protect the innate goodness of the child rather than eradicating an inherent depravity or depending on an external act of God's grace.[21]

Such reflections, which grew in strength during the second half of the nineteenth century, revealed a reversal of generational hierarchies, with children positioned as more spiritual than adults and actually capable of redeeming the adults around them. Since Romanticism emphasized "feeling over reason, the primitive over the sophisticated, the natural over the contrived, and the simple over the complicated," it is clear to see why children trumped adults at every point.[22] Their innocence left them more spiritually sensitive and more closely attuned to God, free from the burdens and corruptions that diminished the adult life. In some ways reacting to the growth of industrial regimentation, Romantics argued that parents and other adults could be spiritually uplifted through the purity, simplicity, and natural joy of their "redeemer" children.[23] As historian Hugh Cunningham helpfully notes, "From being the smallest and least considered of human beings, the child had become endowed with qualities that made it Godlike, fit to be worshipped and the embodiment of hope."[24] In Romanticism, Anne Bradstreet's "serpent's tongue" had been removed, leaving only the child's "pleasing face."

While the Romantic understanding of childhood was always more dominant among Unitarians like Lydia Child and Transcendentalists like Bronson Alcott, this language did begin to pervade the language of those across the theological spectrum, especially by the latter decades of the nineteenth century.[25] Samuel Phillips, who worked in Reformed and Presbyterian churches, described infants as "the most interesting, because the purest, member of the household."[26] In 1872 the American Tract Society published a lengthy tract titled *Our Baby* that included poetry devoted to the earliest years of childhood. Poems such as "Little Angel Visitor" and "The Divine Infant" referred to the young child as a "little cherub" and "bright dawn of our eternal day."[27] Such works spoke not of child sinfulness but of the joy and delight young children could bring to those around them.

Rather than seeking to move young children toward maturity as quickly as possible, as would have been the case in colonial writings, the idea among those with Romantic leanings was to shelter them within the relative innocence of childhood for as long as possible. As the nineteenth century wore on, many began to idealize childhood, to seek to extend it, and to view growing maturity as a loss rather than a gain.[28] As Anne Scott MacLeod explains,

> Early nineteenth-century adults looked on childhood almost entirely as a time of preparation for adult life. They loved and valued their children, to be sure, but they saw childishness as a condition to be outgrown and the irrational aspects of youth as qualities to be replaced as soon as possible by reasoned behavior. By the last decades of the century, childhood had acquired a value in and of itself. Children's innocence, emotionality, and imagination became qualities to be preserved rather than overcome; a child's sojourn in childhood was to be protected, not hastened.[29]

This view was also affirmed within the American Tract Society's poetry. "Mother's Song," for instance, suggested throughout the poem that the child not grow up too quickly:

Don't grow old too fast, my sweet!
Stay a little while
In this pleasant baby land,
Sunned by mother's smile.

Grasp not with thy dimpled hands
At the world outside;
They are still too rosy soft,
Life too cold and wide.[30]

While colonial authors wanted children to resemble adults in their reason, moderation, and faith, many in the Victorian era viewed childhood as a cherished and desirable stage that reflected a godly ideal of purity, innocence, and love. Bushnell suggested, "Tell the child how present God is, how loving he is, how close by he is in all good thoughts, and he will take the sense a great deal better than the adult soul, that is gone a doubting so far, and speculated his mind half away in the false intellectualities miscalled reason."[31] The simplicity of a child's heart and mind was now thought to provide a more receptive soil for the seeds of God's truth.

Of course, both the view of children as malleable and the more Romantic visions of childhood innocence were opposed by strict Calvinists and others who feared the consequences of these changes. Some found in Locke's *tabula rasa* a dangerous dilution of the doctrine of original sin and a potential inroad for more naturalistic approaches to child-rearing. As one put it, "It is the opinion of some, who wish to be accounted philosophers rather than Christians, that human nature, in infancy, is a material which may, by education, be manufactured into almost any thing, that it is like a sheet of white paper, on which you may write good or evil; and of consequence, every corrupt bias of the *man* is the *fruit* of some impure taint, communicated during the process of his education."[32] While a belief in the child's malleability could prompt parents to craft a godly environment in the home, only the Calvinist perspective on original sin, this author argued, could also promote a diligent fight against the corrupt nature and a recognition that success was impossible without the supernatural, cooperating grace of God.[33]

Reactions against the Romantic vision were even more vehement. Heman Humphrey, in his classic work *Domestic Education*, complained that there was much to be found in "bookseller's windows and ladies' parlors" about the "angelic sweetness of infancy."[34] As with many colonial authors, Humphrey feared that parents had lost sight of the real theological status of the child as they focused on the infant's attractiveness. He warned,

> But let us always, when we speak or write on this theme, carefully distinguish between the social affections, and the *state of the heart* in the sight of a holy God, so as not to leave the impression, that there is anything in all this infantile and juvenile loveliness, to set aside the teachers of Scripture in regard to native depravity. When we read of the spotless innocence of childhood, we ought to understand it, as simply expressing those sweet and endearing qualities, which may co-exist with a little heart, that at the same time inherits the corruption of our fallen nature.[35]

S. R. Hall likewise criticized those who "represented children as 'innocent, pure, and perfect,'" arguing instead that children were "conceived in sin" and "estranged from the womb."[36] "What they need," he argued, "is, not so much to be amended and improved as renewed—not so much to be kept from falling into sin, as to be delivered from the reigning power and dominion of sin."[37]

By the mid-nineteenth century, however, such Calvinist rebuttals were clearly in the minority. While all three of these views (original sin, plastic malleability, and child innocence) existed alongside one another throughout the nineteenth century—sometimes even within the same publications—the tides were shifting. Before 1820 it would have been quite common to refer to children as naturally depraved, evil from birth and in need of supernatural grace. Between 1820 and 1850, however, fictional and nonfictional accounts increasingly depicted children as beings with equal potential for good and evil, their direction largely determined by parental training and environmental influences. After 1850 authors more commonly began portraying children as innocent and capable of redeeming the adults around them.[38] As Peter Slater puts it, "The depraved vipers of the Puritans were rivaled by the neutral *tabula rasas* of the Enlightenment and then supplanted by the sweet angels of the Romantic era."[39]

Horace Bushnell and *Christian Nurture*

The upshot of all of these revised perspectives was a belief that young children were easily shaped in the earliest years. For some evangelicals this created a growing sense that children could experience conversion at an earlier age.[40] It was increasingly common by the middle decades of the nineteenth century to argue that younger children—even those between the ages of three and seven—were capable of regeneration.[41] Such beliefs were bolstered not only by more optimistic views of children's ability to respond to external appeals but also by the fact that growing numbers saw conversion as a matter of the heart. While colonial authors tended to locate the catalyst for spiritual awakening within the intellect (and the Holy Spirit's work in enlightening the mind), Protestants in the Victorian era increasingly emphasized an emotional and heart response to God as the engine of transformation, making children the best candidates for conversion because of their tender hearts and trusting natures.[42] This was a function of the rising sentimentalism of this era, but it also tapped into the emotionalism of the Second Great Awakening and its appeal to heart religion. As Charles Finney suggested of young children, "Cannot those who know so well how to depend on a parent, depend on God? . . . Cannot they, whose tender hearts are so ready to trust, be taught to exercise faith in Christ? Why, this is the most likely time in their lives."[43]

While the child's malleability led some to expect earlier conversions, perhaps the more significant result of this new thinking was the belief that the child's spiritual development was largely a result of the environmental impressions of the home. Without question, the most influential spokesperson for this new perspective was Connecticut pastor Horace Bushnell. Bushnell was in many ways a bridge figure between the orthodoxy of Puritan New England and the Romantic ideals emerging in the mid-nineteenth century. He was an active player in many academic debates of his day, but he was perhaps best known in more popular circles for his somewhat controversial approach to raising up children in the faith.[44] In his *Discourses on Christian Nurture* (1847) and in later expansions appearing as *Views of Christian Nurture and of Subjects Adjacent Thereto* (also 1847) and *Christian Nurture* (1861), Bushnell set forth a near perfect articulation of emerging Victorian perspectives on Christian parenting and provided a key reference for those seeking to define their own positions on these issues.[45]

At the core of Bushnell's argument was a strong reaction against the revival system and its implications for Christian parenting. By his historical retelling, the eighteenth-century revivals sparked by Jonathan Edwards, George Whitefield, Gilbert Tennent, and James Davenport had normalized particular patterns within Christianity that emphasized teenage and adult conversion experiences while minimizing the importance of childhood Christian nurture in the home.[46] While he was not opposed in principle to revivals, Bushnell lamented how "everything was brought to the test of the revival state as a standard," and how therefore "it could not be conceived how any one might be in the Spirit, and maintain a constancy of growth, in the calmer and more private methods of duty, patience, and fidelity, on the level of ordinary life."[47] As the Second Great Awakening of the early nineteenth century rekindled this approach to Christian faith—what he called "a piety of conquest rather than love"—Bushnell feared the consequences for the Christian home.[48]

Bushnell was opposed to the belief that God's grace could only be visited on children when they received a "new heart" through a moment-in-time conversion experience.[49] Because revivals emphasized immediate conversion as the central spiritual milestone, parents, he feared, would focus all their energy on this singular event. They would raise their children "in sin," praying and waiting for a future regeneration that would come suddenly through the external agency of the Holy Spirit.[50] Since conversions normally involved "a struggle with sin, a conscious self-renunciation, and a true turning to Christ for mercy," Bushnell worried that parents would think that children could experience God's grace only when they were mature enough for such an awakening.[51] In the meantime, Bushnell felt that parents would treat their children as sinners and "aliens," believing—and reminding their children frequently—that they were unable to do anything "good or acceptable to God" while in their sinful condition.[52] Bushnell labeled this approach the "ostrich nurture" and the nurture "of despair," a spiritual passivity emerging from the sense that the child was capable of sin but incapable of experiencing God's grace until a "new heart" was given by the Spirit.[53]

On the contrary, Bushnell argued that young children could experience God's grace through the character of the parents and the environmental impressions of the home. He believed that there was an "organic connection" of character between parents and children, noting that "the character of one is actually included in that of the other, as a seed is formed in the capsule."[54] Accordingly, he rejected the individualism of Baptists and other revivalists, maintaining that the parents' character and the environmental "spirit of the household" would flow into their children, shaping them in powerful ways from the earliest years.[55] He suggested to parents, "Your character is a stream, a river, flowing down upon your children, hour by hour. What you do here and there to carry an opposing influence is, at best, only a ripple that you make on the surface of the stream. . . . Understand that it is the family spirit, the organic life of the house, the silent power of a domestic godliness, working, as it does, unconsciously and with sovereign effect—this it is which forms your children to God."[56]

For Bushnell, such parental impressions were decisive. He believed that faith was communicated through the parents' eyes, their loving expressions, their character, and their way of life. He was willing to say, in fact, that the Christian gospel was "wrapped up in the life of every Christian parent, and beams out from him as a living epistle, before it escapes from the lips, or is taught in words."[57] As understanding and reason advanced in later childhood and the teen years, age-appropriate teaching would be added. However, it was early, parent-mediated impressions of love and care that were largely determinative in shaping a child's faith development.[58]

Bushnell believed that the focus on parental character and environmental impressions in no way diminished the supernatural nature of transformation in the child's life. He felt it was misguided to think that the Spirit only worked in spectacular and instantaneous acts of conversion. Instead, he reasoned, the Spirit worked in and through parental efforts to form impressions. "This general disposedness to good, which we call a new heart," he suggested, "supposes a work of the Spirit; and, if the parents live in the Spirit as they ought, they will have the Spirit for the child as truly as for themselves, and the child will be grown, so to speak, in the molds of the Spirit, even from his infancy."[59] Therefore, as Peter Slater has argued, while others debated the relative roles of parental and divine influence in the child's life, Bushnell "visualized Christian mothers and fathers as so infused with the divine spirit that God could be represented as directly operative when they formed the juvenile character."[60] The Spirit was still regenerating the child, but this work was completed not through a spiritual experience but through the gradual and natural interactions between parents and children. While this transformative work of the Spirit might understandably look different in children than adults—less dramatic and more incremental—Bushnell argued that it was no less supernatural in nature.[61]

This perspective reinforced Bushnell's most memorable suggestion, that a child growing up within a Christian home should not require a conversion experience but "is to grow up a Christian, and never know himself as being otherwise." "In other words," he claimed, "the aim, effort, and expectation should be, not, as is commonly assumed, that the child is to grow up in sin, to be converted after he comes to a mature age; but that he is to open on the world as one that is spiritually renewed, not remembering the time when he went through a technical experience, but seeming rather to have loved what is good from his earliest years."[62] Bushnell believed—and cited examples such as Richard Baxter and the early Moravians to prove his point—that children should not need a datable conversion "experience" if they grew up within the steady environmental impressions of a nurturing Christian home. He commended the European churches, in fact, for their willingness to define Christian piety as a "habit of life" rather than a "spiritual change in experience."[63] Christian parenting, in the end, was "that which feeds a growth, not that which stirs a revolution."[64]

All of this highlighted the critical nature of early childhood. While many, including his Puritan ancestors, thought infancy and childhood to be less spiritually significant than "youth" (Bushnell noted that many still thought of the young child as a "plaything"), he maintained that the opposite was actually true. Bushnell suggested, in fact, that "the most important age of Christian nurture is the first; that which we have called the age of impressions, just that age, in which the duties and cares of a really Christian nurture are so commonly postponed, or assumed to have not yet arrived. . . . Let every Christian father and mother understand, when their child is three years old, that they have done more than half of all they will ever do for his character."[65] For Bushnell, the parents' control was "absolute" prior to the development of language, and this stage therefore provided an unparalleled opportunity to write in unobstructed fashion on the tablet of the child's heart.[66] He felt that God created the child without a "responsible will" in the earliest years of life so that the impressions forged by the parents would be overwhelming, comprehensive, and determina-tive.[67] "And, to make the work a sure one," he suggested, "the intrusted soul is allowed to have no will as yet of its own, that this motherhood may more certainly plant the angel in the man, uniting him to all heavenly goodness by predispositions from itself, before he is united, as he will be, by choices of his own."[68] Even if children did come to a later conversion experience, Bushnell felt that this seeming change was most likely simply a "resuscitation" of earlier impressions.[69] "What they do not remember still remembers them," he concluded, "and now claims a right in them."[70]

The emphasis on parental impressions and environment in the mid-nineteenth century was actually an important aspect of the larger movement to normalize and routinize childhood nurture in the post-revival era. Bushnell saw the move from a conversion "experience" to gradual domestic nurture as a sign of maturity in the American expression of Christianity. When the Spirit's work would come primarily through "the table and the hearth" rather than through "high scenes of explosive changes," he argued, it was a sign that the church was "growing up," moving from haphazard awakenings to a mature and domesticated faith.[71] Bush-nell argued that widespread family Christian nurture was the pathway to global Protestant expansion. While some saw revivals as the primary engines of Christian evangelism and millennial advancement, he viewed such growth as taking place through "over-populating" the world. Chris-tianizing the world would take place not through individual adult conver-sions but rather as Christian families nurtured their children, gradually reaping a generational harvest that would spread until "the world itself" was "over-populated and taken possession of by a truly sanctified stock."[72]

The Power of Early Impressions

Bushnell's approach to Christian nurture both reflected and inspired the broader changes in advice to Christian parents in the mid- to late nine-teenth century. Between the 1840s and 1880s, many of Bushnell's central themes emerged as commonplace truisms among Protestant authors, although often nuanced in particular ways on the basis of denomina-tional leaning. When pastors and authors made more evangelical appeals for conversions, they tended to locate these experiences earlier, warning parents not to wait for teen or adult maturity. Even prior to Bushnell's book, John S. C. Abbott, Congregationalist pastor and author of the popular *Mother at Home*, noted that "it is to be feared that many parents do not feel their immediate responsibility. They still cherish the impression that their children must attain maturity before they can be decidedly penitent for sin, and the friends of God. But the mother who entertains such feelings as these, is guilty of the most cruel injustice to her child. It is almost impossible that she should be vigilant and faithful in her efforts, unless she expects success."[73] Abbott, and many others like him, recommended that parents work hard to lead their children to receive God's grace through conversion in their earlier years, either at home, in Sunday schools, or as parents toted children along with them to revival meetings.[74]

But the more decided Protestant shift in child-rearing advice after midcentury was to focus, not on a conversion experience, but rather on the gradual growth of faith through the environmental impressions made by parents in the earliest years.[75] Following from John Locke, many believed that the child's character was determined less by the inherited sin nature within than by the cumulative influence of the external impressions stamped on the soft wax of the malleable heart.[76] As one Presbyterian magazine put it, "No matter how sanctimonious our habitual language, no matter how punctilious our external conduct may seem to ourselves to be, there are silent influences streaming out from us constantly, in our actions, words, countenance, attitudes, and in countless untold ways that are moulding the susceptible minds and hearts of our children; just as the sensitive plate in a daguerreotype catches and perpetuates the most transient object that rays its image in silent mystery upon its surface."[77] Parents were thought to be the primary architects of what many called a "domestic environmentalism," constructing a home climate that would gradually seep into the child and form the soul in Christian virtue.[78] Or as popular parenting expert Lydia Sigourney stated, "The soul, the soul of the babe, whose life is nourished by our own! Every trace that we grave upon it, will stand forth at the judgment, when the 'books are opened.'"[79]

This shift had important ramifications for the very nature of Christian parenting. Environmental impressions were routinely described as more spiritually formative than formal religious teaching or practices.[80] Parents' displays of emotion—their voice, their tone, and their facial expressions— were all important, shaping children's perspectives on life and faith. As one pastor put it, "The forming of the character begins sooner than many suppose; and the first book the child begins to read is not the Primer, but the mother's face. The smile and the frown—these are the child's first alphabet!"[81] By the mid-nineteenth century, these emotional impressions were routinely described as more important than formal catechetical training. One author stated bluntly,

> I can conceive how a parent who is entirely *dumb*, by looks, and gestures, and demeanor; by smiles and frowns; by an authority always tempered with love; by the spirit of piety, breathing through the life and shining in the countenance, might govern a child more successfully, and give him better Christian training, than a parent who, with less of personal holiness, less of the genial influence of a pious life, exercises the memory of his child daily in those simple questions, Who was the first man? Who built the ark? Who was in the lion's den? . . . The influence of the life of the parent in forming the character of the child is like that of the sun and the rain in bringing forward the seed. . . . If the cause of Christ is to live and flourish in the world, it must be mainly through this domestic husbandry.[82]

A Presbyterian author concurred: "Not only the general drift of a lifetime, but the most trivial incident, a word, a look, a tear, has determined the destiny of a soul for ever. Nay, we believe it is the common law of humanity, that character, especially in childhood, turns more easily and certainly upon these apparently trivial causes, than upon the more formal and set means on which we are more apt to rely."[83] For a growing number of Protestants, it was the daily and informal parental interactions with their children, rather than formal Christian practices of teaching and worship, that mattered the most.

As many authors elevated the power of environmental impressions, they also began to highlight the spiritual importance of the home's physical space. While colonial authors gave little time and attention to the home as a physical structure, by the mid-nineteenth century it had become commonplace among many to speak of the power of the home's "sacred space."[84] Some spoke of the importance of a home's physical location, with growing numbers suggesting that Christian families live away from the corrupt cities if they wanted to raise children in the best possible environment. As new rail travel in the 1840s and 1850s allowed homes to be constructed at a greater distance from urban centers, this geographical isolation set the ideal family home apart as a sanctuary and retreat from the strains, sins, and immoral "excitements" of city life.[85] In addition to providing more beautiful scenery, rural and suburban locations would provide more outdoor spaces for recreation, peaceful contemplation, and healthy labor within the "pure air" and "under the magnetic and beautiful rays of the sun."[86] These settings would also remove young children from the filth—both physical and moral—of urban life. Protected behind newly appointed fences and gates, such homes established an environment that was set apart from the squalor of the world, thus providing better impressions for malleable children.[87]

While outside scenery was of great value in shaping the tone of the child's character, the house itself was of even greater import for children's spiritual formation. In colonial America, most homes consisted of only one or two rooms with little differentiated space.[88] A growing number of nineteenth-century homes, however, had separate rooms for children that would provide privacy and the "psychic space" necessary for contemplation and quiet reading.[89] In addition, Victorian-era moral and religious leaders believed that home decor and furnishings not only expressed character but helped create it.[90] Houses that were clean, attractive, and beautiful would deeply influence the child's character for good. "It is almost impossible for a child to grow up into loveliness of character, gentleness of disposition and purity of heart amid scenes of slovenliness, untidiness, repulsiveness and filthiness," pastor J. R. Miller suggested. "But a home clean, tasteful, with simple adornments and pleasant surroundings, is an influence of incalculable value in the education of children."[91] Surrounding the child with beauty, in terms of both internal furnishing and external landscaping, had become a central parental duty and a key aspect of a child's Christian nurture. In fulfilling their role as child "architects," parents had to be intentional about the architecture of the home.

This concern for the home's physical environment also extended to the need for religious decor that would create powerful spiritual impressions in children's minds. While the Puritans favored simple dwellings that reflected a Calvinist disdain for adornment, many Protestant homes in the nineteenth century were filled with sacred objects and artifacts. Stitched samplers displaying sacred poems or Bible verses began to grace parlors and bedrooms. Motto card holders and religious bookmarkers, along with embellished crosses of various kinds, were increasingly common. "Chaste and pure" paintings depicting biblical and other refining scenes covered the walls of many parlors in Christian homes.[92] In many households, the "family Bible" assumed a unique importance and was set in a bracket on a special table adorned with richly embroidered tablecloths.[93] While such Bibles could be used for family Bible reading, they were also important as physical objects, containing family birth, death, and marriage records, photographs, and other family memorabilia (locks of hair, pressed flowers from a funeral, etc.) that created strong religious impressions linked to family memories.[94] When the proper mechanism of Christian growth was viewed in terms of instruction and worship—as it was for colonial authors—the venue mattered very little. However, when environmental impressions were charged with a significant role in Christian formation, the home—its larger appearance, culture, and "spirit"—became a critical force for gradual spiritual formation. As Colleen McDannell says, "The house was the center for a new form of liturgy, and the interior furnishings its sacred props."[95]

Because they were concerned about impressions, nineteenth-century pastors and authors also grew far more interested in children's habits of eating, dress, health, and reading that might shape their responsiveness to God.[96] Reflecting new emphases on bodily health in this era, Bushnell spoke to the importance of "wholesome food, clean and sufficient clothing, pure air, and healthful exercise," noting the ways these were linked to preparing the heart for God.[97] Many spoke out against bodily impressions that would lead to excess and thus draw the heart away from God. Charles Finney suggested that since children's wills were influenced by the senses in the earliest years of life, parents must keep their children away from "artificial stimulants" such as tea, coffee, tobacco, spices, and ginger. Simplicity in diet, he suggested, would prevent the development of artificial wants, the kinds that would, by continual satiation, lead to a "beastly intemperance."[98] Others spoke about the importance of simplicity in fashion. In one particularly harrowing tale, a young girl on her deathbed chastised her mother for the negative impressions of her childhood, pointing to her clothes and saying, "These have ruined me."[99] In this era of expanding literacy and the widespread availability of books, many admonished parents who allowed their children to read novels that overstimulated them and sullied their imaginations.[100] Methodist pastor John Power, in fact, warned parents to *"exclude novels from your house, as you would the poison of serpents, or the angel of death!"*[101] Leaders argued that when children opened themselves up to excessive worldly impressions, they would lose their attraction to the faith and fall prey to the corrupting magnetism of empty pleasure.

Because of the power of impressions, authors increasingly worried about the emotions associated with religion in Christian households. They noted that religion in the home must be lived out in a "cheerful" and upbeat manner so that children would associate faith with pleasant feelings.[102] Many leaders, therefore, began arguing against the use of fear and judgment as motivating tools in Christian nurture. Catherine Beecher noted, "The attempt to influence children by fears of hell, of the devil, and of the day of judgment, ordinarily results in false conceptions, that agitate without any compensating healthful results." Beecher spoke of how those children with very "sensitive and nervous" personalities would languish in fear and distress, agonizing over the prospects of damnation. She spoke of her own sister who, when they were children, had read a hymn about the judgment of wicked children that "haunted her in hours of darkness, often banishing sleep, while sometimes, covering her head, she lay sweating with distress and dread."[103] Such impressions, Beecher felt, would tend to push children away from the faith by creating negative religious associations in their minds. The use of fear—a staple of colonial child-rearing—was now considered a threat to the spiritual life.

Hymns and prayers increasingly reflected this desire to create joyful rather than fearful impressions in children's minds.[104] The songs of Isaac Watts continued to be widely used, but popular collections such as Jane Taylor's *Hymns for Infant Minds* (1809) and Cecil Frances Alexander's *Hymns for Little Children* (1848) reflected some of the changing emphases of the day, moving away from fearful warnings about hell to more comforting images of heaven and from depictions of God's wrath to expressions of his love.[105] Such was the emphasis of Anna Bartlett Warner's popular song "Jesus Loves Me," which first appeared in *Say and Seal* (1860), a novel she coauthored with her sister Susan. In the text, the words were addressed to a dying child: "Jesus loves me—this I know, For the Bible tells me so; Little ones to him belong,—They are weak, but he is strong. . . .

Jesus loves me—he will stay, Close beside me all the way. Then his little child will take, Up to heaven for his dear sake."[106] When this was put to music two years later by Baptist choirmaster William Bradbury, he added the now famous chorus, "Yes, Jesus loves me. Yes, Jesus loves me. Yes, Jesus loves me; the Bible tells me so." Such songs, along with more lively and military-inspired tunes after the Civil War, reflected not only a more optimistic view of childhood but also a more general shift toward cheerful celebrations of Christ's love and the certainty of heaven.[107] Poems and prayers about death had not vanished, but they were now designed to lead in a cheerful, rather than a fearful, direction. As David Stannard puts it, "The Puritan child . . . was immersed in death at the earliest age possible: his spiritual well-being required the contemplation of mortality and the terrifying prospects of separation and damnation. The child of the nineteenth century was also taught about death at virtually every turn, but rather than being taught to fear it, he was instructed to desire it, to see death as a glorious removal to a better world and a reunion with departed and soon-to-depart loved ones."[108]

Growing convictions about the power of impressions led many Protestants, like Bushnell, to argue that the youngest years were the most pivotal for faith development. In the colonial era, the years of infancy and early childhood (especially prior to age six or seven) received very little attention, largely because these years predated the language and reason necessary for godly instruction. Most Protestants in the Victorian era, by contrast, believed that the most potent influences in a child's spiritual life took place in the earliest years. John S. C. Abbott asserted that the mother's "secret and silent influence" was largely determinative for the young child, "and the truth is daily coming more distinctly before the public, that the influence which is exerted upon the mind, during the first eight or ten years of existence, in a great degree guides the destinies of that mind for time and eternity."[109] Many now believed that later influences, while no doubt important, were always written on top of the "earlier and more indelible tracing of what was written on the heart, in the fresh, unblotted susceptibility of childhood and youth."[110] As Samuel Phillips concluded, "Spiritual culture belongs eminently to the nursery."[111]

The Determinative Power of Christian Parents

The combination of the young child's impressionable nature and the parents' power to supply such impressions led to a clear conclusion: as "architects," parents largely determined their children's spiritual destinies. While Bushnell had gone out of his way to highlight the fact that it was the Holy Spirit working through the parents that led the young child into faith, many began to blur the lines between God's sovereignty and parental agency. While colonial authors were sure to cite Proverbs 22:6, "Train up a child in the way he should go; / even when he is old he will not depart from it," with a clear caveat that this did not guarantee the godliness of offspring, Victorian-era leaders were much more likely to accept this proverb as unassailable fact. Presbyterian Erastus Hopkins stated of the text that "between parental fidelity and filial rectitude, there is an unfailing connection" because of the "absoluteness" of parental power.[112] As Jacob Abbott stated, "The power of parental influence is almost unbounded . . . and if there is throughout the world an instance of complete, unlimited, absolute power on the one hand, and most entire and helpless submission on the other, it is to be found in the empire which such a parent holds over such a child."[113]

The "absolute" power of Christian parents was a function of the pervasive influence of environmental impressions during childhood. Whereas colonial authors often appealed to God's sovereignty and reminded children not to rely on their parents' faith, by the Victorian era it was far more common for authors to enthusiastically hold parents wholly responsible for their children's spiritual path. Presbyterians Joseph Collier and Rufus Bailey went so far as to contend that Napoleon, if born into a nurturing Christian family, could have been an apostle Paul, while Congregationalist S. R. Hall noted that the infamous Lord Byron would have been godly with the right home environment.[114] Peggy Dow, mother of famed Methodist itinerant Lorenzo Dow, perhaps put it best: "If *mothers* would begin with their *children* when they are *young*, they might mould them into almost any *frame* they chose."[115]

This emerged as a significant issue when nineteenth-century authors addressed the question of why "good" parents sometimes had "bad" children. Colonial authors balanced a belief in the influence of parents with a clear submission to God's will, noting that at times God might allow pious parents to have rebellious children so as to show his divine independence. They also tended to place some of the blame on the children themselves, calling them out for their defiance and letting them know that parents might one day judge them for their disobedience. For Victorian-era Protestants, on the other hand, a child's waywardness was virtually always attributed to parental flaws.[116] In *Christian Nurture*, Bushnell asks "why it is . . . that many persons, remarkable for their piety, have yet been so unfortunate in their children." His answer is clear: "Because, I answer, many persons, remarkable for their piety, are yet very disagreeable persons, and that too, by reason of some very marked defect in their religious character."[117] Even a more dedicated evangelical like Finney, addressing those who were bewildered by the fact that many "good men" had "reprobate children," could state that these men were often guilty of some "capital error" in the training of their children. After all his travels, he indicated the following: "I have seldom, if ever known a family turn out badly, in which, when I searched out the matter, I could not trace it directly or indirectly to the manner in which they had brought the children up—to some fundamental defect in family government."[118]

In fact, Victorian-era authors grew increasingly impatient with those who would blame children's spiritual decline either on the sovereignty of God or on the children themselves. For those wanting to blame God, a piece from the American Tract Society aptly noted, "If training children in the way in which they should go, is a duty of God's appointment, and if he has warranted us to look to him both for assistance and success, we ought certainly to ascribe our failure or success to ourselves, rather than to him."[119] For those wanting to blame the children, another stated clearly, *"If your child is not what you would have it to be, instead of accounting for the evil by charging it to Adam or to an inherent obstinacy—charge the whole sum of it to yourself, and set about a different course of example and of discipline."*[120] Since children were malleable and since the environmental impressions were viewed as the chief source of their development, most drew a straight line between parents' methods and children's outcomes. When children went wrong, nineteenth-century Christians clearly knew where to place the blame.[121]

There were critics of this kind of home-based determinism. Bennet Tyler, a former president of Dartmouth, challenged it from Scripture, noting as colonial authors did that there were many examples of pious parents with godless children in the biblical narrative. While he acknowledged that godly parents generally had godly children, he also noted, "I do not however feel authorized to say, that success is always in exact proportion to fidelity. Some parents are blessed with pious children, who, as far as we can judge, are less faithful than others whose children remain unconverted. . . . Nor do I feel authorized to say, that if parents are equally faithful to all their children, God will make no distinction among them."[122] He noted that in order for parents to ensure success, they would have to be more faithful than Abraham, Isaac, Jacob, Aaron, Samuel, and David. "After all our speculations we must admit, that God is a sovereign," he concluded. "'Therefore, he hath mercy, on whom he will have mercy.'"[123]

In spite of his passion, Tyler's perspective was increasingly rejected. The appeal to parental determinism represented a broader cultural shift from a posture of resignation to God's providence to a more pervasive belief in human agency. Colonial authors had attributed many things to God's providential hand, including children's illnesses, accidents, and deaths. In the face of such tragedies, parents were urged to resign themselves to God's larger plan and to submit to his divine judgments. In the nineteenth century, however, such physical events were increasingly linked to parental failure rather than divine decree. If children fell sick, were injured, or died through diseases or accidents (and death rates were persistently high in this era), parents were far more likely to shoulder the blame for such "preventable" casualties. When children strayed spiritually, the same logic was often applied. As with physical maladies, spiritual "sickness" in children demonstrated parents' failure to follow the proper God-given "natural laws" of parental nurture, a miscarriage of parental faithfulness that could only rightly be attributed to themselves.[124] It is perhaps not surprising, therefore, that the child-rearing literature of this era tended to speak less about the importance of parental prayers for children, focusing more on the home environments that would produce predictable godly outcomes. Nancy Schrom Dye and Daniel Blake Smith's comment regarding mothers' growing responsibility for children's health was equally appropriate for the care of their souls: "Children in early nineteenth century America were gradually slipping out of the hands of God and into their mother's warm, if nervous, embrace."[125]

The Potential and Peril of Architect Parents

In the end, the clear result of these nineteenth-century changes was the growing sense that parents—as home-based "architects"—determined the child's spiritual path. While colonial authors placed little emphasis on the earliest years, Victorian-era Protestants of all stripes began to recognize the pivotal nature of early childhood. Evangelical parents were called on to orchestrate conversion experiences in their younger children's lives. By midcentury, many across the Protestant denominations spoke of how parental impressions in the earliest years of life were determinative, giving parents considerable molding power in their children's lives. These ideas were bolstered by new beliefs about children's spiritual malleability and the sense that infants and very young children were shaped by the impressions around them. Rather than seeing them as wrongly bent by original sin and therefore in need of a new heart, growing numbers of Protestants viewed children as plastic and formed by their environments. When the nineteenth-century child was depicted as either a blank slate or pure and innocent, the emphasis shifted to what parents could do in establishing a nurturing environment and protecting children from the corrosive influences of the world.

The belief in the power of impressions often led nineteenth-century authors to proclaim that the most important factors in spiritual formation, whether for good or ill, existed outside the child. While colonial authors saw children's primary challenges coming from within, rooted in a heart naturally bent toward evil, more and more Protestants viewed the greatest challenges emerging externally, in the environmental impressions that might be inculcated by physically or morally compromising influences. As historian Jay Fliegelman puts it, "Implicitly denying original sin, Lockean sensationalism and the new emphasis on education and nurture it generated temptingly suggested that personal faults of individual character might be better charged to the behavior of one's parents, the character of one's education, or the premature exposure to a corrupting society, rather than to one's own moral failings."[126] This shift from internal to external threats meant that parents' fears were now located in potential sources of environmental corruption rather than within the corrupt hearts of their children.

This perspective surely relieved some fears even as it created new ones. Increasingly, authors believed that parents could create an idyllic Christian home environment that would guarantee an equally idyllic spiritual result. While this may have liberated many from anxieties regarding the inscrutable sovereignty of God, it also meant that parents likely felt a greater weight of responsibility for their children's spiritual outcomes. It was certainly easier, in such a setting, to draw a straight line back from a grown child's spiritual condition to the childhood influences that led—seemingly inevitably—to this outcome. While there was likely some comfort in setting aside God's independent will in the life of the child, there was likely also an overwhelming burden to "get it right" as a parent and an equally potent fear of what "getting it wrong" might mean. If children did not turn out as parents expected, it reflected parents' own failures and could lead to a significant sense of guilt and self-reproach.

For all of their hand-wringing about child-rearing and its challenges, colonial authors never had quite the same confidence in the determinative power of Christian parenting. Their deep-seated belief in providence and their constant appeal to the unseen spiritual world meant that they often realized that there was a larger supernatural framework within which they did their work. While some in the nineteenth century criticized colonial Christians' appeal to divine sovereignty, this doctrine did alleviate some of the sense that parents completely controlled their children's spiritual and eternal destinies. When parents in the nineteenth century, by contrast, were told that their impressions were determinative and that all outcomes could be linked to "the handling of the nursery," this no doubt added a significant burden of expectation and responsibility.[127]

All of this raises important issues related to the control parents have over their children's lives. The emerging Victorian vision certainly reminds parents that they do often play the most significant role in shaping their children and therefore should take their responsibilities very seriously. It also serves as a helpful reminder of the importance of children's pivotal early years. Many Christians who tend to privilege the rational and intellectual aspects of the faith can dismiss the power of early impressions, viewing early childhood as a relatively meaningless prelude to the real work of Christian education and training. By contrast, nineteenth-century authors implored parents not to wait until the later years to be intentional about the family's culture of faith. Since present experiences build into future experiences in ways that can make the child more or less open and responsive to God, parents are not just thinking in terms of some "future" development that will take place "someday." Instead, the impressions of the earliest years shape children's desires toward a certain vision of the good life. Rather than waiting on a future conversion or increased cognitive maturity, therefore, this vision reminds parents that they are called to be faithful and intentional in raising their young children and utilizing all the means provided by God for their growth and development.

The nineteenth-century concern for impressions also highlights the importance of the "hidden curriculum" of the home. While formal instruction and worship are critical teaching venues, the Bushnellian viewpoint emphasizes the fact that spiritual formation is taking place constantly through the environment of the home and the mundane rhythms of the family, either drawing children closer to God's loving arms or potentially driving them away from his presence. The home's physical environment and decor can indeed shape children's understandings of what is most important in that family's life. It can shape desires and set a tone for children's engagement with God and the world that is often beneath conscious awareness. Similarly, scholars who study the spiritual formation of children continue to argue that the home environment and parents' interactions with young children—the tone of speech, the gaze of the eyes, the manner of physical touch—profoundly shape the child's growing understanding of love, grace, and the character of God.[128] A child's early attachments to parents can shape the child's later attachments to God. Though these impressions are not the "stuff" of formal family teaching or worship, parents should nevertheless be intentional about the formation of the household environment. Since children spend so much time in these home spaces, this "hidden curriculum" can indeed be powerful.

At the same time, the belief in parental power has a potential dark side. Many parents assume that if they follow the correct steps and create the ideal environment, children will inevitably develop lives of consistent faith. This is reflected in those Christian parenting techniques that provide "foolproof" approaches to raising godly children. If certain behavioral patterns of teaching, feeding, sleeping, love, and discipline are followed, in other words, parents can guarantee desired spiritual outcomes. This belief also fosters a false confidence that if parents choose the right environments for their children (schools, clubs, churches), they can achieve predictable results.

Within this not-so-subtle behaviorism, parents' sense of spiritual "success" can be wrapped up in the successes and failures of their children. Belief in parents' determinative power can produce pride in those parents whose children conform to Christian cultural ideals and a sense of despair and self-condemnation among those whose children end up on a more circuitous path. Parents can begin to judge themselves by their own children and to judge others by the outcomes of their children. It is easier for "architect" parents to stake their reputations on their children. Since parents "created" them, they can turn their children into trophies if successful and seek to hide their embarrassing flaws if not. Such a belief can even diminish the perceived importance of prayer since parents are able to complete these child "projects" on their own.

This last point highlights a critical issue raised by nineteenth-century changes: the role of God's supernatural power in the child's life. Bushnell's emphasis on the Spirit's work within the ordinary activities and interactions of the Christian home was surely a helpful corrective to the belief that the Spirit works only through immediate and dramatic forms of adult conversion. Bushnell's work reminded parents that, beyond the power of doctrinal teaching, evangelistic appeals, and individual spiritual experiences, children are profoundly shaped by the Spirit's ongoing and daily work of character formation through parental love and example, the environment of the family, and even the physical characteristics of the home's space. The Spirit's supernatural power, Bushnell reminded parents, was at work through these seemingly natural events.

Yet even as it highlighted the ways in which the Spirit worked through natural interactions, Bushnell's views on Christian nurture could also obscure the supernatural role of God's grace in the child's formation. In fact, critiques emerging at the time opposed Bushnell at this very point. Renowned Princeton professor Charles Hodge appreciated aspects of Bushnell's argument, even noting that the discourses were "attractive and hopeful" because they elevated the importance of parental nurture within the home. Yet Hodge also noted that Bushnell's approach was dangerous because it placed too much emphasis on the natural "cause and effect" work of parenting and failed to highlight God's supernatural role in opening the child's heart: "There is all the difference between this theory of conversion, and supernaturalism, that there is between the ordinary growth of the human body and Christ's healing the sick, opening the eyes of the blind, or raising the dead. Both are due to the power of God, but the one to that power acting in the way of nature, and the other to the same power acting above nature."[129] Much of this, Hodge believed, stemmed from a flawed view of human nature, rooted in an inadequate sense of original sin and its debilitating impact. Bushnell's theory, he claimed, "assumes that men are not by nature the children of wrath, that they are not involved in spiritual death, and consequently that they do not need to be quickened by that mighty power which wrought in Christ when it raised him from the dead. The forming influence of parental character and life is fully adequate to his regeneration; education can correct what there is of natural corruption."[130] While Hodge agreed that the Spirit worked through Christian parents, he also wanted parents to know that a special work of regeneration was necessary to move the child from death to life.

Bennet Tyler joined Hodge in ascribing the label of "naturalism" to Bushnell's work. As he put it, "It is God's work to renew the heart. . . . The Christian parent is no more 'able to implant some holy principle' in the heart of his child, than he is to raise the dead, or to create a world."[131] Bushnell's theory, in his estimation, both minimized children's depravity and overemphasized the role of parents (and the environment) in generating true faith. In particular, he felt that the language of "organic connection" would lead to a belief that grace was hereditary, the result of blood connection rather than the alien righteousness achieved by Jesus's death on the cross. In the end, he felt that Bushnell's words would give unsuspecting parents a false confidence in their children's spiritual status, decreasing their urgency in bringing them to a place of decided repentance. He also felt it might lead to a similar delusion among children, who would feel safe in their ethical behavior within the womb of parental faith even if they demonstrated no evidence of a renewed heart. Tyler argued that parents must do the very things that Bushnell despised, suggesting that it was the duty of the parent to "lead his child, as soon as possible, to a knowledge of . . . the wickedness of his heart, and the necessity of a new heart to prepare him for heaven."[132]

In many ways, these critics feared the same kind of false security as their colonial ancestors. In their eyes, the naturalism in Bushnell's theology threatened to diminish the potency of sin, the supernatural power of God in salvation, and the radical nature of the soul's movement from death to life. While they largely agreed with Bushnell's sense that revivals placed too little emphasis on the power of domestic nurture, they also recognized that nurture could undersell the need for a radical awakening of the child's heart. Morality could be substituted for grace with even more conviction since gradual character growth was emphasized over conversion. Reliance on parental faith was also a greater possibility since Bushnell emphasized the organic connection of children and parents and the determinative power of parental impressions. As Margaret Bendroth has noted, within Bushnell's thinking there was always a fine line "between a robust domestic theology and a merely domesticated one."[133]

This battle between parental influence and divine power would emerge again and again as nineteenth-century authors reconsidered the power of family relationships in their child's spiritual formation. Parents were afforded a great deal of influence, but that influence was not equally distributed. The elevated importance of early childhood impressions, coupled with broader cultural and theological changes in this era, led many to a simple conclusion: it was mothers, not fathers, who would serve as the chief architects of their children's faith development.

CHAPTER 6

The Parent as Mother

The Maternal Turn in American Christian Parenting

> The circumstances of our day so correspond to the true characteristics of woman, as to give her the utmost influence in guiding the destinies of the world.
>
> —Alexander T. McGill, "The Present Age, the Age of Woman"[1]

In May of 1851, the popular periodical *Mother's Assistant, Young Lady's Friend & Family Manual* featured a lead article titled "The Era for Mothers." Winner of one of its annual prizes, the piece was written by William Makepeace Thayer, descendant of an original Pilgrim father. Thayer would later become editor of the *Mother's Assistant* and a well-regarded author of juvenile fiction, but at the time he was a new pastor of a Congregational church in Ashland, Massachusetts. A careful observer of the times, he claimed at the outset that the current era was one of unprecedented "crisis," a time of "commingling hopes and fears."[2] Still early in the nation's history, Thayer noted that the eyes of a watching world were waiting to see if the American republican experiment would succeed or collapse under the weight of its newfound freedom. While progress was the "watchword of the day," he proposed that liberty was also threatening to descend into license. Disorder and petty factions ruled the day. Temptations and vice expanded rapidly. The sacred institution of marriage was under attack, and the Sabbath, "that day of days," had been voted down in various conventions, leading Thayer to fear that the nation was careening headlong into a godless void that would echo the direction of "wretched, infidel France." American Christianity, he suggested, seemed ill-equipped for this unprecedented moment.[3]

Yet all was not lost. Thayer's hopeful appeal was to the "three millions of mothers" who had under their charge "three hundred thousand infants," the nation's future judges, senators, statesmen, ministers, and missionaries.[4] In order to infuse both civic and religious life with Christian principles, America's future leaders needed mothers whose "plastic hand and quenchless love" would stir their children (particularly their sons) to godly character in the "morning of life."[5] Thayer stated, "We cannot suppress the feeling, that the present is THE ERA FOR MOTHERS. . . . Yes, to them God has committed, in a measure, the destiny of the world. Around that cradle cluster the hopes and fears of an anxious nation. From that throbbing breast flows the milk of our country's weal or woe."[6] It was mothers who promised to uphold the nation's moral and religious center by raising up their children in virtue and faith.

Christian Formation Is for Mothers

It is intriguing that a leader like Thayer did not appeal, as his Pilgrim ancestors likely would have, to the overriding influence of fathers. His essay, in fact, clearly articulated one of the most significant shifts in the history of American Protestant child-rearing: the growing prominence of mothers in the Christian formation of children. While this trend had begun in the last years of the eighteenth century in halting ways and with considerable anxiety, by the mid-nineteenth century the dominance of the mother had become the normative—indeed the celebrated—pattern of Christian parenting.[7] As early as 1835, pastor and well-known author John S. C. Abbott indicated that "mothers have as powerful an influence over the welfare of future generations as all other causes combined. . . . The world's redeeming influence must come from a mother's lips. . . . It is maternal influence, after all, which must be the great agent, in the hands of God, in bringing back our guilty race to duty and happiness."[8] While many New England communities remained fairly patriarchal up until the 1820s, between the 1830s and 1850s this new perspective was becoming more firmly established.[9] As historian Mary Ryan contends in her important study of central New York in the nineteenth century,

At the close of the Second Great Awakening, Oneida county could no longer be characterized as a community whose central constituting element was the patriarchal household. . . . Within families . . . it was mothers rather than patriarchs who exerted increasing control over the religious allegiances of the young. In other words, a more decidedly privatized and feminized form of religious and social reproduction was beginning to take shape around the relationships between evangelical mothers and converted children. This was perhaps the most significant social change that germinated on the charred landscape of the Burned-Over District.[10]

The growing spiritual dominance of mothers was evident in a number of domains. First, by the mid-nineteenth century, the vast majority of parenting advice literature—a virtual deluge of books, novels, and periodicals in this era of emerging mass media—was now directed toward mothers. In the 1820s and 1830s, much of this consisted of sermons and other didactic literature penned by well-known ministers. By the 1840s and 1850s, however, a host of authors flooded the marketplace with texts effusively praising motherhood, defining its responsibilities, and depicting fictional accounts of its domestic expressions.[11] In fact, while advice manuals continued to exert an important influence, novels composed by and for mothers quickly emerged as a key genre within the domestic advice literature. Female authors such as Lydia Child, Lydia Sigourney, Sarah Hale, Catherine Sedgwick, and Catherine Beecher played a major role in popularizing the idea that mothers had the primary responsibility for the Christian nurture of their children. A parallel literature for fathers was now virtually nonexistent. In fact, in direct contrast to most directives in the seventeenth and eighteenth centuries, authors of the new texts had to remind fathers that they still had a role to play in bringing up their children in the faith.[12]

While maternal literature exploded in this era, organizations also grew up from within the churches devoted to equipping mothers for their responsibilities. In an era that witnessed a steady increase of Christian voluntary and benevolent societies, it was only natural that women would organize themselves in order to promote the advancement of Christian motherhood.[13] While a variety of such groups appeared at the local level, the most prominent were the so-called maternal associations.[14] Emerging within the more evangelically minded Presbyterian, Congregational, and Baptist churches, these groups started in 1815, rapidly multiplied beginning in the 1820s and 1830s, and then gradually declined in the years following the Civil War.[15] By 1836 maternal associations could be found in every Presbyterian church in New York City, and by 1840 such associations existed in every American state and territory in addition to a number of foreign countries.[16]

While many of the voluntary associations of this era directed women outward in benevolence or evangelism, the maternal associations saw motherhood in the home as the key to kingdom advancement. "A third moral revolution remains in which mothers will have a conspicuous part to perform, viz: the introduction of the Millennium," one suggested. "When every nursery shall become a little sanctuary, and not before, will the earth be filled with the knowledge and glory of the Lord."[17] In order to see this come to fruition, the maternal associations did all that they could to promote "an educated ministry of Christian mothers."[18] Most groups included monthly meetings for prayer, mutual encouragement, and instruction. When mothers lost children in death, the members supported the grieving and offered practical help. When mothers faced trials with rebellious children, the members offered prayer and advice. The mothers prayed for the conversion of one another's children. At times groups brought in special speakers, including local pastors, to address parenting topics. They formed libraries of Christian child-rearing literature.[19] In addition, several magazines—including the *Mother's Magazine*, the *Mother's Journal*, and the *Mother's Assistant & Young Lady's Friend*—were formed out of these groups in order to spread parenting advice and encouragement to women across the country.[20] Women viewed such groups as contributing to the larger expansion of the gospel across the globe. "If any one thing is more essential than every thing else for the redemption of the world," one maternal association author argued, "it is early religious education. If any one class of the human family can alone accomplish that work, that class is mothers."[21]

These literary and organizational expressions were matched by the elevation of women as Christian ministers within the home, especially after midcentury. In the seventeenth and eighteenth centuries, fathers were often charged with the chief responsibility for leading family worship, guiding instruction, and exercising authority and discipline. However, by the mid-nineteenth century, mothers played a much larger role in these traditional Christian practices. While fathers still often led at the formal family altar, mothers guided the more informal reading of Scripture and other moral tales with individual children throughout the day. Nineteenth-century paintings often depicted mothers with children either on their laps or pulled in close, reading the Scriptures and other devotional books together, a picture with strong parallels to maternal breastfeeding.[22]

As more personalized nurture and instruction began to be emphasized over formal worship in this era—Colleen McDannell has suggested that the mother as instructor outstripped the father as priest and director of religious ritual—Christian education in the home took on a more maternal cast. Prayer with and for children was also increasingly described as a mother's role. It was the mother's prayers that would pervade children's daily activities, send them to sleep at night, and protect them from physical and moral harm.[23] Thayer, in fact, suggested that the recent American religious revivals had revealed that "scarcely one sinner was brought to the fold of Christ, who was not blest with a prayerful mother."[24] Mothers also frequently took the lead in family singing, and as parlor organs grew increasingly common after midcentury, it was often the matriarch who played and therefore guided this practice. Mothers flooded their homes with samplers, crosses, and other decorations designed to direct children's attention to Jesus.[25] They also took on more of the daily discipline of children, leaving only larger cases to the fathers. In short, mothers in this era often became the central conduits by which Protestant children encountered God in their homes.[26]

To cement this departure from the patriarchal past, many authors now argued that the biblical and historical record demonstrated the determinative role of mothers. Cotton Mather looked to Abraham, David, Job, and other biblical patriarchs to describe the transmission of a godly lineage, but many in the antebellum period chose instead to focus on such matriarchs as Moses's courageous mother and Timothy's mother, Eunice, and grandmother, Lois.[27] Increasingly, authors suggested that historical figures like Augustine, John Wesley, John Newton, and George Washington became the men they were because of their pious mothers.[28] The opposite was also true. Known scoundrels—Lord Byron, David Hume, and others—developed as they did because they lacked godly mothers to guide them in their earliest years. As one put it, "In the circle of our personal observation, if we see a family of sons grow up with noble characters, we shall find they had a noble mother; or if we see a family of sons grow up destitute of moral principle, to be the pests of society, we are almost sure to find that their mother was deficient in the qualities which fit mothers for their station."[29]

"Mother Knows Best": The Sources of Change

The Victorian-era elevation of the mother's Christian child-rearing role was the result of a combination of economic, demographic, and theological factors. Although most Americans still lived in agricultural settings, among northern middle-class families the early stages of industrialization and the growth of a market economy had a number of significant consequences. Up until the 1820s, family industry was the norm as most goods were produced either within the household or by local artisans. Most weaving, soap making, spinning, shoemaking, and food production took place within the home, and most households were largely self-sufficient, requiring the interdependent contributions of all family members. Women, in this setting, made a significant economic contribution to family life.[30]

By midcentury, however, the transportation revolution, sparked by the growth of roads, canals, railways, and steamboats, had connected local economies to an increasingly national commercial network. Goods that had been produced by hand within homes were increasingly manufactured in factories and sold as finished products. As manufacturers took spinning, weaving, and sewing out of women's homes in what Horace Bushnell helpfully called the "transition from mother and daughter power to water and steam-power," the woman's role was irrevocably altered.[31] Working-class and immigrant women were of course far more likely to seek gainful employment outside the home, taking their place in factories or, at times, as domestics in wealthier homes. The middle-class woman's role, however, shifted from production to consumption.[32] As consumers, women now found their primary identity in child-rearing (as mothers) rather than as co-laborers with their husbands (as wives), a clear shift from the colonial era.[33] According to Ruth Bloch, "As women were relieved of much of their former economic role and at the same time left in primary care of children, motherhood understandably came to be a more salient feature of adult female life."[34] Children relied on mothers less for the basic needs of food and clothing and more for the provision of care, nurture, and support.[35] And since mothers were bearing fewer children, they were able to devote more time and attention to each child. In such a context, the woman's role as mother became the defining center of her identity.[36]

The mother's growing importance in her children's Christian nurture was also related to the escalating significance placed on young children in this era. As was mentioned in chapter 5, many religious theorists now argued that the impressions formed in children's earliest years were the most significant factors in their faith development. Because the early years were so pivotal, mothers, who spent the most time with their infants, held a disproportionate spiritual influence in their lives.[37] As Samuel Phillips put it, "She is the center of attraction, the guardian of the infant's destiny. . . . God has fitted her for the work of the nursery. . . . She there possesses the immense force of first impressions. The soul of her child lies unveiled before her, and she makes the stamp of her own spirit and personality upon its pliable nature."[38] "The early years settle what its character will be," J. R. Miller agreed, "and these are the mother's years."[39]

In the midst of these changes, Protestant leaders also began to argue theologically for the inherent gendered superiority of women for this child-rearing task. As Presbyterian pastor Philemon Fowler noted in 1859, "She is 'apt to teach,' constitutionally compassionate and kind, susceptible to spiritual truth, and, 'last at the cross and first at the sepulcher,' glowing with the ardor of her affection in love for the Saviour, and clinging to him with the indissolubleness of her attachments, and losing herself in him in the unsparingness of her sacrifices. She becomes a Christian, humanly speaking, more easily than man."[40] Thayer, in *Life at the Fireside*, similarly suggested, "The female sex have expressed their appreciation of true religion by yielding up their hearts to its power more generally than males have done. . . . Females possess a quicker moral perception than males, and their hearts are less corroded by contact with a wicked world. . . . This fact indicates a wonderful adaptation in Christianity to their natures and wants."[41] It was not surprising to many, therefore, that women dominated in church attendance and also assembled in a number of religious small groups, charitable organizations, and maternal associations.[42] The virtues that accompanied what historians have termed the "Cult of True

Womanhood"—piety, purity, submissiveness, and domesticity—were now viewed as divine gifts bestowed on women specifically for godly child-rearing.[43] The qualities necessary for raising godly children, one author suggested, belonged to women "almost by inheritance."[44]

What is so fascinating about this shift is that some of the maternal qualities heralded by religious leaders in the Victorian era had been disparaged by their colonial forebears. As mentioned, advice literature in the seventeenth and eighteenth centuries tended to critique mothers' emotionalism and indulgence. Such traits were deemed hazardous for the proper Christian nurture of young children, promoting permissiveness and indulgence. By the mid-nineteenth century, however, the evaluation of these qualities had flipped. Rather than being viewed as potentially threatening, mothers were increasingly praised for their natural love, tenderness, emotional vulnerability, and susceptibility to heart impressions.[45] The very qualities considered dangerous signs of weakness and instability within colonial society were now celebrated as the indispensable traits of a nurturing mother.[46]

Mother Love: An Irresistible Force

Mothers were particularly extolled for their natural and seemingly limitless capacity for love, evidenced in the "peculiar, full-born intensity of the maternal affection." Bushnell, in fact, effused that a mother's love was "boundless and fathomless." "Here springs the secret of her maternity," he noted, "and its semi-divine proportions."[47] By the mid-nineteenth century, "mother love" was no longer lamented for its associations with indulgence but was instead linked to the true power of Christian formation. As in the colonial era, men were generally associated with reason while women were connected to the heart. The difference in the nineteenth century, however, was that the affections (not the mind) were now often perceived to be the chief channels through which the child's soul would be transformed. Some of this move to "heart religion" was a product of the Second Great Awakening and its emotional appeals, but this was also more generalized as Romanticism and sentimentalist fiction elevated the subjective and internal aspects of the human person. Because children were most deeply influenced by heart impressions and because mothers were most apt to provide such loving care, mothers and children were increasingly seen as the natural and God-given pairing for Christian nurture. As Samuel Phillips proclaimed, "To the mother especially, is committed the religious education of the child at home. . . . They can better reach and train the heart. Religion is heart-wisdom. . . . And who is better able to storm and carry that inner citadel, and lead its subdued inmates to the Cross, than the pious, tender-hearted, soliciting mother."[48] Contrasting the "frosty indifference, and the rigid severity, of so many fathers" with the "warm impassioned bosom of a mother," Protestants of all stripes increasingly saw mother love as the most powerful force in awakening children's hearts to the things of God.[49]

When describing the power of a mother's love, most authors chose to highlight its sacrificial and selfless nature. Mothers demonstrated a loving spirit of service, devoting themselves to others' well-being while attempting to suppress personal needs and desires.[50] Such sacrifice could be described in terms of the physical labor of mothering (preparing food or caring for children's needs) or in terms of inconspicuous spiritual practices such as prayer for family members.[51] Paradoxically, the mother would exert her greatest influence by rendering herself invisible, serving in the background, shining the spotlight on her husband and children, and looking for reward only through their achievements and in the life to come.[52] Horace Bushnell, in his classic account "The Age of Homespun," nicely articulated this ideal:

> Let no woman imagine that she is without consequence, or motive to excellence, because she is not conspicuous. Oh, it is the greatness of woman that she is so much like the great powers of nature, back of the noise and clatter of the world's affairs, tempering all things with her benign influence only the more certainly because of her silence, greatest in her beneficence because most remote from ambition, most forgetful of herself and fame; a better nature in the world that only waits to bless it, and refuses to be known save in the successes of others, whom she makes conspicuous; satisfied most in the honors that come not to her.[53]

As Catherine Beecher and Harriet Beecher Stowe affirmed, the mother was the "chief minister" of the home, and her "great mission is self-denial."[54]

As historian Jan Lewis has suggested, mothers' servant-hearted love, a love marked by laying down their lives for their families, was set forth as the closest earthly parallel to Christ's sacrificial and atoning love.[55] Repeatedly, authors spoke of the fact that mothers sacrificed themselves—died to themselves—for the sake of their families, especially their perpetually wayward husbands and sons.[56] The mother was frequently portrayed as the family member who would "save" her children through her prayers and self-denying service. In comments clearly alluding to Christ's role, pastor Charles Hall went so far as to affirm that it was typically women who "bear the sins" of the household through their self-forgetting and sacrificial lives, ultimately serving as redemptive models of Christ's love. With a mother's influence, he suggested, the family needed "no other commentary on the Man of Sorrows."[57] It is perhaps not surprising, therefore, that nineteenth-century Protestants—especially liberals but increasingly conservatives as well—emphasized more of God's loving care and his comforting presence, comparing his qualities to that of the nurturing mother. They tended to focus more on Jesus's sacrifice and suffering love than on God's paternal power and wrath. Part of the broader "feminization of Christianity" in this era, these themes highlighted the nurturing affection that best characterized the mother love of this era.[58]

The mother's sacrificial and redemptive love was in many ways seen as most powerful in preserving and rescuing sons who eventually left the household. Countless stories depicted young men who faced temptation upon leaving home but who were saved by tearful and convicting memories of their mother's love and spiritual care. One spoke of memories of his mother's prayers, indicating that they had become a "monitory guardian angel" for him as he traversed the morally perilous terrain of the city.[59] Others mentioned a mother's "last words" or "last prayers" as the instruments God used to soften their hardened hearts.[60] For one young man visiting his childhood home upon the death of his mother, the visual cues of his mother's faithfulness opened the floodgates to spiritual reformation: "The room where she was wont to retire for prayer, and especially the chamber where she last counselled us, and commended us to God, and bade the final farewell to earthly home and kindred, are chapels now, filled with solemn images and a cloud of incense. . . . Thus being dead my mother yet speaks, and scarcely less, perhaps more, than when she was present in the body, continues to influence my thoughts and conduct."[61]

Most were convinced that the mother was the wayward son's only hope.[62] As one author said, "She may fix a grasp upon him which he will never be able to displace. She may entwine cords of truth and affection about his spirit, which he will never succeed in sundering. They will remain, and keep him in all his wanderings, and probably draw him at length, by a gentle constraint, to the feet of Jesus."[63] The strength of the mother's love would bind the child's affections to the mother and her faith, tethering the child's heart to hers so that it would be hard to separate later in life. Several authors commented that the appeal to fathers could not generate the same melting of the heart. In *Narratives of the Spoiled Child*, when one character attempts to reclaim a young man bent on dissipation, an appeal to his father's love for the Bible generates only rebuke. When instead he is asked to consider, not only the father, but also the "mother, who bare you, and nursed you in her bosom, and wept and prayed over you—whose last prayer and sigh were breathed from her dying lips for you," the man immediately bursts into tears and prays for mercy.[64] Contrary to the biblical account, when nineteenth-century prodigals came home, world-weary and weathered by their sinful lifestyles, they always returned broken and repentant to their mothers.

The power of a mother's love perhaps reveals why Protestant authors so vehemently criticized mothers who failed to measure up to the sacrificial standard. Many pointed out the allure of competing social activities for women: dancing, theater, novel reading, card playing, the opera, concerts, parties, and balls.[65] Many worried that mothers, especially those in more affluent circles, would forsake the simple pleasures of home and find themselves captivated by the "frivolities" of fashion and empty amusements. Religious leaders were unrelenting in their critiques of those mothers who sacrificed their maternal responsibilities in order to "make a fair show in the flesh," giving their time to "love of dress," "excessive vanity," and "fondness for light reading" while leaving their children in the care of servants or sending them off to boarding schools.[66] When mothers were captured by such vain and superficial pleasures, they demonstrated an unnatural deficiency in the self-denial and sacrifice required of those embracing the maternal calling. While fathers were given more latitude, many noted that it was maternal failure, more than anything, that threatened to frustrate the Christian nurture of the growing child.

Mother's Purity: Saving the Home and the Nation

While mothers' love provided the necessary disposition for child nurture, it was their purity that promised to protect and nourish the child's growing soul. While colonial authors often viewed women as vulnerable to evil and more susceptible to Satan's schemes, by the nineteenth century they were frequently portrayed as innocent and pure, devoid of immoral appetites and endowed with seemingly innate self-control.[67] As J. R. Miller put it, "It is not possible even to think of true womanhood without purity. . . . Amid the wreck of this world, wrought by sin, there are still some fragments of the beauty of Eden, and among these none is lovelier than the unsullied delicacy of a true woman's heart."[68] Men, who had previously been viewed as masters of rationality, were by contrast now seen as naturally aggressive and unruly. Quoting an unnamed social critic, Thayer stated bluntly, "What I now say may be mortifying to the pride of men, but it is true. We seldom rise quite up to the standard of morality and religion which woman holds before us. We never rise above it."[69] It was pure mothers who, because they were untainted by the world, were best suited to lead and guide impressionable children toward lives of virtue.[70]

Much of this coalesced around the emerging concept that men and women occupied "separate spheres."[71] As late as the 1820s and 1830s, many still viewed the family in patriarchal terms as "a little empire benevolently ruled by a patriarch."[72] Increasingly, however, men were seen to occupy the public sphere, dominated by the impersonal and competitive world of work and politics. Women and children, on the other hand, occupied the private sphere, the domestic realm characterized by gentleness, purity, and love. As historian Paula Fass suggests, the doctrine of separate spheres made it appear that the genders were almost like "different species."[73] While this contrast was certainly overdone and was far closer to reality in urban rather than rural settings, it established a powerful sexual division of labor that exaggerated a sense of both the corruption of the male public sphere and the glorified purity of the maternal home.[74] As Gregg Camfield notes, the sphere of home in the nineteenth century "was defined as one of influence rather than power, of kindness and love rather than work, of educating children, of developing spiritual values in the face of the declining power and importance of church, of maintaining cultural continuity in the home in the face of change in the market—in general, of providing 'a haven in a heartless world.'"[75]

While some women at the time desired to expand female influence into the broader domains of politics and economics, most Protestant authors maintained that women's role should be confined to the private, domestic sphere and to benevolent work that strengthened homes around the world.[76] Nicholas Murray, an Old School Presbyterian pastor in New Jersey, demonstrated the ways this contrast was envisioned:

> God no more designed woman to be a politician, lawyer, soldier, than he designed that the pillars which sustain the house should be made of the vines that adorn it. . . . Her place is to be queen in the home circle. Or, to change the figure, if the father is the sun of that circle, the mother is the moon, and the children are the stars; and as the moon is seen majestically walking among the stars when the sun has retired, so should the mother be seen among her children and household when the father is occupied with the outer and more arduous duties of his profession. . . . The place of woman is the domestic circle, that great laboratory of character.[77]

Such images provided a clear call for women to embrace this maternal role and to see the home as a powerful sphere of soul-shaping work. It was, one author concurred, "in the domestic circle where female excellence shines the brightest."[78]

This restriction of mothers to the "domestic circle" was set forth not as a constraint or limitation but as an expansion of female "influence."[79] Instead of working directly within the political sphere or the world of work, mothers were to influence culture indirectly, developing purified homes and therefore allowing the godly power of domestic life to radiate out into the world through its nurtured boys and men.[80] This role was viewed as absolutely critical within the new republic. In the midst of new freedoms, good public citizenship, it was assumed, would emerge through the strong individual character and moral fiber of America's children.[81] The clarion call to what historian Linda Kerber terms "republican motherhood" reflected the fact that mothers could best serve the nation by making good citizens out of their sons.[82] It was this kind of motivation, in fact, that rested behind the push to make mothers "useful rather than ornamental" and to develop a science of "domestic engineering" to professionalize their work of cooking, cleaning, home decor, child-rearing, and spiritual development.[83] As many spheres of influence were taken away from women—education by schools, care for the sick by professional doctors, and productive domestic labor by factories—children's moral and spiritual nurture became the central location for mothers to shape the destiny of the nation.[84]

Mothers' spiritual role was thought to be even more important because the male public sphere was increasingly characterized by corruption and unbridled greed. More and more, authors depicted women as the only hope for maintaining American moral and religious virtue, mothers establishing Christian homes as a kind of counterbalance to the public sphere of male immorality and vice. In fact, mothers' purity was valorized as the antidote necessary to offset the selfishness of the market economy.[85] Reverend William Buckminster set this forth plainly: "We look to you, ladies, to raise the standard of character in our own sex; we look to you, to guard and fortify those barriers, which still exist in society, against the encroachments of impudence and licentiousness. We look to you for the continuance of domestic purity, for the revival of domestic religion, for the increase of our charities, and the support of what remains of religion in our private habits and public institutions."[86] Most wanted America to continue its march to economic progress, but they also recognized that this was a morally perilous journey. If America was to advance as an economic power and yet also remain a virtuous nation, each mother would need to serve as a bulwark against corruption, her domestic embodiment of love and purity safeguarding her children and her husband from the vices of the public sphere.[87]

In this sense, it is fair to say that the middle-class Christian family model of the Victorian era set up the idea that the good Christian home was built on a radical separation from the evils of the public sphere. Joseph Collier referred to the Christian home as "an oasis in the desert, a garden in the wilderness."[88] It was the home that would guard the purity of mothers and wives, protect vulnerable children, and restore world-weary husbands and fathers who had to go out and do battle in the public sphere. "Home is the citadel in which we are to select our weapons," Jacob Abbott asserted, "and gird on the armor which shall fortify us against the temptations of the world."[89] Only by sheltering the home from the broader society could it serve as a shelter from the turmoil and disorder of the toxic public sphere, erecting "domestic barricades" against the threats of evil and moral contagion.[90]

Such a view could easily lead to a sense that mothers' chief role was to protect children from "the world" by building walls around the purified home and keeping children within its sacred confines. Protection from evil is of course a critical parental task, but viewing the home as refuge from the world could also obscure certain critical realities. At a basic level, the division between the "pure" home and the "evil" public sphere may have limited parents' ability to recognize that sin also existed within the home and within parents' and children's lives. By limiting the concept of protection to keeping children within the sanitized family, parents may have missed out on the need to confront the evils inside the family's "sacred sphere." In addition, such rhetoric may have promoted the idea that religion was associated chiefly with the private sphere of life. As the home became more of a haven from the world and as religion was associated more with mothers and children, it became easier to confine faith to these sacred spaces. If the home was viewed as a setting in which to heal from the wounds of the public sphere, there was maybe less of a sense that the home could play a role in the healing of society's woundedness. The home, in other words, was to provide protection from "the world" rather than a missional engagement with the world. As Rodney Clapp has suggested, this was the equivalent of relegating the Christian faith to the elevation of "household gods" while "the great God Yahweh was tamed, domesticated, housebroken."[91]

Yet mothers themselves did find ways to make a difference in the broader society. As Stephanie Coontz has observed, the mother's "private" sphere was not always equated with the immediate family or the private home.[92] While caring for one's own children was always deemed primary, in the nineteenth century many women engaged in "labor" outside the home through various social movements for moral reform, temperance, missions, and charity.[93] "Despite strict prohibitions on female participation in electoral politics," Coontz notes, "the original notion of domesticity made it socially acceptable—even morally obligatory—for women to play a leading role in public moral discussion."[94] Mothers were often called into Christian social reform as a means of expanding their domestic influence. As Margaret Bendroth has noted, while they would avoid the soiled world of politics, economics, and commerce, women could bring the purified virtues of their homes to the other homes of the world. Women's work in such organizations as the Women's Christian Temperance Union and the various organizations of "home missions" was about protecting the home and helping to bring Christian middle-class home virtues to the poor, to Native Americans, to immigrants, and to freed slaves. Domesticity, in other words, was itself a mission, a place in which mothers could extend the refuge of home to those who were most vulnerable.[95] They could, in the words of Frances Willard, "make the world itself, a larger home."[96]

These maternal ideals, of course, did not always parallel the actual experiences of individual families. Many women, especially immigrants and those of lower economic status, continued to work in factories and as domestics. Many also worked as teachers in this era of the growing common school movement. Furthermore, for rural farming families, the more consistent presence of the father may have curtailed mothers' abilities to assume spiritual authority within the home.[97] Yet by the mid-nineteenth century, the ideological transformation among Northern middle-class families was undeniable. While patriarchy receded at different times in different locations, as historian Mary Ryan has noted, "this change at the level of popular ideology, from patriarchal household to feminine domesticity, was sudden, major, and complete."[98]

From "Pedagogue" to "Playmate": The Declining Spiritual Influence of Fathers

As may already be evident, a significant corollary of the newly elevated maternal role was a relative decline in the father's contribution to Christian parenting. While colonial authors frequently had to remind women of their important maternal role in the spiritual lives of their children, Victorian-era authors often resorted to "special pleading" to urge fathers to carry their load in promoting Christian nurture.[99] Many realized that the emphasis on Christian motherhood, combined with the decline of patriarchal models of parenting, had the potential of marginalizing the father's role within the home. As one pastor put it, "We cannot indeed over-estimate the responsibilities of the maternal relation . . . but on this very account, so much has been written and spoken to mothers, both through the Pulpit and the Press, that we are in danger of forgetting, that the entire responsibility does not rest with her; and it may be questioned, whether, in pursuing the course that has been adopted on this subject, we have not, in some degree, deserted the path which Infinite Wisdom has pointed out."[100] Beginning in the 1830s and rising to a crescendo by midcentury, a number of authors identified a new crisis in Christian parenting: "paternal neglect."[101]

A number of factors were responsible for the father's diminished stature as a familial spiritual guide. Of significance was the gradual decline of patriarchal authority, a process that escalated throughout the eighteenth and early nineteenth centuries. In the seventeenth century, fathers were able to exercise a fair amount of control over their sons because they held ownership of the land that would serve as their inheritance. However, by the mid-eighteenth century the subdivision of land and its declining productivity meant that fathers had less to exchange with their sons in return for their compliance. In addition, the early growth of a market economy meant that more sons began to leave their family plot in search of either educational opportunities or career options in manufacturing, shipping, and trade. This meant that fathers—most of whom were still farmers or local artisans—no longer possessed the keys to unlocking the vocational skills most needed by their sons. Whether sons purchased their own land or left in search of economic opportunities, the authority of the patriarch was compromised. As sons strayed farther from home in search of employment, peer relationships began to eclipse patriarchal authority in terms of influence.[102]

By the mid-nineteenth century, the most common reason given for the loss of paternal influence was the growing market economy that pulled men away from the home.[103] Since many fathers now worked outside the home, they left early in the morning and returned in the evening, leaving only late nights and Sundays available for discipleship in the home.[104] Clerks, businessmen, and professionals such as lawyers and doctors often spent long hours in offices or traveling. Others were away for longer stretches: riverboat captains, miners, politicians, and army and navy officers. Because of the time away, several commented that the home had become for the father little more than a boarding house or hotel. "The god of this world is served with such fidelity that he receives the whole time," noted Thayer, "except what is absolutely demanded for eating and sleeping."[105] This loss of proximity, some indicated, minimized fathers' opportunities for formal teaching, informal mentoring, and spiritual modeling. As well-known Congregationalist pastor and author John S. C. Abbott remarked, "The father, in almost every walk of life, eager in the pursuit of business, toils early and late, and finds no time to fulfill those duties to his children which, faithfully fulfilled, would secure him the richest share of temporal and spiritual blessings."[106]

In this light, leaders saved some of their most caustic rebukes for men who used their limited free time to frequent taverns and clubs rather than investing in their children's spiritual lives. As historian Stephen Frank has suggested, moralists in this era were attempting to change definitions of masculinity such that "manliness" was associated with marriage and fatherhood in the private sphere rather than public male carousing in saloons and clubs. In fact, they hoped that middle-class men would see this as a way to distinguish themselves from working-class and immigrant men who found their identities in these male-dominated domains.[107] Yet this was also an era of expansion for fraternal orders and various eating and drinking clubs. Without question, pastors and other leaders saw these organizations as a blight on the father's proper role as teacher and moral guide. As H. A. Boardman lamented, "To come more directly to the point, the allegation made against these Clubs—made in the name of ten thousand injured wives and mothers and children—is, that they become a sort of rival home to the home *they* occupy."[108] Because they inspired dissipation and a "love of play," these clubs produced in men a "disrelish" for the home and a "spirit which tends to *undomesticate.*"[109]

While they decried the loss of the time quantity, authors also worried that the quality of a father's interactions with children would be compromised by his growing affinity for the values of the public sphere. Because the workplace was dominated by aggressiveness, selfish ambition, and formal bureaucratic relationships, many saw fathers bringing these qualities into the home and thereby compromising their ability to take up a tender and instructive fatherly role. Tainted by the rough-and-tumble world of work, fathers seemed to arrive home impatient, insensitive, and overly formal, lacking the gentle and nurturing spirit increasingly viewed as necessary for engagement with children.[110] Presbyterian pastor James Alexander suggested that the "rage for amassing wealth" and the amount of time absent from the home had generated an "estranging process" in which the father "gradually loses some of that parental tenderness which Providence keeps alive by the presence of those whom we love."[111] Perhaps this is why Mary Ryan could remark that, at times, "a father in a Victorian parlor was something of a bull in a china shop, somewhat ill at ease with the gentle virtues enshrined there."[112]

Operating within the private sphere, it seems, was a significant challenge for men who lived much of their lives in the public. "At best, a man would have to perform an elaborate switch of role and behavior on crossing the threshold of his home," historian John Demos suggests. "At worst, he would have to choose between effectiveness in one 'sphere' or the other."[113] The more typical compromise was for fathers to divide the labor with their wives so that they were fulfilling a specific home role appropriate to their spheres. Fathers took on the external dimensions of life: the development of broad Christian principles (often articulated in formal family devotions), punishment for major acts of disobedience, vocational advice for their sons, and school success. Meanwhile, mothers addressed matters of internal growth and development: Christian piety, individual reading, spiritual disciplines, regular correction, and loving devotion. Thus, even when a father was involved in the Christian formation of his children, that "task" was more formal, principled, and distant.

The loss of time at home and the changing nature of paternal involvement were particularly important in relationships between fathers and sons. Especially in the cities, sons no longer worked alongside their fathers in the fields, settings that for colonial Americans had created a context for both vocational and spiritual modeling. Nineteenth-century fathers still worked to make sure their sons carved out a path to success, but that now came through the selection of clerkships and, increasingly, the willingness to pay for additional education. Growing boys soon found that their emotional, spiritual, and relational needs were met in places other than the father-son bond. In their younger years, they developed intense attachments with their mothers, with whom they spent the bulk of their time. Yet when it came time to break away from their mothers and seek out a pathway to male socialization, they now often turned to their same-age peers rather than their fathers. A host of young men's societies and organizations emerged in the nineteenth century to provide companionship, vocational networking, and spiritual nurture. While fathers were obviously still very concerned about their families, their more "external" focus often led boys elsewhere in their search to develop friendships and a route to Christian manhood.[114]

All of this amounted to nothing less than a wholesale change in Christian fatherly identity. As historian John Demos has helpfully detailed, the vocabulary best used to describe the father's role in the colonial era included such terms as "pedagogue," "benefactor," "controller," "moral overseer," "caregiver," and "example." By the mid-nineteenth century, however, the more appropriate descriptors were "moral support," "playmate," and, perhaps most centrally, "provider."[115] The father was still heralded for his role as a "family man," but that role now placed him in a more external position, fulfilling economic needs, disciplining when needed, helping steer children's vocational directions, and "frolicking" with the children in the evenings after his workday.[116]

Within this new setting, the father's "provider" role came to dominate paternal self-understanding. With the separation of spheres and the sense that mothers now dominated the home's moral space, it was quite natural for fathers with domestic concerns to see their primary identity as a breadwinner, financially providing for children in order to maintain their material needs and class status. Protestant leaders often commented on how fathers excused their lack of spiritual attentiveness by speaking of the need to provide a high standard of living for their families. Furthermore, many felt that the provider role had become an all-encompassing identity, leading to a preoccupation with work and finances even when the father was at home. As one pastor put it, "The influence of the father's daily society is withdrawn from his children. They see him but at his hurried meals. Not only is the whole day given to business, but the evening to the same . . . to such an engrossment of thought in 'the course of this world,' as leaves no liberty of mind or heart for the domestic duty of a Christian father, in charge of the souls of his children."[117]

While the colonial family highlighted the patriarch father as the fountain of religious training, the Victorian-era breadwinning father was viewed more as a support to the mother, an assistant in her work as primary spiritual caregiver. The father's main task, in terms of facilitating his children's faith formation, was therefore to choose a good wife and then to shine an adoring spotlight on her maternal role, giving his approval and support to her domestic centrality. The Reverend M. S. Hutton stated that the father's role was to "honor that mother as the spiritual guide, the angel visitant." He exhorted fathers, "Let your example and your authority be the power around which she may throw her maternal influence, and press it upon the young and yielding hearts which beat responsive to her own."[118] In this setting, based more on "spousal partnership" than on "patriarchal hierarchy," one of the father's most significant roles was that of maternal "cheerleader."[119] This, in fact, was wonderfully captured by an 1847 portrait in which the father was depicted behind his wife, placing a celebratory wreath over her head and admiring her as she attended to their children.[120] As a secondary line of "support," the father receded into the domestic background.

If anything, the father was often depicted as a playful companion with his children, winning their affections through joyful "frolics" in the evenings and on Sundays. Many authors began to argue that fathers must play with their children if they wanted to secure their love and gain a voice in their lives.[121] Increasingly, they viewed this as a singular paternal contribution. This shift from "pedagogue" to "playmate" had significant ramifications for the fatherly role. "Over the course of the century," one historian noted, "middle class men . . . tended to turn their wives into mother figures and their children into playmates, with the result that the Victorian father figure became a curious combination of contradictory images: the stranger, the intruder, the clown, and the biggest child in the family."[122] Such a role promoted a division of labor within the home in which fathers kept children entertained (and gave mothers a break) while mothers were responsible for most of the daily nurture and care. "If paternal play encouraged children to seek companionship from their fathers," one historian notes, "it also directed them toward their mothers for instruction, as well as emotional and physical care."[123]

Fathers did maintain, it should be noted, a kind of formal spiritual authority that may have even been enhanced by their daily absence. Some felt that the father's work may have increased a sense of awe and reverence for the mysterious breadwinner who went into the world to battle on behalf of the family. This point is echoed by historian Bernard Wishy, who surmises, "It may well be, however, that this full day at home (on Sundays) and his few hours at home during the week, made the tangible power and prestige of the near-stranger on those occasions more impressive to the child than a more familiar, easy-going supervision at home during the entire week."[124] In many homes, this authority was reinforced as mothers vested fathers with disciplinary power in more significant infractions. The appeal to "wait for father to come home" could strike fear in the heart of a child, and it reinforced the idea that, as head of the household, he wielded a kind of ultimate formal authority. In addition, despite the mother's overriding spiritual influence in everyday life, reading and praying with individual children, most still acknowledged that fathers would preside over the family altar, leading in the reading of Scripture and prayer.[125] Thus fathers generally maintained a kind of formal spiritual authority as head of the home even as they lost much of their daily spiritual presence and influence. As Catherine Beecher put it, nineteenth-century fathers were like "the heavenly Father who, though unseen, is ever present."[126]

The Ongoing Legacy of the "Maternal Turn"

The shifting understanding of parental gender roles in the mid-nineteenth century certainly reflected a change from earlier colonial models. As understandings of masculinity and femininity began to grow more bounded and defined during the early market and industrial revolutions, the gradual removal of work from the home linked men with the public and women with the private spheres of life. In addition, as conversion and piety were increasingly de-emphasized and replaced by issues of character and virtue, the perceived distinctions between men and women came into stark contrast.[127] Women's purity gave them a new moral authority over men and linked virtue very closely with the domestic sphere they inhabited. Men, more aggressive and wayward, were tainted by the public sphere and thus less qualified to serve as moral models and spiritual leaders within the family. Quite opposed to perceptions in the colonial era, mothers would emerge as the unchallenged centerpiece of the Christian home.

Contemporary research on the Christian family seems to affirm a continued maternal dominance in home-based spiritual nurture. In Barna's recent *Households of Faith* research study, one of the most interesting findings is that mothers far outstrip fathers when it comes to Christian practices with children (praying together, talking about faith issues, confronting each other), providing support (encouragement, advice, and sympathy), talking about hard issues (faith questions, the Bible, politics, and sex), and providing spiritual guidance (encouraging church attendance, teaching about the Bible, teaching about God's forgiveness, and setting an example). When adults were asked whose faith most influenced them, 68 percent indicated mothers while only 46 percent said fathers. In fact, the research indicates that teenagers' siblings were as involved as fathers in providing emotional and spiritual support and encouragement.[128] As the study claims, "In this and other responses throughout the report, it appears that spiritual development in the home is somewhat of a matriarchy."[129]

It was in the middle years of the nineteenth century that this maternal dominance was born. From a time in the colonial period when they were often mistrusted as parental role models, mothers were given a new sense of value and influence within the homes of this era. They were elevated for their love and purity and were venerated for their role in nurturing the nation's future leaders, establishing strong Christian values in their children and reclaiming those threatened by the temptations of the cities and the new market economy. Their influence as spiritual guides was certainly validated as a high calling and gave women a sense of purpose as other vocations in the home were gradually removed. In a culture where individual virtue was seen as the pathway to national flourishing, mothers, as the shepherds of children's souls, were often described as the most important architects of the new social order.

Such a system, however, also created new challenges for mothers and for families. First, the pressure on mothers could be quite strong. They were called on to sacrifice everything for their children, thus demonstrating the sacrificial love of Christ. Since they were the primary Christian nurturers of their children, mothers' sense of significance was inextricably intertwined with their children's spiritual success or failure. When combined with the fact that mothers now rooted their identity in child-rearing and viewed their parenting as determinative in the lives of their children, disillusionment and guilt were near certainties. What Christopher Lasch has termed the "emotional overloading of the parent-child connection" had the potential to raise expectations that the mother-child relationship would supply all emotional and spiritual needs and lead to the "payoff" of children's lifelong obedience and love.[130] Of course, this was not always the case, and when connections were dissolved or Christian faith rejected, the feelings of disappointment and betrayal could be extreme.

In addition, the home-based division of labor was ripe for the gendered double standard that has remained fairly durable since this era. When fathers did take time to teach and nurture their children in the faith, they were applauded for this work. When mothers did the same, they were just "doing their job." Mothers and fathers were also held to different behavioral standards. Placed on a pedestal, mothers (and their daughters) were expected to exhibit a lofty kind of character, a function of their supposed inherent moral superiority and the fact that the society was dependent on their virtue for its proper functioning. Fathers and their sons, on the other hand, were given far more latitude along these lines, with many willing to look the other way at their shortcomings. While men were still called to self-restraint, they had a lower bar of personal holiness, the expectation being that their mothers and wives would both counterbalance their immorality through their own pious lives and rescue them when they strayed beyond proper boundaries. Blame for male moral failure, in fact, was often placed on the mothers who were unable to reign in their husbands' and sons' wayward souls. It was obviously much harder for fathers to see themselves as spiritual guides and exemplars in their families within such a system.

This points to the fact that the separation of spheres could make gendered categories out of qualities that were designed to be true of all Christian parents and children. Sacrificial servanthood, for example, was most often associated with mothers, and it was mothers who were thought to be the reflections of Christ in their unselfish devotion to their families and their disdain for personal acclaim or recognition. Such language was obviously noble, and in many ways accurate to mothers' often thankless work, but this kind of language could also make it seem as if fathers and even children were relieved of such responsibilities. The biblical call for husbands to "love your wives, just as Christ loved the church and gave himself up for her" (Eph. 5:25 NIV) surely implies the kind of sacrificial and self-denying love that was (and still is) often equated with femininity. The call for children to honor their parents (Exod. 20:12) is another species of this larger sacrificial calling, one that seems quite countercultural in more child-centered settings. Such ideals only point to the larger reality that all family members are called to sacrificially put others before themselves— that is, they are called to love one another (Phil. 2:3–4; John 13:34–35). By attaching this calling to mothers alone and arguing that this was somehow located within the female nature, Victorian authors could easily diminish the sense that sacrificial servanthood was a common familial obligation.

Of course, these nineteenth-century shifts also made it more challenging for fathers to determine their precise place in their children's spiritual formation. As they were gradually displaced from the home by work responsibilities, their roles as priests, prophets, and kings gave way to more limited roles as providers, playmates, and moral supports for their wives. In leading family devotions, preparing their children for vocational responsibilities, and providing discipline in cases of significant rebellion, they did maintain a kind of formal authority. Yet their role in the child's internal spiritual development was greatly diminished. Whether this took place willingly or more begrudgingly is difficult to determine. Many advice writers certainly chastised men for their unwillingness to prioritize their children's Christian nurture. At the same time, their new work rhythms, combined with the breathless celebration of motherhood, let fathers off the hook for such work. Fathers, according to many leaders, seemed willing to shirk their own divinely ordained responsibilities because they believed that mothers—who were better equipped temperamentally anyway—were picking up the slack. Before long, cultural expectations for fatherly spiritual nurture had diminished.

In the end, the changing understanding of Christian fatherhood was inextricably linked to the changing understanding of "home" in the male imagination. Because of the time and energy invested in the workplace, it was easy for men to begin viewing the home as a place of rest and recreation rather than pedagogy and nurture. The more men associated their sense of calling and vocation with the world of work outside the home, the more home could be seen as an "avocation," a respite from exertion and a place of relaxation and refreshment. As one put it, "To the man of business, wearied with multiplied perplexities; to the industrious laborer, exhausted with the toil of the day; to the professional man, tired of the competition and strife that beset him on every side . . . how welcome the sight, the sensibilities, the charm of home. . . . Go there, and refresh your wasted spirit at that pure fountain of domestic love."[131] By the logic of the separate spheres vision, the home was a place of work for women but a place of restoration for men. Men did display an interest in religious activities associated with the public sphere, such as the businessmen's revivals that burst on the scene in the 1850s, but the home was less frequently thought of as a place for fatherly discipleship efforts. If home was a refuge and a place of play—an "Elysium" for the soul—then it was less likely to be a place where serious spiritual work was done.[132]

The home thus had a new purpose for men. Many spoke of how the home could heal the wounds inflicted by the world of work, redeeming fathers from both the stresses and the evils of the public sphere. The father at home, freed from his role within the cog of the larger economic machine, could be renewed by what was good and pure while being given a place to reconnect with childlike joys and enthusiasm. Authors even noted how spiritual exercises such as prayer and the family altar could serve as means of "countervailing the hard and selfish world which surrounds him."[133] This "therapeutic" vision of family for men, while helpful in enticing them to return to their home fires each evening, also likely resulted in a diminished call to fatherly teaching and mentoring. As historian Stephen Frank puts it,

> For, if the notion that fatherhood was good for men encouraged positive engagement in family life, it also promoted a therapeutic view of fathering which limited the scope of paternal responsibility. This therapeutic view of fatherhood—what settled domesticity could do for men, rather than what fathers should do for their children—increasingly turned home life into something to be consumed by fathers, a reward for all the hard work they performed elsewhere. . . . Small children could seem at times like little more than toys for masculine amusement. More to the point, fathers who acted primarily as playmates were, by definition, less responsible for a young child's moral and intellectual upbringing.[134]

While many calls for increased fatherly involvement arose, especially around the turn of the twentieth century when fears about Christianity's feminization reached a fever pitch, the maternal turn in Christian nurture would prove difficult to reverse. The nineteenth-century reorientation of mothers' and fathers' roles in Christian parenting would leave a lasting mark on the American Christian family experience.

The power of mothers in this era ultimately "sacralized" the home in significant ways. Their love and purity set up the home as the sanctified sphere that would serve as the primary setting for the child's Christian formation. Set apart from the sordid public sphere and its dangers, the home and its sacred relationships would nourish children in faith and create wonderful memories to keep them in the fold. As authors elevated childhood, the nuclear family, and cherished "family time," they linked children's growth not to distinct Christian practices but rather to the creation of "home sweet home."

CHAPTER 7

The Parent as Memory-Maker

Fashioning the Tight-Knit Christian Family

> Thanks to the man who wrote the imperishable song, Home, Sweet Home! . . . It is a Christian anthem.
>
> —I. W. Wiley, *Religion of the Family*[1]

The nineteenth-century emphasis on environmental impressions and the determinative nature of parenting, coupled with the pervasive influence of mothers, certainly highlighted the spiritual power of the Christian home. While colonial Protestants had obviously seen the household as a critical place of worship, instruction, and discipline, its role as a "little commonwealth" emphasized the house as a functional space in which family members, servants, apprentices, and relatives participated in a number of joint tasks. By the middle of the nineteenth century, many of these educational, medical, and vocational functions were being farmed out to other institutions—common schools, Sunday schools, doctors and hospitals, and factories. As the household's public tasks were gradually removed, its central character was redefined in terms of "home."[2] The Christian home emerged as a sacred private space, a place of cherished and shared family connections built on sentiment and shared memories. The traditional, early modern family centered on deference and patriarchy shifted to a modern nuclear family mode characterized by what historians have called "affective individualism."[3] This new style was rooted in a desire for privacy, more affectionate and democratic relationships (both in marriage and in parenting), and a move toward child-centeredness within the family. The home, in fact, was now seen not as a commonwealth but as a private refuge from the larger world, a pious sanctuary highlighting tight-knit family relationships and protection from the corrosive outside world.

As the home shifted from a center of economic productivity to a spiritual sanctuary, it took on a redemptive role in the lives of American families. Often referred to as the earthly "heaven" and as a replica of the Garden of Eden, the home assumed unprecedented spiritual power in the Protestant imagination. As Horace Bushnell suggested, "The house, having a domestic Spirit of grace dwelling in it, should become the church of childhood, the table and hearth a holy rite, and life an element of saving power."[4] "The house itself," he concluded, "is a converting ordinance."[5] Increasingly, the intimate relationships of the nuclear family were considered critical to children's growth in the faith. Parents were called on to establish warm and affectionate family bonds so that children would associate faith with the happy memories of a loving Christian home. This, authors felt, would help growing children resist the temptations of the world both as they grew up and after they left its cherished confines. The rise of this domestic ideal has had a long-lasting influence on the ways in which contemporary Christian parents think about their roles and about the meaning of the "Christian family" in the modern world.

The Creation of "Home"

The belief that children would be spiritually formed through the creation of tight family relationships was in part a function of the changing nature of the Christian home in the nineteenth century. Perhaps most important was the reduced size of the household. While the average number of children born to a typical white American mother stood at 7.04 in 1800, that number dropped to 5.21 by 1860 and 3.56 by 1900.[6] A mother during the colonial era might have expected to begin bearing children in her early twenties and continue giving birth every two years for up to twenty years while nursing and caring for a broad range of children. A mother in the mid-nineteenth century, by contrast, would have fewer children in a much more compressed period of time.[7] Such declines have been variously attributed to "domestic feminism" (women seeking release from repeated cycles of pregnancy, birth, and nursing), husbands' increasing concern for their wives' health and well-being (since many still died in childbirth), children's more limited economic contributions (linked to the decline of agricultural vocations), and a growing desire to secure a middle-class standard of living for each child.[8] Yet it also seems clear that Protestant parents chose to limit the number of children in the family so as to enhance their ability to provide a concentrated form of nurture for each child. In diminishing the quantity of their children, in other words, many Victorian Protestants saw themselves as increasing the spiritual quality of each child's life.[9] These developments shifted the "extensive" parenting approach of the colonial era—which included many children and many caretakers—to more "intensive" parent-child relationships rooted in strong and intimate parent-child bonds.[10]

This shrinking of family size was also accompanied by a shrinking of family diversity. As mentioned previously, families in colonial New England were large, diverse, and fluid, with children often spending time in multiple households together with a variety of relatives and workers. In the late eighteenth and early nineteenth centuries, families remained somewhat permeable. Within the still-dominant agricultural context, family and work relationships continued to blend nuclear families with kin, servants, boarders, and apprentices.[11] In addition, the nature of evangelical revivalism linked to the Second Great Awakening often placed religious affiliation and affection at the forefront of people's sense of "family." In fact, the revivals generally decentered the nuclear family as the core of religious life, placing more emphasis on individual conversion and at times causing family tensions as women and young people responded more quickly than husbands and fathers to religious appeals.[12] Furthermore, revivals tended to spawn religious societies and associations that became family-like in their intimate relationships, accountability, and care. A. Gregory Schneider has pointed out how, in Methodist societies in the Ohio Valley, class meetings and love feasts drew people into meaningful bonds that transcended blood relations and formed more inclusive communities of faith. Referring to each other as mothers, fathers, brothers, and sisters, such groups collectively provided financial assistance, medical help, care for children, and religious nurture.[13]

However, by the middle decades of the nineteenth century, this more fluid and permeable sense of family began to contract. In fact, one of the most significant modifications in the American middle-class home was its increasing privatization and isolation. The removal of economic work from the household in the nineteenth century began to shrink the home around its nuclear core with the breadwinning father leaving the household for work and the mother staying at home with her children to provide care and nurture. As production was removed from the home (thus reducing women's economic labor) and as the number of children per family began to shrink, the presence of apprentices, servants, and other laborers declined.[14] In the wake of such changes, middle-class Christian homes in the mid-nineteenth century took on the recognizable form of a smaller nuclear family anchored by close and affectionate relationships between parents and children. The more permeable home had made sense when society was anchored by shared religious and moral assumptions, but population growth and increasing religious diversity led many to turn inward, relying on the internal cohesion of the home as a safeguard against the world.[15] As Helena Wall nicely summarizes, "As the relationship between parents and children tightened, the relationship between family and community loosened."[16]

While fewer from outside the nuclear family were now residing in middle-class households, children were also more likely to spend a longer period of time within the home. More consistent and prolonged schooling, combined with the decline of apprenticeships and a delayed entry into the workforce, meant that many children now spent continuous, uninterrupted time in the family home into their late teens and even their twenties.[17] Teenage girls, especially in middle-class households, were less likely to leave home for work in factories and as domestics. With children spending most of their growing up years in the home, free from productive labor outside of simple chores, they took on new roles within the family. Possessing less economic value, children had increasing psychological value in terms of contributing to domestic happiness. Viviana Zelizer has quite appropriately labeled children in the second half of the nineteenth century as "economically 'worthless' but emotionally 'priceless.'"[18]

A key component of this new privatized home, in fact, was its growing child-centeredness, a reality reflected in the expansion of consumer goods and institutions directed toward children. While children's books through the eighteenth century had been largely limited to catechisms, primers, and grammar texts, in the nineteenth century the Rollo series by Jacob Abbott, the Peter Parley tales by Samuel Goodrich, the McGuffey Readers, illustrated children's Bibles, and a host of titles by groups such as the American Sunday School Association and the American Tract Society brought a flurry of didactic "moral tales" to young readers. Likewise, a host of new toys—including dolls, china sets, and music boxes for girls and rocking horses, guns, wagons, swords, and drums for boys—demonstrated a heightened interest in children's play. New furniture for children, such as swings, high chairs, cribs, bassinets, and carriages, was developed and often decorated for children's enjoyment. A variety of institutions— including public schools, Sunday schools, orphanages, reform schools, and children's hospitals—were designed in this era to meet children's unique educational, physical, and religious needs. Such innovations showed a new respect for the importance and uniqueness of the childhood years.[19]

Various changes also revealed a growing appreciation for the individuality of young children. New child-oriented clothing and hairstyles showed a growing consciousness of childhood as a distinct stage.[20] Parents increasingly began to celebrate children's birthdays, making these days more central to the annual family calendar. After the late eighteenth century, as Karin Calvert has pointed out, children were more clearly individualized in portraits, often holding a favorite toy or pet to display their unique amusements.[21] Even child naming became more individualized. On the one hand, the practice of giving children necronyms, the names of deceased siblings, was largely discarded by the nineteenth century, reflecting a new sense that each child possessed an irreplaceable individual identity.[22] In addition, more children received unique names and fewer were given the names of fathers and mothers. According to Daniel Scott Smith, 65.1 percent of first sons and 74.4 percent of first daughters were named for their parents in seventeenth-century Hingham, Massachusetts. By the 1860s and 1870s, however, this was true of only 39.8 percent of sons and 16.8 percent of daughters.[23] Furthermore, the growing universality of middle names and the increasing use of unique pet names for each child (such as "little chick" or "little darling") solidified perceptions of individuality.[24] All of these trends demonstrated the growing sense that children were prized as unique individuals with identities that reflected, but were not constrained by, family heritage.

The changing nature of the home certainly compromised some of the natural avenues of teaching that existed in the colonial era. In the days of the "little commonwealth," the family worked together for a number of important tasks: economic, educational, medical, and the caretaking of children and animals. As each of these was gradually removed, the family's chief purpose centered on creating and sustaining emotional ties and providing a pathway to moral and religious virtue. The loss of these functional tasks, however, removed many of the informal ways in which children could be raised up in the faith. Spiritual lessons in the colonial era were often taught in the midst of productive work that was shared by parents and children. These common tasks provided opportunities for informal teaching that connected truth to life in powerful ways. When this was removed, opportunities for "teachable moments" were a bit harder to find.

At the same time, this era opened up new opportunities for a spiritual formation that was rooted more distinctly in the relational sphere. The Christian formation of children, Victorian authors argued, was now dependent on this new home and its nuclear family relationships. In fact, it was the warm and affectionate relationships between parents and children and between siblings that would strengthen and reinforce the faith in children's lives. Presbyterian pastor Thomas Moore perhaps put it best: "Here is a quiet refuge from the rush and roar of life, where the sunny smile of love, the merry laugh and the joyous prattle of childhood, and the fragrant freshness of untainted young hearts, will melt down the cynical selfishness that the world has engendered."[25] The joys of family connections and the memories of family activities would tether young hearts to the faith, thus making it harder to leave it once they embarked on their own. The home, in short, would sanctify children by becoming a "heaven on earth."

Making the Home a Heaven on Earth

By the middle of the nineteenth century, Protestant leaders were quite certain that the best way to raise Christian children was to make them love and spend time at home as much as possible. While colonial pastors often spoke in terms of the need for parents to restrain their children from negative friendships and the evils of the world, most in the nineteenth century believed that the best way to safeguard their children's faith and morality was to make the home a replacement source of pleasure. Parents would keep their children from dissolute company and the alluring nighttime evils of the streets by making the home the center of joyful fellowship and cherished relationships. The ideal was to construct a home environment that children would enjoy so much that they would have little desire to ever leave its sacred confines. As Presbyterian Joseph Collier put it, "It is also an important fact, which many a parent has learned to his sorrow, when too late to remedy it, that *if happiness be not found at home, it is sure to be sought out elsewhere.* Our streets are filled with those who seek in the company of the vicious and profligate the enjoyment from which they are debarred in the more safe, but sometimes uncongenial, society of the family. . . . Let, then, the home be made the most attractive spot in the world to its occupants—the magnet, towards which their desires and affections shall ever tend."[26]

Those writing about Christian parenting in this era indicated that the key to making the home such a "magnet" was for it to be a cheerful space. As Charles Finney suggested, "There is another fault of parents which I must notice. They do not take sufficient pains to render home happy; and the children not finding friendship and sympathy at home, run about elsewhere in search of it. Their home is not a happy one, and they consequently rove about, and come under bad influences. Now a happy home is one of the principal things at which a parent should aim. The home should be rendered so pleasant that the child would rather remain there than go about."[27] In order to secure such a happy home, authors challenged parents to present a cheerful rather than a dour disposition, one noting that "the whole house should be fragrant with the pervading atmosphere of an affectionate tenderness."[28] Home was to be a place of peace and serenity, a place where children would feel safe, protected, and loved.[29] Many leaders warned parents against the anger and "bickering" between spouses or between parents and children that would repel children from the domestic sphere, commending instead a warm and supportive intimacy represented by chats around the fireside.[30] Happy family evenings were of particular importance, since children were often lured out into the streets at night when they had nothing else to keep them occupied. This, Bushnell noted, was the "field of a mother's greatest art . . . finding how to make a happy and good evening for her children."[31]

Perhaps the chief means by which parents could make the home magnetically happy was to encourage the development of deep bonds of friendship with both parents and siblings. Christian authors denounced parents for participation in outside interests—clubs, taverns, lodges, and charitable organizations—that might lure them away from family time, urging them to make the home the center of their social life.[32] In addition, by the mid-nineteenth century Protestants were routinely recommending that parents spend ample time playing and spending time with their children, entering into their diversions and purchasing toys to enhance their pleasure. Far removed from the colonial concern for hierarchy, reverence, and formal distance, J. R. Miller suggested that parents should "romp and play with them; be a child again among them."[33] Finney likewise noted, "It is a vast mistake in parents, to suppose that money thrown away, or misapplied, that is expended in the purchase of hobby-horses, little carts, wagons, sleds, dolls, sets of furniture for their play houses. . . . You must play with him, take him with you when it is convenient, go into his play room or ground, show him how to use his little blocks, his little tools, his hobby-horse."[34] Critical here was that parents were not simply to serve as exemplars and role models (as they were described in colonial literature) but as friends, entering their children's worlds so as to establish bonds of intimacy and trust. Along with others, Finney suggested that parents become their children's "confidential friends," sharing their secrets, celebrating their joys, and sympathizing with their struggles so that they didn't go elsewhere to look for "confidential companionship."[35] Nathaniel Willis, editor of the popular *Youth's Companion*, put it simply to parents: "Be you their companions and friends, and they will not be anxious to seek foreign ones."[36]

It was also for this reason that authors wanted parents to work hard to encourage sibling friendships.[37] "If you have several children," Finney noted, "study to make them satisfied with each other's society, without feeling a disposition, either to go abroad for companions, or to invite those from abroad to come to them. . . . This then must be a subject of study, of prayer, of much consideration, on your part, how you may make your children love each other, be willing to stay at home, and be satisfied with their books, play things, home, and friends, without roving abroad for amusement or employment."[38] The goal, above all, was to make these sibling relationships so intimate that children would want to spend the bulk of their time with their brothers and sisters. As C. R. Lovell proclaimed in the *Methodist Family Manual*, "Labor to make your children understand that they are a community of themselves, and that they are to depend upon possessions within themselves for happiness here, and not upon the outward excitement of receiving and paying visits, and hearing and sending news."[39] "Such a circle would be a heaven upon earth," Isaac Ferris indicated. "It is one of the suburbs of the new Jerusalem."[40]

As is evident in these appeals, Victorian-era Protestants increasingly associated Christian parenting with the desire to promote family togetherness and "family time." Authors, for example, now called attention to the formative influence of family holidays. Chief among these was Christmas, which enjoyed widespread support from Protestants only after the mid-nineteenth century. The Puritans had rejected Christmas as unbiblical, and Christian disdain for the holiday remained fairly strong into the early 1800s. After the mid-1800s, however, as public support grew, Christmas took on a new role as a sentimental holiday marked by domestic intimacy and centered on the child. Families ate together, played games, and sang newly composed Christmas songs such as "It Came upon the Midnight Clear" (1849), "We Three Kings" (1857), and "O Little Town of Bethlehem" (1868). In a time of great change, Christmas provided a sense of family unity and nostalgia. The blending of Christian themes and family togetherness was also a powerful conduit for family identification around matters of faith.[41]

"The Family That Prays Together": Family Worship as Domestic Bliss

Family worship, often labeled in this period as "the family altar," was also held up as an important source of family togetherness.[42] While there were those, like Horace Bushnell, who sought to downplay the importance of these daily practices in favor of "the open state of prayer and communion with God in the house," most continued to stress the importance of family worship and lamented parental negligence in this area.[43] Legal mandates for such observances were abandoned, but local church leaders still urged parents to attend to these duties. In Methodist circles, for example, class leaders were charged with checking in on families to ensure their compliance.[44] When circuit riders stayed overnight in people's homes, in fact, they could be quite forceful in mandating morning and evening prayer services with the family. On one of his itinerant travels, Methodist leader Peter Cartwright implored a father to lead his family in prayer before bedtime. When the father refused, Cartwright himself led the children in prayer while shaming the parents into obedience. "I told the Lord what a poor weak old man lived there," Cartwright recalled, "and asked the Lord to give him strength and grace to set a better example before his family."[45]

In the eyes of some Protestant authors, the ideal paradigm for family worship closely paralleled the colonial model: morning and evening prayers in which the father read from the Scriptures and led family members and servants in corporate prayer and a hymn.[46] Methodist and Holiness leader Phoebe Palmer described her own family's practice in a way that demonstrated continuity with the colonial past:

> There sat the honored and beloved father of the household, with the large Bible and hymn book on the stand before him. All seated, a portion of the Word of God was reverently read, interspersed occasionally with a few interesting remarks. A holy calm prevailed. Even the infant seemed to know that quietness was the order of the hour. The Bible reading closed, a hymn was given out, every child able to read, having a hymn book, and joining in the song. A sweet anthem of praise rose every morning from that family choir of half a score of blended voices. Then followed the prayer. Thus seeking divine benedictions, the day was commenced. In a similar manner, that is, with a song of praise, reading the Scriptures and prayer, it ended.[47]

Denominational publications revealed certain themes in keeping with their emphases. Presbyterians, for example, often recommended that families use Robert Murray M'Cheyne's daily Bible calendar so that the family could read through the Bible in a year.[48] High-church authors tended to recommend readings from prayer books such as the Book of Common Prayer, and many of these sources followed a liturgical calendar for Bible reading, prayers, and creedal recitation.[49] Low-church Protestants provided space for a good deal of extemporaneous prayer and praise even in the midst of their printed aids.[50] In each case, however, the practices of Scripture reading, prayer, and singing remained the staples of family worship, and a growing number of authors provided written guides, including collections of prayers, Bible readings, and hymns, for parents to use at the family altar.[51]

Perhaps most interesting in this era was the growing consensus within parenting advice literature that family worship was critical precisely because of its ability to promote family togetherness and develop strong family bonds. Authors focused less on the God-centered outcomes of family worship than on the role these experiences could play in fostering a tight-knit Christian family. The family altar, many indicated, would give family members a common "hearth" experience to spark intimacy and affection for one another, especially important now that children and fathers were spread out in schools and jobs throughout the day. It could also smooth over any domestic disputes or hostilities.[52] As popular author Jacob Abbott put it, "All our devotional duties bring with them temporal blessings. . . . It is the oil which removes friction, and causes all the complicated wheels of the family to move smoothly and noiselessly. . . . Can the circle which has been feelingly uniting in the prayer that God would give them control over all their passions, and make them meek and lowly in heart, become at once transformed into a scene of irritation and strife? No! The influence of the hour of prayer must reach onward through the duties of the day. It must promote harmony and affection."[53]

As Abbott's words indicate, authors in this era tended to highlight the ability of family worship to prevent relational strife within the family. As a pathway to a cheerful "domestic harmony," one noted that the family altar "expunges all selfishness, allays petulant feelings and turbulent passions, destroys peevishness of temper, and makes home-intercourse holy and delightful."[54] As family members gathered each morning and evening to read, pray, and sing, they would be far less likely to develop any kind of long-lasting bitterness toward one another. As H. A. Boardman concluded, "To listen, as a family, to the counsels of inspired wisdom; to sing in unison their hymns of praise, and bow down together before the throne of grace. . . . Is it possible to conceive of a service better adapted than this to repress all jealousies and envies, to drive away the gloomy vapors or moroseness, to restore serenity to every clouded brow, to reburnish the chain of affection, and diffuse an air of cheerfulness throughout the house?"[55] Family devotions of this kind, in other words, provided a surefire means of averting family tensions and maintaining loving relationships between family members.

The singing and prayer that took place during these daily exercises were thought to be especially powerful for these ends. Singing hymns together was thought to be one of the chief means of cementing close and intimate family bonds and keeping children happy at home. As A. B. Muzzey proposed, "Let your children be accustomed to sing together, and it will diminish the desire, so common in early life, for a perpetual round of amusements beyond the fireside. . . . Children are incited by it to benefit each other; and a love thus grows up between sisters who have sat side by side at the piano-forte, which no change of times and no length of years will impair."[56] Muzzey further indicated that singing would prevent strife and discord between siblings, noting, "When the voices are once attuned, the inward discord will ere long cease; and the hearts of all, parents and children, will be soon melted into harmony. . . . Words are perhaps insufficient to allay the excitement. But let there be music; call the contending spirits to pause and join in a song, and you need not fear a renewal of their altercations."[57] Prayer would then fortify these bonds. "There is no way in which we can more surely increase mutual love," Presbyterian James Alexander noted, "than by *praying for one another*."[58] Prayer would foster family cohesion and avert resentments by helping each person know he or she was loved and supported by the others in the family circle. This was, in many ways, the nineteenth-century origin of the later colloquial phrase "The family that prays together stays together."

The sense of the family altar as "family time" was likely enhanced by the fact that family worship became more interactive and dialogical in this era, reflecting the democratizing tendencies of the day. While father-led formal worship continued to be the rule in many households, by the mid-nineteenth century a growing number of family devotional aids recommended that family worship become more child-centered, with children assisting in these exercises by reading out loud, praying their own prayers, and choosing the songs to sing.[59] Presbyterian Joseph Collier noted that when families gathered for devotions, children would narrate Bible stories, recite verses, sing some of their own songs, and talk with their parents about the "grand themes of redemption."[60] Authors were increasingly antagonistic toward family worship experiences that were too solemn and adult-centered in their approach. Parents were encouraged to bring these exercises down to the children's level, making them attractive to them in order to excite their interest and establish these times as "cheerful" family activities.

This desire for family togetherness was also evidenced in changing perspectives on the Sabbath after the mid-nineteenth century. Earlier in the century, the recollections of those from more conservative and evangelical homes demonstrated a clear continuity with colonial practice. Famed Baptist pastor and Brown University president Francis Wayland recalled that on the Lord's Day all the children would be asked to "learn a hymn before dinner" (to be repeated to the mother) and a "portion of the Catechism before tea" (to be repeated to the father). After tea the whole family gathered in the parlor, where the father read "some suitable passage of Scripture, which he explained and illustrated, frequently directing the conversation so as to make a personal application to some one or other of us." Singing and prayer followed.[61] Heman Humphrey suggested that on the Sabbath children of all ages "ought not only to be confined within doors, but to be kept still, and to be employed as much of the time as they can be, without real weariness, in reading the Bible and other suitable religious books, and in receiving oral instruction."[62] One author, writing for the American Tract Society, chastised parents who allowed children to be "loitering idly, amusing themselves with ordinary sports, wrestling, playing at ball, roaming place to place, and visiting confectionaries," while also reprimanding parents who would walk in the fields with their children or take a "ride or a sail."[63]

However, for more liberal Protestants—and for a growing number of conservatives after midcentury—the Sabbath shifted to become a day of domestic enjoyment. Many began to argue that play was—at least for children—a form of rest, a proper means of renewal and restoration. Harriet Beecher Stowe, for example, distinguished the Sabbath needs of older people from the needs of children by indicating that the very relaxation and repose that was "invigorating to the disciplined Christian" was at the same time "a weariness to young flesh and bones."[64] For this reason, many argued that a day filled with delightful family activities was more likely to furnish true spiritual rest for children than tedious hours of religious study.[65] In this era, the compromise between strictness and laxity was often found in recommendations for "religious play" on Sundays. Authors increasingly recommended the Sunday use of newly designed children's picture books, diagrams, and toys such as miniature Noah's arks to provide pleasure to children in the absence of their normal amusements. Such playthings were often reserved for the Sabbath alone, setting them apart as special treats. In her 1835 novel *Home*, Catherine Sedgwick spoke of the Barclay family enjoying a Sabbath that included a walk by the seaside to reflect on God's creative beauty, time drawing Bible animals on a slate, and a pretend "class" in which children attempted to stump their parents on Bible trivia questions.[66]

The catechism instruction that previously took place on the Sabbath was often replaced with parent-led storytelling out of new illustrated children's Bibles and the fictional tales churned out by popular presses such as the American Tract Society and the American Sunday School Union.[67] Because the emerging Sunday schools took over biblical and doctrinal instruction, parents increasingly felt that they could give their time instead to these more relational and conversational forms of pedagogy that highlighted the intimacy of the parent-child bond and informal discussions about the life experiences of biblical and fictional characters. While some lamented the loss of more formal doctrinal instruction in the home, others argued that this new mode fit better with the desire to have children learn in a more engaging way that would connect to their experiences and meet their (more concrete) developmental needs.[68] In this kind of reading, as in family devotions, the heartbeat of Protestant home-based instruction was shifting from formal recitation to the more informal and intimate pedagogical interactions between parents (particularly mothers) and their children.[69]

In reality, Christian leaders increasingly spoke of the Sabbath as a day not for isolated study or formal practices but for the "cementing of domestic attachments."[70] In a setting where families were a bit more scattered because of work and school responsibilities, the "domestic Sabbath" was the one day set aside for "family activities," strengthening the cords of affection by spending the whole day with one another.[71] Sunday was now the one day that children could generally count on the presence of fathers in the home, so many authors commented on the ways in which fathers and children could spend quality and playful time together on these days.[72] In addition, by the second half of the nineteenth century, the "Sunday family dinner" had become a central practice, made possible by the gradual elimination of Sunday afternoon church services.[73] Such events became a focal point of family Sabbath togetherness, a means of solidifying family unity through fun family activities. As one historian observes, "The less time families had together, the more certain times came to matter to them—that is, as real time grew scarce, symbolic time loomed ever larger."[74]

All of this reflected a shift in the purposes and motivations of such family Christian practices. While many of the colonial acts of worship also marked Victorian-era Protestant households, the rationale for their importance was in this era rooted more self-consciously in the impact of these rituals on family cohesion and love. Even the language used to describe these practices reflected this change. Colonial authors spoke of family prayer, family worship, and the family sacrifice, each of which was meant to focus attention on the worshipful act and its God-directed purpose. By the mid-nineteenth century, the language of the "family fireside" reflected a more home-focused, relational gathering that put the emphasis on connections between family members. Rather than the Christian home serving primarily as a setting for Christian practices, Christian practices became key means of creating and sustaining the close-knit relationships of the Christian home.

And those family relationships increasingly formed the basis for Christian parents' future hope. The degree to which the home became a type of "heaven" in this era was actually demonstrated by the extent to which Victorian authors described heaven as a celestial "home."[75] Many portrayals of heaven minimized scenes of God-centered worship and highlighted instead the reuniting of family members enjoying their loving relationships in perfected homelike environments (sometimes living together in Victorian cottages complete with such middle-class staples as pianos, favorite food items, and cherished pets). John S. C. Abbott noted, "Parents and children will be associated in heaven. And when the whole household are happily assembled there, when they sit down together in the green pastures and by the still waters; when they go in and out at the mansions which God has prepared for them; then, and not till then, will they experience the fullness of the enjoyment with which God rewards parental fidelity. How full of rapture is the thought, that the whole family may meet again in the world of songs and everlasting joy."[76] Heaven was increasingly envisioned as glorious because it re-established family connections. Many authors concluded their reflections on heaven, in fact, with the family looking around and crying out with blissful excitement, "we are all here!"[77] If the home was depicted as an archetype of heaven, it only stood to reason that heaven would be pictured as the ideal happy home, a perfected family reunion.[78]

The Spiritual Power of Happy Memories

The centrality of these family relationships and activities set the groundwork for one of the novel emphases of nineteenth-century Protestant parenting: the formative power of memory. According to religious leaders, one of the most important forces for sustaining children's faith and safeguarding against wickedness was the deep-seated memory of a loving Christian home. The memory of childhood home relationships, in other words, would last throughout life and serve as a powerful force to keep children tethered to the faith even when they struck out on their own. As J. R. Miller put it, "There is no need for argument to prove the influence of the home memories in the formation of character. When one's childhood home has been true and sweet its memories never can be effaced. . . . Sorrows may quench every joy and hope, and the life may be crushed and broken. But the memory of the early home lives on like a solitary star burning in the gloom of night. . . . There is no surer way to bind them with chains of gold to God's throne."[79]

The importance of memory was linked to the theory of associationism.[80] Congregationalist pastor William Thayer spoke of the "law of association" that "embalms the scenes and events of early life in vivid recollection" and "unites one part of human experience to another, so that the recollection of the one suggests the other."[81] Within the advice literature of the day, parents were charged to create such associations, linking together the joy of family activities with the nurture of faith so that children would always have pleasant associations to draw them back into the fold. As parents played with children, celebrated key holidays, purchased special toys, spent time praying and singing by the fireside, and generally spent more family time together, these all became powerful tools to connect children's memories to the joys of a faith-filled home.[82] As pleasant memories were embedded into the child's very body, they would begin to associate the "mingled love and veneration" of the home and its relationships with religious ideals, creating a memory pathway to sustain the love of God.[83] As Collier indicated, "A happy childhood, passed in a Christian home, is an inestimable blessing; for the memories of our early years are the last to leave us; and when thus associated with the delights of piety, they form through life a winning and powerful plea for the blessedness of serving God."[84]

Memories were even more important in an era when children—especially sons—increasingly left the home for the morally compromised cities. As Presbyterian Thomas Moore suggested, "Even in the scene of temptation, the theatre, the ballroom, and the place of godless pleasure, as the young man remembers that loved ones at home are bending around the family shrine, and quivering lips are uttering the name of the absent child, the holy vision of this evening prayer shall come around the yielding heart as a talisman of resistless power against temptation."[85] This is perhaps why journeys back home were often the critical factors in prompting children's rededication to Christ in their adulthood. Returning to these sacred spaces—seeing the fireplace, holding the family Bible, noting the spot where bedtime prayers took place—would rekindle the pleasant memories of a faith-infused childhood and beckon the child back to the loving nurture of those days.[86] Authors regularly contrasted the pathways of young men who either did or did not have beloved memories to draw on during times of temptation. As H. A. Boardman put it,

> The youth who goes out into the world from a bad home, lacks the best of all restraints and safeguards. . . . He has no *past* to appeal to, or only one whose influences accelerate his downward course. No venerable form of an affectionate father rises up to admonish . . . no mother's hand pressed upon his infant head, as he kneeled at her feet in prayer—no gentle sister ministering to his daily pleasure with her unsolicited offices of kindness—no scenes of boisterous mirth with laughter-loving brothers . . . no jovial vacations—no morning and evening gatherings around the family-altar . . . no reminiscences like these come thronging around him, like a guard of angelic sentinels, to rescue him from impending danger.[87]

To create a home that possessed a family culture of love and togetherness was thus a key spiritual task, not only because it would keep children off the streets, but also because it would furnish powerful memories and associations between a loving family and that family's faith.

The power of memory was in many ways a new emphasis in Christian parenting. For obvious reasons, colonial parents were less apt to call on the value of childhood reminiscences. Many children and parents simply did not live long enough to cultivate such memories. Families were more fluid and permeable, meaning that many children spent time in multiple households with ever-changing combinations of people. Reminiscences were therefore not tied specifically to unique nuclear families or stable home environments in the same way they would be by the mid-nineteenth century.[88] Colonial family celebrations were also rare, eliminating childhood holidays from the cherished memories of adults. In fact, it may be fair to say that the colonial mindset was far more apt to look forward to heaven than to look backward to "heavenly" childhood associations. In the eyes of middle-class Victorian Protestants, however, when the childhood home became a "heaven on earth," the backward gaze became a powerful spiritual tool.

This shift represented a larger transformation in how Protestant child-rearing authors wanted children to experience God's character within the home. While colonial authors tended to highlight God's holiness, truth, and authority, asking parents to emulate these qualities in their own examples, these Victorian authors tended instead to highlight God's love, tenderness, and desire for a tight-knit relationship with his children. They asked parents to form more democratic and affectionate relationships with their children because this is how they wanted children to experience God's loving and even "cheerful" care in their lives. Protestant parenting, in this sense, demonstrated a revised understanding of God as one who was eager to draw near, forming bonds that could not be broken and preserving vulnerable children from being tempted by the false lovers around them. Such a vision, as it turns out, had significant implications for the way authority would be lived out in children's lives.

Discipline, Authority, and the Happy Home

The desire to foster a happy and "cheerful" Christian home, full of fun activities and memories, did not negate the need for parental discipline. However, for many Protestants, even this practice was revised in order to conform to the new ideals of the happy and affectionate home. Nineteenth-century authors emphasized the need for parents to attach authority to intimate and heartfelt relationships between parents and children rather than to formal hierarchy, fear, and deference. Only when discipline was linked to affection, they noted, would godly conduct be truly internalized within the child's life.

Most authors in the mid-nineteenth century still recognized the need for children's obedience, something that appeared far more difficult to secure in the wake of growing democratic and republican freedoms. As Heman Humphrey noted,

> There is, if I am not deceived, a reaction in our unparalleled political freedom, upon our domestic relations. It is more difficult than it was, half, or even a quarter of a century ago, for parents to "command their household after them." Our children hear so much about liberty and equality, and are so often told how glorious it is to be "born free and equal," that it is hard work to make them understand for what good reason their liberties are abridged in the family; and I have no doubt this accounts, in multitudes of instances, for the reluctance with which they submit to parental authority.[89]

Many observers seemed to concur with this assessment. Those from other countries reported that American children were disrespectful, unrestrained, and brazen in their confident willfulness. Attributing some of this to republican sensibilities and the desire for freedom from external authorities, many even commented that parents encouraged willfulness and self-assertiveness within their children, seeing this as a sign of precocious liberty.[90] As the colonial ideals of reverence, obedience, and recompense began to wane amidst calls for more democratic family relationships, many feared the consequences. Presbyterian H. A. Boardman stated bluntly, "Disrespect to parents has come to be one of the prominent characteristics of the times; one which stands out so conspicuously, that he must be blind who does not see it." Recalling the Old Testament and colonial Puritan law that condemned a "stubborn and rebellious son" to death, he concluded, "If such a law were enforced in *our* large cities, executions of this kind would become an every-day affair."[91]

While the need for obedience was clear, the pathway to achieving it was changing. Colonial leaders tended to highlight the perpetual importance of dutiful and submissive obedience to external authorities, but their

Victorian counterparts argued that the formation of "conscience" was the most important aim in a republican society. Drawing from Scottish common sense philosophy and its emphasis on the "moral sense," the goal was to develop what sociologist David Riesman calls the "inner directed" individual, someone who possesses a powerful internal sense of right and wrong derived from early parental training.[92] The motivation to obey, therefore, had less to do with external deference or fear of punishment and more to do with a deep-seated and internalized moral compass, an "internal parent" that would urge the child on to goodness and activate a self-condemning guilt if moral codes were violated. The invisible restraints of "self-control" and "self-government" would serve as the new basis of authority in a society that sought to be governed by noncoercive means. As Humphrey noted,

> Conscience . . . soon establishes her empire in the bosom of the child, so that he cannot be disobedient without a feeling of self-condemnation, which will act as a more powerful restraint, than the most positive requirements and prohibitions. *Command* your child, and if he sees you are in earnest, he will probably obey you. Show him the reason of the command, and he will yield more cheerfully. Appeal to his conscience, get that enlisted on your side, and you have a hold upon him which you never had before. You have gained an auxiliary, that will sometimes help you even when you are asleep yourself, and will often be more efficient when you are absent, than when you are present.[93]

The internal restraints of conscience were critical because many leaders felt that children were growing up in a culture that lacked many of the external restraints of previous eras. Middle-class moralists lamented the new mobile world in which innocent young people were cast adrift in an urban moral wasteland. The loss of key familial, church, and neighborhood moral communities diminished the watchful eyes of fellow community members and, in the eyes of critics, replaced traditional hierarchies with morally precarious peer relationships.[94] As Karen Halttunen has argued, story after story in this era related tales of wholesome rural young men enticed to drunkenness, gambling, and prostitution by urban "confidence men," deceivers who promised friendship to lonely newcomers while gradually leading them to debauchery.[95] One story, for example, told of a young man who was tempted toward immorality by a friendly city dweller, comparing this "friend" to a cat crawling through the grass and ready to pounce on a robin who was too early away from the nest.[96] Organizations such as the YMCA were founded for the purpose of providing a moral ballast for such young men, and a host of pastors wrote guides to protect and preserve those embarking on their adult journeys in this new and destructive moral terrain.[97] Parents, meanwhile, desired to instill strong consciences in their children so that they would be prepared to resist such temptations when they arose.

The appeal to conscience changed the way that many Protestants spoke of the child's willfulness. Among many conservatives, the concept of "subduing the will" maintained a steady following. Baptist leader and former Brown University president Francis Wayland, for example, was immortalized as a paternal disciplinarian by publishing an 1831 account of his extended work subduing the will of his defiant fifteen-month-old son. The process involved withholding food from him for nearly two days until the child finally relented and embraced his father with tears and kisses.[98] John S. C. Abbott, author of *Mother at Home*, similarly spoke of the need for the parent to "conquer" and "subdue" the child, while Charles Finney remarked that parents should "secure the earliest opportunity to get the mastery of the will" by keeping the child "in a state of unqualified submission and obedience."[99] Finney actually maintained the colonial connection between parental will breaking and children's ultimate ability to surrender themselves to Christ.[100]

Such approaches, however, were on the decline, especially after the mid-nineteenth century.[101] Horace Bushnell, in fact, spoke out directly against the "will breaking" mentality that characterized many earlier conservatives, asserting that this approach would either shut down the child with fear (which he called "the lowest of all possible motives") or produce a reactive stubbornness and mean-spiritedness.[102] The proper approach was "not to break, but to bend rather, to draw the will down, or away from self-assertion toward self-devotion, to teach it the way of submitting to wise limitations."[103] The will, for Bushnell and a growing number of Victorian Protestants, was not an intractable evil to be conquered but a pliable and ductile force that could be used to promote virtue and growth as parents harnessed it for good. Bushnell's recommendations regarding willful children served as a fitting counterpoint to Wayland's "battle" with his son:

> Beginning, then, to lift his will in mutiny, and swell in self-asserting obstinacy, refusing to go or come, or stand, or withhold in this or that, let there be no fight begun, or issue made with him, as if it were the true thing now to break his will, or drive him out of it by mere terrors and pains. This willfulness, or obstinacy, is not so purely bad, or evil, as it seems. It is partly his feeling of himself and you, in which he is getting hold of the conditions of authority, and feeling out his limitations. No, this breaking of a child's will to which many well-meaning parents set themselves, with such instant, almost passionate resolution, is the way they take to make him a coward, or a thief, or a hypocrite, or a mean-spirited and driveling sycophant— nothing in fact is more dreadful to thought than this breaking of a will, when it breaks, as it often does, the personality itself, and all highest, noblest firmness of manhood.[104]

While conservatives saw the child's willfulness in negative terms as an indicator of sin, Bushnell recognized the will as an important force of personality and a key means by which the child would develop an internalized conscience. The will, in other words, was necessary for the exercise of internal self-restraint that was so important in securing voluntary obedience. The will did not need to be destroyed, therefore, but rather bent and redirected so that it would serve God's purposes.[105]

It was in this sense that discipline was linked to the tight-knit relational bond between parents and children. Instead of commands and what colonial authors called "admonitions," many suggested that parents simply persuade their children by expressing their wishes. Even Humphrey, who was stronger than most in his appeal to parental authority, claimed that "there is a great advantage in administering family government, by the expression of our *wishes*, rather than by *positive commands*. The most obedient and affectionate children are those that have been accustomed from their cradle, to regard every wish of their mother, as a law of love, and rather to anticipate her desires, than to wait for any less gentle demonstration of her authority."[106] Through an affectionate parent-child bond, therefore, children would obey out of a desire to please their loving parents (and a dread of parental sadness) rather than out of fear or a sense of deference to parents' positional authority.[107] As Catherine Beecher indicated, "Love includes as its main feature *the desire to please* the one loved. The easiest and happiest way to induce obedience to law is so to secure a child's love that it will have a strong desire to please the one who controls."[108] "There is no constraint like that of love," Humphrey concluded. "It is the great law by which the holy family of heaven is sweetly governed."[109]

If obedience was increasingly tied to pleasing parents out of a sense of love, punishment was now linked to the loss of the loving parent-child relationship. Two new disciplinary methods found growing acceptance within this new emphasis: the appeal to wounded love and the threat of emotional and physical withdrawal. The first referred to those strategies that punished children by alerting them to the pain they inflicted on parents through their disobedience. If parents could develop strong emotional ties with their children through loving interactions, then children would develop a keen sensitivity to their parents' emotional states.[110] They would feel a strong sense of guilt when they "wounded" parents' hearts through disobedience, generating an internal motivation to please them and maintain relational harmony.[111] Children's obedience would be developed as they attempted to keep their parents in a happy emotional state, and prodigals would be called back, not through the fearful prospect of eternal torment or a call to restraint, but rather out of what one Baptist publication referred to as a "sacred regard to [parents'] feelings."[112]

The "invisible" punishment of "wounded love" was viewed as a powerful tool to restrain children from disobedience. When Thomas Teller recounted the story of his father reading each Saturday out of pink and black books in which were written all of their good and bad deeds for the week, he noted that he and his siblings were "much more impressed and punished by the deep distress we saw it gave him when there was much in the black book, than by anything else that could have been done to us."[113] In the fictional *Mother's Jewels*, an exchange between mother and child reflected a similar appeal: "Oh dear mother. I was thinking how dreadful it would be if I should be a bad boy. It would make you so sorry," the young son remarks. Encouraging this sentiment, the mother replies, "Yes, my son, it would almost break my heart. But as long as you are afraid of it, I do not think it will happen."[114] As historian Mary Ryan summarizes, "The magic of the parent's smile would win ready compliance, and the merest sign of displeasure upon a beloved parental countenance would restrain any improper action. The infant would become the emotional marionette of its parents."[115]

The second approach to discipline—emotional and physical withdrawal—threatened the young child with a loss of parents' affection or presence. Appealing to the loving parent-child relationship, parents believed that a child would be punished by removing this affection for a period of time. Colonial pastors like Cotton Mather actually experimented with this with their own children, but by the mid-nineteenth century it had become a very common practice. In one typical fictional account, a mother responds to her son's disobedience with a threat of emotional withdrawal: "I should not give you sweet kisses, I should not smile upon you, I should not receive your flowers, but I should have to separate you from my company." The son's response reveals the power of such an approach: "Mother, I should rather have your sweet kisses, and your pleasant smiles, than ten rolls of gingerbread. . . . I could not be happy if you did not love me."[116] Such approaches exploited the parent-child bond and the potent childhood fear of losing the parents' affection in order to secure a heartfelt obedience. "A child, gently trained by a gentle parent, receives the most poignant wounds through the heart," noted pastor Theodore Dwight. "I have seen a slight expression of disapprobation from such a parent produce a flood of tears in a young child. . . . The love of his parent and his Maker should be the leading strings of a child, and the fear of losing it a sufficient motive to deter them from evil."[117]

The increasing popularity of physical removal to one's room or a different part of the house—equivalent to contemporary approaches of "time out"—also reflected this emphasis. John S. C. Abbott noted that if a child was in an "excited state," the parent should "give him a comfortable seat by the fire, and tell him that he must not leave the chair for half an hour."[118] In a popular fictional account, Catherine Sedgwick told the story of Wallace Barclay, a ten-year-old boy who killed his sister's cat. As a punishment, the father informed Wallace that he must retire to his room because he had "forfeited [his] right to a place among us."[119] He was told that he was to stay isolated from the family until he gained control of his "hasty temper" and was willing to own and confess his sin. Two weeks of silence were required to reclaim the offender, who finally broke down and returned to his parents' presence. Parents clearly felt that the time of separation would both provide space for the workings of conscience and generate a longing for a happy reunion. The period of withdrawal was generally followed by a tearful confession and by a reinstatement accompanied by an outpouring of parental love and affection.[120] While colonial Protestants spoke mostly of disobedience as a breach against God's law that could alienate children from him (thus sparking the need for parental restraint), Victorian-era authors were far more likely to speak of obedience as fostering a good relationship with parents and misbehavior as causing a rift in the parent-child relationship. If children were to make their parents sad or lose their affection or presence, that would be its own punishment.

Because of the growing emphasis on strong and intimate parent-child relationships and the desire for a cheerful home, corporal punishment was increasingly rejected.[121] Physical punishment was of course still implemented, but discussions about this showed more hesitancy, urged more caution, and gave the rod a definitive "last resort" status. Autobiographical accounts across a wide variety of geographical, economic, and religious backgrounds rarely mention physical punishment as a common part of childhood experience.[122] Such punishment, Samuel Goodrich suggested, had been "altogether discarded by many, as degrading to human nature and injurious to the subjects of such discipline."[123] Many argued that physical punishment would create an emotional breach between parents and children, threatening the relationship and therefore the basis for ongoing parental influence. While colonial parents rejected severe punishment because of its impact on the child's view of God, it was the threat to the parent-child bond that served as a basis for much of the resistance to physical punishment after the mid-nineteenth century.[124]

These changes in parental discipline paralleled similar theological shifts in the ways people related to God.[125] Christian authors in the mid-nineteenth century tended to highlight God's loving care and the human need to respond to that love out of obedience. As Erastus Hopkins put it, "If your children love you, they will delight to please you, and they will feel sorrowful when they displease you. This is the way that we should all feel toward God; and this is the way you should train your little children to feel toward you."[126] Instead of fearing God's wrathful punishment in response to sin, authors encouraged a fear of disappointing a loving God, integrating into the divine relationship the "wounded love" paradigm of the parent-child bond.

Of course, comfort with these changes existed on a theological contin-
uum. Presbyterians and other Calvinists, maintaining stronger convictions
about the inherent sinfulness of children, were more likely to advocate
for strict discipline, parental deference, and corporal punishment. One
Presbyterian pastor lamented the "levelling system of the present age,"
noting that parents ought to utilize the rod and to exercise an authority
that was *early, absolute, and entire*."[127] "There is a growing disposition to
regard all punishment, and especially all corporal punishment, as cruel,
the relic of a barbaric age, and inconsistent with the benign era in which
we live," Presbyterian Thomas Moore noted. To dispense with the rod, he
warned, and to "attempt to govern children by moral suasion entirely, is
a thing as futile and foolish in a family as it would be in the state, and in
the end will bring a far heavier punishment on both parent and child."[128]
More liberal groups, on the other hand, tended to be more lenient with
regard to discipline, trusting that a parents' loving relationship would
lead to the development of a strong internal sense of right and wrong
without the need for the imposition of fear, autocratic commands, or
physical punishment. Most found themselves somewhere in the middle,
but among many groups discipline was evolving toward a gentler process
rooted in parental affection and the maintenance of strong relationships
between parents and children.[129]

It is important to note that the new forms of discipline were not
intended as means of diminishing parental authority. Instead, they were
envisioned as new and more effective tools for ensuring children's compliance.[130] Authors indicated that the new discipline was both a more
fitting mechanism of control in a democratic society and a more powerful
and long-lasting means of securing obedience. The locus of authority
changed from an external source of control with a power to punish to an
internal authority that also threatened to punish through the pangs of
unmitigated guilt. Children were still expected to obey their parents, but
they were now expected to do this out of love, gratitude, and relational
closeness rather than out of fear and deference. While foreign visitors
might scoff at the seeming impudence of "republican" children, therefore,
American religious leaders and child-rearing experts were quite insistent
that these approaches would bear greater and more enduring moral and
spiritual fruit. As Catherine Sedgwick argued, these children "might not
appear so orderly as they whose parents are like drill-sergeants, and who,

while their eyes are on the fugel-man, appear like little prodigies; but, deprived of external aid or restraint, the self-regulating machine shows its superiority."[131]

Focusing on the Family: Prospects and Pitfalls

After the mid-nineteenth century, Christian parents were increasingly called on to develop warm, affectionate, close-knit home relationships that would bind children to the nuclear family and that family's faith. By forming deep companionships, making memories through family time, and even setting up obedience as a desire to please loving parents, authors hoped that children would be woven into a loving fabric of "home sweet home" that would enfold them into their parents' faith.

The isolation, privatization, and sacralization of the "happy" nineteenth-century home had a number of long-lasting consequences that continue to shape the experience of Christian parenting. By emphasizing the importance of intimate relationships between parents, children, and siblings, Victorian authors displayed a growing recognition that the transmission of faith was not merely cognitive and didactic but also affective and relational in nature. In contrast to a colonial system in which distance was heralded as a means of fostering "reverence," these new approaches highlighted the ability of parents to identify with their children, to "get on their turf" and see the world from their point of view. Parents could show children that they were not just religious projects but loved and cherished companions worthy of time and investment outside formal Christian activities. The desire for parents to share their lives rather than just their teaching reflected Paul's own maternal metaphor in 1 Thessalonians 2:8 (NIV): "Because we loved you so much, we were delighted to share with you not only the gospel of God but our lives as well." Such a posture surely built relational trust that encouraged sharing and vulnerability through "confidential companionship." Parental modeling, in such a setting, had the potential to represent not just imitation but identification forged through close and supportive relationships.

Contemporary research on the Christian home has demonstrated that the transmission of faith from parents to children seems to be connected to these kinds of close-knit relationships.[132] Vern L. Bengtson, for example, recently found that children's likelihood of embracing parents' faith was very closely related to the degree of warmth and intimacy experienced between parent and child. He notes, "While most parents wanting to transmit their faith understand that their own examples and actions as parents are important in achieving success, some may not be aware that it is the nature and quality of the relationship they have with their child that is crucial—perhaps as much or more than what parents do or teach religiously."[133] Warm, affirming parenting, Bengtson suggests, is far more likely to lead to faith transmission than cold, distant, or authoritarian parenting, ambivalent or mixed-message parenting, or strained and preoccupied parenting. In his research, even children who strayed from the faith were more likely to return to the fold if they had close-knit relationships with their parents.[134] As Christian Smith and Amy Adamczyk recently confirmed, "Crucial in the parental transmission of religion to children is having generally *warm, affirming relations* with them."[135]

Likewise, Barna's 2019 research on Christian families, summarized in *Households of Faith*, revealed that spiritually vital families tended to be those that engaged in activities together, including games, reading, singing, and sports. Intentionality in relationship building, in other words, tended to "cross categories" so that the relational warmth forged through "quality time" bled over into a spiritual connectedness.[136] "Good fun, good work, and good faith seem to go hand in hand," the study's authors suggest, "indicating spiritual growth is yet another way of being present, interested and engaged in the lives of those around you."[137] Such studies seem to validate the nineteenth-century Protestant belief that the overall relational vitality of the home—including the good memories associated with "home sweet home"—is central to fostering and perpetuating faith across the generations. Such relationships seem to cement Christian convictions within children and make them harder to cast off as they grow.

Yet for all its advantages, this intensifying of the nuclear family "greenhouse" also may have diminished the communal resources available to parents and set the stage for an idolatry of the family unit. Victorian authors increasingly argued that parents had all the resources necessary within the nuclear family to raise their children up in the faith. A helpful image for understanding this shift comes in John Gillis's metaphor of the "temporal convoy," a descriptor he borrows from sociologist David Cheal. Gillis defines a temporal convoy as the "individuals who share a common sense of time, sustaining one another through challenges of life."[138] Gillis indicates that, for those in colonial New England, this convoy included the church and the local covenant community of faith. While one's nuclear family and kin were of course important, these Christians found their primary allegiance, loyalty, and sense of "family" together with their fellow believers. Such a communal convoy likely diluted the intensity of nuclear family relationships but also provided children access to a wide array of "religious archetypes and communal exemplars," people who could serve as mentors and models of "good life and good death."[139]

By the mid-nineteenth century, however, the nuclear family had become the clear "temporal convoy" for many Protestant Christian parents and children. The spiritual isolation of the home created a context in which one's parents were the chief teachers, mentors, and exemplars of the Christian faith. Of course, the church and the emerging Sunday schools played a role in educating children in the faith, but when it came to the people who shared a key role in the child's spiritual development, the nuclear family took more exclusive responsibility.[140] This posture tended to minimize the importance of the larger "family of God," shrinking the relational scope of Christian child-rearing to the confines of the individual home. As historian Margaret Bendroth puts it, "Each parent was, in the end, a lone priest and each child a single congregant in an isolated domestic church."[141]

This shift to the spiritual exclusivity of the nuclear family resulted in a diminishing sense that the larger church was the "first family" of the Christian disciple, a posture that continues to shape American Christian parenting.[142] It is in the nuclear family that many parents trace their true identity, linked to blood ties more than a shared adoption as sons and daughters of God. It is in the nuclear family that many parents locate their responsibilities, limiting spiritual and physical care to the members of their own household and minimizing commitments to the larger community of faith. It is in the nuclear family that many parents seek to build a legacy, viewing children and grandchildren as the solitary reference points for success and spiritual "fruit." It is even in the nuclear family that many seek spiritual validation and commendation—perhaps even their salvation. Yet Jesus himself decentered the nuclear family as the core source of human identity. When a woman cried out to him, "Blessed is the womb that bore you, and the breasts at which you nursed," his response was,

"Blessed rather are those who hear the word of God and keep it" (Luke 11:27–28). When someone told him that his mother and brothers wanted to speak to him, he said the following: "Whoever does the will of my Father in heaven is my brother and sister and mother" (Matt. 12:50). He noted that he had come to "set a man against his father, and a daughter against her mother," noting that at times "a person's enemies will be those of his own household" (Matt. 10:34–36). While none of this reflected a lack of appreciation for family relationships (Jesus, after all, loved his own mother deeply and appeared to his brother James after the resurrection), it did manifest a call to locate one's primary identity in God himself and in the larger spiritual family of believers.

All of this highlights the importance of seeing Christian parenting as a shared endeavor of the entire family of God. When parents bring their child before the congregation for baptism or dedication, this ceremony is often accompanied by the congregation's affirmation that they will help shepherd the child in the faith. This declaration serves as a reminder that the child is now embraced within the larger family of God, a reality that promises a host of spiritual brothers and sisters, aunts and uncles, parents and grandparents.[143] Parents are not meant to—and really cannot—walk this journey alone. As social beings, children need a larger web of mentoring relationships to nurture them in the faith through the various stages of their lives.[144] As James K. A. Smith notes, "One of the terrible lies of our culture—and even the rhetoric of 'family values'—is the crippling myth that our homes are self-sufficient incubators for child rearing."[145] This represents a challenge to our isolation, privacy, and autonomy. At the same time, as Smith indicates, it offers a hopeful sense of mutual support: "We don't have to raise these kids on our own!"[146]

The deep connection in the Victorian era between family intimacy and the child's Christian growth also created a setting ripe for idolatry. Colonial authors repeatedly warned parents to be very careful about idolizing their children and spouses, reminding them that God must be first in their hearts. By the mid-nineteenth century, however, such warnings had essentially vanished. As the Christian life was linked so closely to the fellowship between parents and children, it was just a short journey to the place where the family itself became the object of worship.[147] Some of this came in the worship of family members: the saintly mother, the godly father, or the angelic offspring in child-centered homes. Some of it came in the worship of the family unit, viewing family relationships and time together as uniquely spiritual and precious. All of this reflected G. K. Chesterton's observation of Victorian England that "theirs was the first generation that ever asked its children to worship the hearth without the altar."[148]

Of course, the altar was still present, and most families continued practices of corporate worship both in the church and in the home. The calls to sustain such practices, however, had changed in focus and tone. When family worship was envisioned more as a means of enhancing family togetherness than as a means of connecting children to God, it revealed a shift at the heart of Christian parenting. When obedience was linked to pleasing parents and disobedience to hurting parents' feelings, it seemed to prioritize the sacred parent-child bond over divine decree. The colonial home was called a "little church" because it housed practices of worship that were designed to lead children into the very presence of God. In the Victorian era, however, the home became "the church of childhood" because it set them within family relationships that were increasingly described as the "end" of the Christian life.[149] In fact, Christian practices were often described as instrumental means to achieve these familial ends.

In many ways, as Colleen McDannell has argued, the sacralization of the home led directly to the deification of human love. As she points out, it was the home, not the church, that was the archetype of heaven because it was the closest reflection of the "romantic love, family life, and Christian values" that were now so esteemed.[150] And heaven itself was anticipated because it would carry these joys into eternity. While this certainly gave people an earthly reference point for understanding the joys of heaven, it may have also decentered the worship of God as the principal source of heavenly ecstasy. In order to protect themselves from a false idolatry and preserve God's centrality, Christian parents in the seventeenth and eighteenth centuries continually reminded themselves that their earthly relationships were but temporal echoes of the greater intimacy with Christ that awaited them in eternity.[151] Beginning in the nineteenth century, however, it became far more common to view the treasured relationships of the nuclear family as eternal in nature, continuing into the heavenly realm and in many ways constituting its greatest joys. Family bonds, particularly those between parents and children, had become the primary source of eschatological anticipation for a growing number of Protestant Christians.

Such idolatry, of course, could lead to an inward-looking focus on one's own nuclear family. It could limit hospitality as well as evangelism and service to those beyond the walls of the home. Victorian-era writers seemed to devote most of their parenting advice to the creation of parent-child intimacy, giving little space to engaging children in a mission outside the family. A focus on the family revealed a desire to harness the power of close-knit family relationships to foster children's faith, loyalty, and obedience. At the same time, it had the potential to reduce a child's vision of Christianity to the narrow "temporal convoy" of one's own parents and siblings. When family intimacy became the primary purpose of the "heavenly" home, it also had the potential to become the primary purpose of the Christian faith.

Conclusion

The Legacy and Future of Christian Parenting

> Above and beyond any other effect on children's religion is the
> influence of their parents.
>
> —Christian Smith and Amy Adamczyk,
> *Handing Down the Faith*[1]

The overarching shift in Christian parenting advice from the colonial era through much of the nineteenth century was from a model
that emphasized content-heavy household religious practices to one
that emphasized the development of a nurturing and relational home
environment. The colonial pastors who gave out advice through printed
sermons and lectures had a very clear picture of what it meant to be a
"good" Christian parent. Colonial parents were to be evangelists, alerting
their children to their sinful state and to the perils of eternal damnation while urging them to come to Christ for salvation. They were to be
priests, praying for their children, guiding them in morning and evening
worship (Bible reading, singing, and prayer), supervising their Sabbath
practices in church and at home, and leading them into their own practices of devotion. These parents were also to serve as prophets, teaching
biblical and doctrinal truths both formally through reading and the catechism and informally in the midst of children's activities. Finally, parents
were to assume authoritative positions as kings, leading children toward
reverence, obedience, and recompense while also correcting children's
disobedience through admonition, restraint, and the rod. From the early
seventeenth century to the middle years of the eighteenth century, parents,
as stewards representing God's purposes, sought to utilize these postures

and practices to foster conversion—a Spirit-empowered awakening—in their children's lives.

By the mid-nineteenth century, much of the advice literature of the day communicated a new vision of good Christian parenting. Composed by pastors but also by women and other laypeople, new resources emphasized the determinative power of the impressions generated within the home by loving parents. Authors told parents that children were most deeply formed in the earliest years by the physical environment of the home, the intentional nurture and love of parents, and the deep relationships forged among family members. The home itself became a sacred space in which shared family activities (both religious and nonreligious) would create wonderful memories that children would associate with the family's faith. Parents were directed to spend ample time with children and to encourage sibling friendships so that the faith would be embedded into children's lives in an enduring way. Even traditional practices such as worship, teaching, and discipline were rooted in this relational space, derived from and contributing to the home's relational bonds. The relationship between children and their mothers, in particular, was held up as formative in nature. Mothers' sacrificial love and purity would nurture children in their younger years and then protect them (especially sons) when they left home for more dangerous settings. For these authors, the relational environment of "home sweet home" was the best means of raising children up in the faith. Some coupled these newer ideas with traditional desires for conversion, while others saw God at work more within the natural and nurturing interactions of the Christian home.

Even when common practices were engaged across these time periods, there were decided changes in parenting styles. When colonial Christian authors described parents as evangelists, priests, prophets, and kings, they saw them as authorities, teachers, and leaders, people who would proclaim, warn, teach, correct, and exemplify the faith for their children. When Victorian-era authors described parents as architects, mothers, and memory-makers, they saw them as nurturers, companions, and mentors, loving guides who would establish a warm and supportive environment within which impressionable children would develop in faith and obedience through early emotional connections. Of course, both styles existed across this entire time period. Colonial parents loved their children and delighted in them even as they engaged in the daily practices of faith.

Likewise, nineteenth-century Christian parents still engaged in Christian practices, including the family altar. Yet the relative importance attributed to more formal and hierarchical "content-centered practices" and more informal and democratic "impression-centered relationships" was clearly shifting across these years.

These different visions of Christian parenting clearly shaped the way parents engaged in their roles. With regard to teaching, colonial parents sought to instruct their children in the biblical and theological foundations of the faith, both directly through Bible reading and catechism training and indirectly in the midst of everyday life experiences. Children whose minds were corrupted by sin needed regular doses of truth, teaching that would help them understand God, themselves, and their world while opening the door to the Holy Spirit's transformative work. With the rise of Sunday schools and changing beliefs about children, nineteenth-century authors tended to focus on more indirect forms of teaching, coming chiefly through the "hidden curriculum" of household impressions and the more relational pedagogy of discussion and storytelling. Viewing children as radically open to environmental shaping, they tended to see the entire scope of a child's physical and relational world as "teaching" the child about God, about themselves, and about the Christian faith as a whole.

With regard to authority, colonial parents saw themselves as possessing a God-given governance within the hierarchy of creation that was meant to lead children toward reverent obedience to external authority. In asking parents to "subdue" children's wills, authors were directing them to furnish a context in which children would willingly surrender themselves to God in conversion. In times of disobedience, parents sought to teach and admonish, restrain, and, if all else failed, correct through the rod. Victorian authors, while still encouraging obedience, wanted this to come voluntarily through the development of an internalized conscience. This conscience would be activated through a relational intimacy with parents that would make children always want to please and never want to disappoint them or lose their favor and presence. Since more felt that the will was to be bent rather than broken, love and affection became more critical tools than fear and authority. In fact, many began to compare this to the way that humans should relate to God, obeying him not out of fear of punishment but out of a desire to please—and never disappoint—this loving and divine Parent. Less hierarchical and more democratic, this form of authority was more clearly grounded in the parent-child relationship than submission to external commands.

Finally, with regard to worship and spiritual formation, colonial parents saw much of this happening through distinct worshipful practices centered within the home and through parental prayer. As families gathered for the daily "sacrifice," they engaged God through Bible reading, psalm and hymn singing, and prayers that reflected the redemptive story of the gospel. On the Sabbath, such activities were extended and combined with lengthy church services. Parents prayed for their children's salvation, sanctification, and protection, recognizing their own inability to bring about these supernatural results. While nineteenth-century authors also recommended the daily family altar, they often spoke of this "fireside" activity as a time of family connection and an antidote to family squabbles. Sabbaths were more often used for family activities that would deepen family relationships. In fact, family time was itself seen as a powerful means of spiritual formation, a way in which children would develop memories associated with family members that would keep them tethered to the family's faith. These authors also gave a good deal more attention to the power of the home environment, both in the sense of the physical space and in the sense of parents' examples and daily interactions with their children. Daily and more individualized reading and discussion times with mothers began to eclipse formal father-led devotions in relative importance within children's lives.

These alternative visions of Christian parenting reflected a number of cultural and theological changes. From the cultural angle, homes were clearly changing. Colonial homes were physically small, but they housed a large number of children and a diverse group of people. Though families were still nuclear in structure (parents and children living in the same home, rarely with multiple families or generations), boundaries between private and public spheres were quite porous, with children often spending time in other households and sharing space with servants, apprentices, and relatives. Family relationships were hierarchical and patriarchal, with parents, especially fathers, possessing a governing authority in their children's lives. Such a context encouraged an approach to Christian parenting that was more deferential and rooted in formal practices.

By the mid-nineteenth century, Northern middle-class households looked quite different. Some of this related to a growing privacy and isolation, as families tended to shrink around the nuclear core. Fewer children left the home, and fewer servants and relatives came to live within the home. Parents also had fewer children, meaning they could devote more time and relational nurture to each one. Hierarchies diminished as family relationships grew more democratic, egalitarian, and child-centered. Patriarchy also declined as fathers lost some of the power of inheritance and also began working in settings removed from the home. Freed from their former contributions to the family economy, mothers now located their central identities in child-rearing and in their children's moral and spiritual formation. All of these changes tended to highlight the nuclear family's relational bonds, placing these front and center in a Christian parent's toolbox.

Theologically, these disparate visions were connected to shifting views of children and God. For colonial authors, children were stained by original sin and therefore existed in a state of eternal spiritual peril. Children's greatest "problem" was internal, a "dead" soul in need of salvation. The goal, therefore, was conversion, the Holy Spirit's work of alerting them to their sin and awakening them to their need for a Savior. Children were blind and thus in need of the spiritual "sight" of Jesus. Their minds were corrupted and so in need of Spirit-illumined doctrinal truth. They were naturally willful and so in need of restraint. The parenting practices colonial authors encouraged were designed to lead children to these places. Parents' warnings would alert children to their perilous state. Their prayers would open children's eyes. Family worship would help them confess their sin and encounter the beauty of Christ. Catechetical teaching would help them understand their condition and Christ's work on their behalf. Authority and discipline would subdue children's wills, placing children under their parents' rule and preparing them to do the same with God as they grew. Much emphasis was placed on "youth," in part because by that age children were able to understand more of the gospel and also respond to the convicting presence of the Holy Spirit. In fact, since parents saw their children as belonging to God, all of these parental postures were designed to prepare children to submit to Christ as their ultimate evangelist, priest, prophet, and king. Parents wanted their children to see God as someone who desired their salvation, who was worthy of their worship, who was himself the Truth, and who deserved a reverent obedience. He was to be their herald, their sacrifice, their teacher, their ruler. Parents echoed these roles for their children, but their real goal was to place them in his saving arms.

By the mid-nineteenth century, beliefs about children's natures were far more varied and complex, ranging from continued affirmations of total depravity to breathless celebrations of their angelic innocence. Amidst the various perspectives emerging at the time, however, the general shift was to diminish the gravity of original sin and to emphasize instead the radical openness of children to the shaping power of the environment. Whether children were viewed as blank slates or idyllic cherubs, children's greatest threat was external, a corrupting environment that would skew them in unhelpful ways. This is what in many ways fostered the belief that the environmental impressions of the home would be the most powerful forces for spiritual development, pressing goodness into the soft wax of children's souls so that they would be gradually shaped in Christian character and prepared to face the challenges beyond the home. It is also what precipitated the emphasis on early childhood as the most pivotal moment for spiritual impact.

This call for a nurturing and relational environment reflected changing perspectives on God in this era. Emerging cultural and theological changes worked to promote a view of God as less wrathful, more congenial, and more given to relate to humanity through love rather than fear. This certainly highlighted the maternal virtues that operated in the private sphere of nurture and loving sacrifice. In general, however, it also emphasized a loving relationship with God that would be cultivated through intimate parent-child and family relationships. Parents wanted their children to see God as someone who desired a close-knit relationship with them, an affectionate bond that would ensure their voluntary and heartfelt desire to stay with him through all of life. As in the colonial era, parents were to reflect God's nature to their children. The nature of that God, however, had shifted in significant ways.

Protestant Parenting and the Challenges of the "Modern" Family

As Americans entered the early decades of the 1900s, Protestant parenting advice literature again began to shift, though in ways that still bore the marks of these earlier visions. In part, the changes in the twentieth century were a function of new authorship. While parenting advice was communicated chiefly by pastors in the colonial era and by a combination of ministers, women, and other lay leaders in the nineteenth century, by the early twentieth century a new cadre of parenting "experts" had emerged. Beginning in the late nineteenth century, a host of psychologists, sociologists, educators, and doctors began to conduct serious inquiry into the nature and status of the child. Professionalizing what had been the work of lay "child savers" in the late nineteenth century, these "child study" theorists worked to bring the academic rigor of the new social sciences to the study of child development.[2] Many viewed parents as incapable, on their own, of raising healthy and flourishing children. In a move toward what Christopher Lasch has called the "proletarianization of parenthood," authors began arguing that mothers and fathers must avoid their own "common sense wisdom" and instead place their confidence in experts, both the specialized professionals in outside institutions (teachers, doctors, counselors, etc.) and trusted scholars (especially psychologists and sociologists) who would provide parenting advice based on empirical research.[3] "Mother love" was not enough and in some cases might even be dangerous to the child's emotional health. Instead, mothers needed science to tell them how they should raise their children.[4]

And those experts were abundant. Medical professionals, now specialized within the new field of "pediatrics," provided wisdom on issues of feeding, nutrition, sleep schedules, disease prevention, and sex education.[5] Child psychologists, following the lead of G. Stanley Hall, provided insights into a child's developmental stages, looking specifically at issues of personality, mental and emotional health, and behavioral problems.[6] Not to be outdone, professionals in the new field of "religious education" drew chiefly on the social sciences of psychology, sociology, and education to provide directives on how parents should meet children's spiritual needs in keeping with best practices.[7] As Lasch has argued, the "socialization of production," in which labor was removed from the household and collectivized in factories, was followed by the "socialization of reproduction," in which child-rearing wisdom was removed from the home and given over to teachers, psychiatrists, child guidance counselors, doctors, religious professionals, and other experts.[8] This trend reached a tipping point in the early twentieth century as the home's monopoly over childhood was broken and its functions increasingly redistributed to other professionals and organizations.

One of the clear implications of the move toward expertise in this era was the growing push to professionalize Christian parenting through intentional parent education. Stemming from the work of groups such as the Parent and Teachers Association (PTA) of America (formerly the National Congress of Mothers) and the National Council of Parent Education, many Protestant churches, especially in the mainline denominations, developed national committees promoting parent education and also sponsored a broad array of educational seminars in local congregations in order to bring scientific insights to Christian parents.[9] In some cases, Sunday schools took this up, providing parent seminars or adult education classes devoted to home issues. In New York, a number of parent-education study groups were formed in local churches (one study mentioned seventy-five of these representing six denominations), looking at such issues as parent-child relationships, religion, sex education, home life, and mental and physical health.[10] Regarding the need for experts, George Walter Fiske noted, "We need them to teach parents how to teach religion to their children. . . . Our parents need expert guidance, that they themselves may become expert guides."[11]

By the 1920s, much of this "expert" parenting literature described the challenges faced by families as they attempted to develop faith within their children. Chief among the threats was the "centrifugal" nature of modern society, a force that thrust both parents and children outside the home for the majority of the day.[12] Parents, many argued, had fallen prey to the jazz-era "go-craze," mothers giving their time to theater, opera, and bridge, while fathers left the home for their clubs, lodges, and rounds of golf. Busy school, work, and activity schedules meant that less time was available for shared meals and religious exercises. Children, the recipients of increased leisure time, were lured out of the home by the growing world of public entertainment. Theaters, dance halls, sports venues, and other commercialized amusements provided novel and alluring spaces for youth to gather without their parents.[13] Because cars now allowed young people to stray beyond their homes and local communities, youth were afforded a degree of moral anonymity that loosened the built-in restraints of communal watchfulness.[14] In fact, while nineteenth-century "courting" required the couple to enjoy structured time in close proximity to family members, the advent of "dating" in the 1920s meant that relationship formation now often took place in locations outside the home and far beyond parents' watchful eyes.[15] As one Christian leader put it, "When young people are permitted the use of automobiles to go where they please and to park in secluded places at night and engage in familiarities which would not be tolerated in true love or a Christian home, we cannot help but say that the automobile is a great tool of Satan and that these practices are the enemy of the home."[16]

Many were especially concerned about the ways in which these centrifugal forces were influencing the Sabbath. More and more people were called on to work on Sunday, reflecting the loss of this day's unique status. Children were more likely to use Sunday to complete homework for Monday school classes.[17] More importantly, the availability of a growing number of outside amusements made it more challenging to maintain the Sunday emphasis on sacred activities. The pull of commercial amusements, many of which were now open on Sundays, proved difficult to resist. While museums and libraries began opening up on Sundays in the second half of the nineteenth century, by the 1920s these were joined by a growing number of theaters, amusement parks, saloons, golf courses, and baseball parks.[18] As railways and streetcars expanded service, traveling to parks and beaches became popular Sunday activities. In addition, by the 1920s the allure of the "Sunday drive" was often quite strong, pulling people away from the home and from opportunities for church involvement, reading, prayer, and family devotions.[19] All of this led popular Christian author Margaret Sangster to lament that Sundays had become "holidays" rather than "holy days."[20]

Religious critics worried that life in the early twentieth century had become too consumed with frenetic activity, stifling opportunities for family reading, devotions, and other spiritual activities. Some, in fact, indicated that the insatiable longing for entertainment rendered children and youth unable to participate attentively in family religious exercises. George Walter Fiske spoke of how young people would come home and "immediately switch on the radio" because the "quiet in the place seems to oppress them."[21] Parents complained that children had a harder time sitting through family devotions or engaging in prolonged prayer. In fact, Presbyterian James Smylie pointed to the 1916 publication of *God's Minute: A Book of 365 Daily Prayers Sixty Seconds Long for Home Worship* as a clear indicator of what children would tolerate when it came to the practice of family devotions.[22] The main concern here was that children were so overstimulated by the delights of the world outside the home that they could no longer be content with the more subdued tones of family religious practice. "This eager generation is living by the speedometer rather than the compass," Fiske pointed out. "Too much ginger dulls the appetite for bread."[23]

Even when families did share space, many found that homes were less conducive to parental guidance in spiritual formation. The growth of electric power meant that family members no longer needed to gather around a central light source or fireplace but could spread out in different rooms of the home. The introduction of innovations such as the radio, telephone, and television threatened to isolate and distract family members by consuming their time with individualized activities that appealed to their lower natures. Some also noted that urban families, now living more often in cramped homes and apartments, desired to flee these confining environments for outside pleasures.[24] As homes themselves became more casual, efficient, and functional, parlors were replaced by living rooms and much of the religious decor was removed.[25] In short, what had been lost was the "home-centered life" that nineteenth-century families had set up as the pinnacle of a Christian upbringing.[26] In such a context, authors feared, there was little opportunity to develop common interests and life experiences that would establish the loving connections and memories—and the deep environmental impressions—required for strong parental nurture.

Closely related to this, authors on Christian parenting recognized that more and more of children's Christian formation was shifting to outside organizations. While the home had been the assumed center of children's religious training through the nineteenth century, by the 1920s other institutions began to eclipse parental dominance in this arena. Sunday schools continued to grow and professionalize. Public schools increasingly offered programs of "released time" religious education in which ministers of various faiths and denominations provided teaching to students during the school day, many granting academic credit for successful completion.[27] Beginning with such groups as Christian Endeavor in the 1880s, a host of clubs and organizations, some denominational and others more national in scope (e.g., Boy Scouts, Girl Scouts, Boys' Brigade, Pioneer Girls, YMCA, and YWCA), emerged to guide children and youth in matters of faith. This "exporting" of Christian nurture left many concerned about parents' ongoing roles in their children's faith formation. While the nineteenth-century household had surrendered many of its educational, medical, and vocational tasks, it now seemed as if families were ready to contract even further by farming out children's religious lives to other institutions. By relying on a specialized professional to oversee their children's spiritual formation, Fiske quipped that parents were essentially saying, "'Here is my check, Lord; send him!' 'Here is my paid minister, my hired director of religious education, my paid church-school teacher—now make my child religious!'"[28]

With a host of new commercial amusements competing for children's time and a variety of organizations taking over the religious functions of the household, the home was defined not as the center of a child's life but as a space to quickly rest and refuel before re-entering the public sphere. "The transition is now complete," one lamented. "The home is simply that item in the economic machinery which will best furnish us storage for our sleeping bodies and our clothes!"[29] In such a setting, where parents saw themselves as facilitating their children's engagement with outside ministries, a "parent as chauffeur" metaphor seemed more and more appropriate. In addition, in a context where children now experienced "crosscutting sources of identity" in their various institutional involvements, parents were increasingly called on to serve not as teachers but as interpreters and coordinators, helping children navigate the various beliefs and opinions competing for their loyalty.[30]

Some of this parental crisis involved the changing values of this new era. A number of critics worried that fewer couples seemed eager to enter into responsibilities of marriage and parenting. Several spoke out against the growing tendency for young adults—male "marriage slackers" and female "bachelor maids"—to delay marriage or avoid it altogether, blaming much of this on the selfish pursuit of pleasure.[31] Fiske contended that young men and women increasingly acted like "self-indulgent children, accustomed always to make 'a good time' their chief end in life." "It is time," he argued, "they grew up, settled down and began to take life seriously, instead of regarding it as one big amusement park, run for their childish pleasure."[32] Furthermore, some railed against the emerging popularity of "companionate marriage," an arrangement in which couples married purely for personal and sexual pleasure without the promise of permanence (divorce rates were rising in this era) and without a commitment to the bearing and raising of children. Sociologist Ernest Groves called this new pattern "the arrested family," one in which individual interests and pursuits trumped the formation of a cohesive spiritual unit.[33] Further declines in birthrates in this era were often blamed on parents who felt that children would inhibit their financial progress or stifle their passion for entertainment. "If any are willfully childless, choosing to have it so, to escape the pain and trouble and interference with their own pleasures," Presbyterian George Luccock noted, "they commit a great sin."[34]

Critics were hardest on women, claiming that their new affinity for higher education and career aspirations had blunted their maternal instincts. In commenting that "it takes three graduates of Bryn Mawr to produce one child, or five of the honors scholars of Wellesley," Fiske highlighted the reticence of highly educated women to marry and have children.[35] Many feared that the increasing standard of living fueled by a double-income family would create an ongoing appetite for consumer goods, continued employment for both parents, and the loss of family time.[36] The key for most was that a working mother, gone for many hours from the home and weary upon her return, could not invest the time and energy in her children to nurture them in the faith. "Even when at home," Groves concluded, "the mother is likely to be too tired to deal wisely with her children or to give them a normal expression of mother-love."[37] Some lamented that mothers relied more on older children to care for their younger siblings, thus depriving them of concentrated maternal attention. All of this seemed to indicate that the primary maternal quality of "sacrifice" was eroding as women grew more autonomous, independent, and concerned for their own economic and social advancement. Many Christian authors felt that this "industrialization of womanhood" threatened to undermine the mother-centered framework of Christian nurture that had bolstered the nineteenth-century home.[38]

While these issues threatened the separate spheres ideology that celebrated women's domestic contributions, other factors led some to question whether the qualities of "true womanhood" were vanishing altogether in the wake of the new youth culture of the 1920s. Both the sacrificial love and the radical purity of mothers appeared threatened by the rise of the 1920s "flapper." Many saw the immorality of girls and young women, whether viewed in terms of immodesty in dress, dancing, drinking and smoking, or the use of foul language, as symbolic of the utter demise of

American culture because of the critical moral role ascribed to mothers in the society. In a culture that had glorified the purity of women and the need for this to compensate for male immorality, the blurring of male and female spheres was indeed a significant cause for concern.[39] As Paula Fass states so precisely, "Gazing at the young women of the period, the traditionalist saw the end of American civilization as he had known it. Its firm and robust outlines, best symbolized by the stable mother secure in her morality and content in her home, were pushed aside and replaced by the giddy flapper, rouged and clipped, careening in a drunken stupor to the lewd strains of a jazz quartet."[40] Groves stated in the 1920s that many women, drawn to the allurements of leisure and luxury, became "discontented, restless, parasitic, shirking, and intolerant of home obligations."[41] The intoxicating brew of personal freedom and moral laxity, according to many, had raised expectations for personal fulfillment and decimated the maternal moral impulse.

Conflicting messages for fathers continued to be the norm. In the late nineteenth and early twentieth centuries, many were concerned that the church (and Christianity in general) had become overly "feminized," plagued by a weak and effeminate vision of Jesus and given over to the sentimental and maternal vision of love, emotional vulnerability, and relational intimacy that seemed to favor women and children while dampening the vigor of the male character. The growing calls for men in the early twentieth century to facilitate the masculine socialization of their sons were in part related to the fear that boys were growing up either too effeminate (owing to the continual presence of mothers and female teachers) or too delinquent (owing to their attempts to express their masculinity in unhelpful ways). Christian fathers, many argued, could help this "boy problem" by developing masculine traits within their sons while also channeling these qualities in fruitful ways for the kingdom of God. Fathers, many argued, must show their boys that Christianity could be both masculine and pure, drawing on the athletic, business, military, and medieval metaphors of the day to promote a vigorous and manly pursuit of both personal and social goodness. A host of new boys' clubs and organizations gave men a chance to socialize their sons in a more "muscular" vision of Christ.[42]

By the 1920s, some of this call for "muscular Christianity" had dissipated. As social science appeals to mental health and personality eclipsed calls for sex-role socialization, fathers were again relegated to the background. Scientific experts directed their child-rearing advice to mothers, leading fathers to feel less competent in this domain. Fathers' breadwinning function only increased as families in a flourishing economy became more reliant on consumer goods and experiences to anchor both status and happiness. In addition, within this more democratic age, many began to argue that significant paternal authority was detrimental to children's growing personalities. Far more beneficial, experts argued, was a kind of playful companionship that furnished a healthy camaraderie. While fathers were often described as role models, therefore, the most frequent label by the 1920s was that of "pal." Continuing the trends begun in the nineteenth century, the "culture of daddyhood" between 1916 and 1930 was based on the idea that fathers were best suited for playful banter, sports, and leisure-time activities than for any kind of nurture or instruction.[43]

Polarized Parenthood:
The Ongoing Influence of Colonial and Victorian Models

With all these challenges facing Christian parents in this era, there emerged two distinct camps—fundamentalists and modernists—that interpreted both the parenting crisis and its potential solutions in vastly different ways.[44] On the one hand, Protestant conservatives and fundamentalists tended to see the family and the broader culture descending into moral chaos. They therefore urged parents to defend their children against the godless and immoral trends around them by recapturing what authors often called "the old-fashioned home." By this they seemed to imply something like a combination of the colonial vision and select components of the Victorian approach. They wanted parents to teach biblical and doctrinal truth to their children as a means of combatting modernist heresy. "Home Bible reading" in this era, according to Colleen McDannell, "marked one as a conservative Protestant" who was opposed to modern and progressive trends.[45] In an era when many complained about the loss of the "family altar," they wanted to restore and strengthen the practice of daily family worship. William Edward Biederwolf, a popular evangelist and later director of the famous Winona Lake Bible Conference, formed the Family Altar League in 1909 to inspire parents to return to the "old-time" practice of family worship, asking members to commit to reading Scripture and praying with their families.[46] Many on the conservative side wanted to maintain as much of the Victorian Sabbath as possible. While most agreed that the Puritan Sabbath was too restrictive and burdensome, they clearly maintained the importance of keeping this as a day set apart for religious activities. Clarence Benson, a professor at Moody Bible Institute, instructed parents, "The Sabbath should always be different from other days. Clean clothes and everything that is new and best should appear on Sunday, and Bible books and Bible games should be held in reserve for this particular day."[47]

Conservatives also wanted to see a return to the nineteenth-century gendered division of labor that had anchored the Christian family. They wanted fathers to be restored to their priestly roles, and they wanted mothers to resist the allure of outside careers so that they could return to their roles as virtuous homemakers.[48] Fundamentalists did not, however, tend to base their call for intensive mothering on the presumed spiritual superiority of women. While nineteenth-century Protestants had invested women with unique spiritual sensitivity, purity, and love, fundamentalists wanted to preserve men's spiritual stature and argued more in terms of the fact that God had uniquely fitted women for the home.[49] George R. Stuart, addressing attendees at the Winona Lake Bible Conference, suggested that woman was made by God for the home while man was made for the public world of work. Just as a duck was made to thrive in the water rather than on the land or in the air, he noted, the woman was made to thrive within her sphere of the home. "If God had intended the woman to share the burdens of men and the men to share the burdens of women equally," Stuart remarked, "he would have divided the milk!"[50] While they did not sacralize the home or elevate mothers to angelic status like many in the nineteenth century, fundamentalists did see Victorian gender roles as an important means by which families could preserve strong Christian parenting in turbulent times.[51] Not surprisingly, they also commended parents—especially fathers—who upheld authority and were willing to impose strict discipline in order to restrain children from their sinful impulses. In these ways, conservatives and fundamentalists hoped that the home could again become a bastion of Christian holiness that would serve as a shelter from the evils of both godless modernism and the moral decay they saw all around them.[52]

Liberals and modernists, on the other hand, saw 1920s social changes as ushering in a new age of progress and possibility. Rather than defending their homes against evil, liberals hoped that parents would assist children in their adaptation to the changes of the new world. They were more concerned with the social relationships and daily interactions between family members than they were with formal religious practices.[53] Liberal Protestants often believed, in fact, that the family altar of the "old-fashioned home" was a barrier to true religious growth. Drawing quite explicitly from Horace Bushnell, they viewed systematic Bible teaching and the teaching of doctrine as too disconnected from the problems of family and social life. Modernists hoped to lean into the scientific and democratic postures of the day in order to supplant traditional Protestant family worship within the home. One of their chief innovations was a move to problem-based group discussions within the family. Drawing from the contributions of John Dewey and the progressive education movement, liberal religious educators recommended that families start, not with Christian content, but with a set of social or personal problems to be solved. True Christian teaching, one noted, was "more apt to flow from some vital discussion of family problems."[54] Gathering around the fireside for "group thinking," the family could discuss a sibling's college choice, how to respond to a difficult friend, and many other vexing questions, using the Bible not as a text to be learned and memorized but as one potential resource for solving such problems.[55]

Appealing to such democratic ideals, modernists tended to see fathers and mothers sharing Christian parenting responsibilities. They spoke out against father-led devotions, urging all family members, including children, to contribute so that each had a chance to provide an opinion before coming to a collective decision. In such gatherings, religious educator Henry Cope suggested, "the father may cease to be the 'high priest' for his family and becomes a worshiper along with the other members."[56] Perhaps not surprisingly, modernists were far more positive about women's outside employment, though they certainly desired mothers to embrace the critical importance of their domestic role, hoping that they would also see this as a legitimate "career."[57]

These democratic ideals also deeply influenced the liberal Protestant approach to authority. Instead of subduing the child's will, early twentieth-century liberal Protestants saw the will as an important ally in the fight for Christian growth. The goal, both reflecting and extending Bushnell's proposal, was for parents to allow a strong will to develop while also attempting to channel that will in profitable directions. "We have been accustomed to thinking the child must be wrong in asserting his will," Cope suggested. "Instead of being a wrong or a sin his opposition may be the expression of a power which is the backbone of virtue. It is ours to train and develop rather than to repress this power."[58] Modernists tended to condemn strict discipline, one noting that "it was not because of this rigid, austere type of discipline, but in spite of it, that the old-time home with its noble ideals and religious spirit succeeded in developing sturdy character for generations."[59] As Margaret Bendroth has indicated, "Their goal was to create a wholesome set of relationships within a Christian family, not to police certain behavior. The Christian child was not a Scripture-quoting, rule-abiding model of comportment but a growing individual psychologically well-adjusted and internally well equipped to face the challenges of modern life."[60]

In keeping with nineteenth-century trends, modernist Christian authors were clear in asserting that the home would need to increase its entertainment value if it wanted to maintain an influence in children's lives. If parents could not slow the pace of the 1920s "go-craze," they could at least make the home a central gathering place where children and their friends would want to be. Many authors recommended the expansion of family play through the development of "game nights."[61] They pressed for more sports at home, focusing specifically on the athletic bond between father and son. They also commended the use of the automobile for family outings, picnics, and beach excursions. Cope recommended that parents provide for a fun family Sunday, constructing a "*Family Book*" that would help in the creation of shared memories.[62] The key was to find ways to enhance family connections by providing fun activities for the children that would avoid moral compromise, to "find pleasures that will leave no regrets."[63] For these liberals, Christian parenting was less about furnishing Christian practices than it was about facilitating healthy relationships within the home that would prepare children to live well in the modern world.

In many ways the fundamentalist-modernist divide on Christian parenting reflected the competing postures assumed by colonial and Victorian-era authors. Fundamentalists placed more of an emphasis on distinct and God-directed Christian practices within the Christian home. They cherished the vision of the father-led family altar, a place where men would lead their wives and children in Bible reading and prayer. They commended Christian instruction in the home as a way to guide children against what they perceived to be false teaching. They desired strong parental authority, seeing this as a remedy to the weak-willed parenting that failed to protect children from immorality and vice. They tended to maintain a darker vision of children's nature, viewing them as sinful from birth and in need of a Spirit-empowered conversion experience. Modernists, on the other hand, were far more likely to emphasize the importance of home-based socialization and parental impressions. Drawing on Bushnell, they highlighted family relationships and the importance of these as the basis of Christian nurture. They rejected harsh discipline and encouraged forms of authority that emphasized the capacity to channel impulses in the right direction. They retained more optimistic views of children and their potential, welcoming their participation in family government.

These early twentieth-century groups were not clones of the colonial and Victorian versions, of course. Fundamentalists embraced the power of mothers in a manner far beyond their colonial counterparts. Likewise, modernists had less confidence in the Bible and relied more on science than those within more liberal nineteenth-century groups. Yet the distinctions echoed many of these earlier paradigms, attempting to adapt both the colonial and Victorian ideals to the modern world. As the twentieth century dawned, some of the shared consensus that had characterized nineteenth-century Protestant parenting was harder to find as increasing polarization caused parents to move in one direction or the other.

These fault lines in many ways continued to shape advice on Christian parenting through the remainder of the twentieth century. As Margaret Bendroth has noted, despite sporadic efforts to provide for more formal Christian teaching within the home (including the well-regarded Presbyterian "Christian Faith and Life" curriculum of the 1950s), mainline Protestants continued to view Christian parenting in terms of family "togetherness." Surveys revealed that families identified activities such as family recreation and vacations as the most critical for Christian growth, far above any teaching that would communicate the distinct content of the faith.[64] Although liberal Protestants were in many ways the leaders in the Christian family emphasis from the mid-nineteenth century to the mid-twentieth century, their interest in family religion experienced a dramatic decline between the 1960s and the 1980s. Commitment to the family altar had crumbled, replaced in many circles by appeals to the need for a "family night" or family discussions. Denominational commitment to family programming also declined precipitously. A growing number gave up on the belief that parents could—or even should—instruct their children in the Christian faith, many arguing that the church and its experts should assume this work. With divorce rates rising and the decline of nuclear families with working fathers and stay-at-home mothers, the child-centered impulse of the redemptive family seemed a bit more difficult to sustain.[65]

Conservative Protestants in many ways picked up the "family-centered" mantle beginning at this very time. Starting in the 1940s and escalating through the 1980s, fundamentalists and neo-evangelicals elevated the family as a critical stronghold against a secularizing culture. Many, including well-known authors such as John R. Rice, Bill Gothard, and James Dobson, advocated for increased parental authority and discipline (including spanking) as an antidote to the more permissive models that had been popularized by theorists such as John Holt and Benjamin Spock.[66] Most called for a renewed commitment to the family altar, with daily family devotions increasingly viewed as a nonnegotiable staple of the Christian home. The evangelical "pro-family" movement of the 1980s launched a vigorous attack on "secular humanism" and its corrosive fruit: teen pregnancies, feminism, moral relativism, abortion, homosexuality, and general lack of discipline among children. At the individual level, many saw parents' best response as one of retreat and withdrawal, creating a Christian parallel culture that included Christian schools, home schools, and a host of Christian books, magazines, music, movies, and games. At a more public level, however, issues of "family values" fueled a political agenda that brought many evangelicals into positions of cultural power.[67]

Yet the full story of conservative Protestant parenting advice since the 1960s reveals more of a blending of the colonial and Victorian approaches. As Bendroth so helpfully points out, as much as late twentieth-century conservative advice on Christian parenting refreshed traditional colonial themes of family worship, teaching, authority, and the need for conversion, there was a growing measure of Bushnellian sentiment mixed in as well. Many spoke of the power of the home environment, both the physical characteristics of the home and the need to be alert to early childhood impressions, including habits of eating, sleeping, and reading. Many focused a great deal on the power of fun and tight-knit family relationships, stressing the need to create warm and affectionate associations between faith and the family. Echoing themes of the sacred home and redemptive domesticity, the conservative "focus on the family" also at times minimized the importance of the larger "family of God," highlighting the power of the nuclear family in children's lives over the larger church community. Many also tended to see the family environment as determinative, providing a sense of certainty in good spiritual outcomes if the proper environment was created.[68]

Perhaps this blending anticipated what research has revealed about the status of Protestant parenting in twenty-first-century America. In his recent study on the nature of "religious parenting" in America, sociologist Christian Smith and two of his doctoral students looked at parents' approaches to transmitting faith and values to their children. Expecting to find significant diversity among competing groups, they instead discovered a widely shared set of parental "assumptions, hopes, and strategies" that cut across differences of "religious tradition, race and ethnicity, social class, gender, household type, and rural-urban background."[69] In other words, they documented among religious parents a kind of American "consensus" regarding what they wanted to see happen in the lives of their children and the particular approaches they believed were most likely to produce these outcomes.

Among many fascinating findings, a few reveal intriguing links with this historical overview. First, Smith and his team found that, when it comes to the practice of faith formation in the home, the typical method is one that centers on parental example and the environment of the home. Most parents feel that spiritual formation is a gradual process in which children absorb, almost unconsciously, their parents' approach to religious faith. In labeling this a "semivoluntary socialization," Smith and his colleagues suggested that most religious parenting consists of setting a good example and then hoping that children will be attracted to a certain way of life. There is very little expectation of a radical religious experience or conversion. As they put it, "Almost no parents spoke about 'religious experiences' either positively or negatively. Religion for nearly all of them is mostly about being a good person, not a dramatic enlightenment or personal encounter with God, Jesus, or any other superhuman force."[70] In addition, they note, such parenting rarely includes a "didactic teaching program," few seeing religious instruction as part of the parental job description. For most religious parents, faith is not a content to be transmitted but a posture toward life that is better caught than taught.[71]

Second, Smith and his colleagues found that many see family relationships and togetherness as the essence of what it means to be a family of faith. Parents prize faith because they believe that it helps foster family unity and solidarity. Because parents so value warm relationships with their children, they see a common faith as a critical aspect of relational cohesion. They view faith as a powerful bonding agent, a "glue" that holds parents and children together, provides a sense of unity, and minimizes conflict. Discussions of heaven and eternity, therefore, tend to focus on the fact that family members will experience a joyous reunion in the afterlife. Faith is important, in other words, because it brings families together and sustains them over time.[72]

Third and finally, Smith and his team found that religious parents see their own roles as determinative. Parents view their responsibility not as a shared venture with relatives, friends, and fellow church members but rather as a solitary project in which they act alone. Contrary to the idea that parents have abdicated their roles to other institutions and organizations, this study found that parents see themselves as the chief architects of their children's faith. Most believe that if children turn out poorly, it is the parents' fault. Along with this, they have very low expectations of what religious congregations can contribute to their child's faith development and therefore low commitments to children's participation in congregational activities. At best, most parents think, congregations can support parents by providing a fun environment and teaching that reinforces parental convictions. All of this speaks to the solitary nature of religious parenting in the contemporary era. As Smith and his colleagues note, this view "contrasts sharply with other historically widespread approaches to parenting" that see children "as the shared responsibility of the tribe, village, or kinship network." Today, alternatively, "nearly all of the responsibility for the raising of children religiously rests on [parents'] shoulders alone. Their children are their own projects to organize, implement, and hopefully bring to successful realization." "Such an understanding of parenting," they conclude, "begs for further research and explanation about the historically changing nature of society and family that would bring such an approach into being."[73]

In light of the history of American Protestant parenting, it appears that this contemporary approach owes a great deal to the emerging Bushnellian synthesis in which formation was connected more to parental impressions, modeling, and the environment of the home than to explicit teaching, worship, or desired conversion experiences. Faith was connected to a desire for close family relationships, and many saw family togetherness as a critical goal of sharing faith together. Parental determinism was also a clear outcome of the sacralization of the home in the nineteenth century, building on the notion that parents were the primary architects of children's faith. Contemporary parents seem to have embraced a division of labor in which the church is responsible for teaching, worship, and evangelism, while the home is responsible for cultivating warm and affectionate relationships, parental modeling, and the creation of environmental impressions that can shape the heart toward positive values. This approach has essentially taken the various emphases of colonial and nineteenth-century Christian parenting and divided them between the church and the home. And most of this happens without much of a partnership between these two formative institutions.

Building on the Long Legacy of American Protestant Parenting

In the end, perhaps the true potential of Protestant parenting relates to the possibility of holding both the colonial and the nineteenth-century visions together. On the one hand, parents can effectively teach, train, exhort, and discipline their children and yet neglect the critical environmental and relational aspects of nurture and care. One the other hand, parents can be loving nurturers, orchestrating a tight-knit setting for family togetherness, and yet miss out on viewing the home as a place of instruction, worship, and proper authority. Twentieth-century Protestants seemed to carry split visions along these lines, and more contemporary approaches seem to reflect the nineteenth-century approach more exclusively. Yet each of these approaches offers wisdom to contemporary Christians attempting to think more holistically about the parenting task.

First, while colonial authors put most of their emphasis on formal Christian practices of worship and teaching, Victorian authors tended to highlight the informal and day-to-day rhythms of family life—parent-child interactions, modeling, home impressions, and time spent in play and family activities. In reality, both serve important purposes. It is in the formal spaces of daily Bible reading, prayer, study, singing, and teaching that children are exposed, in a systematic way, to the truth of God and to the posture of regular worship. The teaching of biblical and doctrinal truth is an important means of providing a vocabulary that can fortify children as they face the false narratives of the broader culture. These formal liturgical rhythms not only reinforce certain patterns of belief but also immerse children in a particular story of the world that shapes their "loves." Worship, prayer, and singing also connect children more distinctly to a dialogical relationship with God that involves both speaking and listening—a participation in the "with-God life." At the same time, as James K. A. Smith reminds us, "Every household has a 'hum,' and that hum has a tune that is attuned to some end, some *telos*."[74] The rhythms and schedules and habits and relationships of the household are all communicating ideals and values to children, often beneath conscious awareness. These can either reinforce or subvert the more formal inputs children receive through daily religious exercises. Both formal teaching and the informal cadences of the household—the "hidden curriculum"—are spiritually formative and require parental intentionality. As Smith suggests, parents might consider taking an "audit" of the family's daily routines, asking what stories, values, and visions of the good life are carried in these everyday rhythms.[75] From both the formal and the informal approaches of the past, parents can take away the sense that Christian teaching in the home is far richer and more comprehensive than usually imagined.

In a closely related way, while nineteenth-century authors tended to focus more on God's work through natural parent-child interactions and colonial pastors tended to highlight God's supernatural work through Scripture, doctrine, and spiritual experiences, both are actually critical. One of Horace Bushnell's contributions was to remind Christian parents that the Holy Spirit was at work not only in instantaneous works of conversion (as revivalists highlighted) but also in the regular interactions between parents and children in the flow of life. He wanted parents to know that they did not have to wait for some future act of immediate transformation. God was already at work, pouring out his grace on children from the time of birth through the organic interactions between parents and children. This is an important reminder, especially for those parents in traditions that tend to focus heavily on individual spiritual events and therefore downplay the importance of God's presence and activity in seemingly "natural" human relationships. At the same time, the colonial emphasis on God's supernatural work in conversion and the need for the Spirit to awaken dead souls is a necessary complement to this reality. It is easy for Bushnell's perspective to grow into an unhelpful naturalism that places all hope in environmental socialization and neglects God's work in opening blind eyes and rescuing souls from "the dominion of darkness" (Col. 1:13 NIV). Without this, parents can begin to assess the child's Christian growth as mere ethical improvement and behavioral conformity. Colonial fears over the false security of substituting morality for regenerating grace recognized this trap, and it was this realization of the need for supernatural grace that moved colonial parents to their knees in prayer. To really embrace the Spirit's work in all of life, both perspectives are critical.

The visions of these two eras can also alert contemporary parents to the pendulum swings related to the relative importance attributed to mothers and fathers. Colonial pastors addressed most of their comments to fathers (or to both parents), occasionally reminding mothers that their parenting role was also significant. By the mid-nineteenth century, these roles were reversed, with literature addressing the pivotal place of mothers and some authors pleading with fathers to maintain a presence within the home. Theologically, colonial fathers were given priority as patriarchs and masters who governed, taught, and led their families in worship. As cultural and theological currents shifted in the nineteenth century, mothers were held up as naturally loving, sacrificial, and pure, making them the best parents to shepherd their children's hearts toward either conversion or nurture. In the end, however, both of these alternatives tended to downplay the importance of one of the parents, giving either the mother (in the colonial era) or the father (in the nineteenth century) a diminished standing with regard to the tasks of Christian child-rearing. Yet Scripture clearly affirms the importance of both. Proverbs 1:8–9 (NIV) exhorts children as follows: "listen . . . to your father's instruction / and do not forsake your mother's teaching," as does Proverbs 23:22 (NIV):

"listen to your father, who gave you life, / and do not despise your mother when she is old." In addition to "honoring" (Exod. 20:12; Eph. 6:2–3) and "obeying" (Eph. 6:1; Col. 3:20) both mother and father, it is clear that many passages speak universally of parents playing roles as teachers and mentors for their children (Prov. 22:6; Deut. 6:6–7). It is telling that Paul could speak of his own ministry work with the Thessalonians using both paternal (exhorting, encouraging, and charging) and maternal (gentleness and care) images (1 Thess. 2:7, 12), stressing the need for both "modes" in the work of spiritual shepherding and care.

With regard to authority, colonial authors tended to emphasize the hierarchical and positional authority of parents, especially fathers. In highlighting the key virtues of reverence, obedience, and recompense, they stressed the distance between parents and children and the need for submission to parental commands. While they did also mention the need for love in addition to fear ("sugar" to sweeten the "salt") and spoke against severity, the clear priority was for parents to subdue their children's wills. Mid-nineteenth-century Protestants, on the other hand, increasingly urged parents to foster self-government within their children, a strong conscience that would serve as an internal monitor against evil. They also attached disciplinary methods to their loving relationships with their children, appealing either to wounded love or to threats of emotional or physical withdrawal. There was not much in the way of permissive parenting in either era among Northern Protestants, but the two time periods did witness a relative shift from external to internal sources of authority and from fear to love as the motivation for obedience. The middle ground, what Isaac Ambrose called "a loving Fear, and a fearing Love," was a hard balance to strike, but it was a charge meant to echo the loving discipline of God:

> My son, do not despise the LORD's discipline
>   or be weary of his reproof,
> for the LORD reproves him whom he loves,
>   as a father the son in whom he delights. (Prov. 3:11–12)

Since Christians are called both to fear and reverence God and to love and desire to please him, both aspects seem critical for holistic Christian parenting. In this sense, the desire is something like what contemporary theorists have called an "authoritative" parenting style. This style represents a posture that combines high behavioral standards and high affectionate support and is often set in contrast to an "authoritarian" style (high behavioral standards and low affectionate support), a "permissive" style (low behavioral standards and high affectionate support), and a "neglectful" style (low behavioral standards and low affectionate support).[76] Recent research indeed seems to demonstrate that authoritative parenting is connected to the more effective transmission of faith from parents to children, especially if parents themselves are highly religious.[77]

Finally, these eras set forth contrasting visions of what determines children's ultimate path of faith. Colonial authors tended to place the emphasis here on God's sovereignty and power, also commending the roles of parents and the church. Nineteenth-century authors tended to see parental nurture through impressions and relationships as more determinative in children's lives. In reality, both seem to be important. Many recent research studies confirm that parents are the most important factors in transmitting faith to children. Christian Smith and Amy Adamczyk connect the critical importance of parents to the time they spend with children, the modeling of priorities, and the capacity to talk with children about faith in the midst of everyday life.[78] Christian parents, therefore, should indeed consider the power and the high calling of parenting and not attempt to pass off responsibility to other institutions. At the same time, the importance of parenting should not be taken to imply that parents completely control their children's spiritual lives or that they are meant to do this work in isolation. The power of parenting must sit alongside the pervasive power of God to work in the child's life, driving parents to their knees in dependence on his power and grace. The power of parenting must also sit alongside the importance of the larger family of God—the believer's "first family"—and the broad fellowship of people who can serve as mentors, teachers, and models for children.[79] In other words, Christian parenting is powerful—and parents live into this with bold intentionality—but it is not independent. It humbly acknowledges a dependence on God and an interdependence with others in the family of faith. Combining these two perspectives, such "humble boldness" is the true posture of a Christian parent.

So what does it mean to be a good Christian parent? The combined wisdom of American Protestants over the past several centuries seems to point to the expansive nature of true parental love. This love warns because it desires children's eternal salvation. It prays because it knows that true spiritual blessing depends on God's lavish grace in their lives. It teaches because it wants to help children understand true goodness and avoid the perils of Satan's lies and the "hollow and deceptive philosophies" of the world (Col. 2:8 NIV). It admonishes and restrains because it wants to protect children from things that can keep them from true pleasure and joy. It creates environments to put God's love on display in both formal and informal ways. It creates strong relationships with family members and the church community so that children can experience the corporate nature of God's love. It shares life with children because it wants them to realize the tender depth of a love that, like Christ, crosses boundaries in order to demonstrate care. It displays Christ's love through sacrifice, giving up self for the good of others. It continues to press on with children even when they resist parental appeals, showing that this love can even love an enemy (Matt. 5:44).

Ultimately, this kind of love will drive parents not to idolatry but to gratitude for God's good gifts and to a sacrificial willingness to offer children to God so that he can fulfill his greater purposes in their lives. The privilege of such parenting is to serve as Christ's ambassadors, to place children into the loving arms of the God who created them, and therefore to help children see, embrace, and experience the one love that will never fail (Ps. 13:5).

Notes

Introduction

1. Among a number of studies, see, for example, Vern L. Bengtson, *Families and Faith: How Religion Is Passed Down across Generations* (New York: Oxford University Press, 2013); Christian Smith, Bridget Ritz, and Michael Rotolo, *Religious Parenting: Transmitting Faith and Values in Contemporary America* (Princeton: Princeton University Press, 2020); Christian Smith and Amy Adamczyk, *Handing Down the Faith: How Parents Pass Their Religion on to the Next Generation* (New York: Oxford University Press, 2021), 53–54, 71–72, 83–85; Christian Smith, *Soul Searching: The Religious and Spiritual Lives of American Teenagers* (New York: Oxford University Press, 2005); Scott M. Myers, "An Interactive Model of Religiosity Inheritance: The Importance of Family Context," *American Sociological Review* 61 (1996): 858–66; Christopher Bader and Scott A. Desmon, "Do as I Say and as I Do: The Effects of Consistent Parental Beliefs and Behaviors upon Religious Transmission," *Sociology of Religion* 67 (2006): 313–29.

2. Smith, *Soul Searching*, 56–57; Christian Smith, *Souls in Transition: The Religious and Spiritual Lives of Emerging Adults* (New York: Oxford University Press, 2009), 215.

3. Bengtson, *Families and Faith*, 54–67.

4. Smith and Adamczyk, *Handing Down the Faith*, 69.

5. Smith and Adamczyk, *Handing Down the Faith*, 69–92. See also Smith, Ritz, and Rotolo, *Religious Parenting*, 5–7.

6. Besides a few comparative references, this work does not address Christian parenting in the American South in this time period. In that region of the country, different living conditions, family structures, economic realities, and the growth of

slavery led to fewer and different kinds of conversations about Christian parenting. See, for example, Edmund S. Morgan, *Virginians at Home: Family Life in the Eighteenth Century* (Charlottesville, VA: Dominion Books, 1952); Daniel Blake Smith, *Inside the Great House: Planter Family Life in Eighteenth-Century Chesapeake Society* (Ithaca, NY: Cornell University Press, 1980); Lauren F. Winner, *A Cheerful and Comfortable Faith: Anglican Religious Practice in the Elite Households of Eighteenth-Century Virginia* (New Haven: Yale University Press, 2010); Elizabeth Fox-Genovese, *Within the Plantation Household: Black and White Women of the Old South* (Chapel Hill: University of North Carolina Press, 1989); Scott Stephan, *Redeeming the Southern Family: Evangelical Women and Domestic Devotion in the Antebellum South* (Athens: University of Georgia Press, 2008); Jean Friedman, *The Enclosed Garden: Women and Community in the Evangelical South, 1830–1900* (Chapel Hill: University of North Carolina Press, 1985); Christine Leigh Heyrman, *Southern Cross: The Beginnings of the Bible Belt* (New York: Knopf, 1998).

7. Philip Greven, *The Protestant Temperament: Patterns of Child-Rearing, Religious Experience, and the Self in Early America* (Chicago: University of Chicago Press, 1977).

8. Rowan Williams, *Why Study the Past? The Quest for the Historical Church* (Grand Rapids: Eerdmans, 2005), 24–25.

9. C. S. Lewis, introduction to *The Incarnation of the Word of God*, by Athanasius (New York: Macmillan, 1946), 7.

10. Don S. Browning and Bonnie J. Miller-McLemore, *Children and Childhood in American Religions* (New Brunswick, NJ: Rutgers University Press, 2009), 12.

11. Among many helpful resources on the history of childhood and the family, see Steven Mintz, *Huck's Raft: A History of American Childhood* (Cambridge, MA: Belknap, 2004); Steven Mintz and Susan Kellogg, *Domestic Revolutions: A Social History of American Family Life* (New York: Free Press, 1988); Paula S. Fass, *The End of American Childhood: A History of Parenting from Life on the Frontier to the Managed Child* (Princeton: Princeton University Press, 2016); Paula S. Fass and Mary Ann Mason, eds., *Childhood in America* (New York: New York University Press, 2000); David Peterson Del Mar, *The American Family* (New York: Palgrave Macmillan, 2011); Linda Pollock, *Forgotten Children: Parent-Child Relations from 1500 to 1900* (New York: Cambridge University Press, 1983); N. Ray Hiner and Joseph M. Hawes, eds., *Growing Up in America: Children in Historical Perspective* (Urbana: University of Illinois Press, 1985); Joseph M. Hawes and N. Ray Hiner, eds., *American Childhood: A Research Guide and Historical Handbook* (Westport, CT: Greenwood, 1985).

12. Among many important single-era works, see Edmund S. Morgan, *The Puritan Family: Religion and Domestic Relations in Seventeenth-Century New England* (New York: Harper & Row, 1966); James Axtell, *The School upon a Hill: Education and Society in Colonial New England* (New York: Norton, 1974); James Marten, ed., *Children in Colonial America* (New York: New York University Press, 2007); Jacqueline S. Reinier,

From Virtue to Character: American Childhood, 1775–1850 (New York: Twayne, 1996); Colleen McDannell, *The Christian Home in Victorian America, 1840–1900* (Bloomington: Indiana University Press, 1986); Steven Mintz, *A Prison of Expectations: The Family in Victorian Culture* (New York: New York University Press, 1985); Priscilla Ferguson Clement, *Growing Pains: Children in the Industrial Age, 1850–1890* (New York: Twayne, 1997). Marcia Bunge's excellent edited collection, *The Child in Christian Thought* (Grand Rapids: Eerdmans, 2001), does address historical perspectives on children and religion, but this work looks at single figures and is focused on a broader historical and geographical context.

13. For example, many of the popular "history of Christian education" texts mention almost nothing about Christian education and formation in the home. See Kenneth O. Gangel and Warren S. Benson, *Christian Education: Its History and Philosophy* (Chicago: Moody, 1983); James E. Reed and Ronnie Prevost, *History of Christian Education* (Nashville: B&H Academic, 1998); Michael J. Anthony and Warren S. Benson, *Exploring the History and Philosophy of Christian Education* (Grand Rapids: Kregel, 2003).

14. Robert Orsi, "Beyond the Niebuhrs: An Interview with Robert Orsi on Recent Trends in American Religious History," in *Recent Themes in American Religious History: Historians in Conversation*, ed. Randall J. Stephens (Columbia: University of South Carolina Press, 2009), 25. On this theme, see Mintz, *Huck's Raft*, vii–viii; Randall J. Stephens, "Roundtable: Children and Family in the History of Modern American Christianity," *Fides et Historia* 45, no. 2 (Summer/Fall 2013): 55–56.

15. McDannell, *Christian Home*, 151.

16. Margaret Bendroth, "Bad Children," *Fides et Historia* 45, no. 2 (Summer/Fall 2013): 57.

17. Margaret Bendroth, *Growing Up Protestant: Parents, Children, and Mainline Churches* (New Brunswick, NJ: Rutgers University Press, 2002).

18. Carl N. Degler notes that the middle-class character of most parenting source materials in the nineteenth century does not limit their usefulness, because up to three-fifths of the population could be considered "middle class," and because it was this population that set the tone for larger discussions among most literate Americans at this time. *At Odds: Women and the Family in America from the Revolution to the Present* (New York: Oxford University Press, 1980), 82–83.

19. On this theme, see Jay Mechling, "Advice to Historians on Advice to Mothers," *Journal of Social History* 9, no. 1 (Autumn 1975): 44–63; Catherine M. Scholten, *Childbearing in American Society: 1650–1850* (New York: New York University Press, 1985), 69.

20. Peter Laslett, "The Character of Familial History, Its Limitations, and the Conditions for Its Proper Pursuit," *Journal of Family History* 12, no. 1–2 (March 1987): 263–84.

21. Henry Clay Trumbull, *The Sunday-School: Its Origin, Mission, Methods, and Auxiliaries* (New York: Charles Scribner's Sons, 1888), 179–83.

The Parent as Evangelist

1. William Cooper, *God's Concern for a Godly Seed. As it was shewed in the Forenoon Sermon*, in *Two Sermons Preached in Boston, March 5, 1723 on a Day of Prayer*, by Benjamin Colman and William Cooper (Boston: S. Kneeland, 1723), 32.

2. Colman and Cooper, *Two Sermons*, i.

3. Colman and Cooper, *Two Sermons*, iii. For other examples of days set apart for prayer for the rising generation, see Joseph Belcher, *Two Sermons Preached in Dedham N. E. The First On a Day Set Apart for Prayer with Fasting, To Implore Spiritual Blessings On the Rising Generation* [. . .] (Boston: B. Green, 1710); Increase Mather, *Pray for the Rising Generation, or A Sermon Wherein Godly Parents are Encouraged, to Pray and Believe for their Children* [. . .] (Boston: John Foster, 1679); Increase Mather, *The Duty of Parents to Pray for their Children* [. . .] (Boston: B. Green and J. Allen, 1703); Cotton Mather, *The Duty of Children Whose Parents have Pray'd for them, or, Early and Real Godliness Urged; Especially upon Such as Are Descended from Godly Ancestors* (Boston: B. Green and J. Allen, 1703).

4. Cooper, *God's Concern*, 30–31.

5. Cooper, *God's Concern*, 14.

6. Benjamin Colman, *The Duty of Parents to pray for their Children, And especially to ask God for them the Spiritual Blessing*, in Colman and Cooper, *Two Sermons*, 3–5.

7. Colman, *Duty of Parents*, 4, 19–20.

8. Colman and Cooper, *Two Sermons*, iv.

9. Eleazer Mather, *A Serious Exhortation to the Present and Succeeding Generation in New England* [. . .] (Cambridge, MA: S. G. and M. T., 1671), 16. See also Benjamin Wadsworth, *The Well-Ordered Family* [. . .] (Boston: B. Green, 1712), 85.

10. Steven Mintz, *Huck's Raft: A History of American Childhood* (Cambridge, MA: Belknap, 2004), 30–31. See also Samuel Willard, *Covenant-Keeping the Way to Blessedness* [. . .] (Boston: James Glen, 1682), 117.

11. Perry Miller, *Errand into the Wilderness* (Cambridge, MA: Belknap, 1956).

12. John Cotton, *God's Promise to His Plantations* [. . .] (Boston: Samuel Green, 1686), 19.

13. Colman, *Duty of Parents*, 33–34.

14. E. Mather, *Serious Exhortation*, 20. See also Joseph Sewall, *Desires that Joshua's Resolution May Be Revived, or Excitations to the Constant and Diligent Exercise of Family Religion* (Boston: B. Green, 1716), i; Benjamin Colman, *An Argument for and Persuasive unto the Great and Important Duty of Family Worship: With Rules and Directions for the Due Performance of It* (Boston: Gamaliel Rogers, 1728), 38–39; Steven Ozment, *When Fathers Ruled: Family Life in Reformation Europe* (Cambridge, MA: Harvard University Press, 1985), 132.

15. Cotton Mather, *A Family Well-Ordered. Or An Essay To Render Parents and Children Happy in one another* [. . .] (Boston: B. Green & J. Allen, 1699), 6.

16. As Margo Todd has argued, Puritans were not unique with regard to their views on household religion. Puritans, Anglicans, and Catholics in the 1500s drew on both humanist and biblical sources in crafting a common perspective on Christian parenting. However, by the early seventeenth century, both Anglicans (under the influence of Archbishop Laud) and Catholics (after the Council of Trent) had shifted to a more clerical, church-oriented perspective, rendering the Puritans unique in their strong commendation of the spiritualized household. See "Humanists, Puritans, and the Spiritualized Household," *Church History* 49, no. 1 (March 1980): 18–34.

17. James Axtell, *The School upon a Hill: Education and Society in Colonial New England* (New York: Norton, 1974), 21; Lawrence A. Cremin, *American Education: The Colonial Experience, 1607–1783* (New York: Harper & Row, 1970), 135; Maris Vinovskis, "Family and Schooling in Colonial and Nineteenth-Century America," *Journal of Family History* 12, no. 1 (1987): 22.

18. Cooper, *God's Concern*, 32. See also George Selement, *Keepers of the Vineyard: The Puritan Ministry and Collective Culture in Colonial New England* (Lanham, MD: University Press of America, 1984).

19. C. John Sommerville, *The Discovery of Childhood in Puritan England* (Athens: University of Georgia Press, 1992), 23. Lawrence Stone also contends that most of the popular child-rearing handbooks in the seventeenth century were written by Puritans, who he notes were "abnormally concerned about children and their upbringing." *The Family, Sex, and Marriage in England, 1500–1800* (New York: Harper & Row, 1977), 125.

20. This regularity was likely due to the contraceptive effects of nursing, and only one in twelve women was childless in colonial New England. See Steven Mintz and Susan Kellogg, *Domestic Revolutions: A Social History of American Family Life* (New York: Free Press, 1988), 12–13; John Demos, *A Little Commonwealth: Family Life in Plymouth Colony* (New York: Oxford University Press, 1970), 68; Laurel Thatcher Ulrich, *Good Wives: Image and Reality in the Lives of Women in Northern New England, 1650–1750* (New York: Vintage Books, 1991), 135.

21. Karin Calvert, *Children in the House: The Material Culture of Early Childhood, 1600–1900* (Boston: Northeastern University Press, 1992), 23. Because of lower life expectancies, in fact, it was also not unusual for one or both parents to have died before all their children reached adulthood.

22. Stephen M. Frank, *Life with Father: Parenthood and Masculinity in the Nineteenth-Century American North* (Baltimore: Johns Hopkins University Press, 1998), 18.

23. Mintz, *Huck's Raft*, 12–13.

24. Benjamin Colman, *Some of the Honours that Religion Does unto the Fruitful Mothers in Israel* [. . .] (Boston: B. Green, 1715), 5. See also Ulrich, *Good Wives*, 159–61; Ozment, *When Fathers Ruled*, 100.

25. Demos, *Little Commonwealth*, 132; Philip J. Greven Jr., *Four Generations: Population, Land, and Family in Colonial Andover, Massachusetts* (Ithaca, NY: Cornell University Press, 1970), 25–26; Gerald F. Moran and Maris A. Vinovskis, *Religion, Family, and the Life Course: Explorations in the Social History of Early America* (Ann Arbor: University of Michigan Press, 1992), 34–35; Joseph E. Illick, "Child-Rearing in Seventeenth Century England and America," in *The History of Childhood*, ed. Lloyd deMause (New York: Harper Torchbooks, 1974), 305. Demos suggests about one birth in thirty resulted in the death of the mother; see *Little Commonwealth*, 66.

26. David E. Stannard, *The Puritan Way of Death: A Study in Religion, Culture, and Social Change* (New York: Oxford University Press, 1977), 53–56. The years "beyond infancy and prior to adolescence" were particularly susceptible to certain diseases, such as the throat distemper that raged in the 1730s (Greven, *Four Generations*, 190). Moran and Vinovskis note that adult mortality rates were far better in New England than in England: "A person who survived to age twenty in seventeenth-century Plymouth Colony . . . might expect to live another forty or fifty years." *Religion, Family, and the Life Course*, 33.

27. Peter G. Slater, "From the *Cradle* to the *Coffin*: Parental Bereavement and the Shadow of Infant Damnation in Puritan Society," in *Growing Up in America: Children in Historical Perspective*, ed. N. Ray Hiner and Joseph M. Hawes (Urbana: University of Illinois Press, 1985), 27–43; Mintz, *Huck's Raft*, 14; Mintz and Kellogg, *Domestic Revolutions*, 2, 14; Catherine Brekus, *Sarah Osborn's World: The Rise of Evangelical Christianity in Early America* (New Haven: Yale University Press, 2013), 79, 137–69. Cotton Mather believed—and regularly stated—that about half of all people in Boston died before the age of seventeen; see *The Words of Understanding. Three Essays* [. . .] (Boston: S. Kneel, 1724), 9, and *Corderius Americanus: An Essay Upon The Good Education of Children* [. . .] (Boston: John Allen, 1708), 17–20. He also noted that "Ten times more Dy before Twenty than after Sixty." *The Young Man Spoken To: Another Essay, To Recommend & Inculcate the Maxims of Early Religion, Unto Young Persons; And Especially the Religion of the Closet* [. . .] (Boston: T. Green, 1712), 8.

28. John Duffy, *Epidemics in Colonial America* (Baton Rouge: Louisiana State University Press, 1953), 33–37.

29. Judith S. Graham, *Puritan Family Life: The Diary of Samuel Sewall* (Boston: Northeastern University Press, 2000), 102; N. Ray Hiner, "Cotton Mather and His Children: The Evolution of a Parent Educator, 1686–1728," in *Regulated Children/Liberated Children: Education in Psychohistorical Perspective*, ed. Barbara Finkelstein (New York: Psychohistory, 1979), 30.

30. Stannard, *Puritan Way of Death*, 55–56.

31. Anne Bradstreet, "Upon a Fit of Sickness, Anno 1632 *Aetatis Suae*, 19," in *The Works of Anne Bradstreet*, ed. Jeannine Hensley (Cambridge, MA: Belknap, 2010), 241. The fragility of his children's lives was so palpable to Samuel Sewall that he literally dreamed

that all but one of his children had died. M. Halsey Thomas, ed., *The Diary of Samuel Sewall, 1674–1729* (New York: Farrar, Straus & Giroux, 1973), 1:328.

32. Demos, *Little Commonwealth*, 183–84.

33. Demos, *Little Commonwealth*. Demos derives this phrase from English Puritans. See William Gouge, *Of Domesticall Duties, Eight Treatises*, 2nd ed. (London: John Beale, 1626), 10.

34. Edmund S. Morgan, *The Puritan Family: Religion and Domestic Relations in Seventeenth-Century New England* (New York: Harper & Row, 1966), 68. See also Carole Shammas, *A History of Household Government in America* (Charlottesville: University of Virginia Press, 2002), 35.

35. John R. Gillis, *A World of Their Own Making: Myth, Ritual, and the Quest for Family Values* (Cambridge, MA: Harvard University Press, 1996), 33.

36. Gillis, *World of Their Own Making*, 36–37.

37. Henry Gibbs, *Godly Children their Parents' Joy* [. . .] (Boston: S. Kneeland & T. Green, 1727), 55; William Homes, *The Good Government of Christian Families Recommended: As that which will contribute greatly to their Peace and true Happiness* [. . .] (Boston: D. Henchman, 1747), 74–76.

38. Helena Wall, *Fierce Communion: Family and Community in Early America* (Cambridge, MA: Harvard University Press, 1990), 96–125.

39. Morgan, *Puritan Family*, 77. See also Demos, *Little Commonwealth*, 120. Such an arrangement did not always imply complete separation from the child's family. When possible, children were placed in the homes of close relatives who would be more willing to maintain family connections. If in the same town, many masters allowed children to return home to visit their families during slower work seasons. See Morgan, *Puritan Family*, 73–76.

40. Graham, *Puritan Family Life*, 135.

41. Gillis, *World of Their Own Making*, 30.

42. On this contrast, see, for example, Lauren F. Winner, *A Cheerful and Comfortable Faith: Anglican Religious Practice in the Elite Households of Eighteenth-Century Virginia* (New Haven: Yale University Press, 2010), 35–37; Philip Greven, *The Protestant Temperament: Patterns of Child-Rearing, Religious Experience, and the Self in Early America* (Chicago: University of Chicago Press, 1977), 266–68.

43. Thomas Cobbett, *A Fruitfull and Usefull Discourse Touching The Honour due from Children to Parents, and the Duty of Parents toward their Children* (London: S. G. for John Rothwell, 1656), 2; Morgan, *Puritan Family*, 12.

44. Wall, *Fierce Communion*; Michael Zuckerman, *Peaceable Kingdoms: New England Towns in the Eighteenth Century* (New York: Norton, 1970). For similar practices among the Quakers, see J. William Frost, *Quaker Family in Colonial America* (New York: St. Martin's Press, 1973).

45. Mary P. Ryan, *Cradle of the Middle Class: The Family in Oneida County, New York, 1790–1865* (New York: Cambridge University Press, 1981), 40, 43. It is important

to note that such a theory did not imply willing participation on the part of all families. See, for example, David D. Hall, *Worlds of Wonder, Days of Judgment: Popular Religious Belief in Early New England* (Cambridge, MA: Harvard University Press, 1989), 14–20.

46. On this theme, see Colman, *Some of the Honours*, 8, 17–20; Cotton Mather, *Help for Distressed Parents. Or, Counsels & Comforts for Godly Parents Afflicted with Ungodly Children* [. . .] (Boston: John Allen, 1695), 40–42; Belcher, *Two Sermons*, 29–30.

47. Colman, *Some of the Honours*, 8.

48. Jay Fliegelman, *Prodigals and Pilgrims: The American Revolution against Patriarchal Authority, 1750–1800* (New York: Cambridge University Press, 1982), 68; Catherine Brekus, "Writing as a Protestant Practice: Devotional Diaries in Early New England," in *Practicing Protestants: Histories of Christian Life in America, 1630–1965*, ed. Laurie F. Maffly-Kipp, Leigh E. Schmidt, and Mark Valeri (Baltimore: Johns Hopkins University Press, 2006), 25; Brekus, *Sarah Osborn's World*, 165–67.

49. John Cotton, *A Practical Commentary, or An Exposition with Observations, Reasons, and Uses Upon the First Epistle General of John* (London: R. I. and I. C. for Thomas Parkhurst, 1661), 200.

50. Richard Baxter, *The Godly Home*, ed. Randall J. Pederson (Wheaton, IL: Crossway, 2010), 118.

51. Deodat Lawson, *The Duty and Property of a Religious Householder* [. . .] (Boston: B. Green, 1693), 31.

52. Wadsworth, *Well-Ordered Family*, 50–51; I. Mather, *Duty of Parents*, 36–38; Cotton Mather, *Parentalia: An Essay Upon the Blessings and Comforts Reserved for Pious Children After the Death of their Pious Parents* [. . .] (Boston: J. Allen, 1715), 27; Cotton Mather, *Orphanotrophium. Or, Orphans Well-provided for* [. . .] (Boston: B. Green, 1711), 31–39.

53. Sewall, *Joshua's Resolution*, 69; William Cooper, *How and Why Young People Should Cleanse Their Way, in Two Sermons* [. . .] (Boston: B. Green, 1716), 37.

54. C. Mather, *Family Well-Ordered*, 9–10.

55. Daniel Lewes, *The Joy of Children walking in Truth* [. . .] (Boston: Henchman, 1723), 14; Sewall, *Joshua's Resolution*, 50–69; Gibbs, *Godly Children*, 15–16, 26–27; W. Gouge, *Domesticall Duties*, 305; Benjamin Colman, *Parents and grown Children should be together at the Lord's Table* [. . .] (Boston: S. Gerrish, 1727), 18–19; Homes, *Good Government*, 86–87.

56. *The New-England Primer Enlarged* (Boston: S. Kneeland and T. Green, 1727), 8.

57. William Williams, *The Duty of Parents to Transmit Religion to their Children* [. . .] (Boston: B. Green, 1721), 9. See also N. Ray Hiner, "The Cry of Sodom Enquired Into: Educational Analysis in Seventeenth-Century New England," *History of Education Quarterly* 13, no. 1 (Spring 1973): 7; Sommerville, *Discovery of Childhood*, 28, 83.

58. Cotton Mather, *Vita Brevis. An Essay, Upon Withering Flowers* [. . .] (Boston: John Allen, 1714), 28–29; I. Mather, *Pray for the Rising Generation*, 16.

59. Benjamin Wadsworth, "The Nature of Early Piety," in *A Course of Sermons on Early Piety. By the Eight Ministers Who Carry on the Thursday Lecture in Boston* (Boston: S. Kneeland, 1731), 10. See also Cotton Mather, *The A, B, C of Religion. Lessons Relating to the Fear of God, Fitted unto the Youngest & Lowest Capacities* [. . .] (Boston: Timothy Green, 1713), 24; I. Mather, *Duty of Parents,* 8–9; Cotton Mather, *Parental Wishes and Charges. Or, The Enjoyment of a Glorious Christ, Proposed, as the Great Blessedness, which Christian Parents desire, both for Themselves, and for their Children* [. . .] (Boston: T. Green, 1705), 23–24, 44; Cotton Mather, *Cares about the Nurseries* [. . .] (Boston: T. Green, 1702), 31; Cotton Mather, *Addresses to Old Men, and Young Men, and Little Children* [. . .] (Boston: R. Pierce, 1694), 117; Cotton Mather, *Man Eating the Food of Angels: The Gospel of the Manna, To be Gathered in the Morning* [. . .] (Boston: T. Green, 1710), 35–36, 59.

60. Thomas Shepard, *The Sincere Convert: Discovering the Small Number of True Believers and the great Difficulty of Saving Conversion* (Cambridge, 1664), 36. See also Richard Osmer, "The Christian Education of Children in the Protestant Tradition," *Theology Today* 56, no. 4 (2000): 511.

61. Bradstreet, "Of the Four Ages of Man," in Hensley, *Works of Anne Bradstreet,* 58.

62. *The Works of Jonathan Edwards,* vol. 4, ed. C. C. Goen (New Haven: Yale University Press, 1972), 394.

63. Stannard, *Puritan Way of Death,* 49, 52. See also Peter Gregg Slater, *Children in the New England Mind: In Death and in Life* (Hamden, CT: Archon Books, 1977), 21.

64. Descriptions of hell were less common in the first half of the seventeenth century, but by the late seventeenth and early eighteenth centuries Puritan leaders consistently reminded children of the terrors of hell that awaited the unregenerate. See Brekus, *Sarah Osborn's World,* 145.

65. Michael Wigglesworth, *The Day of Doom: or, A Poetical Description of the Great and Last Judgment. With a short Discourse about Eternity,* 6th ed. (Boston: John Allen, 1715).

66. The book was definitely a bestseller, averaging more than 450 copies sold per year. See Hugh Amory and David D. Hall, *A History of the Book in America* (Chapel Hill: University of North Carolina Press, 2007), 1:107–8.

67. Wigglesworth, *Day of Doom,* 41.

68. *The Works of Jonathan Edwards,* vol. 13, ed. Thomas A. Schafer (New Haven: Yale University Press, 1994), 169.

69. On the confidence of infant salvation for godly parents, see Slater, *Children,* 30–31; C. Mather, *Cares about the Nurseries,* 55–56; C. Mather, *Addresses to Old Men,* 112; Cotton Mather, *Meat Out of the Eater. Or, Funeral-Discourses Occasioned By the Death of several Relatives* [. . .] (Boston, 1703), 27–28, 96–98; Benjamin Colman, *A Devout Contemplation on the Meaning of Divine Providence, in the Early Death of Pious and Lovely Children* [. . .] (Boston: John Allen, 1714), 10.

70. Demos, *Little Commonwealth*, 136–37; Philip Greven, *Spare the Child: The Religious Roots of Punishment and the Psychological Impact of Physical Abuse* (New York: Knopf, 1990). British historian Lawrence Stone likewise claimed that, because of its rejection of good within the child, the doctrine of original sin could only lead to repression as the basis of educational philosophy. Stone, *Family, Sex, and Marriage*, 125.

71. I. Mather, *Duty of Parents*, 24–25. Playing on real parental fears, Mather noted that "slavery" to the devil was far worse than if children had been taken captive by "Turks" or "Indians" (24–25).

72. Wadsworth, *Well-Ordered Family*, 71–73. On this theme, see also C. Mather, *Family Well-Ordered*, 10–13; Slater, *Children*, 41.

73. John Dod and Robert Cleaver, *A Godly Forme of Household Government, For the Ordering of Private Families, According to the Direction of God's Word* (London: R. Field, 1598), unnumbered page. See also Ozment, *When Fathers Ruled*, 163; Slater, "From the Cradle to the Coffin," 29.

74. C. Mather, *Family Well-Ordered*, 11. See also I. Mather, *Duty of Parents*, 11–12.

75. Increase Mather, *A Call from Heaven To the Present and Succeeding Generations* [. . .] (Boston: J. Foster, 1679), 85. See also Charles Hambrick-Stowe, *The Practice of Piety: Puritan Devotional Disciplines in Seventeenth-Century New England* (Chapel Hill: University of North Carolina Press, 1982), 21; Hiner, "Cry of Sodom," 5; Anne S. Brown and David D. Hall, "Family Strategies and Religious Practice: Baptism and the Lord's Supper in Early New England," in *Lived Religion in America: Toward a History of Practice*, ed. David D. Hall (Princeton: Princeton University Press, 1997), 45; Cremin, *American Education*, 49.

76. Hambrick-Stowe, *Practice of Piety*, 54–90.

77. David Levin, *Cotton Mather: The Young Life of the Lord's Remembrancer, 1663–1703* (Cambridge, MA: Harvard University Press, 1978), 15–16.

78. Cotton Mather, *Conversion Exemplified* (Boston, 1703); Brown and Hall, "Family Strategies," 45; Edmund Morgan, *Visible Saints: The History of a Puritan Idea* (New York: Cornell University Press, 1965), 68–69, 88; Patricia Caldwell, *The Puritan Conversion Narrative: The Beginnings of American Expression* (New York: Cambridge University Press, 1985); Charles Lloyd Cohen, *God's Caress: The Psychology of Puritan Religious Experience* (New York: Oxford University Press, 1986), 75–110.

79. For the development of this requirement, see Morgan, *Visible Saints*, 93–112; Norman Pettit, *The Heart Prepared: Grace and Conversion in Puritan Spiritual Life* (New Haven: Yale University Press, 1966).

80. Pettit, *Heart Prepared*, 155.

81. Thomas Hooker, *The Unbeleevers Preparing for Christ* (London: T. Cotes, 1638), 200. It appears that women were converted in greater numbers and at earlier ages than men. For many, this was coordinated in time with marriage and church membership and was potentially seen developmentally as a link to full maturity. During revivals, ages of

conversion dropped and more single men and women were converted. See Moran and Vinovskis, *Religion, Family, and the Life Course*, 20–32. Stephen R. Grossbart, "Seeking the Divine Favor: Conversion and Church Admission in Eastern Connecticut, 1711–1832," *William and Mary Quarterly* 46, no. 4 (October 1989): 696–740.

82. Stannard, *Puritan Way of Death*, 50.

83. *Works of Jonathan Edwards*, 4:158.

84. As Catherine Brekus contends, it may have been precisely because these children were "on the brink of death" that they were able to experience an earlier conversion. *Sarah Osborn's World*, 48.

85. James Janeway and Cotton Mather, *A Token For Children. Being An Exact Account of the Conversion, Holy and Exemplary Lives and Joyful Deaths of Several Young Children, To which is Added, A Token, for the Children of New England* (Boston: Nicholas Boone, 1700).

86. Catherine Brekus, "Children of Wrath, Children of Grace: Jonathan Edwards and the Puritan Culture of Child Rearing," in *The Child in Christian Thought*, ed. Marcia J. Bunge (Grand Rapids: Eerdmans, 2001), 313.

87. Thomas Hooker thought it important that people not limit conversion to a particular age of life, since this might root conversion in human attributes rather than God's sovereign design. See Hooker, *Unbeleevers Preparing for Christ*, 195. Belief in the possibility of earlier conversion likely expanded in the eighteenth century when early evangelicals began emphasizing the importance of the heart. See Brekus, "Children of Wrath," 314.

88. C. Mather, *A, B, C of Religion*, 19.

89. I. Mather, *Duty of Parents*, 43.

90. Morgan, *Puritan Family*, 1–3.

91. I. Mather, *Call from Heaven*, 32.

92. Cotton Mather, *The Best Ornaments of Youth. A Short Essay, on the Good Things, Which are found in Some, and should be found in All, Young People* [. . .] (Boston: Timothy Green, 1707), 27. See also Richard P. Gildrie, *The Profane, the Civil, and the Godly: The Reformation of Manners in Orthodox New England, 1679–1749* (University Park: Pennsylvania State University Press, 1994), 108.

93. Colman, *Parents and Grown Children*, 24; Cotton Mather, *The Wayes and Joyes of Early Piety. One Essay more, To Describe and Commend, A Walk in the Truth Of our Great Saviour, Unto the Children of His People* [. . .] (Boston: B. Green, 1712), 48. See also C. Mather, *A, B, C of Religion*, 34, 39; C. Mather, *Vita Brevis*, 26–30; C. Mather, *Corderius Americanus*, 17.

94. This came from the 1737 edition. See Paul Leicester Ford, ed., *The New-England Primer: A History of Its Origin and Development* (New York: Dodd, Mead, 1897), 46. On this theme, see Mintz, *Huck's Raft*, 20.

95. C. Mather, *Young Man Spoken To*, 7.

96. Cotton Mather, *Early Religion, Urged in a Sermon, The Duties Wherein, and the Reasons Wherefore, Young People Should Become Religious* [. . .] (Boston: B. D., 1694), 32–33, 54; Benjamin Bass, *Parents and Children Advised and Exhorted to their Duty* [. . .] (Newport, RI, 1729), 7.

97. Ford, *New-England Primer*, 233–37.

98. Thomas Gouge, *The Young Man's Guide, Through the Wilderness of this World, To the Heavenly Canaan* [. . .] (Boston: J. Draper, 1742), 9.

99. C. Mather, *Early Religion*, 57.

100. C. Mather, *Early Religion*, 32. See also C. Mather, *Wayes and Joyes*, 21–23; C. Mather, *Best Ornaments of Youth*, 33; I. Mather, *Duty of Parents*, 51, 53; T. Gouge, *Young Man's Guide*, A2, 3–44; Morgan, *Puritan Family*, 96–97; Bass, *Parents and Children*, 7; Lewes, *Joy of Children*, 12, 24–25; Gibbs, *Godly Children*, 34–36, 73.

101. See also Cotton, *Practical Commentary*, 92; Bass, *Parents and Children*, 7.

102. T. Gouge, *Young Man's Guide*, 18.

103. T. Gouge, *Young Man's Guide*, A2. See also C. Mather, *Vita Brevis*, 13.

104. Samuel Phillips, *Children Well Imployed, and, Jesus much delighted; or, The Hosannahs of Zion's Children, Highly Pleasing to Zion's King* [. . .] (Boston: S. Kneeland, 1739), 23; C. Mather, *Cares about the Nurseries*, preface.

105. T. Gouge, *Young Man's Guide*, 6.

106. C. Mather, *Vita Brevis*, 12.

107. I. Mather, *Pray for the Rising Generation*, 12. See also I. Mather, *Duty of Parents*, 19–20.

108. C. Mather, *Duty of Children*, 32.

109. Cooper, *God's Concern*, 16.

110. C. Mather, *Help for Distressed Parents*, 13–14.

111. C. Mather, *Help for Distressed Parents*, 5.

112. Morgan, *Visible Saints*, 128.

113. On the "half-way covenant," see Robert G. Pope, *The Half-Way Covenant: Church Membership in Puritan New England* (Eugene, OR: Wipf & Stock, 1969); Brown and Hall, "Family Strategies," 52.

114. Mark Noll, *America's God: From Jonathan Edwards to Abraham Lincoln* (New York: Oxford University Press, 2002), 40–41. Others gave the "half-way covenant" a theological rationale. Rev. Chauncy Graham, for example, noted that the efficacy of baptism was not dependent on the spiritual state of the parents, which was in any case unknowable. Instead, as an ordinance it maintained its own power and authority rooted in the work of Christ. *Children fœderally Holy, A Sermon, Shewing that the Holiness of Children, arises from one, or, both of their Parents being in Covenant with God* [. . .] (New York: Samuel Brown, 1765), 8.

115. *The Works of Jonathan Edwards*, vol. 12, ed. David D. Hall (New Haven: Yale University Press, 1994), 316.

116. *Works of Jonathan Edwards*, 12:318.

117. Brown and Hall, "Family Strategies," 42.

118. C. Mather, *Cares about the Nurseries*, 55–56. Mather was sure that youth, those over the age of twelve, were responsible for their own faith "in the reckoning of God" (56). See also Ross W. Beales, "In Search of the Historical Child: Miniature Adulthood and Youth in Colonial New England," *American Quarterly* 27, no. 4 (October 1975): 388–91.

119. While most resisted declaring a specific age of accountability for children to be held responsible before God, age fourteen did appear to be the closest approximation. Legal standards also seemed to confirm this general cutoff for minority status. In some cases, fourteen was declared the minimum age to be admitted to the Lord's Table. In his descriptions of childhood conversions during the eighteenth-century revivals, Jonathan Edwards designated fourteen as the upper limit of childhood. See Beales, "In Search of the Historical Child," 384–85.

120. Brekus, *Sarah Osborn's World*, 143–51. See also Joseph Kett, *Rites of Passage: Adolescence in America, 1790 to the Present* (New York: Basic Books, 1977), 62–85.

121. John F. Walzer, "A Period of Ambivalence: Eighteenth-Century American Childhood," in deMause, *History of Childhood*, 370; Sandford Fleming, *Children and Puritanism: The Place of Children in the Life and Thought of the New England Churches, 1620–1847* (New Haven: Yale University Press, 1933), 66, 90, 153.

122. George Marsden, *Jonathan Edwards: A Life* (New Haven: Yale University Press, 2003), 26.

123. Janeway and Mather, *Token For Children*, preface.

124. I. Mather, *Call from Heaven*, 28. See also C. Mather, *Words of Understanding*, 31; C. Mather, *Help for Distressed Parents*, 53; Increase Mather, *An Earnest Exhortation to the Children of New-England, To Exalt the God of their Fathers* (Boston, 1711), 35.

125. T. Gouge, *Young Man's Guide*, 55. See also I. Mather, *Duty of Parents*, 28, 30–31, 50, 52.

126. Graham, *Puritan Family Life*, 70–72.

127. Cited in Fleming, *Children and Puritanism*, 158.

128. Janeway and Mather, *Token For Children*, preface. For the Puritans, songs and poems about death for children tended to be "monitory" (cautionary tales in verse) rather than "consolatory" (focusing on the heavenly promises of Christ). Jeffrey VanderWilt, "Singing about Death in American Protestant Hymnody," in *Wonderful Words of Life: Hymns in American Protestant History and Theology*, ed. Richard J. Mouw and Mark A. Noll (Grand Rapids: Eerdmans, 2004), 181–82.

129. Cited in Brekus, "Children of Wrath," 321.

130. Paul David Tripp, *Parenting: 14 Gospel Principles That Can Radically Change Your Family* (Wheaton, IL: Crossway, 2016), 11–20.

131. Wadsworth, *Well-Ordered Family*, preface.

The Parent as Priest

1. John Dod and Robert Cleaver, *A Godly Forme of Household Government, For the Ordering of Private Families, According to the Direction of God's Word* (London: R. Field, 1598), preface.

2. On this theme, see *Luther's Works*, ed. Jaroslav Pelikan and Helmut Lehman (Philadelphia: Fortress; St. Louis: Concordia, 1955–1986), 45:46.

3. Benjamin Wadsworth, *The Well-Ordered Family* [. . .] (Boston: B. Green, 1712), 6; Isaac Backus, *Family Prayer Not to be Neglected* [. . .] (Newport: Samuel Hall, 1766), 11.

4. Thomas Hooker, *The Application of Redemption, by the Effectual Work of the Word, and Spirit of Christ, for the Bringing Home of Lost Sinners to God* (London: Peter Cole, 1656), 357.

5. Steven Mintz, *Huck's Raft: A History of American Childhood* (Cambridge, MA: Belknap, 2004), 15; Anne S. Brown and David D. Hall, "Family Strategies and Religious Practice: Baptism and the Lord's Supper in Early New England," in *Lived Religion in America: Toward a History of Practice*, ed. David D. Hall (Princeton: Princeton University Press, 1997), 53.

6. Daniel Scott Smith, "Child-Naming Patterns and Family Structure Change: Hingham, Massachusetts 1640–1880," *Newberry Papers in Family and Community History*, Paper 76-5 (January 1977): 3.

7. Joseph E. Illick, "Child-Rearing in Seventeenth Century England and America," in *The History of Childhood*, ed. Lloyd deMause (New York: Harper Torchbooks, 1974), 324; Laurel Thatcher Ulrich, *Good Wives: Image and Reality in the Lives of Women in Northern New England, 1650–1750* (New York: Vintage Books, 1991), 150–51.

8. Mintz, *Huck's Raft*, 15.

9. Daniel Scott Smith, "Continuity and Discontinuity in Puritan Naming: Massachusetts, 1771," *William and Mary Quarterly* 51 (January 1994): 67.

10. Worthington Chauncey Ford, ed., *The Diary of Cotton Mather* (repr., New York: Frederick Unger, 1911), 1:218.

11. M. Halsey Thomas, ed., *The Diary of Samuel Sewall, 1674–1729* (New York: Farrar, Straus & Giroux, 1973), 1:324. Cited in Judith S. Graham, *Puritan Family Life: The Diary of Samuel Sewall* (Boston: Northeastern University Press, 2000), 38.

12. Dod and Cleaver, *Godly Forme*, unnumbered page.

13. Ulrich, *Good Wives*, 151–52.

14. Cited in David D. Hall, *Puritans in the New World: A Critical Anthology* (Princeton: Princeton University Press, 2004), 38–39.

15. Illick, "Child-Rearing," 324–25; Ross Beales, "The Child in Seventeenth-Century America," in *American Childhood: A Research Guide and Historical Handbook*, ed. Joseph M. Hawes and N. Ray Hiner (Westport, CT: Greenwood, 1985), 26–27.

16. Smith, "Continuity and Discontinuity," 6.

17. As Mark Noll has pointed out, the language of covenant served to frame the understanding of all spiritual realities. Salvation was defined as entry into the covenant of grace. Obedience consisted of "keeping covenant," while rebellion was defined as willful "covenant breaking." Those joining the church entered into covenant, and they would collectively renew the covenant to reaffirm their corporate allegiance to God. *America's God: From Jonathan Edwards to Abraham Lincoln* (New York: Oxford University Press, 2002), 39.

18. Cotton Mather, *Cares about the Nurseries* [. . .] (Boston: T. Green, 1702), 61–69; William Williams, *The Obligations of Baptism and the Duty of Young Persons to Recognize them* [. . .] (Boston: B. Green, 1721), 4; William Cooper, *How and Why Young People Should Cleanse Their Way, in Two Sermons* [. . .] (Boston: B. Green, 1716), ii, 17. See also David D. Hall, *Worlds of Wonder, Days of Judgment: Popular Religious Belief in Early New England* (Cambridge, MA: Harvard University Press, 1989), 153–54; Brown and Hall, "Family Strategies," 47–49.

19. C. John Sommerville, *The Discovery of Childhood in Puritan England* (Athens: University of Georgia Press, 1992), 75; Catherine Brekus, *Sarah Osborn's World: The Rise of Evangelical Christianity in Early America* (New Haven: Yale University Press, 2013), 79.

20. Cotton Mather, *The Duty of Children Whose Parents have Pray'd for them, or, Early and Real Godliness Urged; Especially upon Such as Are Descended from Godly Ancestors* (Boston: B. Green and J. Allen, 1703), 69. See also Williams, *Obligations of Baptism*, 5.

21. Richard Baxter, *The Godly Home*, ed. Randall J. Pederson (Wheaton, IL: Crossway, 2010), 118.

22. Cotton Mather, *Corderius Americanus: An Essay Upon The Good Education of Children* [. . .] (Boston: John Allen, 1708), 10; Cotton Mather, *Bonifacius: An Essay Upon the Good* [. . .] (Boston: B. Green, 1710), 53; Cotton Mather, *Young Man Spoken To: Another Essay To Recommend & Inculcate the Maxims of Early Religion Unto Young Persons; And Especially the Religion of the Closet* [. . .] (Boston: T. Green, 1712), 20.

23. Samuel Phillips, *Children Well Imployed, and, Jesus much delighted; or, The Hosannahs of Zion's Children, Highly Pleasing to Zion's King* [. . .] (Boston: S. Kneeland, 1739), 41.

24. Wadsworth, *Well-Ordered Family*, 60–61; Joseph Sewall, *Desires that Joshua's Resolution May Be Revived, or Excitations to the Constant and Diligent Exercise of Family Religion* (Boston: B. Green, 1716), 34–35.

25. Charles Hambrick-Stowe, *The Practice of Piety: Puritan Devotional Disciplines in Seventeenth-Century New England* (Chapel Hill: University of North Carolina Press, 1982), 93–135. By the eighteenth century, as church structures and the supply of clergy grew and stabilized, the church assumed increasing importance as an educational force. See Lawrence A. Cremin, *American Education: The Colonial Experience, 1607–1783* (New York: Harper & Row, 1970), 237; Patricia Bonomi, *Under the Cope of Heaven: Religion, Society, and Politics in Colonial America* (New York: Oxford University Press, 2003), 6–10, 87–127.

26. Wadsworth, *Well-Ordered Family*, 61. See also Joseph Belcher, *Two Sermons Preached in Dedham N. E. The First On a Day set apart for Prayer with Fasting, To Implore Spiritual Blessings On the Rising Generation* [. . .] (Boston: B. Green, 1710), 12.

27. Dod and Cleaver, *Godly Forme*, unnumbered page.

28. Sewall, *Joshua's Resolution*, 35. See also Henry Gibbs, *Godly Children their Parents' Joy* [. . .] (Boston: S. Kneeland & T. Green, 1727), 44.

29. Franklin Bowditch Dexter, ed., *New Haven Town Records, 1662–1684* (New Haven: New Haven Colony Historical Society, 1919), 2:379. Cited in Helena Wall, *Fierce Communion: Family and Community in Early America* (Cambridge, MA: Harvard University Press, 1990), 8. Colonial authors were especially hard on children who "mocked" ministers. See Cotton Mather, *Man Eating the Food of Angels: The Gospel of the Manna, To be Gathered in the Morning* [. . .] (Boston: T. Green, 1710), 40–41; Samuel Phillips, *Advice to a Child, or Young People Solemnly Warn'd both against Enticing, and Consenting when Enticed to Sin* [. . .] (Boston: J. Phillips, 1729), 22.

30. William Homes, *The Good Government of Christian Families Recommended: As that which will contribute greatly to their Peace and true Happiness* [. . .] (Boston: D. Henchman, 1747), 44; Wadsworth, *Well-Ordered Family*, 60–61.

31. Deodat Lawson, *The Duty and Property of a Religious Householder* [. . .] (Boston: B. Green, 1693), 50; William Cooper, *God's Concern for a Godly Seed. As it was shewed in the Forenoon Sermon*, in *Two Sermons Preached in Boston, March 5, 1723 on a Day of Prayer*, by Benjamin Colman and William Cooper (Boston: S. Kneeland, 1723), 11. Margo Todd traces the idea of the household as a "little church" to the humanist tradition. "Humanists, Puritans, and the Spiritualized Household," *Church History* 49, no. 1 (March 1980): 23–24.

32. Sewall, *Joshua's Resolution*, 30.

33. Cooper, *God's Concern*, 11. See also John Barnard, *A Call to Parents, and Children. Or, The Great Concern of Parents; And The Important Duty of Children* [. . .] (Boston: T. Fleet, 1737), 4.

34. Increase Mather, *Returning unto God the Great Concernment of a Covenant People* [. . .] (Boston: John Foster, 1680), 20.

35. Benjamin Colman, *An Argument for and Persuasive unto the Great and Important Duty of Family Worship: With Rules and Directions for the Due Performance of it* (Boston: Gamaliel Rogers, 1728), 2–3; Increase Mather, *Some Important Truths Concerning Conversion* [. . .], 2nd ed. (Boston: Samuel Green, 1684), 105–6; Lawson, *Duty and Property*, 40, 55–56.

36. Cotton Mather, *A Family-Sacrifice. A Brief Essay to Direct and Excite Family-Religion* [. . .] (Boston: B. Green and J. Allen, 1703); I. Mather, *Some Important Truths*, 7; William Seward, *Family-Religion Revived: Or, An Attempt to Promote Religion and Virtue in Families* [. . .] (New Haven: James Parker, 1755), 10; Barnard, *Call to Parents*,

14–15; Thomas Gouge, *Young Man's Guide Through the Wilderness of this World, To the Heavenly Canaan* [. . .] (Boston: J. Draper, 1742), 69.

37. C. Mather, *Family-Sacrifice*, 7, 15.

38. Homes, *Good Government*, 20–21.

39. Barnard, *Call to Parents*, 15. See also George Whitefield, *The Great Duty of Family Religion* [. . .] (Boston: T. Fleet, 1739), 12–13.

40. C. Mather, *Family-Sacrifice*, 32–33. See also C. Mather, *Man Eating the Food of Angels*, 12.

41. Seward, *Family-Religion Revived*, 5.

42. Richard Osmer, "The Christian Education of Children in the Protestant Tradition," *Theology Today* 56, no. 4 (2000): 508–9; John Morgan, *Godly Learning: Puritan Attitudes towards Reason, Learning, and Education, 1560–1640* (New York: Cambridge University Press, 1988), 155–56.

43. Thomas, *Diary of Samuel Sewall*, 1:113. Cited in Edmund S. Morgan, *The Puritan Family: Religion and Domestic Relations in Seventeenth-Century New England* (New York: Harper & Row, 1966), 137.

44. Thomas, *Diary of Samuel Sewall*, 1:308. Cited in Morgan, *Puritan Family*, 137.

45. Thomas, *Diary of Samuel Sewall*, 1:364. Cited in Graham, *Puritan Family Life*, 67.

46. "Directions of the General Assembly, Concerning Secret and Private Worship, And Mutual Edification; For Cherishing Piety, For Maintaining Unity, and Avoiding Schism and Division," August 24, 1647, Session 10. For examples of this, see Joel R. Beeke and Mark Jones, *A Puritan Theology: Doctrine for Life* (Grand Rapids: Reformation Heritage Books, 2012), 866–70.

47. Samuel Hopkins, *The Life and Character of the Late Reverend, Learned, and Pious Mr. Jonathan Edwards, President of the College of New Jersey. Together with a Number of his Sermons on Various Important Subjects* (Boston: S. Kneeland, 1765), 43.

48. Cotton Mather, *Family-Religion Urged. Or, Some Serious Considerations offer'd to the Reason and Conscience of Every Prayerless Householder* [. . .] (Boston: Benjamin Harris, 1709), 17–18. The music in John Bayly's *Practice of Piety*, for example, used child-birth metaphors to prompt reflection on the caring hand of God in bringing the family out of the darkness into the light of a new day. See Hambrick-Stowe, *Practice of Piety*, 146–47; Sewall, *Joshua's Resolution*, 33.

49. C. Mather, *Family-Sacrifice*, 34. See also Hambrick-Stowe, *Practice of Piety*, 115; Baxter, *Godly Home*, 81.

50. Cited in Mark A. Noll, "The Defining Role of Hymns in Early Evangelicalism," in *Wonderful Words of Life: Hymns in American Protestant History and Theology*, ed. Richard J. Mouw and Mark A. Noll (Grand Rapids: Eerdmans, 2004), 5.

51. Christopher N. Phillips, "Cotton Mather Brings Isaac Watts's Hymns to America; or, How to Perform a Hymn without Singing It," *New England Quarterly* 85, no. 2 (June 2012): 203. See also Esther Rothenbusch Crookshank, "We're Marching to Zion: Isaac

Watts in Early America," in Mouw and Noll, *Wonderful Words of Life*, 23–25; William L. Joyce et al., eds., *Printing and Society in Early America* (Worcester, MA: American Antiquarian Society, 1983), 21–23; Hambrick-Stowe, *Practice of Piety*, 113–14. Edwards also promoted Watts's hymns in the colonies. Noll, "Defining Role," 4.

52. For changes in church music in the eighteenth century, see Mark Noll, "The Significance of Hymnody in the First Evangelical Revivals," in *Revival, Renewal, and the Holy Spirit*, ed. Dyfed Wyn Roberts (Colorado Springs: Paternoster, 2009), 45–64; Stephen A. Marini, "Rehearsal for Revival: Sacred Singing and the Great Awakening in America," in *Sacred Sound: Music in Religious Thought and Practice*, ed. Joyce Irwin (Chico, CA: Scholars Press, 1983).

53. This work was also called "Divine Songs Attempted in Easy Language for the Use of Children." A popular collection of twenty-two Watts hymns (taken from the 1709 edition of his hymns) and Cotton Mather's "The Body of Divinity Versify'd" came together as *Honey Out of the Rock, Flowing to Little Children That They May Know to Refuse the Evil and Chuse the Good*. See Crookshank, "We're Marching to Zion," 30.

54. Crookshank, "We're Marching to Zion," 32; Harry Escott, *Isaac Watts: Hymnographer* (London: Independent Press, 1962), 199–216; Cremin, *American Education*, 277–78.

55. Hambrick-Stowe, *Practices of Piety*, 147–50. On this theme, see also I. Mather, *Some Important Truths*; Kenneth Silverman, *The Life and Times of Cotton Mather* (New York: Harper & Row, 1984), 265.

56. On this, see Seward, *Family-Religion Revived*, 9–10; *An Address of the Pastors of the Churches of the Western District in the County of New-London, to the Families of their Charge; On the Subject of Family Religion* (New-London, CT: Timothy Green, 1765), 44–48.

57. Dod and Cleaver, *Godly Forme*, unnumbered page.

58. C. Mather, *Family-Sacrifice*, 28.

59. Hambrick-Stowe, *Practice of Piety*, 147–48; *Address of the Pastors*, 37; Mary Cable, *The Little Darlings: A History of Child Rearing in America* (New York: Scribner's, 1975), 8.

60. *Address of the Pastors*, 37.

61. Homes, *Good Government*, 25; Backus, *Family Prayer*, 13.

62. Lawson, *Duty and Property*, 46.

63. C. Mather, *Family-Sacrifice*, 29.

64. Seward, *Family-Religion Revived*, 21.

65. Colman, *Duty of Family Worship*, 20. See also Lawson, *Duty and Property*, 28.

66. Seward, *Family-Religion Revived*, 21. See also Wadsworth, *Well-Ordered Family*, 21–22.

67. Seward, *Family-Religion Revived*, 22.

68. Seward, *Family-Religion Revived*, 20. See also Paul Sangster, *Pity My Simplicity: The Evangelical Revival and the Religious Education of Children, 1738–1800* (London: Epworth, 1963), 72–74.

69. Lawson, *Duty and Property*, 29.

70. Wadsworth, *Well-Ordered Family*, 63; Colman, *Duty of Family Worship*, 21.

71. C. Mather, *Family-Sacrifice*, 44.

72. C. Mather, *Family-Sacrifice*, 46.

73. C. Mather, *Family-Sacrifice*, 45, 46.

74. Wall, *Fierce Communion*, 13–29.

75. Alexis McCrossen, *Holy Day, Holiday: The American Sunday* (Ithaca, NY: Cornell University Press, 2001), 10–12.

76. Hambrick-Stowe, *Practice of Piety*, 51–52, 203; Lawson, *Duty and Property*, 33.

77. Ford, *New-England Primer*, 118. McCrossen, *Holy Day, Holiday*, 11–13; Benjamin Bass, *Parents and Children Advised and Exhorted to their Duty* [...] (Newport, RI, 1729), 12. Parents and local governmental agents ("selectmen" and "tithingmen") were responsible for ensuring that their children and servants remained engaged in both private and public worship on the Sabbath, restraining them from inappropriate work and play. James Axtell notes that parents were responsible for their children by enforcing the Sabbath until age fourteen, at which time children themselves could be fined for Sabbath violations. See *The School upon a Hill: Education and Society in Colonial New England* (New York: Norton, 1974), 99. On this theme, see also Dod and Cleaver, *Godly Forme*, 10–11; Sewall, *Joshua's Resolution*, 33; Isaac Ambrose, *The Well-Ordered Family* [...], reprinted ed. (Boston: S. Kneeland, 1762), 6; Bonomi, *Under the Cope of Heaven*, 5–6; Samuel Checkley, *Little Children Brought to Jesus Christ* [...] (Boston: Rogers and Fowle, 1741), 20, 23.

78. Cable, *Little Darlings*, 18.

79. Ford, *New-England Primer*, 59.

80. Cooper, *God's Concern*, 10.

81. Colman, *Duty of Family Worship*, 24. Colman even commended the practice of extending family prayer to four times on Sabbath days since the law had directed the Israelites to double their sacrifices on these weekly occasions (18–19).

82. Cooper, *God's Concern*, 10.

83. Cotton Mather, *Magnalia Christi Americana; or, The Ecclesiastical History of New England* [...] (Hartford: Silas Andrus & Son, 1853), 536. See also Lawson, *Duty and Property*, 32.

84. Wadsworth, *Well-Ordered Family*, 17.

85. Benjamin Colman, *The Duty of Parents to pray for their Children, And especially to ask God for them the Spiritual Blessing*, in Colman and Cooper, *Two Sermons*, 21–22; Lawson, *Duty and Property*, 51; Colman, *Duty of Family Worship*, 28.

86. Cotton Mather, *Family Religion Excited and Assisted: The Third Impression* (Newport, RI: Printed by Ann Franklin, 1740), 6. While no one wrote as voluminously as Mather when it came to the topic of prayer for children, it was nonetheless a common Puritan theme. See, for example, Ambrose, *Well-Ordered Family*, 13–14; Thomas Cobbett, *A Fruitfull and Usefull Discourse Touching The Honour due from Children to Parents*,

and the Duty of Parents toward their Children (London: S. G. for John Rothwell, 1656), 56, 235; William Gouge, *Of Domesticall Duties, Eight Treatises*, 2nd ed. (London: John Beale, 1626), 283.

87. C. Mather, *Family-Religion Urged*, 9.

88. Increase Mather, *The Duty of Parents to Pray for their Children* [. . .] (Boston: B. Green and J. Allen, 1703), 12–13.

89. Increase Mather, *Pray for the Rising Generation, or A Sermon Wherein Godly Parents are Encouraged, to Pray and Believe for their Children* [. . .] (Boston: Samuel Green, 1678), 14. See also Wadsworth, *Well-Ordered Family*, 59.

90. Cremin, *American Education*, 314; I. Mather, *Duty of Parents*, preface; C. Mather, *Duty of Children*; C. Mather, *Family-Sacrifice*.

91. Cotton Mather, *A Family Well-Ordered. Or An Essay To Render Parents and Children Happy in one another* [. . .] (Boston: B. Green & J. Allen, 1699), 37.

92. Colman, *Duty of Parents*, 23–24. Increase Mather spoke of how his mother, a "very Holy praying woman," prayed for him "day and night" while exhorting him to pursue both God's grace and learning. M. G. Hall, ed., "The Autobiography of Increase Mather," *American Antiquarian Society Proceedings* 71 (October 1961): 278.

93. Ambrose, *Well-Ordered Family*, 11.

94. Belcher, *Two Sermons*, 8. Thomas Gouge recommended that parents pray for each child after conception, "especially if they observe them to bee quicke in the wombe." *Young Man's Guide*, 283.

95. Brekus, *Sarah Osborn's World*; Gibbs, *Godly Children*, 40–42.

96. C. Mather, *Family Well-Ordered*, 33.

97. C. Mather, *Family Well-Ordered*, 34.

98. C. Mather, *Family-Sacrifice*, 20; C. Mather, *Family Well-Ordered*, 34. See also Cooper, *God's Concern*, in Cooper and Colman, *Two Sermons*, 8–9.

99. Cotton Mather, *Help for Distressed Parents. Or, Counsels & Comforts for Godly Parents Afflicted with Ungodly Children* [. . .] (Boston: John Allen, 1695), 21.

100. Ford, *Diary of Cotton Mather*, 2:455; C. Mather, *Bonifacius*, 54.

101. Ford, *Diary of Cotton Mather*, 2:351.

102. For the patristic source of Mather's interest in such prayers, fasting, and vigils, see Richard Lovelace, *The American Pietism of Cotton Mather* (Eugene, OR: Wipf & Stock, 2007), 126.

103. On Puritan "conference," see Joanne J. Jung, *Godly Conversation: Rediscovering the Puritan Practice of Conference* (Grand Rapids: Reformation Heritage Books, 2015). Often this practice would include the child who was the special focus of prayer for the day. See, for example, Ford, *Diary of Cotton Mather*, 2:351.

104. C. Mather, *Family Well-Ordered*, 35–36. See also Gibbs, *Godly Children*, 42.

105. C. Mather, *Bonifacius*, 61.

106. Ford, *Diary of Cotton Mather*, 1:240. See also 2:203, 230.

107. This was also the practice in Cotton Mather's childhood home with his father, Increase. See David Levin, *Cotton Mather: The Young Life of the Lord's Remembrancer, 1663–1703* (Cambridge, MA: Harvard University Press, 1978), 12.

108. C. Mather, *Family Well-Ordered*, 34.

109. Lovelace, *American Pietism*, 124–27.

110. R. A. Bosco, ed., *Paterna: The Autobiography of Cotton Mather* (New York: Scholar's Facsimilies & Reprints, 1976), 233–37.

111. Ford, *Diary of Cotton Mather*, 1:294.

112. Ford, *Diary of Cotton Mather*, 2:234.

113. Ford, *Diary of Cotton Mather*, 1:283.

114. Cited in Lovelace, *American Pietism*, 123. See also Ford, *Diary of Cotton Mather*, 1:336–37.

115. Ford, *Diary of Cotton Mather*, 2:480.

116. Ford, *Diary of Cotton Mather*, 2:612.

117. Ford, *Diary of Cotton Mather*, 2:485.

118. Ford, *Diary of Cotton Mather*, 2:485–86.

119. Ford, *Diary of Cotton Mather*, 2:489.

120. C. Mather, *Help for Distressed Parents*, 30–32.

121. C. Mather, *Family Well-Ordered*, 34. On this theme, see also Hambrick-Stowe, *Practice of Piety*, 177.

122. C. Mather, *Help for Distressed Parents*, 34.

123. Cotton Mather, *Orphanotrophium. Or, Orphans Well-provided for* [. . .] (Boston: B. Green, 1711), 33–34; Cotton Mather, *Parentalia: An Essay Upon the Blessings and Comforts Reserved for Pious Children After the Death of their Pious Parents* [. . .] (Boston: J. Allen, 1715), 19–20. See also Increase Mather, *A Call from Heaven To the Present and Succeeding Generations* [. . .] (Boston: J. Foster, 1679), 24; Gibbs, *Godly Children*, 66–70; Ambrose, *Well-Ordered Family*, 14.

124. Cooper, *God's Concern*, in Cooper and Colman, *Two Sermons*, 8.

125. Cotton Mather, *The Words of Understanding. Three Essays* [. . .] (Boston: S. Kneel, 1724), 17, 16.

126. C. Mather, *Words of Understanding*, 16. See also Colman, *Duty of Parents*, 29–30.

127. Homes, *Good Government*, 90.

128. C. Mather, *Bonifacius*, 58. This was Cotton Mather's own practice as a child, one of his biographers noting that there was a time he read fifteen chapters of the Bible each day, five in the morning, five at noon, and five at night, also withdrawing for secret prayer "several times a day." Levin, *Cotton Mather*, 10.

129. Ford, *Diary of Cotton Mather*, 2:81.

130. C. Mather, *Bonifacius*, 57.

131. Hambrick-Stowe, *Practice of Piety*, 176.

132. C. Mather, *Corderius Americanus*, 11. Mather taught his own children how to turn Scripture into prayer. See, for example, Ford, *Diary of Cotton Mather*, 2:251.

133. C. Mather, *Family Religion Excited*, 9.

134. Cotton Mather, *Early Religion, Urged in a Sermon, The Duties Wherein, and the Reasons Wherefore, Young People Should Become Religious* [. . .] (Boston: B. D., 1694), 25–26.

135. C. Mather, *Bonifacius*, 57; C. Mather, *Family Religion Excited*, 10. In one sermon, Mather commended the experience of a young man who noted that he never let a passage of Scripture pass by without a "pertinent ejaculation thereupon." *Early Religion*, 25.

136. C. Mather, *Man Eating the Food of Angels*, 12; C. Mather, *Early Religion*, 25.

137. C. Mather, *Family-Religion Urged*, 11; C. Mather, *Cares about the Nurseries*, 25.

138. C. Mather, *Bonifacius*, 57.

139. C. Mather, *Family-Religion Urged*, 12.

140. Cooper, *Young People*, 23.

141. Cooper, *Young People*, 26.

142. Cooper, *Young People*, 26.

143. Cotton Mather, *Addresses to Old Men, and Young Men, and Little Children* [. . .] (Boston: R. Pierce, 1694), 78–79.

144. Benjamin Colman, *Some of the Honours that Religion Does unto the Fruitful Mothers in Israel* [. . .] (Boston: B. Green, 1715), 14–15.

145. Benjamin Colman, *A Devout Contemplation on the Meaning of Divine Providence in the Early Death of Pious and Lovely Children* [. . .] (Boston: John Allen, 1714), 27.

146. Samuel Willard, *The Just Man's Prerogative* [. . .] (Boston: B. Green, 1706), 5; Colman, *Devout Contemplation*, 8.

147. C. Mather, *Orphanotrophium*, 12.

148. Cited in Silverman, *Life and Times*, 272.

149. James K. A. Smith, *You Are What You Love: The Spiritual Power of Habit* (Grand Rapids: Brazos, 2016), 130.

150. James K. A. Smith, *Imagining the Kingdom: How Worship Works* (Grand Rapids: Baker Academic, 2013), 109–10.

151. On the importance of prayer for children in the midst of everyday experience, see Catherine Stonehouse and Scottie May, *Listening to Children on the Spiritual Journey: Guidance for Those Who Teach and Nurture* (Grand Rapids: Baker Academic, 2010), 41–54.

152. Christian Smith, *Soul Searching: The Religious and Spiritual Lives of American Teenagers* (New York: Oxford University Press, 2005), 165.

The Parent as Prophet

1. Increase Mather, *Some Important Truths Concerning Conversion* [. . .], 2nd ed. (Boston: Samuel Green, 1684), 47. On this theme, see also James Axtell, *The School upon a Hill: Education and Society in Colonial New England* (New York: Norton, 1974), 12.

2. Cotton Mather, *A Family-Sacrifice. A Brief Essay to Direct and Excite Family-Religion* [. . .] (Boston: B. Green and J. Allen, 1703), 35.

3. C. Mather, *Family-Sacrifice*, 35, 37.

4. Richard Baxter, *The Godly Home*, ed. Randall J. Pederson (Wheaton, IL: Crossway, 2010), 76–77.

5. J. Lewis Wilson, "Catechisms and Their Use among the Puritans," in *One Steadfast High Intent: Report of The Puritan and Reformed Studies Conference* (London, 1966), 34–35.

6. Edmund Morgan, *The Puritan Family: Religion and Domestic Relations in Seventeenth-Century New England* (New York: Harper & Row, 1966), 97.

7. William Orme, *The Practical Works of the Rev. Richard Baxter* (London: James Duncan, 1830), 8:21.

8. Cotton Mather, *Cares about the Nurseries* [. . .] (Boston: T. Green, 1702), 43.

9. William Cooper, *God's Concern for a Godly Seed. As it was shewed in the Forenoon Sermon*, in *Two Sermons Preached in Boston, March 5, 1723 on a Day of Prayer*, by Benjamin Colman and William Cooper (Boston: S. Kneeland, 1723), 6; George Whitefield, *The Great Duty of Family Religion* [. . .] (Boston: T. Fleet, 1739), 12.

10. Benjamin Wadsworth, *The Well-Ordered Family* [. . .] (Boston: B. Green, 1712), 71. See also Cooper, *God's Concern*, 6.

11. Hugh Amory and David D. Hall, *A History of the Book in America* (Chapel Hill: University of North Carolina Press, 2007), 1:120; Gerald F. Moran and Maris A. Vinovskis, *Religion, Family, and the Life Course: Explorations in the Social History of Early America* (Ann Arbor: University of Michigan Press, 1992), 119–20. As a practice, reading was viewed in very positive terms in this era. See Courtney Weikle-Mills, *Imaginary Citizens: Child Readers and the Limits of American Independence, 1640–1868* (Baltimore: Johns Hopkins University Press, 2013), 32–62.

12. Wadsworth, *Well-Ordered Family*, 60.

13. Deodat Lawson, *The Duty and Property of a Religious Householder* [. . .] (Boston: B. Green, 1693), 43.

14. *Records of the Governor and Company of the Massachusetts Bay in New England*, ed. Nathaniel B. Shurtleff (Boston: William White, 1853), 2:203. While all of the communities complied with the order to establish grammar schools, only about one-third started primary schools, indicating that they were willing to rely on home-based training for basic literacy. In addition, up until the eighteenth century, the population in New England was so dispersed that forming such schools proved challenging. Many more complied in the eighteenth century when population density made this more possible. See Moran and Vinovskis, *Religion, Family, and the Life Course*, 124–26.

15. Literacy rates did expand among white men from about 60 percent in the mid-seventeenth century to close to 85 percent by the mid-eighteenth century. See Kenneth A. Lockridge, *Literacy in Colonial America: An Enquiry into the Social Context of Literacy*

and Social Development in the Early Modern West (New York: Norton, 1974); Amory and Hall, *History of the Book*, 1:119–31. While rates were lower for women, it is notable that female literacy was also deemed critically important among New England's colonial Christians. It was just as important for girls to read (though not write) so that they could access the Scriptures and prepare for a future motherhood in which they would be teaching their children how to imbibe its divine truths. See E. Jennifer Monaghan, *Learning to Read and Write in Colonial America* (Amherst: University of Massachusetts Press, 2005). White men had achieved nearly universal literacy by the end of the eighteenth century, while women also made significant gains, especially in urban areas. See Lockridge, *Literacy in Colonial America*, 38–42; Amory and Hall, *History of the Book*, 1:380–81. Historical records seem to demonstrate that mothers indeed played a significant role in teaching basic literacy to children. Many, in fact, may have followed Increase Mather's pattern: "I learned to read of my mother. I learned to write of Father, who also instructed me in grammar learning, both in the Latin and the greeke tongues." M. G. Hall, ed., "The Autobiography of Increase Mather," *American Antiquarian Society Proceedings* 71 (October 1961): 278.

16. Most households had five or fewer books, with collections over twenty mostly reserved for ministers and magistrates. The bestselling books in New England were hornbooks, primers, psalm books, and catechisms. After 1730, spelling books also grew in popularity. In the early eighteenth century, a coalition of clergy and civil government worked to make sure all households had a Bible. Amory and Hall, *History of the Book*, 1:125–26. See also David H. Watters, "'I Spake as a Child': Authority, Metaphor and *The New-England Primer*," *Early American Literature* 20, no. 3 (1985–1986): 193–213. The *New England Primer* was one of the chief ways Puritan children learned to read and memorize the Bible. See Daniel L. Dreisbach, *Reading the Bible with the Founding Fathers* (New York: Oxford University Press, 2016), 36–37.

17. The *New England Primer* was developed by Benjamin Harris, a London printer who fled England once the Catholic James II ascended to the throne. Arriving in Boston in 1686, he sought a market for his instructional manual for Protestant children, *The Protestant Tutor*. To make it more marketable, he shortened its length, emphasized its potential as a textbook, and appealed to local pride by calling it *The New England Primer*. See Paul Leicester Ford, ed., *The New-England Primer: A History of Its Origin and Development* (New York: Dodd, Mead, 1897), 12–19.

18. While it is difficult to precisely trace its decline, the *New England Primer* had certainly fallen out of widespread usage by the mid-nineteenth century. Editions were continuously published until at least 1886, but its use as a schoolbook diminished as other texts, including Noah Webster's *Blue-Backed Speller* and William Holmes McGuffey's *Eclectic Readers*, took its place. See Ford, *New-England Primer*, 12–19.

19. Ford, *New-England Primer*, 47.

20. Cotton Mather, *A Family Well-Ordered. Or An Essay To Render Parents and Children Happy in one another* [. . .] (Boston: B. Green & J. Allen, 1699), 19.

21. Cotton Mather, *Corderius Americanus: An Essay Upon The Good Education of Children* [. . .] (Boston: John Allen, 1708), 5; Cotton Mather, *Addresses to Old Men, and Young Men, and Little Children* [. . .] (Boston: R. Pierce, 1694), 84. See also Worthington Chauncey Ford, ed., *The Diary of Cotton Mather* (repr., New York: Frederick Unger, 1911), 2:234.

22. Ford, *Diary of Cotton Mather*, 2:149. See also Cotton Mather, *Bonifacius: An Essay Upon the Good* [. . .] (Boston: B. Green, 1710), 58.

23. See, for example, Daniel Lewes, *The Joy of Children walking in Truth* [. . .] (Boston: Henchman, 1723), 19; Henry Gibbs, *Godly Children their Parents' Joy* [. . .] (Boston: S. Kneeland & T. Green, 1727), 37–39; John Barnard, *A Call to Parents, and Children. Or, The Great Concern of Parents; And The Important Duty of Children* [. . .] (Boston: T. Fleet, 1737), 22–23, 45–46; Wadsworth, *Well-Ordered Family*, 54, 62.

24. Lawson, *Duty and Property*, 27.

25. Ian Green, *The Christian's ABC: Catechisms and Catechizing in England, 1530–1740* (Oxford: Clarendon, 1996); Lawrence A. Cremin, *American Education: The Colonial Experience, 1607–1783* (New York: Harper & Row, 1970), 130–31; Axtell, *School upon a Hill*; Morgan, *Puritan Family*, 98–99; Barnard, *Call to Parents*, 23–24.

26. Wadsworth, *Well-Ordered Family*, 83–84; C. Mather, *Addresses to Old Men*, 119.

27. Wadsworth, *Well-Ordered Family*, 63. See also C. Mather, *Family Well-Ordered*, 19.

28. In Norwich, Connecticut, all males eight to nine years old were to come to the church on the Sabbath to be catechized until they were thirteen. See Sandford Fleming, *Children and Puritanism: The Place of Children in the Life and Thought of the New England Churches, 1620–1847* (New Haven: Yale University Press, 1933), 110–11. Cotton Mather regularly visited families to pose questions to youth on the catechism and to use their answers to make "as lively Applications unto them as I could." In later years, it appears he would often invite youth together into his home for monthly catechism instruction. See Cremin, *American Education*, 156; Fleming, *Children and Puritanism*, 111. When churches maintained both a "pastor" and a "teacher," as many churches did in the seventeenth century, the teacher would often be involved in the preparation of the catechisms. See Vergel V. Phelps, "The Pastor and Teacher in New England," *Harvard Theological Review* 4, no. 3 (July 1911): 390.

29. Axtell, *School upon a Hill*, 26.

30. Morgan, *Puritan Family*, 88. In 1650, Connecticut's General Court made similar provision, followed closely by nearly identical statements in New Haven (1655), New York (1665), and Plymouth (1671) (Axtell, *School upon a Hill*, 23; Cremin, *American Education*, 125). Of course, not all parents engaged this work with equal fervor. The laws requiring such training and the need of selectmen and tithingmen to enforce such laws imply that external threats were necessary to ensure faithful compliance. Deodat

Lawson observed that there were many who were twelve, fourteen, or sixteen years old "who can read little, understand less of holy scriptures, are strangers to catechetical instruction, and so ignorant of the principles of Christian religion that are necessary for the saving of their souls" (*Duty and Property*, 45–46). This was still an issue by the time of Jonathan Edwards, who likewise suggested that there was a "great want of care and pains in instructing children and instilling principles of religion into 'em." *The Works of Jonathan Edwards*, vol. 17, ed. Mark Valeri (New Haven: Yale University Press, 1999), 92.

31. Stephen M. Frank, *Life with Father: Parenthood and Masculinity in the Nineteenth-Century American North* (Baltimore: Johns Hopkins University Press, 1998), 11; Maris Vinovskis, "Family and Schooling in Colonial and Nineteenth-Century America," *Journal of Family History* 12, no. 1 (1987): 22–23.

32. Cotton Mather, *Ornaments for the Daughters of Zion, or, The Character and Happiness of a Vertuous Woman* [. . .] (Cambridge: S. G. and B.G, 1692), 94–95.

33. William Williams, *The Duty of Parents to Transmit Religion to their Children* [. . .] (Boston: B. Green, 1721), 11. See also C. Mather, *Cares about the Nurseries*, 44.

34. Steven Mintz, *Huck's Raft: A History of American Childhood* (Cambridge, MA: Belknap, 2004), 16.

35. C. Mather, *Ornaments for the Daughters of Zion*, 93.

36. Laurel Thatcher Ulrich, *Good Wives: Image and Reality in the Lives of Women in Northern New England, 1650–1750* (New York: Vintage Books, 1991), 35–50.

37. Ulrich, *Good Wives*, 126–45.

38. Ulrich, *Good Wives*, 157.

39. Cremin, *American Education*, 130.

40. For a complete list of New England catechisms, see Wilberforce Eames, *Early New England Catechisms* (Worcester, MA: Press of Charles Hamilton, 1898). Benjamin Keach developed a Baptist catechism (for which he was tried) that was used by many and enjoyed a long run. See Ford, *New-England Primer*, 9.

41. Cited in Eames, *Early New England Catechisms*, 89. Anglicans were actually far less given to developing catechisms, likely both because they had standardized church catechisms and because they relied more on embodied traditions and habits than the word-centered Puritans and their allies. See C. John Sommerville, *The Discovery of Childhood in Puritan England* (Athens: University of Georgia Press, 1992), 135–37; Williams, *Duty of Parents*, 10–12.

42. John Cotton, *Spiritual Milk for Boston Babes in either England: drawn out of the breasts of both Testaments for their Souls nourishment. But may be of like use to any Children* (Boston, 1684).

43. Elizabeth A. Francis, "American Children's Literature, 1646–1880," in *American Childhood: A Research Guide and Historical Handbook*, ed. Joseph M. Hawes and N. Ray Hiner (Westport, CT: Greenwood, 1985), 190.

44. Ford, *New-England Primer*, 41. This catechism was incorporated somewhere between 1690 and 1701.

45. Josiah Smith, *The Duty of Parents to Instruct their Children* [. . .] (Boston: D. Henchman, 1730), 14.

46. Isaac Watts, *Discourse on the Way of Instruction by Catechisms, and of the Best Manner of Composing Them*, 3rd ed. (London: Printed for Richard Ford and Richard Hett, 1736), 12.

47. Matthew Henry, *Family Religion* (Fearn, UK: Christian Focus, 2008), 72.

48. Increase Mather, *An Earnest Exhortation to the Children of New-England, To Exalt the God of their Fathers* (Boston, 1711), 17.

49. Cotton Mather, *Magnalia Christi Americana; or, The Ecclesiastical History of New England* [. . .] (Hartford: Silas Andrus & Son, 1853), 550.

50. Watts, *Way of Instruction*, 15.

51. Watts, *Way of Instruction*, 15. On this theme, see also Patricia Demars, *Heaven upon Earth: The Form of Moral and Religious Children's Literature, to 1850* (Knoxville: University of Tennessee Press, 1993), 53.

52. J. Smith, *Duty of Parents*, 14.

53. Wadsworth, *Well-Ordered Family*, 64; C. Mather, *Cares about Nurseries*, 18–19. See also C. Mather, *Corderius Americanus*, 10.

54. Barnard, *Call to Parents*, 23. See also Increase Mather, *A Call from Heaven to the Present and Succeeding Generations* [. . .] (Boston: J. Foster, 1679), 92. Whitefield spoke of the "seducers" who attempt to "sap the very foundation of our most holy religion." *Great Duty*, 11.

55. Sommerville, *Discovery of Childhood*, 136.

56. Benjamin Bass, *Parents and Children Advised and Exhorted to their Duty* [. . .] (Newport, RI, 1729), 11; N. Ray Hiner, "The Cry of Sodom Enquired Into: Educational Analysis in Seventeenth-Century New England," *History of Education Quarterly* 13, no. 1 (Spring 1973): 11.

57. C. Mather, *Cares about the Nurseries*, 20. See also Joseph Sewall, *Desires that Joshua's Resolution May Be Revived, or Excitations to the Constant and Diligent Exercise of Family Religion* (Boston: B. Green, 1716), 27.

58. C. Mather, *Cares about the Nurseries*, 6, 23.

59. Samuel Hopkins, *The Life and Character of the Late Reverend, Learned, and Pious Mr. Jonathan Edwards, President of the College of New Jersey. Together with a Number of his Sermons on Various Important Subjects* (Boston: S. Kneeland, 1765), 43.

60. Barnard, *Call to Parents*, 24.

61. C. Mather, *Family-Sacrifice*, 36. Mather also utilized a method first championed by Herbert Palmer that required children to provide yes or no answers to the catechism responses. See C. Mather, *Family Well-Ordered*, 19; C. Mather, *Cares about the Nurseries*; C. Mather, *Corderius Americanus*, 10. Isaac Watts rejected this method, noting that a

simple yes or no answer would do little to enhance understanding since the child may simply guess the right answer (*Way of Instruction*, 59). See also Sommerville, *Discovery of Childhood*, 135–37; Green, *Christian's ABC*, 263.

62. C. Mather, *Cares about the Nurseries*, 6.

63. Cotton Mather, *Family-Religion Urged. Or, Some Serious Considerations offer'd to the Reason and Conscience of Every Prayerless Householder* [. . .] (Boston: Benjamin Harris, 1709), 12.

64. Green, *Christian's ABC*.

65. C. Mather, *Cares about Nurseries*, 38.

66. Lewes, *Joy of Children*, 19.

67. Lewes, *Joy of Children*, 20. See also C. Mather, *Family Well-Ordered*, 21.

68. Lawson, *Duty and Property*, 28.

69. *The Works of Jonathan Edwards*, vol. 4, ed. C. C. Goen (New Haven: Yale University Press, 1972), 200. Bartlett's conversion was validated when she developed a heart of evangelism for her siblings, a love for the Sabbath, a love for attending church, a delight in spiritual conversation, and a reflexive hatred for sin that emerged after inadvertently stealing plums from a neighbor's tree (200–205).

70. For examples in this tradition, see John Demos, *A Little Commonwealth: Family Life in Plymouth Colony* (New York: Oxford University Press, 1970); Michael Zuckerman, *Peaceable Kingdoms: New England Towns in the Eighteenth Century* (New York: Norton, 1970); Joseph Kett, *Rites of Passage: Adolescence in America, 1790 to the Present* (New York: Basic Books, 1977); Fleming, *Children and Puritanism*.

71. Zuckerman, *Peaceable Kingdoms*, 72–80; Demos, *Little Commonwealth*.

72. Fleming, *Children and Puritanism*, 59–60.

73. Cited in Moran and Vinovskis, *Religion, Family, and the Life Course*, 120.

74. Catherine Brekus, *Sarah Osborn's World: The Rise of Evangelical Christianity in Early America* (New Haven: Yale University Press, 2013), 38.

75. David E. Stannard, *The Puritan Way of Death: A Study in Religion, Culture, and Social Change* (New York: Oxford University Press, 1977), 69.

76. Benjamin Colman, *A Devout Contemplation on the Meaning of Divine Providence in the Early Death of Pious and Lovely Children* [. . .] (Boston: John Allen, 1714), 5.

77. J. Smith, *Duty of Parents*, 10.

78. Cited in Anne Lombard, *Making Manhood: Growing Up Male in Colonial New England* (Cambridge, MA: Harvard University Press, 2003), 21.

79. C. Mather, *Cares about the Nurseries*, 52.

80. Karin Calvert, *Children in the House: The Material Culture of Early Childhood, 1600–1900* (Boston: Northeastern University Press, 1992), 46. Calvert also indicates that boys could be put back in petticoats as punishment for immaturity or misbehavior, indicating a loss of status.

81. Lombard, *Making Manhood*, 30.

82. Lombard, *Making Manhood*, 30. See also Ralph Larossa, *The Modernization of Fatherhood: A Social and Political History* (Chicago: University of Chicago Press, 1996), 24; Steven Ozment, *When Fathers Ruled: Family Life in Reformation Europe* (Cambridge, MA: Harvard University Press, 1985), 132.

83. Lombard, *Making Manhood*, 29–30.

84. Peter Bulkeley, *The Gospel-Covenant; or, The Covenant of Grace Opened* (London: Matthew Simmons, 1651), 162.

85. Isaac Ambrose, *The Well-Ordered Family* [. . .], reprinted ed. (Boston: S. Kneeland, 1762), 11–12.

86. Ambrose, *Well-Ordered Family*, 12. See also C. Mather, *Family Well-Ordered*, 20.

87. C. Mather, *Addresses to Old Men*, 93.

88. Watts, *Way of Instruction.* Page references appear in the text.

89. Watts also argued that such catechisms should avoid denominational disputes and controversies, focusing on areas of common agreement.

90. See, for example, Isaac Watts, *The First Set of Catechisms and Prayers: or, The Religion of Little Children Under Seven or Eight Years of Age*, 9th ed. (Boston: Printed for J. Blanchard, 1745); Watts, *The Second Sett of Catechisms and Prayer: or, Some Helps to the Religion of Children, and their Knowledge of the Scripture, from seven to twelve Years of Age*, 7th ed. (Boston: Rogers and Fowle, 1748).

91. Calvert, *Children in the House*, 19–38.

92. Sommerville, *Discovery of Childhood*, 45.

93. C. Mather, *Corderius Americanus*, 18.

94. William Cooper, *How and Why Young People Should Cleanse Their Way, in Two Sermons* [. . .] (Boston: B. Green, 1716), iii–iv.

95. Mintz, *Huck's Raft*, 10.

96. Eleazer Mather, *A Serious Exhortation to the Present and Succeeding Generation in New England* [. . .] (Cambridge, MA: S. G. and M. T., 1671), 20.

97. Barnard, *Call to Parents*, 25–26.

98. *The Works of Jonathan Edwards*, vol. 22, ed. Harry S. Stout and Nathan O. Hatch (New Haven: Yale University Press, 1994), 453.

99. James Janeway and Cotton Mather, *A Token For Children. Being An Exact Account of the Conversion, Holy and Exemplary Lives and Joyful Deaths of Several Young Children, To which is Added, A Token, for the Children of New England* (Boston: Nicholas Boone, 1700). See also Sommerville, *Discovery of Childhood*, 50–56.

100. Janeway and Mather, *Token For Children*, front matter.

101. Morgan, *Puritan Family*, 97–98.

102. Kenneth Silverman, *The Life and Times of Cotton Mather* (New York: Harper & Row, 1984), 266.

103. Ford, *Diary of Cotton Mather*, 2:151.

104. Ford, *Diary of Cotton Mather*, 2:182, 262.

105. Wadsworth, *Well-Ordered Family*, 65.

106. Ford, *Diary of Cotton Mather*, 2:104.

107. C. Mather, *Family-Sacrifice*, 43. See also Silverman, *Life and Times*, 182.

108. Ian Murray, *Jonathan Edwards: A New Biography* (Carlisle, PA: Banner of Truth, 1987), 402.

109. M. Halsey Thomas, ed., *The Diary of Samuel Sewall, 1674–1729* (New York: Farrar, Straus & Giroux, 1973), 1:249.

110. George Marsden, *Jonathan Edwards: A Life* (New Haven: Yale University Press, 2003), 321.

111. Wadsworth, *Well-Ordered Family*, 65–66. See also C. Mather, *Corderius Americanus*, 18; Cotton Mather, *Man Eating the Food of Angels: The Gospel of the Manna, To be Gathered in the Morning* [. . .] (Boston: T. Green, 1710), 33; Cotton Mather, *Young Man Spoken To: Another Essay To Recommend & Inculcate the Maxims of Early Religion Unto Young Persons; And Especially the Religion of the Closet* [. . .] (Boston: T. Green, 1712), 8; Cotton Mather, *The Wayes and Joyes of Early Piety. One Essay more, To Describe and Commend, A Walk in the Truth Of our Great Saviour, Unto the Children of His People* [. . .] (Boston: B. Green, 1712), 48–50; Cotton Mather, *Things that Young People Should Think Upon. Or, The Death of Young People Improved, In Some Lively Admonitions to the Living* [. . .] (Boston: B. Green & J. Allen, 1700). When a fourteen-year-old boy in their neighborhood was crushed by a cart and killed, Cotton Mather used the occasion to provide "more than ordinarily importunate Admonitions" for his son "to become serious, and prayerful and afraid of Sin." *Vita Brevis. An Essay, Upon Withering Flowers* [. . .] (Boston: John Allen, 1714), 26–30.

112. Carl N. Degler, *At Odds: Women and the Family in America from the Revolution to the Present* (New York: Oxford University Press, 1980), 71.

113. Ford, *Diary of Cotton Mather*, 2:219. See also Cotton Mather, *Genethlia Pia; or, Thoughts on a Birth-Day* [. . .] (Boston: B. Green, 1719).

114. J. M. Lloyd Thomas, ed., *The Autobiography of Richard Baxter* (London: J. M. Dent & Sons, 1925), 10.

115. Christian Smith, Bridget Ritz, and Michael Rotolo, *Religious Parenting: Transmitting Faith and Values in Contemporary America* (Princeton: Princeton University Press, 2020), 180.

116. Christian Smith, *Souls in Transition: The Religious and Spiritual Lives of Emerging Adults* (New York: Oxford University Press, 2009), 81.

117. On this theme, see Nicholas Wolterstorff, *Educating for Responsible Action* (Grand Rapids: Eerdmans, 1980), 7–15; Kenda Creasy Dean, *Almost Christian: What the Faith of Our Teenagers Is Telling the American Church* (New York: Oxford University Press, 2010), 117–20.

118. James K. A. Smith, *You Are What You Love: The Spiritual Power of Habit* (Grand Rapids: Brazos, 2016), 3. See also James K. A. Smith, *Desiring the Kingdom: Worship, Worldview, and Cultural Formation* (Grand Rapids: Baker Academic, 2009).

119. C. Smith, *Souls in Transition*, 154.

120. Christian Smith and Amy Adamczyk, *Handing Down the Faith: How Parents Pass Their Religion on to the Next Generation* (New York: Oxford University Press, 2021), 53–54, 71–72, 83–85.

121. Smith and Adamczyk, *Handing Down the Faith*, 83.

122. Smith and Adamczyk, *Handing Down the Faith*, 225.

123. Peter Berger and Thomas Luckmann, *The Social Construction of Reality* (New York: Anchor/Doubleday, 1967), 152–54. On this theme, see also Amanda Hontz Drury, *Saying Is Believing: The Necessity of Testimony in Adolescent Spiritual Development* (Downers Grove, IL: IVP Academic, 2015).

124. Smith and Adamczyk, *Handing Down the Faith*, 84.

125. Dean, *Almost Christian*, 119.

The Parent as King

1. Jonathan Edwards, *The Works of President Edwards, in Four Volumes* (New York: Leavitt, Trow, 1844), 399.

2. *The Works of Jonathan Edwards*, vol. 25, ed. Willson H. Kimnach (New Haven: Yale University Press, 2006), 484.

3. *The Works of Jonathan Edwards*, vol. 17, ed. Mark Valeri (New Haven: Yale University Press, 1999), 92.

4. *The Works of Jonathan Edwards*, vol. 19, ed. M. X. Lesser (New Haven: Yale University Press, 2001), 54.

5. *The Works of Jonathan Edwards*, vol. 22, ed. Harry S. Stout and Nathan O. Hatch (New Haven: Yale University Press, 1994), 333.

6. Catherine Brekus, "Children of Wrath, Children of Grace: Jonathan Edwards and the Puritan Culture of Child Rearing," in *The Child in Christian Thought*, ed. Marcia J. Bunge (Grand Rapids: Eerdmans, 2001), 308.

7. On this case, see George Marsden, *Jonathan Edwards: A Life* (New Haven: Yale University Press, 2003), 292–302; Ava Chamberlain, "Bad Books and Bad Boys: The Transformation of Gender in Eighteenth Century Northampton, Massachusetts," *New England Quarterly* 75, no. 2 (June 2002): 179–203.

8. *Works of Jonathan Edwards*, 25:458.

9. *Works of Jonathan Edwards*, 25:485.

10. *Works of Jonathan Edwards*, 25:484.

11. *Works of Jonathan Edwards*, 25:484.

12. Benjamin Colman, *An Argument for and Persuasive unto the Great and Important Duty of Family Worship: With Rules and Directions for the Due Performance of it* (Boston: Gamaliel Rogers, 1728), 4.

13. John Norton, *Abel Being Dead Yet Speaketh; or The Life and Death of that Deservedly Famous Man of God, Mr. John Cotton* (London: Tho. Newcomb, 1658), 8.

14. Deodat Lawson, *The Duty and Property of a Religious Householder* [. . .] (Boston: B. Green, 1693), 59–60.

15. Benjamin Bass, *Parents and Children Advised and Exhorted to their Duty* [. . .] (Newport, RI, 1729), 2; Joseph Sewall, *Desires that Joshua's Resolution May Be Revived, or Excitations to the Constant and Diligent Exercise of Family Religion* (Boston: B. Green, 1716), 37.

16. John Dod and Robert Cleaver, *A Godly Forme of Household Government, For the Ordering of Private Families, According to the Direction of God's Word* (London: R. Field, 1598); Joseph Buckminster, *Heads of Families to Resolve for their Households, No Less than for Themselves, That They Will Serve the Lord* [. . .] (Boston: S. Kneeland, 1759); Samuel Davies, "The Necessity and Excellency of Family Religion," in *Sermons on Important Subjects* (New York: Robert Carter and Brothers, 1851), 2:42–43 (originally published 1758).

17. Colman, *Duty of Family Worship*, 4; Sewall, *Joshua's Resolution*, 37–38; Benjamin Wadsworth, *The Well-Ordered Family* [. . .] (Boston: B. Green, 1712), 47–49.

18. See, for example, Wadsworth, *Well-Ordered Family*; Cotton Mather, *A Family Well-Ordered. Or An Essay To Render Parents and Children Happy in one another* [. . .] (Boston: B. Green & J. Allen, 1699); Isaac Ambrose, *The Well-Ordered Family* [. . .], reprinted ed. (Boston: S. Kneeland, 1762); *Memoirs of Captain Roger Clap* (Boston, 1731), 5. On the theme of hierarchical order and duty, see also Patricia Demars, *Heaven upon Earth: The Form of Moral and Religious Children's Literature, to 1850* (Knoxville: University of Tennessee Press, 1993), 35–39.

19. Dod and Cleaver, *Godly Forme*, unnumbered page.

20. Steven Ozment, *When Fathers Ruled: Family Life in Reformation Europe* (Cambridge, MA: Harvard University Press, 1985).

21. John Demos, "Digging Up Family History: Myths, Realities, and Works-in-Progress," in *Major Problems in the History of American Families and Children*, ed. Anya Jabour (Boston: Houghton Mifflin, 1980), 7.

22. Harry Stout, *The New England Soul: Preaching and Religious Culture in Colonial New England* (New York: Oxford University Press, 1986), 22; Lisa Wilson, *Ye Heart of a Man: The Domestic Life of Men in Colonial New England* (New Haven: Yale University Press, 1999), 126; N. Ray Hiner, "The Cry of Sodom Enquired Into: Educational Analysis in Seventeenth-Century New England," *History of Education Quarterly* 13, no. 1 (Spring 1973): 13; John Barnard, *A Call to Parents, and Children* (Boston: T. Fleet, 1737), 13; Anne

Lombard, *Making Manhood: Growing Up Male in Colonial New England* (Cambridge, MA: Harvard University Press, 2003), 22–27.

23. William Gouge, *Of Domesticall Duties, Eight Treatises*, 2nd ed. (London: John Beale, 1626), 275.

24. Mary P. Ryan, *Cradle of the Middle Class: The Family in Oneida County, New York, 1790–1865* (New York: Cambridge University Press, 1981), 31–43.

25. William Homes, *The Good Government of Christian Families Recommended: As that which will contribute greatly to their Peace and true Happiness* [. . .] (Boston: D. Henchman, 1747), 11.

26. Philip J. Greven Jr., *Four Generations: Population, Land, and Family in Colonial Andover, Massachusetts* (Ithaca, NY: Cornell University Press, 1970); Ralph Larossa, *The Modernization of Fatherhood: A Social and Political History* (Chicago: University of Chicago Press, 1996), 25; John Demos, *A Little Commonwealth: Family Life in Plymouth Colony* (New York: Oxford University Press, 1970), 44; Lombard, *Making Manhood*, 7; E. Anthony Rotundo, "American Fatherhood: A Historical Perspective," *American Behavioral Scientist* 29, no. 1 (September/October 1985): 8; Steven Mintz and Susan Kellogg, *Domestic Revolutions: A Social History of American Family Life* (New York: Free Press, 1988), 9.

27. Demos, *Little Commonwealth*, 46; Catherine M. Scholten, *Childbearing in American Society: 1650–1850* (New York: New York University Press, 1985), 56–57; Carole Shammas, *A History of Household Government in America* (Charlottesville: University of Virginia Press, 2002), 24–52. Some historians contend that patriarchy actually increased in the early modern era because of the waning influence of kinship ties and the declining power of church leaders owing to the Protestant doctrine of the priesthood of all believers.

28. Lombard, *Making Manhood*, 8–17. See also Cotton Mather, *Parentalia: An Essay Upon the Blessings and Comforts Reserved for Pious Children After the Death of their Pious Parents* [. . .] (Boston: J. Allen, 1715), 31; W. Gouge, *Domesticall Duties*, 307; Cotton Mather, *Youth in its Brightest Glory: An Essay, Directing them that are Young in Age, To Become Strong in Grace, By the Word of God Abiding in them* (Boston: T. Green, 1709), 19.

29. Demos, *Little Commonwealth*, 45.

30. Cited in Philip J. Greven, *Child-Rearing Concepts, 1628–1861* (Itasca, IL: Peacock, 1973), 11.

31. Lombard, *Making Manhood*, 5; Catherine Brekus, *Sarah Osborn's World: The Rise of Evangelical Christianity in Early America* (New Haven: Yale University Press, 2013), 54–57.

32. Benjamin Colman, *The Duty and Honour of Aged Women* [. . .] (Boston: B. Green, 1711), ii–iii. See also Steven Mintz, *Huck's Raft: A History of American Childhood* (Cambridge, MA: Belknap, 2004), 26–27.

33. Amanda Porterfield, *Female Piety in Puritan New England: The Emergence of Religious Humanism* (New York: Oxford University Press, 1992), 118; Gerald F. Moran and Maris A. Vinovskis, *Religion, Family, and the Life Course: Explorations in the Social History of Early America* (Ann Arbor: University of Michigan Press, 1992), 31, 131; Laurel Thatcher Ulrich, "Vertuous Women Found: New England Ministerial Literature, 1668–1735," *American Quarterly* 28, no. 1 (Spring 1976): 31; Lonna M. Malmsheimer, "Daughters of Zion: New England Roots of American Feminism," *New England Quarterly* 50, no. 3 (September 1977): 487–92. Cotton Mather thought this imbalance might be the result of the "*Curse*" faced by women in submission and childbearing, along with the concomitant "*Tenderness* of their Disposition." As early as 1691, in fact, Mather indicated that "there are far more *godly Women* in the world, than there are *godly Men*." See Cotton Mather, *Ornaments for the Daughters of Zion, or, The Character and Happiness of a Vertuous Woman* [...] (Cambridge: S. G. and B. G., 1692), 44. He suggested that the fear of death in childbearing was a source of religious motivation for women. See Cotton Mather, *Tabitha Rediviva. An Essay To Describe and Commend the Good Works of a Vertuous Woman* [...] (Boston: J. Allen, 1713), 22. See also Richard D. Shiels, "The Feminization of American Congregationalism," *American Quarterly* 33, no. 1 (1981): 46–62.

34. Brekus, *Sarah Osborn's World*, 55.

35. Demos, *Little Commonwealth*, 45.

36. Laurel Thatcher Ulrich, *Good Wives: Image and Reality in the Lives of Women in Northern New England, 1650–1750* (New York: Vintage Books, 1991), 154–55; Dod and Cleaver, *Godly Forme*, 23.

37. Dod and Cleaver, *Godly Forme*, unnumbered page.

38. Cotton Mather, *Help for Distressed Parents. Or, Counsels & Comforts for Godly Parents Afflicted with Ungodly Children* [...] (Boston: John Allen, 1695), 30.

39. Thomas Cobbett, *A Fruitfull and Usefull Discourse Touching The Honour due from Children to Parents, and the Duty of Parents toward their Children* (London: S. G. for John Rothwell, 1656), 3–6; W. Gouge, *Domesticall Duties*, 266–68; Ozment, *When Fathers Ruled*, 151–52.

40. Edmund S. Morgan, *The Puritan Family: Religion and Domestic Relations in Seventeenth-Century New England* (New York: Harper & Row, 1966), 106–8.

41. C. Mather, *Family Well-Ordered*, 59–60.

42. Cobbett, *Fruitfull and Usefull Discourse*, 99.

43. Wadsworth, *Well-Ordered Family*, 90–91.

44. Cobbett, *Fruitfull and Usefull Discourse*, 89–90; W. Gouge, *Domesticall Duties*, 256–57; Wadsworth, *Well-Ordered Family*, 91–92.

45. S. E. Dwight, *The Life of President Edwards* (New York: G. & C. & H. Carvill, 1830), 129.

46. Wadsworth, *Well-Ordered Family*, 91. See also C. Mather, *Family Well-Ordered*, 61.

47. Wadsworth, *Well-Ordered Family*, 93.

48. Wayne J. Urban, Jennings L. Wagoner, and Milton Gaither, *American Education: A History*, 6th ed. (New York: Routledge, 2019), 30–31. Steven Mintz confirms that not many court proceedings resulted from these laws, and the one child who was tried under this law was whipped, not hanged. "Regulating the American Family," *Journal of Family History* 14, no. 4 (1989): 391.

49. John Barnard spoke of "natural, spiritual, and civil parents." *Call to Parents*, 53. See also Samuel Phillips, *Advice to a Child, or Young People Solemnly Warn'd Both Against Enticing, and Consenting When Enticed to Sin* (Boston: J. Phillips, 1729), 23–25; Cotton Mather, *Man Eating the Food of Angels: The Gospel of the Manna, To be Gathered in the Morning* [. . .] (Boston: T. Green, 1710), 40.

50. Wilson, *Ye Heart of a Man*, 127.

51. Barnard, *Call to Parents*, 20, 53; Cotton Mather, *Cares about the Nurseries* [. . .] (Boston: T. Green, 1702), 11.

52. W. Gouge, *Domesticall Duties*, 300; C. Mather, *Family Well-Ordered*, 17.

53. Wadsworth, *Well-Ordered Family*, 53.

54. Cobbett, *Fruitfull and Usefull Discourse*, 30–31; Homes, *Good Government*, 110; Henry Gibbs, *Godly Children their Parents' Joy* [. . .] (Boston: S. Kneeland & T. Green, 1727), 32–33.

55. Barnard, *Call to Parents*, 29; Homes, *Good Government*, 11.

56. Peter N. Stearns, "Obedience and Emotion: A Challenge in the Emotional History of Childhood," *Journal of Social History* 47, no. 3 (2014): 593.

57. C. Mather, *Family Well-Ordered*, 41–42.

58. Ambrose, *Well-Ordered Family*, 2. See also C. Mather, *Help for Distressed Parents*, 60; John R. Gillis, *A World of Their Own Making: Myth, Ritual, and the Quest for Family Values* (Cambridge, MA: Harvard University Press, 1996), 35; Brekus, *Sarah Osborn's World*, 50.

59. Gibbs, *Godly Children*, 49, 48.

60. Robert Ashton, ed., *The Works of John Robinson, Pastor of the Pilgrim Fathers* (London: John Snow, 1851), 247. Cited in Greven, *Child-Rearing Concepts*, 14.

61. Samuel Hopkins, *The Life and Character of the Late Reverend, Learned, and Pious Mr. Jonathan Edwards, President of the College of New Jersey. Together with a Number of his Sermons on Various Important Subjects* (Boston: S. Kneeland, 1765), 43.

62. Dwight, *Life of President Edwards*, 129.

63. Philip Greven, *The Protestant Temperament: Patterns of Child-Rearing, Religious Experience, and the Self in Early America* (Chicago: University of Chicago Press, 1977), 65, 99.

64. Ambrose, *Well-Ordered Family*, 24; C. Mather, *Family Well-Ordered*, 62–65.

65. Ambrose, *Well-Ordered Family*, 24; C. Mather, *Family Well-Ordered*, 65.

66. Homes, *Good Government*, 110.

67. C. Mather, *Help for Distressed Parents*, 59.

68. Colman, *Duty of Family Worship*, 31–33; Homes, *Good Government*, 1–5. See also Gibbs, *Godly Children*, 50.

69. C. Mather, *Family Well-Ordered*, 4.

70. Morgan, *Puritan Family*, 145–47; Ann Braude, *Sisters and Saints: Women and American Religion* (New York: Oxford University Press, 2001), 6–7; Bernard Farber, *Guardians of Virtue: Salem Families in 1800* (New York: Basic Books, 1972).

71. *Records of the Governor and Company of Massachusetts Bay*, 5:241. Mather favored strengthening the power of the community tithingmen in order to halt unruly youth, especially on the Sabbath. Worthington Chauncey Ford, ed., *The Diary of Cotton Mather* (repr., New York: Frederick Unger, 1911), 1:76, 101. See also Shammas, *Household Government*, 47–48.

72. Mintz, "Regulating the American Family," 390.

73. Shammas, *Household Government*, 48. For information on the role of tithingmen, see Morgan, *Puritan Family*, 148–50; Mintz, *Huck's Raft*, 14, 29.

74. Jay Fliegelman, *Prodigals and Pilgrims: The American Revolution against Patriarchal Authority, 1750–1800* (New York: Cambridge University Press, 1982); Lombard, *Making Manhood*; Stephen M. Frank, *Life with Father: Parenthood and Masculinity in the Nineteenth-Century American North* (Baltimore: Johns Hopkins University Press, 1998).

75. As David D. Hall has noted, the population of New England at the beginning of the eighteenth century was "astonishingly youthful," maintaining a median age of just sixteen ("New England, 1660–1730," in *The Cambridge Companion to Puritanism*, ed. John Coffey and Paul C. H. Lim [New York: Cambridge University Press, 2008], 145). Some historians seem to believe that there was little conception of the importance of the teenage years in colonial New England. See John Demos and Virginia Demos, "Adolescence in Historical Perspective," *Journal of Marriage and the Family* 31, no. 4 (November 1969): 632; Joseph Kett, *Rites of Passage: Adolescence in America, 1790 to the Present* (New York: Basic Books, 1977), 12. Kett claims that colonial Americans failed to distinguish between children and youth, viewing the differences between a seven-year-old and a seventeen-year-old as "unimportant." Other historians have recognized the concept of adolescence in the colonial era. See, for example, Barbara A. Hanawalt, "Historical Descriptions and Prescriptions for Adolescence," *Journal of Family History* 17, no. 4 (1992): 341–51, and Hiner, "Cry of Sodom," 15–16.

76. Cited in Ross Beales, "The Child in Seventeenth-Century America," in *American Childhood: A Research Guide and Historical Handbook*, ed. Joseph M. Hawes and N. Ray Hiner (Westport, CT: Greenwood, 1985), 35–36.

77. C. Mather, *Cares about the Nurseries*, 57.

78. Beales, "Child in Seventeenth-Century America," 36. Cotton Mather urged young people not to wait until they were "Twice Seven Years Old" before becoming "seriously Religious." *Words of Understanding* (Boston: S. Kneel, 1724), 10.

79. C. Mather, *Cares about the Nurseries*, 52–53.

80. C. Mather, *Cares about the Nurseries*, 52.

81. Cotton Mather, *Early Religion, Urged in a Sermon, The Duties Wherein, and the Reasons Wherefore, Young People Should Become Religious* [. . .] (Boston: B. D., 1694), 115–17. Mather apparently initiated a society of this kind during his own youth at the age of sixteen. See also Cotton Mather, *Religious Societies* (Boston: S. Kneeland, 1724); M. M. Ramsbottom, "Religion, Society, and the Family in Charlestown, Massachusetts, 1630–1740" (PhD diss., Yale University, 1987), 205–38. Patricia Tracy sees such societies in Jonathan Edwards's era as weakening family government and the direct spiritual ties between parents and children (substituting pastoral and peer authority for parental authority). *Jonathan Edwards, Pastor: Religion and Society in Eighteenth-Century Northampton* (Eugene, OR: Wipf & Stock, 2006), 111.

82. On girls, see Cotton Mather, *The Best Ornaments of Youth. A Short Essay, on the Good Things, Which are found in Some, and should be found in All, Young People* [. . .] (Boston: Timothy Green, 1707); Mather, *Man Eating the Food of Angels*, 36. Puritans were not always averse to some of the educational achievements that aimed at female refinement (Mather taught his daughters cooking, needlework, instrumental and vocal music, science, and Hebrew), but they were clear that such accomplishments were of secondary importance when compared to the pious practice of prayer, catechism training, and spiritual reading.

83. Cotton Mather, *Addresses to Old Men, and Young Men, and Little Children* [. . .] (Boston: R. Pierce, 1694), 57.

84. C. Mather, *Addresses to Old Men*, 57.

85. C. Mather, *Early Religion*, 5. On this theme, see also Glenn Wallach, *Obedient Sons: The Discourse of Youth and Generations in American Culture, 1630–1860* (Amherst: University of Massachusetts Press, 1997), 10–32.

86. On the relation of passion and "the profane" in New England, see Richard P. Gildrie, *The Profane, the Civil, and the Godly: The Reformation of Manners in Orthodox New England, 1679–1749* (University Park: Pennsylvania State University Press, 1994). This privileging of age over youth seems to have been somewhat reversed in the ministry of Jonathan Edwards. See Kenneth Minkema, "Old Age and Religion in the Writings and Life of Jonathan Edwards," *Church History* 70, no. 4 (December 2001): 674–704.

87. Thomas Foxcroft, *Cleansing Our Way in Youth Press'd, As of the Highest Importance* [. . .] (Boston: S. Kneeland, 1719), 16. See also C. Mather, *Addresses to Old Men*, 69–70.

88. Barnard, *Call to Parents*, 29.

89. William Cooper, *How and Why Young People Should Cleanse Their Way, in Two Sermons* [. . .] (Boston: B. Green, 1716), 7–13.

90. C. Mather, *Addresses to Old Men*, 71. Such sins were aggravated, he noted, by the "promiscuous dancing" favored by young people and by a growing tolerance for masturbation (self-pollution), a practice that served to make their hearts "the *Ovens* that have the impure flames of Hell constantly flaming there" (73). See also C. Mather, *Early*

Religion, 8–9; Cotton Mather, *The Pure Nazarite* [. . .] (Boston: T. Fleet, 1723); Greven, *Protestant Temperament*, 65–73.

91. Daniel Scott Smith and Michael S. Hindus, "Premarital Pregnancy in America, 1640–1971: An Overview and Interpretation," *Journal of Interdisciplinary History* 5, no. 4 (Spring 1975): 537–70. On this theme, see also Brekus, *Sarah Osborn's World*, 45. These rates were much lower in the seventeenth century and also declined in the nineteenth century. See Mintz, *Huck's Raft*, 29.

92. Lombard, *Making Manhood*, 47–52. On the association of passion and the female nature, see also Malmsheimer, "Daughters of Zion," 487–88. The Puritan disdain for excessive passion was coupled somewhat incongruously with their heralding of passionate religion. On this theme, see Richard Lovelace, *The American Pietism of Cotton Mather* (Eugene, OR: Wipf & Stock, 2007).

93. C. Mather, *Youth in its Brightest Glory*, 19. Increasingly, the sexual double standard was beginning to take hold as allowances were made for male sexual indiscretions. See Chamberlain, "Bad Books and Bad Boys," 179–203. Cotton Mather also labeled self-pollution as "effeminate" in *Nicetas. Or, Temptations to Sin, And Particularly to the Sin wherewith Youth Is most Usually and Easily Ensnared* [. . .] (Boston: Timothy Green, 1705), 40. Lombard makes a similar point in noting that "the opprobrious term *effeminate* referred not to a man with homosexual feelings but to one with 'a strong heterosexual passion.'" *Making Manhood*, 63.

94. Patricia Tracy notes that youth in the eighteenth century had fewer opportunities for informal gatherings because of the decline of common field agriculture, barn raisings, and corn huskings. She sees this as spawning the less desirable youthful gatherings that were disparaged by people like Mather and, later, Jonathan Edwards. *Jonathan Edwards, Pastor*, 106.

95. Mintz, *Huck's Raft*, 29. Roger Thompson notes that youth in New England were not as organized or institutionalized as in Europe. "Adolescent Culture in Colonial Massachusetts," *Journal of Family History* 9, no. 2 (Summer 1984): 127–41.

96. Lombard, *Making Manhood*, 47–48, 52; Cotton Mather, *The Young Mans Preservative: Serious Advice to All, and Especially to Young People, About their Company* [. . .] (Boston: Timothy Green, 1701), 10, 28, 33.

97. Gibbs, *Godly Children*, 66–67.

98. Ford, *Diary of Cotton Mather*, 2:466.

99. C. Mather, *Help for Distressed Parents*, 18–19. Because Mather believed in a kind of "symbolic judgment," he felt that the sins of children often represented a direct punishment of parental sins. As James Sears McGee has indicated, Puritans believed that God—as a God of order—often sent afflictions that reflected the nature of the particular sins. This "boomerang principle" revealed that God wanted to alert his children to the nature of their sin through the particular "cross" that he sent. *The Godly Man in Stuart England: Anglicans, Puritans, and the Two Tables, 1620–1670* (New Haven: Yale University Press, 1976), 36–37.

100. C. Mather, *Help for Distressed Parents*, 17.

101. Ambrose, *Well-Ordered Family*, 12.

102. C. Mather, *Help for Distressed Parents*, 17.

103. C. Mather, *Help for Distressed Parents*, 16.

104. C. Mather, *Help for Distressed Parents*, 19–21.

105. Dwight, *Life of President Edwards*, 128–29.

106. C. Mather, *Family Well-Ordered*, 24.

107. Barnard, *Call to Parents*, 32.

108. *Works of Jonathan Edwards*, 19:55.

109. *Works of Jonathan Edwards*, 19:55. See also Gibbs, *Godly Children*, 48.

110. Lombard, *Making Manhood*, 55; Mintz, *Huck's Raft*, 28; Wadsworth, *Well-Ordered Family*, 57.

111. Barnard, *Call to Parents*, 25.

112. Thomas Gouge, *The Young Man's Guide Through the Wilderness of this World, To the Heavenly Canaan* [. . .] (Boston: J. Draper, 1742), 167.

113. C. Mather, *Young Mans Preservative*, 21.

114. C. Mather, *Young Mans Preservative*, 43–44.

115. Cotton Mather, *The Wayes and Joyes of Early Piety. One Essay more, To Describe and Commend, A Walk in the Truth Of our Great Saviour, Unto the Children of His People* [. . .] (Boston: B. Green, 1712), 44. See also Wadsworth, *Well-Ordered Family*, 57–58.

116. Barnard, *Call to Parents*, 30. See also William Seward, *Family-Religion Revived: Or, An Attempt to Promote Religion and Virtue in Families* [. . .] (New Haven: James Parker, 1755), 86–87.

117. Hopkins, *Mr. Jonathan Edwards*, 44.

118. *Works of Jonathan Edwards*, 19:56.

119. Barnard, *Call to Parents*, 32–33.

120. William Williams, *The Duty of Parents to Transmit Religion to their Children* [. . .] (Boston: B. Green, 1721), 15–16.

121. C. Mather, *Help for Distressed Parents*, 28. Helena Wall notes that corporal punishment was "widely sanctioned" in colonial New England. *Fierce Communion: Family and Community in Early America* (Cambridge, MA: Harvard University Press, 1990), 117.

122. Margo Todd, "Humanists, Puritans, and the Spiritualized Household," *Church History* 49, no. 1 (March 1980): 28–29.

123. W. Gouge, *Domesticall Duties*, 310.

124. Cotton Mather, *Bonifacius: An Essay Upon the Good* [. . .] (Boston: B. Green, 1710), 59–60. See also Sewall, *Joshua's Resolution*, 73.

125. Gibbs, *Godly Children*, 52–54. See also Gloria L. Main, *Peoples of a Spacious Land: Families and Cultures in Colonial New England* (Cambridge, MA: Harvard University Press, 2001), 130–37.

126. *The Works of Jonathan Edwards*, vol. 14, ed. Kenneth P. Minkema (New Haven: Yale University Press, 1997), 503.

127. According to Philip Greven, "moderates" and "genteels" were less rigorous in faith, more approving of the self, and more open to limited authority than their "evangelical" counterparts. While Greven does not speak in terms of chronological or generational change along these lines, the growth of moderate and genteel forms seems to have accelerated in the eighteenth century. See *Protestant Temperament*, esp. 151–91 and 265–95.

128. C. Mather, *Help for Distressed Parents*, 29–30; Williams, *Duty of Parents*, 14, 16.

129. C. Mather, *Help for Distressed Parents*, 20.

130. C. Mather, *Family Well-Ordered*, 24.

131. Seward, *Family-Religion Revived*, 87.

132. Philip Greven, *Spare the Child: The Religious Roots of Punishment and the Psychological Impact of Physical Abuse* (New York: Knopf, 1990).

133. Brekus, *Sarah Osborn's World*, 59–77.

134. Ashton, *Works of John Robinson*, 246–47.

135. Seward, *Family-Religion Revived*, 80–81.

136. Wadsworth, *Well-Ordered Family*, 57.

137. Gibbs, *Godly Children*, 54.

138. Barnard, *Call to Parents*, 34; Bosco, *Paterna*, 194–95. See also Morgan, *Puritan Family*, 104–5; Moran and Vinovskis, *Religion, Family, and the Life Course*, 116.

139. Wadsworth, *Well-Ordered Family*, 57.

140. W. Gouge, *Domesticall Duties*, 312.

141. Sewall, *Joshua's Resolution*, 40–41; Barnard, *Call to Parents*, 31–35.

142. C. Mather, *Help for Distressed Parents*, 25. See also C. Mather, *Family Well-Ordered*, 25.

143. Gibbs, *Godly Children*, 54.

144. Dod and Cleaver, *Godly Forme*, 40.

145. John H. Ellis, ed., *Works of Anne Bradstreet* (Charlestown, MA: A. E. Cutter, 1867), 50.

146. Wadsworth, *Well-Ordered Family*, 55.

147. C. Mather, *Family Well-Ordered*, 22.

148. Ambrose, *Well-Ordered Family*, 23.

The Parent as Architect

1. Horace Bushnell, *Christian Nurture* (New York: Charles Scribner, 1861), 236.

2. Catherine Brekus, *Sarah Osborn's World: The Rise of Evangelical Christianity in Early America* (New Haven: Yale University Press, 2013), 9–11. Brekus indicates that evangelicals embraced many aspects of the Enlightenment, such as progress, humanitarian zeal, the elevation of the individual, and the importance of the affections, but modified these to reflect their beliefs.

3. Brekus, *Sarah Osborn's World*, 8. See also Mark Noll, *America's God: From Jonathan Edwards to Abraham Lincoln* (New York: Oxford University Press, 2002), 93–113.

4. H. Shelton Smith, *Changing Conceptions of Original Sin: A Study in American Theology Since 1750* (New York: Charles Scribner's Sons, 1955), 10–86; Peter Gregg Slater, *Children in the New England Mind: In Death and in Life* (Hamden, CT: Archon Books, 1977), 51–67.

5. Margaret Bendroth, *Growing Up Protestant: Parents, Children, and Mainline Churches* (New Brunswick, NJ: Rutgers University Press, 2002), 20–24. See also Jacqueline S. Reinier, *From Virtue to Character: American Childhood, 1775–1850* (New York: Twayne, 1996), 72–83.

6. Margaret Bendroth, "Children of Adam, Children of God: Christian Nurture in Early Nineteenth-Century America," *Theology Today* 56, no. 4 (January 2000): 495.

7. Brekus, *Sarah Osborn's World*, 145.

8. Slater, *Children*, 49–90.

9. John Taylor, *The Scripture-Doctrine of Original Sin Proposed to Free and Candid Examination*, 4th ed. (London: M. Waugh, 1767). On this theme, see also H. Smith, *Changing Conceptions*, 10–36; Merle Curti, *Human Nature in American Thought: A History* (Madison: University of Wisconsin Press, 1980).

10. Bendroth, "Children of Adam," 496–98; Slater, *Children*, 51–55, 81–84; M. J. G., "Parents the Medium of Divine Favor or Frown on their Children," *Father's and Mother's Manual* 1, no. 4 (October 1848): 97–106; Kathryn Kish Sklar, *Catherine Beecher: A Study in American Domesticity* (New York: Norton, 1976), 13.

11. Samuel Webster, *A Winter Evening's Conversation Upon the Doctrine of Original Sin* (Boston, 1757), 9.

12. "Dissertation on the Sinfulness of Infants," *Christian Disciple* 8, no. 2 (August 1814): 245–50.

13. Slater, *Children*, 63. Edwards's views on original sin were complex. He seemed to hold that children were born neutral but began to sin as soon as they were capable, which for Edwards was so soon after birth that they were culpable from the beginning. See Catherine Brekus, "Children of Wrath, Children of Grace: Jonathan Edwards and the Puritan Culture of Child Rearing," in *The Child in Christian Thought*, ed. Marcia J. Bunge (Grand Rapids: Eerdmans, 2001), 309–10.

14. Slater, *Children*, 76–81; Noll, *America's God*, 298–99; Anne M. Boylan, "Sunday Schools and Changing Evangelical Views of Children in the 1820s," *Church History* 48, no. 3 (September 1979): 328.

15. Anne M. Boylan, *Sunday School: The Formation of an American Institution, 1790–1880* (New Haven: Yale University Press, 1988), 145; Reinier, *From Virtue to Character*, 87–88.

16. Jay Fliegelman, *Prodigals and Pilgrims: The American Revolution against Patriarchal Authority, 1750–1800* (New York: Cambridge University Press, 1982), 167–68. See also H. Smith, *Changing Conceptions*.

17. Anne Scott MacLeod, *American Childhood: Essays on Children's Literature in the Nineteenth and Twentieth Centuries* (Athens: University of Georgia Press, 1994), 102, 146; Slater, *Children*, 128–58; Todd M. Brenneman, "A Child Shall Lead Them: Children and New Religious Groups in the Early Republic," in *Children and Youth in a New Nation*, ed. James Marten (New York: NYU Press, 2009), 109–14.

18. Catherine Beecher, *Religious Training of Children in the School, the Family, and the Church* (New York: Harper & Brothers, 1864), 190.

19. MacLeod, *American Childhood*, 94; Sklar, *Catherine Beecher*, 81; Reinier, *From Virtue to Character*, 97–98.

20. Lydia Child, *The Mother's Book* (Boston: Carter, Hendee and Babcock, 1831), 3.

21. Child, *Mother's Book*, 9. See also Boylan, *Sunday School*, 165. It was common for those with Romantic sensibilities to explain child deaths in these terms, noting that these children were "too fair" to remain within the corruption of the world. See, for example, Pat Jalland, *Death in the Victorian Family* (New York: Oxford University Press, 1996).

22. Carl N. Degler, *At Odds: Women and the Family in America from the Revolution to the Present* (New York: Oxford University Press, 1980), 68.

23. Boylan, *Sunday School*, 149. See, for example, W. S. T., "A Father and Mother Converted Through the Influence of a Sabbath School Scholar," *Sunday School Advocate* 8, no. 14 (April 17, 1849): 111; Bernard Wishy, *The Child and the Republic: The Dawn of Modern American Child Nurture* (Philadelphia: University of Pennsylvania Press, 1968), 81–181. Literary works often reflected these themes, depicting infants and children who would elevate their parents spiritually by their very presence. See, for example, T. S. Arthur, *The Angel of the Household* (Philadelphia: J. W. Bradley, 1854).

24. Hugh Cunningham, *Children and Childhood in Western Society Since 1500*, 3rd ed. (New York: Routledge, 2020), 59.

25. Charles Strickland, "A Transcendentalist Father: The Child-Rearing Practices of Bronson Alcott," *History of Childhood Quarterly* 1, no. 1 (1973): 11.

26. Samuel Phillips, *The Christian Home, as it is in the Sphere of Nature and the Church* (Springfield, MA: Gurdon Bill, 1865), 94.

27. *Our Baby* (New York: American Tract Society, 1872), 14, 184.

28. Karin Calvert, *Children in the House: The Material Culture of Early Childhood, 1600–1900* (Boston: Northeastern University Press, 1992), 104–10; Wishy, *The Child and the Republic*, 81–169.

29. MacLeod, *American Childhood*, 156. See also John R. Gillis, *A World of Their Own Making: Myth, Ritual, and the Quest for Family Values* (Cambridge, MA: Harvard University Press, 1996), 82–87.

30. *Our Baby*, 36.

31. Horace Bushnell, *God's Thoughts Fit Bread for Children: A Sermon Preached Before the Connecticut Sunday School Teachers' Convention, March 2, 1869* (Boston: Nichols and Noyes, 1869), 25.

32. *To Parents* (New York: American Tract Society, 1828), 181.

33. *To Parents*, 182. See also John M. Lowrie, "The Christian in the Family," in *Home, the School, and the Church; or the Presbyterian Education Repository*, ed. C. Van Rensselaer (Philadelphia: C. Sherman & Son, 1850–1860), 7:10.

34. Heman Humphrey, *Domestic Education* (Amherst, MA: J. S. & C. Adams, 1840), 48.

35. Humphrey, *Domestic Education*, 48–49.

36. S. R. Hall, *Practical Lectures on Parental Responsibility, and the Religious Education of Children* (Boston: Pierce and Parker, 1833), 30.

37. Hall, *Practical Lectures*, 29.

38. MacLeod, *American Childhood*, 146; Wishy, *The Child and the Republic*.

39. Slater, *Children*, 50. See also Priscilla J. Brewer, "'The Little Citizen': Images of Children in Early Nineteenth-Century America," *Journal of American Culture* 7, no. 4 (1984): 45.

40. Nancy F. Cott sees a belief in childhood malleability as the source of both evangelical moves toward early conversion and more liberal beliefs in the power of impressions in shaping young children ("Notes toward an Interpretation of Antebellum Childrearing," *Psychohistory Review* 6, no. 4 [1978]: 4–20). See also Reinier, *From Virtue to Character*, 72. For examples of earlier conversions, see Ada, "Conversation between Catherine and her Mother," *Sabbath School Messenger* 2, no. 3 (August 1838): 57–59; "The Conversion of My Little Daughter," *Mother's Assistant & Young Lady's Friend*, April 1844, 74–81; "Hint to Parents," *Baptist Memorial & Monthly Record* 8 (January 1849): 277.

41. Boylan, *Sunday School*, 143–46. See also Reiner, *From Virtue to Character*, 72–73; Mary P. Ryan, *Cradle of the Middle Class: The Family in Oneida County, New York, 1790–1865* (New York: Cambridge University Press, 1981), 91.

42. Boylan, *Sunday School*, 138–46.

43. Charles Finney, "The Conversion of Children: A Lecture Delivered on Monday, Dec. 16, 1850 by the Rev. C. G. Finney at the Tabernacle, Moorfields," in *The Penny Pulpit*, https://www.gospeltruth.net/1849-51Penny_Pulpit/501216pp_conversion_of_chi.htm. On this, see also Claudia Stokes, *The Altar at Home: Sentimental Literature and Nineteenth-Century American Religion* (Philadelphia: University of Pennsylvania Press, 2014), 21–66.

44. Robert Bruce Mullin, *The Puritan as Yankee: A Life of Horace Bushnell* (Grand Rapids: Eerdmans, 2002), 25–26.

45. Bushnell's original 1847 work, *Discourses on Christian Nurture*, was published by the conservative Massachusetts Sabbath School Society. While initial response was largely favorable, emerging theological opposition led the society to suspend publication, forcing Bushnell to republish the book on his own, defending his perspectives and

adding a series of older talks on revivalism and organic Christian growth. See Mullin, *Puritan as Yankee*, 117–20.

46. Horace Bushnell, *Views of Christian Nurture and of Subjects Adjacent Thereto* (Hartford: Edwin Hunt, 1847), 67–69; Bushnell, *Christian Nurture*, 187–92. See also Mullin, *Puritan as Yankee*, 121. Bushnell suggested that Edwards himself later in life recognized the flaws within the revival standard, addressing more and more the importance of family nurture as the "chief means of grace" (*Christian Nurture*, 188–89). See also James D. Bratt, *Antirevivalism in Antebellum America* (New Brunswick, NJ: Rutgers University Press, 2006), 137–49.

47. Horace Bushnell, *An Argument for "Discourses on Christian Nurture," Addressed to the Publishing Committee of the Massachusetts Sabbath School Society* (Hartford: Edwin Hunt, 1847), 20. These ideas came out of Bushnell's earlier work, in which he argued that Christianity should develop through growth, not conquest. See "The Kingdom of Heaven as a Grain of Mustard Seed," *New Englander* (October 1844): 600–619.

48. Bushnell, *Christian Nurture*, 13.

49. Bushnell, *Views of Christian Nurture*, 12, 17.

50. Bushnell, *Views of Christian Nurture*, 171.

51. Bushnell, *Christian Nurture*, 73; Bushnell, *Views of Christian Nurture*, 12, 17. See also Bendroth, *Growing Up Protestant*, 22; John Krahn, "Nurture vs. Revival: Horace Bushnell on Religious Education," *Religious Education* 70, no. 4 (July 1975): 375–82.

52. Bushnell, *Argument*, 73.

53. Bushnell, *Christian Nurture*, 65–89.

54. Bushnell, *Views of Christian Nurture*, 21, 145. Bushnell's language certainly echoed the language of covenant, but while the Puritans placed their confidence in the Abrahamic promises, Bushnell focused his confidence on the parent-child relationship and the godly home environment that surrounded the growing child. Interestingly, Bushnell claimed that his beliefs about Christian nurture were consistent with the Puritans and that he was attempting to reclaim their legacy of covenantal family relationships and home-based Christian nurture over against revivalist innovations. Mullin, *Puritan as Yankee*, 120–26.

55. This critique of individualism also rested behind Bushnell's affirmation of infant baptism and his rejection of believer's baptism. Because children existed within the matrix of the parents' faith, he believed children could be baptized with the assumption of their place within the church. See Bushnell, *Christian Nurture*, 53, 145. See also Mullin, *Puritan as Yankee*, 117–20.

56. Bushnell, *Christian Nurture*, 118–19. In a manner not fully explained, Bushnell even felt that this organic connection began prenatally, bringing the influence of previous ancestors into the life of the child (97–100).

57. Bushnell, *Christian Nurture*, 22. See also Asa D. Smith, "Parental Faithfulness," *Mother's Magazine & Family Monitor*, March 1851, 94.

58. James D. Bratt, "The Reorientation of American Protestantism, 1835–1845," *Church History* 67, no. 1 (March 1998): 52–82.

59. Bushnell, *Christian Nurture*, 239.

60. Slater, *Children*, 154.

61. Bushnell, *Christian Nurture*, 383.

62. Bushnell, *Christian Nurture*, 10. Bushnell affirmed a version of the doctrine of original sin, but he noted that the sin inherited from parents was not blameworthy but rather something that merely "inclines" the child to evil. See also Bushnell, *Views of Christian Nurture*, 18; Norman Pettit, "Infant Piety in New England: The Legacy of Horace Bushnell," *New England Quarterly* 75, no. 3 (September 2002): 444–65.

63. Bushnell, *Views of Christian Nurture*, 20.

64. Bushnell, *Christian Nurture*, 381.

65. Bushnell, *Christian Nurture*, 248–49; see also 236.

66. Bushnell, *Christian Nurture*, 93.

67. Bushnell, *Christian Nurture*, 238.

68. Bushnell, *Christian Nurture*, 237.

69. Bushnell, *Views of Christian Nurture*, 171.

70. Bushnell, *Christian Nurture*, 247.

71. Bushnell, *Views of Christian Nurture*, 119.

72. Bushnell, *Christian Nurture*, 205.

73. John S. C. Abbott, *The Mother at Home; or The Principles of Maternal Duty* (Boston: Crocker & Brewster, 1833), 140.

74. Reinier, *From Virtue to Character*, 76.

75. Bendroth, *Growing Up Protestant*, 26; Boylan, *Sunday School*, 147–49.

76. Steven Mintz, *A Prison of Expectations: The Family in Victorian Culture* (New York: New York University Press, 1985), 28–29; Fliegelman, *Prodigals and Pilgrims*, 12–23.

77. M. B. H., "Transmission of Parental Character," *Presbyterian Magazine* 1, no. 4 (April 1851): 177. See also John H. Power, *Discourse on Domestic Piety and Family Government* (Cincinnati: L. Swormstedt & A. Poe, 1854), 109; William Bacon, *Parental Influence, Authority, And Instruction: Their Power and Importance* (New York: Miller, Orton & Mulligan, 1856), 39; "Maternal Influence," *Mother's Magazine*, April 1841, 83–91.

78. Katherine C. Grier, *Culture and Comfort: Parlor Making and Middle-Class Identity, 1850–1930* (Washington, DC: Smithsonian Books, 1988), 6–9.

79. L. H. Sigourney, *Letters to Mothers* (Hartford: Hudson and Skinner, 1838), viii. William M. Thayer noted that "no early impression is effaced from the tablet of memory" (*Life at the Fireside* [Boston: Congregational Board of Publication, 1857], 262). On this theme, see also Thomas Gallaudet, *The Child's Book on the Soul: Two Parts in One* (New York: American Tract Society, 1836).

80. Wishy, *The Child and the Republic*, 30; Barbara Finklestein, "Casting Networks of Good Influence: The Reconstruction of Childhood in the United States, 1790–1870," in

American Childhood: A Research Guide and Historical Handbook, ed. Joseph M. Hawes and N. Ray Hiner (Westport, CT: Greenwood, 1985), 124–28; Anne M. Boylan, "Growing Up Female in Young America, 1800–1860," in Hawes and Hiner, *American Childhood*, 154–58.

81. Daniel Baker, *An Affectionate Address to Mothers* (Philadelphia: Presbyterian Board of Publication, 1850), 6.

82. J. P. Thompson, "Domestic Husbandry," *Mother's Magazine and Family Monitor*, April 1851, 132.

83. M. B. H., "Transmission of Parental Character," 178.

84. Romanticism, through its elevation of nature, its appreciation of aesthetic display, and the prominence given to sentiment, created a ripe setting for the growing significance of material culture as a key element of spiritual formation. See Colleen McDannell, *The Christian Home in Victorian America, 1840–1900* (Bloomington: Indiana University Press, 1986), 164–70.

85. Mary P. Ryan, *The Empire of the Mother: American Writing about Domesticity, 1830–1860* (New York: Harrington Park, 1985), 109. Because they allowed men working in the cities to raise families in the "country," Catherine Beecher called the railroads a "special blessing." Catherine Beecher and Harriet Beecher Stowe, *The American Woman's Home: Or, Principles of Domestic Science; Being a Guide to the Formation and Maintenance of Economical, Healthful, Beautiful and Christian Homes* (New York: J. B. Ford, 1869), 25.

86. Beecher and Stowe, *American Woman's Home*, 24. On the importance of space and fresh air, see Witold Rybczynski, *Home: A Short History of an Idea* (New York: Penguin Books, 1987), 123–43.

87. Ryan, *Empire of the Mother*, 110.

88. David Freeman Hawke, *Everyday Life in Early America* (New York: Harper & Row, 1988), 47–57; Jack Larkin, *The Reshaping of Everyday Life, 1790–1840* (New York: Harper Perennial, 1989), 118.

89. Clifford Edward Clark, *The American Family Home, 1800–1960* (Chapel Hill: University of North Carolina Press, 1986), 29–30; Rybczynski, *Home*, 15–49; Jane Nylander, *Our Own Snug Fireside: Images of the New England Home, 1760–1860* (New York: Knopf, 1993); McDannell, *Christian Home*, 25–26.

90. Grier, *Culture and Comfort*, 6–11. See also J. R. Miller, *Weekday Religion* (Philadelphia: Presbyterian Board of Publication, 1880), 265–81.

91. J. R. Miller, *Home-Making* (Philadelphia: Presbyterian Board of Publication, 1882), 110. See also Susan A. Tucker, "Homely Hints," *Mother's Assistant & Young Lady's Friend*, November 1844, 104.

92. Miller, *Weekday Religion*, 271.

93. Since the parlor was a room that served to mediate between the public sphere beyond the home and the private sphere of the home's personal space, the Bible could serve both as a statement of family piety and as a showpiece demonstrating a sense of

refinement. See Grier, *Culture and Comfort*, 91, 98; Paul C. Gutjahr, *An American Bible: A History of the Good Book in the United States, 1777–1880* (Stanford, CA: Stanford University Press, 1999), 71.

94. Colleen McDannell, *Material Christianity: Religion and Popular Culture in America* (New Haven: Yale University Press, 1995), 67–102, 90–91. See also Phillips, *Christian Home*, 82–84; Susan M. Stabile, *Memory's Daughters: The Material Culture of Remembrance in Eighteenth-Century America* (Ithaca, NY: Cornell University Press, 2004). In order to capitalize on these strong family associations, publishers began marketing specific "family Bibles" by highlighting their beauty and the supplementary pages connected to family religious life. Gutjahr, *American Bible*, 35; McDannell, *Material Christianity*, 72–98.

95. McDannell, *Christian Home*, 49.

96. Thomas Moore, "God's University; or, The Family Considered as a Government, a School, and a Church," in Van Rensselaer, *Home, the School, and the Church*, 6:17.

97. Bushnell, *Christian Nurture*, 271–93. See also B. M. Smith, *Family Religion, or the Domestic Relations as Regulated by Christian Principles* (Philadelphia: Presbyterian Board of Publication, 1859), 69–71; Nicholas Murray, *The Happy Home* (New York: Harper & Brothers, 1858), 28–38.

98. Charles Finney, "Letters to Parents, No. 3," *Advocate of Moral Reform* 6, no. 22 (November 16, 1840): 171. On this theme, see Cott, "Antebellum Childrearing," 4–20.

99. Joseph Belcher, *The Clergy of America: Anecdotes Illustrative of the Character of Ministers of Religion in the United States* (Philadelphia: J. P. Lippincott, 1849), 424.

100. David Paul Nord, *Faith in Reading: Religious Publishing and the Birth of Mass Media in America* (New York: Oxford University Press, 2004), 116–18; Cathy N. Davidson, *Revolution and the Word: The Rise of the Novel in America* (New York: Oxford University Press, 1986); Candy Gunther Brown, *The Word in the World: Evangelical Writing, Publishing, and Reading in America, 1789–1880* (Chapel Hill: University of North Carolina Press, 2005); Hall, *Practical Lectures*, 156–63; Joseph A. Collier, *The Christian Home, or Religion in the Family* (Philadelphia: Presbyterian Board of Publication, 1859), 182–85; Thayer, *Life at the Fireside*, 227–30.

101. Power, *Discourse on Domestic Piety*, 51.

102. On this theme, see, for example, Murray, *Happy Home*, 185–90; Isaac Ferris, *Home Made Happy*, 2nd ed. (New York: M. W. Dodd, 1848).

103. Beecher, *Religious Training*, 41–42.

104. Mark A. Noll, "The Defining Role of Hymns in Early Evangelicalism," in *Wonderful Words of Life: Hymns in American Protestant History and Theology*, ed. Richard J. Mouw and Mark A. Noll (Grand Rapids: Eerdmans, 2004), 4; Samuel L. Rogal, *The Children's Jubilee: A Bibliographical Survey of Hymnals for Infants, Youth, and Sunday Schools Published in Britain and America, 1655–1900* (Westport, CT: Greenwood, 1983); Esther Rothenbusch Crookshank, "We're Marching to Zion: Isaac Watts in Early America," in

Mouw and Noll, *Wonderful Words of Life*, 33. While Protestants from all denominations took part in home-based singing, the Methodists seemed particularly drawn to this practice. Presbyterian James Alexander, in fact, was concerned that the Methodists had a leg up on his own denomination because of their proclivity for family singing. See Alexander, *Thoughts on Family-Worship* (Philadelphia: Presbyterian Board of Publication, 1847), 223.

105. Candy Gunther Brown, "Singing Pilgrims: Hymn Narratives of a Pilgrim Community's Progress from This World to That Which Is to Come, 1830–1880," in *Sing Them Over Again to Me: Hymns and Hymnbooks in America*, ed. Mark A. Noll and Edith L. Blumhofer (Tuscaloosa: University of Alabama Press, 2006), 194–213; Stephen Marini, "From Classical to Modern: Hymnody and the Development of American Evangelicalism, 1737–1970," in *Singing the Lord's Song in a Strange New Land: Hymnody in the History of North American Protestantism*, ed. Edith L. Blumhofer and Mark A. Noll (Tuscaloosa: University of Alabama Press, 2004), 1–38. In contrast to the focus on death and hell that marked his contemporaries, Watts leaned in the direction of a more benevolent faith and a "pleasant piety" (Harry Escott, *Isaac Watts: Hymnographer* [London: Independent Press, 1962], 213). However, these shifts were never complete, even for Watts, and most hymnals used in Sunday schools and families continued to include selections that ran the gamut of topics from fearful reminders of hell to reflections on heavenly bliss. See Heather D. Curtis, "Children of the Heavenly King: Hymns in the Religious and Social Experience of Children, 1780–1850," in Noll and Blumhofer, *Sing Them Over Again to Me*, 214–34; Brekus, *Sarah Osborn's World*, 38–39.

106. Anna Bartlett Warner and Susan Warner, *Say and Seal* (Philadelphia: J. B. Lippincott, 1860), 115–16.

107. On this trend within the Sunday school movement, see Robert W. Lynn and Elliott Wright, *The Big Little School: 200 Years of the Sunday School* (New York: Harper & Row, 1971), 68–88.

108. David E. Stannard, *The Puritan Way of Death: A Study in Religion, Culture, and Social Change* (New York: Oxford University Press, 1977), 188–89.

109. John Abbott, *Mother at Home*, 14.

110. Moore, "God's University," 6:16.

111. Phillips, *Christian Home*, 149. See also Thayer, *Life at the Fireside*, 58; Jacob Abbott, *Fire-Side Piety, or The Duties and Enjoyments of Family Religion* (New York: Leavitt, Lord, 1834), 56.

112. Erastus Hopkins, *The Family a Religious Institution; or Heaven Its Model* (Troy, NY: Elias Gates, 1840), 200–201. See also "What is Meant by Christian Education?," *Mothers' Monthly Journal*, April 1836, 49; Hall, *Practical Lectures*, 143–51.

113. Jacob Abbott, "The Influence of Parental Example," *Mother's Magazine*, November 1847, 331.

114. Collier, *Christian Home*, 24; Rufus W. Bailey, *Domestic Duties, or The Family a Nursery for Earth and Heaven* (Philadelphia: Presbyterian Board of Publication, 1837), 84–85; Hall, *Practical Lectures*, 143.

115. Lorenzo Dow, *Vicissitudes in the Wilderness; Exemplified in the Journey of Peggy Dow*, 5th ed. (Norwich, CT: William Faulkner, 1833), 84.

116. A few continued to hold out the possibility that God, in his sovereignty, might allow for deeply pious parents to have a reprobate child. John S. C. Abbott, in his popular *The Mother at Home*, notes that a pious mother with a dissolute child may have to "bow before the sovereignty of her Maker." But even here, he notes that "such cases are rare" and that "Profligate children are generally the offspring of parents, who have neglected the moral and religious education of their family" (16). He also states of the mother, "She ought even to feel that if her child does not give early evidence of piety, much of the blame rests with her" (140).

117. Bushnell, *Christian Nurture*, 48–49.

118. Charles Finney, "Letters to Parents, No. 7," *Christian Palladium* 9, no. 21 (March 1, 1841): 321; Charles Finney, "Family Government: A Sermon Delivered on Monday Evening, Dec. 23, 1850 by the Rev. C. G. Finney at the Tabernacle, Moorfields," in *The Penny Pulpit*, https://www.gospeltruth.net/1849-51Penny_Pulpit/501223pp_family_govt.htm.

119. *To Parents*, 183. For similar perspectives, see "Hints on Early Religious Culture," *Mothers' Monthly Journal*, October 1839, 145.

120. "Parental Duties," *Christian Messenger* 1, no. 10 (January 7, 1832): 76. See also Collier, *Christian Home*, 193; Thayer, *Life at the Fireside*, 52–90.

121. On this theme, see "Where's the Defect?," *Sabbath School Instructor* 1, no. 12 (August 1831): 48; T. Atkinson, "The Expectation and Duty of Christian Parents," in Van Rensselaer, *Home, the School, and the Church*, 7:22, 27; Thayer, *Life at the Fireside*, 53; Collier, *Christian Home*, 193–94; Baker, *Affectionate Address to Mothers*, 34.

122. Bennet Tyler, *Letters to the Rev. Horace Bushnell, Containing Strictures on his book Entitled "Views of Christian Nurture, and Subjects Adjacent Thereto"* (Hartford: Brown & Parsons, 1848), 25.

123. Tyler, *Letters to the Rev. Horace Bushnell*, 25. See also P. H. Fowler, "The Salvation of Children Pledged to Faithful Parents," *Mother's Magazine & Family Monitor*, February 1851, 39–41.

124. On this theme, see Charles Hambrick-Stowe, *Charles G. Finney and the Spirit of American Evangelicalism* (Grand Rapids: Eerdmans, 1996), 274–75.

125. Nancy Schrom Dye and Daniel Blake Smith, "Mother Love and Infant Death, 1750–1920," *Journal of American History* 73, no. 2 (September 1986): 329–53.

126. Fliegelman, *Prodigals and Pilgrims*, 2.

127. Bushnell, *Christian Nurture*, 241. See also William G. McGloughlin, "Evangelical Child Rearing in the Age of Jackson: Francis Wayland's Views on When and How to Subdue the Willfulness of Children," in *Growing Up in America: Children in Historical*

Perspective, ed. N. Ray Hiner and Joseph M. Hawes (Urbana: University of Illinois Press, 1985), 96.

128. Scottie May et al., *Children Matter: Celebrating Their Place in the Church, Family, and Community* (Grand Rapids: Eerdmans, 2005), 152–53.

129. Charles Hodge, "Discourses on Christian Nurture," *Biblical Repertory and Princeton Review* 19, no. 4 (October 1847): 533, 530.

130. Hodge, "Discourses on Christian Nurture," 536.

131. Tyler, *Letters to the Rev. Horace Bushnell*, 14.

132. Cited in Pettit, "Infant Piety in New England," 448.

133. Bendroth, "Children of Adam," 496.

The Parent as Mother

1. Alexander T. McGill, "The Present Age, the Age of Woman," in *Home, the School, and the Church; or the Presbyterian Education Repository*, ed. C. Van Rensselaer (Philadelphia: C. Sherman & Son, 1850–1860), 10:59.

2. William Thayer, "The Era for Mothers," *Mother's Assistant, Young Lady's Friend & Family Manual*, May 1851, 129.

3. Thayer, "Era for Mothers," 131.

4. Thayer, "Era for Mothers," 133.

5. Thayer, "Era for Mothers," 133.

6. Thayer, "Era for Mothers," 133–34.

7. Carl N. Degler, *At Odds: Women and the Family in America from the Revolution to the Present* (New York: Oxford University Press, 1980), 73–74. Henry Ward Beecher called the mother's room in the house "the holy of holies." *Norwood, or Village Life at Home* (New York: Charles Scribner's Sons, 1868), 12.

8. John S. C. Abbott, *The Mother at Home; or The Principles of Maternal Duty* (Boston: Crocker & Brewster, 1833), 149.

9. Nancy Cott, *The Bonds of Womanhood: "Woman's Sphere" in New England, 1780–1835* (New Haven: Yale University Press, 1977); A. Z., "The Christian Mother," *Mother's Magazine*, April 1833, 53–55; G. W. B., "The Christian Mother," *Mothers' Monthly Journal*, August 1836, 115–17.

10. Mary P. Ryan, *Cradle of the Middle Class: The Family in Oneida County, New York, 1790–1865* (New York: Cambridge University Press, 1981), 104.

11. Mary P. Ryan, *The Empire of the Mother: American Writing about Domesticity, 1830–1860* (New York: Harrington Park, 1985).

12. Loyal Young, "The Religious Influence and the Appliances of the Parental Relation," in Van Rensselaer, *Home, the School, and the Church*, 5:18.

13. Charles I. Foster, *An Errand of Mercy: The Evangelical United Front* (Chapel Hill: University of North Carolina Press, 1960). See also Whitney Cross, *The Burned-Over District: The Social and Intellectual History of Enthusiastic Religion in Western New York, 1800–1850* (New York: Harper Torchbooks, 1965).

14. In addition to maternal associations, some churches recommended "maternal concerts," in which groups of mothers would agree to pray for each other's children every day. See E. D. Kinney, "Maternal Concerts," *Mother's Magazine & Family Journal*, October 1850, 296–98.

15. Ryan, *Cradle of the Middle Class*, 142–44.

16. Unlike many evangelical associations at the time, it seems these received most support from the lower middle class. See Richard A. Meckel, "Educating a Ministry of Mothers: Evangelical Maternal Associations, 1815–1860," *Journal of the Early Republic* 2, no. 4 (Winter 1982): 416–17, 423. According to Mary Ryan, artisan wives in Utica outnumbered professional wives two to one, indicating that perhaps women in the midst of a bustling household economy needed this the most. The women grew very close, and in many groups they pledged to raise the children of any deceased mother. See Ryan, *Cradle of the Middle Class*, 89–91.

17. Cited in Meckel, "Educating a Ministry of Mothers," 412.

18. Meckel, "Educating a Ministry of Mothers," 416.

19. "The Maternal Meeting," *Mother's Magazine & Family Monitor*, January 1851, 6–8.

20. Meckel, "Educating a Ministry of Mothers," 417.

21. Josiah Holbrook, "Domestic Education," *Mother's Magazine*, August 1838, 188.

22. Samuel G. Goodrich, *Fireside Education* (New York: F. J. Huntington, 1838), frontispiece.

23. See, for example, *The Mother's Hand* (New York: Thomas Nelson, 1854), 5–8; Thomas Searle, *A Companion for the Season of Maternal Solicitude* (New York: Moore & Payne-Collins & Hannay, 1834), 33–35; Miss Grierson, *Pious Mother's Love Illustrated* (Boston: James Loring's Sabbath School Bookstore, 1829), 18–27; Catherine M. Scholten, *Childbearing in American Society: 1650–1850* (New York: New York University Press, 1985), 81; Anne Kuhn, *The Mother's Role in Childhood Education, New England Concepts, 1830–1860* (New Haven: Yale University Press, 1947), 80–82; Cott, *Bonds of Womanhood*, 130.

24. William M. Thayer, *Life at the Fireside* (Boston: Congregational Board of Publication, 1857), 265.

25. Colleen McDannell, *The Christian Home in Victorian America, 1840–1900* (Bloomington: Indiana University Press, 1986), 127–36.

26. Scholten, *Childbearing in American Society*, 50–66, 67–97; McDannell, *Christian Home*, 128.

27. Thayer, *Life at the Fireside*, 367; "The Mothers of the Bible," *Mrs. Whittelsey's Magazine for Mothers and Daughters*, January 1851, 26–28; William Bacon, *Parental*

Influence, Authority, and Instruction: Their Power and Importance (New York: Miller, Orton & Mulligan, 1856), 17–18.

28. Thayer, *Life at the Fireside*, 55; Nathan Bangs, "Influence of Female Character," *Ladies' Repository*, May 1848, 144–46.

29. "Illustrations of the Power of Maternal Influence," *Mrs. Whittelsey's Magazine for Mothers*, January 1850, 152.

30. Ann Douglas, *The Feminization of American Culture* (New York: Knopf, 1977), 50. In many locations there were intermediate steps in this transformation. As Mary Ryan points out, factories would often share responsibilities with families, taking over just the processing component. At other times, whole families went to work together in factories. All of this, however, presaged the ultimate separation of work and home characterized by a wage-earning system. Ryan, *Cradle of the Middle Class*, 43–51.

31. Horace Bushnell, "The Age of Homespun," in *Litchfield Country Centennial Celebration* (Hartford, 1851), 376.

32. Bushnell, "Age of Homespun," 383. See also Douglas, *Feminization of American Culture*, 48–56; Glenna Matthews, *Just a Housewife: The Rise and Fall of Domesticity in America* (New York: Oxford University Press, 1987), 11; Steven Mintz, *A Prison of Expectations: The Family in Victorian Culture* (New York: New York University Press, 1985), 19–20. Early in the nineteenth century, a number of rural young women did assume employment in factory communities such as Lowell, but by midcentury most of these roles were taken by working-class and immigrant women. It became far less socially acceptable for middle-class women to take such positions. Cott, *Bonds of Womanhood*, 19–62.

33. Laurel Thatcher Ulrich, *Good Wives: Image and Reality in the Lives of Women in Northern New England, 1650–1750* (New York: Vintage Books, 1991), 157.

34. Ruth Bloch, "American Feminine Ideals in Transition: The Rise of the Moral Mother, 1785–1815," *Feminist Studies* 4, no. 2 (June 1978): 115. Jennifer Popiel, "Making Mothers: The Advice Genre and the Domestic Ideal, 1760–1830," *Journal of Family History* 29 (2004): 339–50.

35. Douglas, *Feminization of American Culture*, 74.

36. Ann Braude, "Women's History *Is* American Religious History," in *Retelling U.S. Religious History*, ed. Thomas A. Tweed (Berkeley: University of California Press, 1997), 94–95.

37. Jan Lewis, "Mother's Love: The Construction of an Emotion in Nineteenth-Century America," in *Social History and Issues in Human Consciousness: Some Interdisciplinary Considerations*, ed. Andrew E. Barnes and Peter N. Stearns (New York: New York University Press, 1989); Daniel Baker, *An Affectionate Address to Mothers* (Philadelphia: Presbyterian Board of Publication, 1850), 6.

38. Samuel Phillips, *The Christian Home, as it is in the Sphere of Nature and the Church* (Springfield, MA: Gurdon Bill, 1865), 144.

39. J. R. Miller, *Home-Making* (Philadelphia: Presbyterian Board of Publication, 1882), 124.

40. P. H. Fowler, *Woman's Sphere of Usefulness* [. . .] (Utica, NY: Roberts, Book & Job, 1859), 13.

41. Thayer, *Life at the Fireside*, 370–71. John Wolffe suggests that evangelicals may have diminished the language of separate spheres because of leveling theological convictions related to conversion. The argument here is that it was more difficult within evangelicalism for women to be portrayed as pure and angelic when they were still viewed as sinners in need of saving grace. However, many evangelicals did still speak of women in exalted tones. See Wolffe, *The Expansion of Evangelicalism: The Age of Wilberforce, More, Chalmers, and Finney* (Downers Grove, IL: InterVarsity Press, 2007), 144–46.

42. The percentage of women in Congregationalist churches appeared to rise slightly in the early nineteenth century. See Richard D. Shiels, "The Feminization of American Congregationalism, 1730–1835," *American Quarterly* 33, no. 1 (1981): 46–62.

43. Barbara Welter, "The Cult of True Womanhood, 1820–1860," *American Quarterly* 18, no. 2 (Summer 1966): 151–74. See also Shiels, "Feminization," 46–62.

44. *Aunt Grace's Home; or Early Days in New Hampshire* (Boston: Massachusetts Sabbath School Society, 1855), 46.

45. Daniel Chaplin, *A Discourse Delivered before the Charitable Female Society in Groton (Massachusetts), October 19, 1814* (Andover, 1814), 9.

46. On this theme, see Bloch, "American Feminine Ideals in Transition."

47. Horace Bushnell, *Christian Nurture* (New York: Charles Scribner, 1861), 236–37.

48. Phillips, *Christian Home*, 189. See also Charles H. Hall, *The Church of the Household* (New York: Hurd & Houghton, 1878), 173.

49. *Sketches of the History, Disposition, Accomplishments, Employments, Customs and Importance of the Fair Sex* [. . .] (Boston: Joseph Bumstead, 1807), 105. See also Kathryn Kish Sklar, *Catherine Beecher: A Study in American Domesticity* (New York: Norton, 1976), 135–37; B. M. Smith, *Family Religion, or the Domestic Relations as Regulated by Christian Principles* (Philadelphia: Presbyterian Board of Publication, 1859), 78–80.

50. Cott, *Bonds of Womanhood*, 70–72; Popiel, "Making Mothers," 340; Mintz, *Prison of Expectations*, 51; Barbara Z. Thaden, *The Maternal Voice in Victorian Fiction: Rewriting the Patriarchal Family* (New York: Garland, 1997), 51–52. As Thaden indicates, "During the Victorian period, the idealized middle-class mother's function became providing for the health, happiness, and peace of all family members while appearing to have no needs of her own. . . . The ideal of service insists that the mother's personality, desires, and frustrations be entirely invisible to the occupants of her household" (51).

51. John H. Power, *Discourse on Domestic Piety and Family Government* (Cincinnati: L. Swormstedt & A. Poe, 1854), 69–72.

52. On this theme, see Bangs, "Influence of Female Character," 144–46; A. E., "The Christian Mother's Privilege," *Mother's Magazine & Family Monitor*, October 1852,

314–15; "Maternal Influence," *Mother's Magazine*, April 1841, 85. Daughters were also explicitly trained for this future sacrificial maternal role. One author spoke of the Christian daughter who "welcomes her father from his daily toil—who, unasked, has drawn up for him the easy chair, and brought the slippers, and stands patiently to brush his aching head." H. C. C., "The Christian Young Lady," *Mother's Monthly Journal*, January 1839, 1.

53. Bushnell, "Age of Homespun," 398–99. This spirit was often displayed in the didactic novels of the era as well. See, for example, *The Carpenter's Children: A New England Story* (Boston: Hilliard, Gray, 1836), 5. On this theme, see also Sklar, *Catherine Beecher*, 135–36; Rufus W. Bailey, *Domestic Duties, or The Family a Nursery for Earth and Heaven* (Philadelphia: Presbyterian Board of Publication, 1837), 56–57.

54. Catherine Beecher and Harriet Beecher Stowe, *The American Woman's Home: Or, Principles of Domestic Science; Being a Guide to the Formation and Maintenance of Economical, Healthful, Beautiful and Christian Homes* (New York: J. B. Ford, 1869), 19.

55. Lewis, "Mother's Love." See also Ann Taves, "Mothers and Children and the Legacy of Mid-Nineteenth-Century American Christianity," *Journal of Religion* 67, no. 2 (April 1987): 203–19.

56. Kuhn, *Mother's Role*, 75; Ann Braude, *Sisters and Saints: Women and American Religion* (New York: Oxford University Press, 2001), 49.

57. Hall, *Church of the Household*, 175 (Hall notes that he is quoting "Sir E. Stuckey"). See also "Death of a Christian Mother," *Home Missionary and American Pastor's Journal* 12, no. 12 (April 1840): 288.

58. Douglas, *Feminization of American Culture*; Taves, "Mothers and Children," 207–19. See also Henry Bacon, "As One Whom His Mother Comforteth," *Ladies' Repository*, March 1852, 338–43.

59. "The Effect of a Mother's Prayer," *Mother's Magazine & Family Journal*, December 1850, 371–72.

60. See, for example, H. M. D., "A Mother's Grave," *Mother's Magazine*, June 1837, 138; "A Dying Mother's Last Prayer," *Advocate of Moral Reform & Family Guardian*, August 15, 1850, 123–24.

61. "Our Family—The Changes of Home," *Mother's Magazine*, April 1846, 126.

62. "My Mother's Last Prayer," *Pupil's Monitor*, March 1834, 49–50; J. P. Thompson, "The Prisoner's Death-Bed," *Mother's Magazine & Family Monitor*, May 1851, 133–35; S. T. Martyn, "Maternal Faithfulness," *Ladies' Repository & Gatherings of the West: A Monthly Periodical Devoted to Literature and Religion*, November 1842, 337–38; J. C. P., "Early Recollections," *Ladies' Repository*, July 1847, 200; J. M'D., "Parental Duties," *Ladies' Repository*, May 1846, 132–34.

63. "Modes of Parental Training," *Religious Magazine*, June 15, 1835, 398. See also Baker, *Affectionate Address to Mothers*, 11–22; E. W. Hooker, "Maternal Fidelity," *Mother's Assistant & Young Lady's Friend*, March 1848, 58–59; Phillips, *Christian Home*, 18.

64. *Narratives of the Spoiled Child; David Baldwin and the General's Widow* (New York: American Tract Society, 1833–1846), 40. See also Thayer, *Life at the Fireside*, 262; Hall, *Church of the Household*, 173; Joseph A. Collier, *The Christian Home, or Religion in the Family* (Philadelphia: Presbyterian Board of Publication, 1859), 8.

65. Thomas A. Morris, *Miscellany: Consisting of Essays, Biographical Sketches, and Notes of Travel* (Cincinnati: L. Swormstedt and J. H. Power, 1852), 37.

66. A. H. S., "Parents' Desire for the Conversion of their Children. Number Two," *Mother's Journal & Family Visitant*, April 1846, 111; James R. Hughes, *Family Religion* (Philadelphia: Presbyterian Board of Publication, 1853), 15.

67. Betty A. DeBerg, *Ungodly Women: Gender and the First Wave of American Fundamentalism* (Macon, GA: Mercer University Press, 2000), 20.

68. Miller, *Home-Making*, 197.

69. Thayer, *Life at the Fireside*, 339.

70. Mark Noll, *America's God: From Jonathan Edwards to Abraham Lincoln* (New York: Oxford University Press, 2002), 215.

71. According to Ruth Bloch, separate spheres ideology emerged out of the combined influences of evangelical Protestantism, Scottish moral philosophy, and sentimental fiction in the nineteenth century. *Gender and Morality in Anglo-American Culture, 1650–1800* (Berkeley: University of California Press, 2003), 144–53.

72. Ryan, *Empire of the Mother*, 23.

73. Paula S. Fass, *The End of American Childhood: A History of Parenting from Life on the Frontier to the Managed Child* (Princeton: Princeton University Press, 2016), 34. The separation of spheres also provided space for the development of very intimate and significant friendships and networks among women. See Caroll Smith-Rosenberg, "The Female World of Love and Ritual: Relations between Women in Nineteenth-Century America," *Signs: Journal of Women in Culture and Society* 1, no. 1 (Autumn 1975): 1–29.

74. Sklar, *Catherine Beecher*, 135–37; Bloch, *Gender and Morality*, 136–53.

75. Gregg Camfield, *Necessary Madness: The Humor of Domesticity in Nineteenth-Century American Literature* (New York: Oxford University Press, 1997), 15.

76. Sklar, *Catherine Beecher*, 135–37.

77. Nicholas Murray, *The Happy Home* (New York: Harper & Brothers, 1858), 93–95. This critique would become a staple of early fundamentalism. See DeBerg, *Ungodly Women*, 50–58.

78. Bangs, "Influence of Female Character," 145. On this theme, see also Thayer, *Life at the Fireside*, 339–49; Mary Kelley, *Private Woman, Public Stage: Literary Domesticity in Nineteenth-Century America* (New York: Oxford University Press, 1984). Elizabeth Fox-Genovese notes that Southern women could never approach this emphasis on separation and purity because of the fact that the home remained a center of production and slave management. Southern women continued to bear more children than their

Northern counterparts, and fathers remained more integrally involved in the operation of the home. See Fox-Genovese, *Within the Plantation Household: Black and White Women of the Old South* (Chapel Hill: University of North Carolina Press, 1989), 38. On this theme, see also Scott Stephan, *Redeeming the Southern Family: Evangelical Women and Domestic Devotion in the Antebellum South* (Athens: University of Georgia Press, 2008); Jean Friedman, *The Enclosed Garden: Women and Community in the Evangelical South, 1830–1900* (Chapel Hill: University of North Carolina Press, 1985).

79. Douglas, *Feminization of American Culture*, 77; Claudia Nelson, *Invisible Men: Fatherhood in Victorian Periodicals* (Athens: University of Georgia Press, 1995), 44–46.

80. See, for example, *Hints for Mothers* (New York: John S. Taylor, 1845), vii.

81. Anne Scott MacLeod, *American Childhood: Essays on Children's Literature in the Nineteenth and Twentieth Centuries* (Athens: University of Georgia Press, 1994), 87–98; B. Edward McClellan, *Moral Education in America: Schools and the Shaping of Character from Colonial Times to the Present* (New York: Teachers College Press, 1999); Jacqueline S. Reinier, *From Virtue to Character: American Childhood, 1775–1850* (New York: Twayne, 1996), 20–45; Cott, *Bonds of Womanhood*, 96.

82. Linda Kerber, *Women of the Republic: Intellect and Ideology in Revolutionary America* (New York: Norton, 1986), 269–88. See also Sarah Robbins, "'The Future Good and Great of Our Land': Republican Mothers, Female Authors, and Domesticated Literacy in Antebellum New England," *New England Quarterly* 75, no. 4 (December 2002): 562–91; Bloch, *Gender and Morality*, 136–53; Lewis, "Mother's Love," 212–14; Carl Kaestle, *Pillars of the Republic: Common Schools and American Society, 1780–1860* (New York: Hill & Wang, 1983), 79. Many actually defended their calls for increasing female education on the basis of this critical maternal role. See Andrea L. Turpin, *A New Moral Vision: Gender, Religion, and the Changing Purposes of American Higher Education, 1837–1917* (Ithaca, NY: Cornell University Press, 2016), 37–62.

83. Christopher Lasch, *Haven in a Heartless World: The Family Besieged* (New York: Norton, 1995), 6. On "domestic engineering," see Catherine W. Beecher, *A Treatise on Domestic Economy for the Use of Young Ladies at Home and at School* (New York: Harper & Brothers, 1856).

84. McGill, "Present Age," 62.

85. Kuhn, *Mother's Role*, 154.

86. *Sermons by the Late Rev. Joseph S. Buckminster with a Memoir of His Life and Character* (Boston: Wells and Lilly, 1815), 328.

87. Cott, *Bonds of Womanhood*, 64–74; Thayer, *Life at the Fireside*, 370; Sklar, *Catherine Beecher*, 163. Some, especially earlier in the century, maintained a more patriarchal emphasis. See Theodore Dwight Jr., *The Father's Book; or Suggestions for the Government and Instruction of Young Children, on Principles Appropriate to a Christian Country*, 2nd ed. (Springfield, MA: G. and C. Merriam, 1835); Heman Humphrey, *Domestic Education* (Amherst, MA: J. S. & C. Adams, 1840).

88. Collier, *Christian Home*, 8.

89. Jacob Abbott, *Fire-Side Piety, or The Duties and Enjoyments of Family Religion* (New York: Leavitt, Lord, 1834), 145.

90. Ryan, *Empire of the Mother*, 40. See also Brigitte Berger and Peter L. Berger, *The War over the Family: Capturing the Middle Ground* (New York: Anchor, 1983), 95.

91. Rodney Clapp, *Families at the Crossroads: Beyond Traditional and Modern Options* (Downers Grove, IL: InterVarsity Press, 1993), 65. Edmund S. Morgan found this to be true of the later Puritans as well. He claimed that they left behind their ideal to be a "beacon to the world" and moved toward "tribalism," concerned mostly for their own children. See Morgan, *The Puritan Family: Religion and Domestic Relations in Seventeenth-Century New England* (New York: Harper & Row, 1966), 173.

92. Stephanie Coontz, *The Way We Never Were: American Families and the Nostalgia Trap* (New York: Basic Books, 1992), 65.

93. Marguerite Van Die, "The Rise of the Domestic Ideal in the United States and Canada," in *Turning Points in the History of American Evangelicalism*, ed. Heath W. Carter and Laura Rominger Porter (Grand Rapids: Eerdmans, 2017), 100–101.

94. Coontz, *Way We Never Were*, 101.

95. Margaret Bendroth, *Growing Up Protestant: Parents, Children, and Mainline Churches* (New Brunswick, NJ: Rutgers University Press, 2002), 42–50.

96. Cited in Bendroth, *Growing Up Protestant*, 44. See also David W. Bebbington, *The Dominance of Evangelicalism: The Age of Spurgeon and Moody* (Downers Grove, IL: IVP Academic, 2005), 256; Margaret Marsh, *Suburban Lives* (New Brunswick, NJ: Rutgers University Press, 1990), 22.

97. Stephen M. Frank, *Life with Father: Parenthood and Masculinity in the Nineteenth-Century American North* (Baltimore: Johns Hopkins University Press, 1998); Shawn Johansen, *Family Men: Middle-Class Fatherhood in Industrializing America* (New York: Routledge, 2001).

98. Ryan, *Empire of the Mother*, 20.

99. John Demos, *Past, Present, and Personal: The Family and the Life Course in American History* (New York: Oxford University Press, 1986), 50.

100. M. S. Hutton, "Thoughts for Fathers," *Mother's Magazine & Family Monitor*, January 1852, 6. See also Miller, *Home-Making*, 99.

101. John S. C. Abbott, "Paternal Neglect," *Parents' Magazine*, March 1842, 147.

102. Steven Mintz and Susan Kellogg, *Domestic Revolutions: A Social History of American Family Life* (New York: Free Press, 1988), 17–23, 44–45; Anne Lombard, *Making Manhood: Growing Up Male in Colonial New England* (Cambridge, MA: Harvard University Press, 2003), epilogue; E. Anthony Rotundo, "American Fatherhood: A Historical Perspective," *American Behavioral Scientist* 29, no. 1 (September/October 1985): 9–10.

103. J. N. Danforth, "Nurture and Admonition," *Mother's Magazine & Family Journal*, June 1850, 183–84.

104. "The Christian Mother," *Mothers' Monthly Journal*, August 1836, 115.

105. Thayer, *Life at the Fireside*, 190. See also Miller, *Home-Making*, 99–102; H. A. Boardman, *The Bible in the Family; or, Hints on Domestic Happiness*, 7th ed. (Philadelphia: Lippincott, Grambo, 1853), 185.

106. John Abbott, "Paternal Neglect," 148. Critics likely overestimated the time colonial fathers had with their children and underestimated the possibilities of continued fatherly interaction within the new economic setting. Even in colonial families, fathers' agricultural labors often kept them busy for much of the day. Children were also frequently apprenticed out to other families, limiting fatherly guidance for long stretches of time. In addition, recent scholarship seems to indicate that even those fathers working outside the home in the nineteenth century had opportunities to combine home and work responsibilities. See Johansen, *Family Men*, 31–44; Nancy F. Cott, "Notes toward an Interpretation of Antebellum Childrearing," *Psychohistory Review* 6, no. 4 (1978): 4–20.

107. Frank, *Life with Father*, 85–88.

108. Boardman, *Bible in the Family*, 191.

109. Boardman, *Bible in the Family*, 194, 192.

110. Nelson, *Invisible Men*, 59.

111. James Alexander, *Thoughts on Family-Worship* (Philadelphia: Presbyterian Board of Publication, 1847), 54.

112. Ryan, *Cradle of the Middle Class*, 232.

113. Demos, *Past, Present, and Personal*, 55.

114. Lombard, *Making Manhood*, epilogue.

115. Demos, *Past, Present, and Personal*, 41–60.

116. On this theme, see Frank, *Life with Father*, 113–38; Johansen, *Family Men*, 75–76.

117. McIlvaine, "Influence of Excessive Attention to Business on Family Religion," *Sunday School Journal* 9, no. 8 (October 17, 1838): 414.

118. Hutton, "Thoughts for Fathers," 8.

119. Frank, *Life with Father*, 3, 118. See also John Abbott, *Mother at Home*, 164.

120. A. B. Muzzey, *The Fireside: An Aid to Parents* (Boston: Crosby, Nichols, 1854), frontispiece. Frank makes the observation that most artistic renderings of parents and children in this era depict mothers alone with their offspring. Fathers are almost never portrayed alone with their children, thus implying that the father's role only made sense in supportive partnership with the mother. In addition, depictions of mothers and children were most often framed inside the house, while those including fathers often moved out of doors, implying that the home was the mother's unique sphere. See Frank, *Life with Father*, 39–43.

121. J. A. T., "The Christian Father, Exemplified by Wilberforce," *Oberlin Evangelist* 6, no. 12 (June 5, 1844): 96.

122. John R. Gillis, *A World of Their Own Making: Myth, Ritual, and the Quest for Family Values* (Cambridge, MA: Harvard University Press, 1996), 124.

123. Frank, *Life with Father*, 138.

124. Bernard Wishy, *The Child and the Republic: The Dawn of Modern American Child Nurture* (Philadelphia: University of Pennsylvania Press, 1968), 26.

125. McDannell, *Christian Home*, 108–16; Colleen McDannell, "Parlor Piety: The Home as Sacred Space in Protestant America," in *American Home Life, 1880–1930: A Social History of Spaces and Services*, ed. Jessica H. Foy and Thomas J. Schlereth (Knoxville: University of Tennessee Press, 1992), 170–72. This emulated the famous "Cotter's Saturday Night," a poem about a Scottish family participating in worship with its "priest-like father" that gained wide popularity in this era. See "The Cotter's Saturday Night," in *Home Scenes; or, Lights and Shadows of the Christian Home* (New York: American Tract Society, 1865), 136–38. On this, see also Bendroth, *Growing Up Protestant*, 51.

126. Catherine Beecher, *Religious Training of Children in the School, the Family, and the Church* (New York: Harper & Brothers, 1864), 33.

127. Sklar, *Catherine Beecher*, 83–85.

128. Barna Group, *Households of Faith: The Rituals and Relationships That Turn a Home into a Sacred Space* (Ventura, CA: Barna Group, 2019), 105–12.

129. Barna Group, *Households of Faith*, 39.

130. Lasch, *Haven in a Heartless World*, 6.

131. J. N. Danforth, "Various Aspects of Family," *Mother's Magazine & Family Journal*, April 1850, 103–4.

132. John Mather Austin, *A Voice to the Married; Being a Compendium of Social, Moral, and Religious Duties, Addressed to Husbands and Wives* (Boston: A Tompkins, 1847), 38. Cited in Ryan, *Cradle of the Middle Class*, 147.

133. Alexander, *Thoughts on Family-Worship*, 55.

134. Frank, *Life with Father*, 177.

The Parent as Memory-Maker

1. I. W. Wiley, *Religion of the Family* (Cincinnati: Hitchcock and Walden, 1872), 7.

2. Arlene Skolnick, *Embattled Paradise: The American Family in an Age of Uncertainty* (New York: Basic Books, 1991), 28

3. See, for example, Lawrence Stone, *The Family, Sex, and Marriage in England, 1500–1800* (New York: Harper & Row, 1977), 149–80; Skolnick, *Embattled Paradise*, 27–30. Interestingly, many of these ideals were nourished in the various "associations" that formed outside the home in the 1830s and 1840s. These groups—including Bible societies, tract societies, missionary societies, moral reform societies, Methodist class meetings and love feasts, and maternal associations—moved away from the patriarchal and deferential modes of "family" relationship and embraced more affectionate and egalitarian bonds of intimacy. As both A. Gregory Schneider and Mary Ryan have

indicated, such groups paved the way for the nuclear family to embrace these forms. See Schneider, *The Way of the Cross Leads Home: The Domestication of American Methodism* (Bloomington: Indiana University Press, 1993); Ryan, *Cradle of the Middle Class: The Family in Oneida County, New York, 1790–1865* (New York: Cambridge University Press, 1981).

4. Horace Bushnell, *Christian Nurture* (New York: Charles Scribner, 1861), 19–20.

5. Bushnell, *Christian Nurture*, 77.

6. Stephen M. Frank, *Life with Father: Parenthood and Masculinity in the Nineteenth-Century American North* (Baltimore: Johns Hopkins University Press, 1998), 18–19; Daniel Scott Smith, "Family Limitation, Sexual Control, and Domestic Feminism in Victorian America," *Feminist Studies* 1 (1973): 44. While this decline encompassed most nineteenth-century Americans, urban families had lower fertility rates than their rural counterparts. In addition, higher economic status (especially for those involved in business and the professions) generally correlated with a sharper decline in birthrate when compared to the families of skilled or unskilled laborers and farmers. Immigrant parents typically maintained a higher birthrate than native-born whites. See Ryan, *Cradle of the Middle Class*, 155–56; Tamara K. Hareven and Maris A. Vinovskis, eds., *Family and Population in Nineteenth-Century America* (Princeton: Princeton University Press, 1978); Joseph Kett, *Rites of Passage: Adolescence in America, 1790 to the Present* (New York: Basic Books, 1977), 115.

7. Steven Mintz, *Huck's Raft: A History of American Childhood* (Cambridge, MA: Belknap, 2004), 79; Glenna Matthews, *Just a Housewife: The Rise and Fall of Domesticity in America* (New York: Oxford University Press, 1987), 29.

8. See Gloria Main, "Rocking the Cradle: Downsizing the New England Family," *Journal of Interdisciplinary History* 37, no. 1 (Summer 2006): 35–58; D. Smith, "Family Limitation"; Carl N. Degler, *At Odds: Women and the Family in America from the Revolution to the Present* (New York: Oxford University Press, 1980), 178–79. See also Daniel Scott Smith, "'Early' Fertility Decline in America: A Problem in Family History," *Journal of Family History* 12 (1987): 73–84.

9. Donald H. Parkerson and Jo Ann Parkerson, "'Fewer Children of Greater Spiritual Quality': Religion and the Decline of Fertility in Nineteenth-Century America," *Social Science History* 12, no. 1 (Spring 1988): 49–70. See also Robert V. Wells, "Family History and Demographic Transition," in *Growing Up in America: Children in Historical Perspective*, ed. N. Ray Hiner and Joseph M. Hawes (Urbana: University of Illinois Press, 1985), 61–77; Morton Owen Schapiro, *Filling Up America: An Economic-Demographic Model of Population Growth and Distribution in the Nineteenth-Century United States* (Greenwich, CT: JAI Press, 1986).

10. Steven Mintz, *A Prison of Expectations: The Family in Victorian Culture* (New York: New York University Press, 1985), 190. See also Brigitte Berger and Peter L. Berger, *The War over the Family: Capturing the Middle Ground* (New York: Anchor, 1983), 92–104.

11. Paul Johnson, *A Shopkeeper's Millennium: Society and Revivals in Rochester, New York, 1815–1837* (New York: Hill & Wang, 1990).

12. Margaret Bendroth, *Growing Up Protestant: Parents, Children, and Mainline Churches* (New Brunswick, NJ: Rutgers University Press, 2002), 20–21. See also Christine Leigh Heyman, *Southern Cross: The Beginnings of the Bible Belt* (New York: Knopf, 1997), 125.

13. Schneider, *Way of the Cross*.

14. Mintz, *Prison of Expectations*, 13–16. Even when middle-class families maintained servants, they made increasingly clear distinctions between the nuclear family unit and the domestic "help," often relegating servants to parts of the home that were removed from the family's central living spaces. In previous eras, many servants had been closely related to the family—the mother's younger sister or cousin or a close neighbor's daughter. However, by the early to mid-nineteenth century, more of the servant class came from the unrelated ranks of the immigrant working class, making it less likely that mothers would entrust children to their long-term care.

15. Helena Wall, *Fierce Communion: Family and Community in Early America* (Cambridge, MA: Harvard University Press, 1990), 126–50.

16. Wall, *Fierce Communion*, 131.

17. Mintz, *Prison of Expectations*, 14–15.

18. Viviana A. Zelizer, *Pricing the Priceless Child: The Changing Social Value of Children* (Princeton: Princeton University Press, 1994), 3; Shawn Johansen, *Family Men: Middle-Class Fatherhood in Industrializing America* (New York: Routledge, 2001), 87.

19. Monica Kiefer, *American Children through Their Books* (Philadelphia: University of Pennsylvania Press, 1948); Candy Gunther Brown, *The Word in the World: Evangelical Writing, Publishing, and Reading in America, 1789–1880* (Chapel Hill: University of North Carolina Press, 2005), 27–33; Priscilla Ferguson Clement, *Growing Pains: Children in the Industrial Age, 1850–1890* (New York: Twayne, 1997); Karin Calvert, *Children in the House: The Material Culture of Early Childhood, 1600–1900* (Boston: Northeastern University Press, 1992), 79–147.

20. Calvert, *Children in the House*, 91.

21. Calvert, *Children in the House*, 87–94; Bendroth, *Growing Up Protestant*, 17.

22. Joseph E. Illick, "Child-Rearing in Seventeenth Century England and America," in *The History of Childhood*, ed. Lloyd deMause (New York: Harper Torchbooks, 1974), 324–25; Degler, *At Odds*, 71.

23. Daniel Scott Smith, "Child-Naming Patterns and Family Structure Change: Hingham, Massachusetts 1640–1880," *Newberry Papers in Family and Community History*, Paper 76-5 (January 1977): 29. See also Daniel Scott Smith, "Child-Naming Practices, Kinship Ties, and Change in Family Attitudes in Hingham, Massachusetts, 1641 to 1880," *Journal of Social History* 18, no. 4 (Summer 1985): 541–66. Samuel Phillips lamented that many by the mid-nineteenth century were pulling children's names from novels rather

than from the Bible. *The Christian Home, as it is in the Sphere of Nature and the Church* (Springfield, MA: Gurdon Bill, 1865), 137.

24. Johansen, *Family Men*, 69; Mintz, *Huck's Raft*, 59.

25. Thomas Moore, "God's University; or, The Family Considered as a Government, a School, and a Church," in *Home, the School, and the Church; or the Presbyterian Education Repository*, ed. C. Van Rensselaer (Philadelphia: C. Sherman & Son, 1850–1860), 6:7. See also Katherine C. Grier, *Culture and Comfort: Parlor Making and Middle-Class Identity, 1850–1930* (Washington, DC: Smithsonian Books, 1988).

26. Joseph A. Collier, *The Christian Home, or Religion in the Family* (Philadelphia: Presbyterian Board of Publication, 1859), 110–11. See also Schneider, *Way of the Cross*, 156–57; Charles Finney, "Letters to Parents, No. 4," *Oberlin Evangelist* 2, no. 21 (October 7, 1840): 163; Phillips, *Christian Home*, 199; William M. Thayer, *Life at the Fireside* (Boston: Congregational Board of Publication, 1857), 355.

27. Charles Finney, "The Conversion of Children: A Lecture Delivered on Monday, Dec. 16, 1850 by the Rev. C. G. Finney at the Tabernacle, Moorfields," in *The Penny Pulpit*, https://www.gospeltruth.net/1849-51Penny_Pulpit/501216pp_conversion_of_chi.htm. For a fictional account of this, see *The History of Thomas Frankland* (New York: American Tract Society, 1828–1833), 8.

28. J. M. Crowell, *Religion in the Household* (Philadelphia: J. P. Skelly, 1868), 11. See also J. R. Miller, *Weekday Religion* (Philadelphia: Presbyterian Board of Publication, 1880), 77–79; *Narratives of the Spoiled Child: David Baldwin and the General's Widow* (New York: American Tract Society, 1833–1846), 28–30.

29. Jacob Abbott, *Fire-Side Piety, or The Duties and Enjoyments of Family Religion* (New York: Leavitt, Lord, 1834), 212–13.

30. *The Family Instructor; or, A Manual of the Duties of Domestic Life* (New York: Harper & Brothers, 1844), 34–48; *The Two Homes Compared; or, The Advantages of Cleanliness* (Philadelphia: American Sunday-School Union, 1850), 28.

31. Bushnell, *Christian Nurture*, 345.

32. H. A. Boardman, *The Bible in the Family; or, Hints on Domestic Happiness*, 7th ed. (Philadelphia: Lippincott, Grambo, 1853), 123–27; Jacob Abbott, *Fire-Side Piety*, 131–58.

33. J. R. Miller, *Home-Making* (Philadelphia: Presbyterian Board of Publication, 1882), 229.

34. Finney, "Letters to Parents, No. 4," 163.

35. Finney, "Letters to Parents, No. 4," 163. See also S. R. Hall, *Practical Lectures on Parental Responsibility, and the Religious Education of Children* (Boston: Pierce and Parker, 1833), 52.

36. Cited in Paul B. Ringel, *Commercializing Childhood: Children's Magazines, Urban Gentility, and the Ideal of the Child Consumer in the United States, 1823–1918* (Amherst: University of Massachusetts Press, 2015), 42.

37. On sibling rivalry, see Thayer, *Life at the Fireside*, 113–29.

38. Finney, "Letters to Parents, No. 4," 163.

39. C. R. Lovell, *Methodist Family Manual: Containing the Doctrines and Moral Government of the Methodist Church* (Cincinnati: H. S. & J. Applegate, 1852), 177–78. See also "Fraternal Love," *Youth's Companion*, May 5, 1837, 202; Ansel D. Eddy, "The Relation of Brothers and Sisters," *Mother's Magazine & Family Journal*, June 1850, 169–73; Collier, *Christian Home*, 71–72.

40. Isaac Ferris, *Home Made Happy*, 2nd ed. (New York: M. W. Dodd, 1848), 5.

41. Timothy Larsen, "The Nineteenth Century," in *The Oxford Handbook of Christmas*, ed. Timothy Larsen (New York: Oxford University Press, 2020), 35–50; Gary Cross, "Just for Kids: How Holidays Became Child Centered," in *We Are What We Celebrate: Understanding Holidays and Rituals*, ed. Amitai Etzioni (New York: New York University Press, 2004), 61–73.

42. Bendroth, *Growing Up Protestant*, 50–55.

43. Bushnell, *Christian Nurture*, 388.

44. Joseph P. Tarkington, *Autobiography of Rev. Joseph Tarkington, One of the Pioneer Methodist Preachers of Indiana* (Cincinnati: Curtis and Jennings, 1899), 26; W. P. Strickland, ed., *Autobiography of Rev. James B. Finley* (Cincinnati: Methodist Book Concern, 1854), 259.

45. Charles L. Wallis, ed., *Autobiography of Peter Cartwright* (New York: Abingdon, 1956), 148.

46. Bendroth, *Growing Up Protestant*, 51; Colleen McDannell, *The Christian Home in Victorian America, 1840–1900* (Bloomington: Indiana University Press, 1986), 108–16.

47. Richard Wheatley, *The Life and Letters of Mrs. Phoebe Palmer* (New York: W. C. Palmer, Jr., 1876), 16–17.

48. See James Alexander, *Thoughts on Family-Worship* (Philadelphia: Presbyterian Board of Publication, 1847).

49. McDannell, *Christian Home*, 80–81.

50. Charles F. Deems, *The Home-Altar: An Appeal in Behalf of Family Worship; with Prayers and Hymns, and Calendar of Lessons from Scripture, for Family Use*, 4th ed. (New York: Funk and Wagnalls, 1867).

51. Bendroth, *Growing Up Protestant*, 51. For examples, see Deems, *Home-Altar*; Henry A. Miles, ed., *The Altar at Home: Prayers for the Family and the Closet. By Clergymen in and near Boston*, 2nd ed. (Boston: American Unitarian Association, 1855); S. G. Winchester, *The Importance of Family Religion; with a Selection of Prayers and Hymns Adapted to Family Worship, and Tables for the Regular Reading of the Scriptures*, 2nd ed. (Philadelphia: J. B. Lippincott, 1856).

52. James Wood, "Household Religion," in Van Rensselaer, *Home, the School, and the Church*, 8:16.

53. Jacob Abbott, *Fire-Side Piety*, 25. See also Deems, *Home-Altar*, 30.

54. Phillips, *Christian Home*, 172.

55. Boardman, *Bible in the Family*, 231–32.

56. A. B. Muzzey, *The Fireside: An Aid to Parents* (Boston: Crosby, Nichols, 1854), 232.

57. Muzzey, *Fireside*, 231–32.

58. Alexander, *Thoughts on Family-Worship*, 97. For a similar perspective, see Ferris, *Home Made Happy*, 11–12.

59. Bendroth, *Growing Up Protestant*, 52.

60. Collier, *Christian Home*, 54.

61. Francis Wayland Jr. and H. L. Wayland, *A Memoir of the Life and Labors of Francis Wayland, the Late President of Brown University* (New York: Sheldon, 1867), 1:15.

62. Heman Humphrey, *Domestic Education* (Amherst, MA: J. S. & C. Adams, 1840), 165.

63. Frances M. Caulkins, *Do Your Children Reverence the Sabbath?* (New York: American Tract Society, 1836), 1–2. See also *Clara's Childhood* (Philadelphia: American Sunday-School Union, 1843), 37–51; Caroline Cowles Richards, *Village Life in America, 1852–1872* (New York: Henry Holt, 1912), 80–81; Susan Warner, *The Wide, Wide World*, 4th ed. (New York: George P. Putnam, 1851), 18.

64. Harriet Beecher Stowe, *The May Flower, and Miscellaneous Writings* (New York: Phillips, Sampson, 1855; Boston: Ticknor and Fields, 1866), 132. Citation from the Ticknor and Fields edition.

65. See, for example, Theodore Dwight Jr., *The Father's Book; or Suggestions for the Government and Instruction of Young Children, on Principles Appropriate to a Christian Country*, 2nd ed. (Springfield, MA: G. and C. Merriam, 1835), 89.

66. Catherine Sedgwick, *Home* (Boston: James Monroe, 1841), 54–66. See also Lydia Child, *The Mother's Book* (Boston: Carter, Hendee and Babcock, 1831), 64–86.

67. There were a number of reasons for the decline of catechism instruction. The rise of the Sunday school in this era led some parents to abdicate their teaching roles, seeing these responsibilities fulfilled as they transported children to their classes. In a democratic and populist age, many also began to argue that people should read the Bible for themselves rather than depending on the filtered interpretations of educated elites. Still others, reflecting a desire for Protestant unity, rejected what they perceived as the sectarianism of most catechisms, locking children into particular theological frameworks rather than broad Christian truths. Some began to argue that catechisms were developmentally inappropriate for children, Bushnell suggesting that "very small children are more likely to be worried and drummed into apathy by dogmatic catechisms, than to get any profit from them" (*Christian Nurture*, 368). In line with the evolving educational philosophies of individuals like Johann Heinrich Pestalozzi and Friedrich Froebel, some began to argue that true education must be linked to life experience rather than "storing the mind" with doctrinal facts. On these themes, see J. I. Packer and Gary A. Parrett, *Grounded in the Gospel: Building Believers the Old-Fashioned Way* (Grand Rapids: Baker Books, 2010), 51–74; McDannell, *Christian Home*, 152; "Leading Children To God," *Mother's Assistant & Young Lady's Friend*, December 1846, 141–42;

M. O. Stevens, "The Restored Family," *Mother's Assistant & Young Lady's Friend*, May 1844, 99; T. Atkinson, "The Expectation and Duty of Christian Parents," in Van Rensselaer, *Home, the School, and the Church*, 7:27; John S. C. Abbott, *The Mother at Home; or The Principles of Maternal Duty* (Boston: Crocker & Brewster, 1833), 204. Story-based teaching was obviously dependent on the growth of the print industry for children's Bibles and literature. On this, see David Paul Nord, *Faith in Reading: Religious Publishing and the Birth of Mass Media in America* (New York: Oxford University Press, 2004), 61–88; Paul C. Gutjahr, *An American Bible: A History of the Good Book in the United States, 1777–1880* (Stanford, CA: Stanford University Press, 1999), 35; Ringel, *Commercializing Childhood*, 1; Anne Scott MacLeod, *American Childhood: Essays on Children's Literature in the Nineteenth and Twentieth Centuries* (Athens: University of Georgia Press, 1994).

68. For a critique of Sunday schools taking over parenting teaching, see Charles Hodge, "Training of the Children," *Biblical Repertory and Princeton Review* 35, no. 1 (January 1863): 93.

69. McDannell, *Christian Home*, 152.

70. Boardman, *Bible in the Family*, 230.

71. Colleen McDannell, *Heaven: A History* (New York: Vintage, 1990), 273. See also Stevens, "Restored Family," 111–12; Thayer, *Life at the Fireside*, 131, 135.

72. Frank, *Life with Father*, 69–72; Boardman, *Bible in the Family*, 228–29.

73. Alexis McCrossen, *Holy Day, Holiday: The American Sunday* (Ithaca, NY: Cornell University Press, 2001), 127–29.

74. John R. Gillis, *A World of Their Own Making: Myth, Ritual, and the Quest for Family Values* (Cambridge, MA: Harvard University Press, 1996), 87.

75. McDannell, *Heaven*; Erastus Hopkins, *The Family a Religious Institution; or Heaven Its Model* (Troy, NY: Elias Gates, 1840). See also Marguerite Van Die, "The Rise of the Domestic Ideal in the United States and Canada," in *Turning Points in the History of American Evangelicalism*, ed. Heath W. Carter and Laura Rominger Porter (Grand Rapids: Eerdmans, 2017), 98.

76. John Abbott, *Mother at Home*, 157. See also Phillips, *Christian Home*, 370–71; Wood, "Household Religion," 19–20; Jacob Abbott, *Fire-Side Piety*, 18–19; Albert Barnes, "A Family in Heaven," *Mother's Assistant & Young Lady's Friend*, April 1850, 82–83; Thayer, *Life at the Fireside*, 377; J. N. Danforth, "Various Aspects of the Family," *Mother's Magazine and Family Journal*, April 1850, 104.

77. See Collier, *Christian Home*, 171; Phillips, *Christian Home*, 26; Thayer, *Life at the Fireside*, 23.

78. McDannell, *Christian Home*, 83; McDannell, *Heaven*; Jacob Abbott, *Fire-Side Piety*, 18–19; Grier, *Culture and Comfort*, 4; Lindsley, "Re-union in Heaven," *Ladies' Garland: Devoted to Literature, Amusement, and Instruction*, September 1839, 75; Barnes, "Family in Heaven." Perhaps the quintessential fictional example of this domesticated heaven came in Elizabeth Stuart Phelps's popular novel *The Gates Ajar* (Boston:

Fields, Osgood, 1869). Studying nineteenth-century hymns, Susan VanZanten Gallagher suggests that this theme was expressed differently among the oppressed and marginalized. Gallagher suggests that the democratization of American Christianity, which highlighted hymn-writing contributions from Baptists, Methodists, and Holiness groups of more modest means, actually served to foster an image of heaven, not as an idealized home, but as a "better home in the world to come." "Domesticity in American Hymns, 1820–1870," in *Sing Them Over Again to Me: Hymns and Hymnbooks in America*, ed. Mark A. Noll and Edith L. Blumhofer (Tuscaloosa: University of Alabama Press, 2006), 235–50.

79. Miller, *Home-Making*, 284, 285, 289. See also Stevens, "Restored Family," 112.

80. Susan M. Stabile, *Memory's Daughters: The Material Culture of Remembrance in Eighteenth-Century America* (Ithaca, NY: Cornell University Press, 2004), 30–32, 55–56.

81. Thayer, *Life at the Fireside*, 179; see also 276–81.

82. Stabile, *Memory's Daughters*, 30–32; J. N. Danforth, "Nurture and Admonition," *Mother's Magazine & Family Journal*, June 1850, 182.

83. Alexander, *Thoughts on Family-Worship*, 140, 102.

84. Collier, *Christian Home*, 109.

85. Moore, "God's University," 6:25.

86. Colleen McDannell, *Material Christianity: Religion and Popular Culture in America* (New Haven: Yale University Press, 1995).

87. Boardman, *Bible in the Family*, 215–16.

88. John H. Gillis, "Gathering Together: Remembering Memory through Ritual," in Etzioni, *We Are What We Celebrate*, 90–91.

89. Humphrey, *Domestic Education*, 22–23.

90. MacLeod, *American Childhood*, 128–29; Priscilla J. Brewer, "'The Little Citizen': Images of Children in Early Nineteenth-Century America," *Journal of American Culture* 7, no. 4 (1984): 46. As Paula S. Fass has argued, in the decades immediately following the Revolution, children appear to have been given more independence and responsibility. Much of this had changed by the mid-nineteenth century, when children were more doted on by parents, sheltered from the world of work, and viewed as needing protection from the corrupting influences of the world. See Fass, *The End of American Childhood: A History of Parenting from Life on the Frontier to the Managed Child* (Princeton: Princeton University Press, 2016), 13–44.

91. Boardman, *Bible in the Family*, 62–63. See also Fass, *End of American Childhood*, 18; Bernard Wishy, *The Child and the Republic: The Dawn of Modern American Child Nurture* (Philadelphia: University of Pennsylvania Press, 1968), 12; Ferris, *Home Made Happy*, 33

92. David Riesman, Reuel Denny, and Nathan Glazer, *The Lonely Crowd* (New Haven: Yale University Press, 1950). See also Ryan, *Cradle of the Middle Class*, 160–61; John P. Carter, "Religious Instruction at Home," in Van Rensselaer, *Home, the School, and the*

Church, 2:9; B. Edward McClellan, *Moral Education in America: Schools and the Shaping of Character from Colonial Times to the Present* (New York: Teachers College Press, 1999), 26.

93. Humphrey, *Domestic Education*, 47.

94. Rodney Hessinger, *Seduced, Abandoned, and Reborn: Visions of Youth in Middle Class America, 1780–1850* (Philadelphia: University of Pennsylvania Press, 2005), 125–47. While many narratives dealt with youth leaving for the city or for further education, another archetypal prodigal was the sailor, the son who left the purified and stable confines of the country home to strike out on the (literally and morally) tempestuous seas.

95. Karen Halttunen, *Confidence Men and Painted Women: A Study of Middle-Class Culture in America, 1830–1870* (New Haven: Yale University Press, 1982). See also *The Bad Boy: A Story of Edward Winthrop* (Philadelphia: American Baptist Publication Society, 1876).

96. Beriah Bishop Hotchkin, *Manliness for Young Men and their Well-Wishers* (Philadelphia: Presbyterian Board of Publication, 1864). See also *Alfred Raymond; or, A Mother's Influence* (Philadelphia: American Sunday-School Union, 1854).

97. See, for example, Henry Ward Beecher, *Seven Lectures to Young Men, on Various Important Subjects* (Indianapolis: Thomas B. Cutler, 1844); William Alcott, *The Young Man's Guide* (Boston: T. R. Marvin, 1843; 1st ed. 1833); William Alcott, *Familiar Letters to Young Men* (Buffalo: Geo. H. Derby, 1850; 1st ed. 1849); Timothy Shay Arthur, *Advice to Young Men on Their Duties and Conduct in Life* (Philadelphia: John E. Potter, 1848); A. B. Muzzey, *The Young Man's Friend* (Boston: James Monroe, 1836).

98. Francis Wayland, *The Elements of Moral Science* (Boston: Gould, Kendall, and Lincoln, 1844), 330; William G. McGloughlin, "Evangelical Child Rearing in the Age of Jackson: Francis Wayland's Views on When and How to Subdue the Willfulness of Children," in *Growing Up in America: Children in Historical Perspective*, ed. N. Ray Hiner and Joseph M. Hawes (Urbana: University of Illinois Press, 1985).

99. John Abbott, *Mother at Home*, 43; Charles Finney, "Letters to Parents, No. 3," *Advocate of Moral Reform* 6, no. 22 (November 16, 1840): 41.

100. Finney, "Conversion of Children."

101. Wishy, *The Child and the Republic*, 42–49, 94–104.

102. Bushnell, *Christian Nurture*, 245–46.

103. Bushnell, *Christian Nurture*, 245.

104. Bushnell, *Christian Nurture*, 244–45.

105. Philip Greven, *The Protestant Temperament: Patterns of Child-Rearing, Religious Experience, and the Self in Early America* (Chicago: University of Chicago Press, 1977), 166–67.

106. Humphrey, *Domestic Education*, 46. See also Hopkins, *Family a Religious Institution*, 90; MacLeod, *American Childhood*, 99–113.

107. Hall, *Practical Lectures*; Hopkins, *Family a Religious Institution*, 89; Catherine Beecher, *Religious Training of Children in the School, the Family, and the Church* (New York: Harper & Brothers, 1864), 18; Mintz, *Prison of Expectations*, 32.

108. Beecher, *Religious Training*, 25.

109. Humphrey, *Domestic Education*, 48. See also Frank, *Life with Father*, 116; Degler, *At Odds*, 89; Hopkins, *Family a Religious Institution*, 117.

110. Mintz, *Prison of Expectations*, 32.

111. Beecher, *Religious Training*, 26.

112. "My Dear Young Friend," *Christian Baptist* (Cincinnati) 7, no. 1 (August 3, 1829): 599. See also Beecher, *Religious Training*, 18.

113. Thomas Teller, *A Parents' Offering* (New Haven: S. Babcock, 1845), 17.

114. *Mother's Jewels* (Philadelphia: American Sunday-School Union, 1827–1853), 8.

115. Mary P. Ryan, *The Empire of the Mother: American Writing about Domesticity, 1830–1860* (New York: Harrington Park, 1985), 51–52. See also Mintz, *Prison of Expectations*, 37.

116. "Little Frank—Or the Affectionate Child," *Mother's Magazine*, February 1833, 26. Cited in Ryan, *Cradle of the Middle Class*, 159.

117. Dwight, *Father's Book*, 114–15.

118. John Abbott, *Mother at Home*, 51. See also Wishy, *The Child and the Republic*, 101.

119. Sedgwick, *Home*, 17.

120. Ryan, *Empire of the Mother*, 54.

121. Frank, *Life with Father*, 119; Lyman Cobb, *The Evil Tendencies of Corporal Punishment as a Means of Moral Discipline in Families and Schools, Examined and Discussed* (New York: Mark H. Newman, 1847); Myra Glenn, "School Discipline and Punishment in Antebellum America," *Journal of the Early Republic* 1, no. 4 (Winter 1981): 395–408.

122. MacLeod, *American Childhood*, 107–8; Johansen, *Family Men*, 98; Frank, *Life with Father*, 113–38.

123. Samuel G. Goodrich, *Fireside Education* (New York: F. J. Huntington, 1838), 124.

124. Nancy F. Cott, "Notes toward an Interpretation of Antebellum Childrearing," *Psychohistory Review* 6, no. 4 (1978): 15–20.

125. Hopkins, *Family a Religious Institution*, 112.

126. Hopkins, *Family a Religious Institution*, 116.

127. Rev. Loyal Young, "The Religious Influence and the Appliances of the Parental Relation," in Van Rensselaer, *Home, the School, and the Church*, 4:16. For a similar perspective, see James R. Hughes, *Family Religion* (Philadelphia: Presbyterian Board of Publication, 1853), 6; Crowell, *Religion in the Household*, 8–12.

128. Moore, "God's University," 6:10.

129. Even Timothy Dwight, very much a Calvinist, spoke of the primacy of love, affection, and tenderness in Christian discipline, placing love over fear as a motivational tool. See Peter Gregg Slater, *Children in the New England Mind: In Death and in Life* (Hamden, CT: Archon Books, 1977), 102–14.

130. Jay Fliegelman, *Prodigals and Pilgrims: The American Revolution against Patriarchal Authority, 1750–1800* (New York: Cambridge University Press, 1982), 13.

131. Sedgwick, *Home*, 27.

132. Christian Smith and Amy Adamczyk, *Handing Down the Faith: How Parents Pass Their Religion on to the Next Generation* (New York: Oxford University Press, 2021), 5, 37–61; Vern L. Bengtson, *Families and Faith: How Religion Is Passed Down across Generations* (New York: Oxford University Press, 2013), 71–98.

133. Bengtson, *Families and Faith*, 196.

134. Bengtson, *Families and Faith*, 71–98. Bengtson surmises that this is perhaps one reason why evangelicals, Mormons, and Jews are particularly successful in generational faith transmission. In these traditions, family closeness is highly valued and emphasized within their faith communities.

135. Smith and Adamczyk, *Handing Down the Faith*, 5.

136. Barna Group, *Households of Faith: The Rituals and Relationships That Turn a Home into a Sacred Space* (Ventura, CA: Barna Group, 2019), 61–62.

137. Barna Group, *Households of Faith*, 63.

138. Gillis, *World of Their Own Making*, 43.

139. Gillis, *World of Their Own Making*, 43–44. For Cheal's work, see David Cheal, "The Ritualization of Family Ties," *American Behavioral Scientist* 31, no. 6 (July/August 1988): 632–43.

140. On the metaphorical shift from "family of God" to "family," see Schneider, *Way of the Cross*, 122–35.

141. Bendroth, *Growing Up Protestant*, 36.

142. Rodney Clapp, *Families at the Crossroads: Beyond Traditional and Modern Options* (Downers Grove, IL: InterVarsity Press, 1993), 67–88.

143. Trevecca Okholm, "Reimagining the Role of Family in Twenty-First Century Family Faith Practices," in *Bridging Theory and Practice in Children's Spirituality: New Directions for Education, Ministry, and Discipleship*, ed. Mimi L. Larson and Robert J. Keeley (Grand Rapids: Zondervan, 2020), 102–3.

144. Catherine Stonehouse and Scottie May, *Listening to Children on the Spiritual Journey: Guidance for Those Who Teach and Nurture* (Grand Rapids: Baker Academic, 2010), 123–38.

145. James K. A. Smith, *Discipleship in the Present Tense* (Grand Rapids: Calvin College Press, 2013), 150–51.

146. James K. A. Smith, *You Are What You Love: The Spiritual Power of Habit* (Grand Rapids: Brazos, 2016), 116–17.

147. Gillis, *World of Their Own Making*, 63, 71.

148. *The Autobiography of G. K. Chesterton* (New York: Sheed & Ward, 1936), 20. See also John Wolffe, *The Expansion of Evangelicalism: The Age of Wilberforce, More, Chalmers, and Finney* (Downers Grove, IL: InterVarsity Press, 2007), 158.

149. See William G. McLoughlin, *The Meaning of Henry Ward Beecher: An Essay on the Shifting Values of Mid-Victorian America, 1840–1870* (New York: Knopf, 1970), 176.

150. McDannell, *Heaven*, 274. See also M. S. Hutton, "Thoughts for Fathers," *Mother's Magazine & Family Monitor*, January 1852, 7.

151. Bendroth notes that some evangelicals, such as Phoebe Palmer, still saw family relationships as an "impediment to full religious consecration" (*Growing Up Protestant*, 21). Even Palmer, however, noted very clearly that "a religion that would lead to coolness of affection, or want of attachment to family endearments, or domestic ties, in any of its various relations, is not of God." Wheatley, *Life and Letters of Mrs. Phoebe Palmer*, 159. Cited in Anne C. Loveland, "Domesticity and Religion in the Antebellum Period: The Career of Phoebe Palmer," *Historian* 39, no. 3 (May 1977): 460.

Conclusion

1. Christian Smith and Amy Adamczyk, *Handing Down the Faith: How Parents Pass Their Religion on to the Next Generation* (New York: Oxford University Press, 2021), 224.

2. Ann Hulbert, *Raising America: Experts, Parents, and a Century of Advice about Children* (New York: Vintage Books, 2003); Barbara Beatty, Emily D. Cahan, and Julia Grant, *When Science Encounters the Child: Education, Parenting, and Child Welfare in 20th-Century America* (New York: Teachers College Press, 2006); Elliott West, *Growing Up in Twentieth-Century America: A History and Reference Guide* (Westport, CT: Greenwood, 1996). For a version of this from a more conservative Christian educator, see Clarence Benson, *An Introduction to Child Study* (Chicago: Bible Institute Colportage Association, 1927), 77–78.

3. Christopher Lasch, *Haven in a Heartless World: The Family Besieged* (New York: Norton, 1995), 12.

4. Julia Grant, *Raising Baby by the Book: The Education of American Mothers* (New Haven: Yale University Press, 1998); Rima Apple, *Perfect Motherhood: Science and Child-rearing in America* (New Brunswick, NJ: Rutgers University Press, 2006); Rebecca Jo Plant, *Mom: The Transformation of Motherhood in Modern America* (Chicago: University of Chicago Press, 2010), 88–97.

5. Peter N. Stearns, *Anxious Parents: A History of Modern Childrearing in America* (New York: New York University Press, 2002), 40–49.

6. Hulbert, *Raising America*, 29–40.

7. See, for example, Stephen Schmidt, *A History of the Religious Education Association* (Birmingham, AL: Religious Education Press, 1983); George Albert Coe, *A Social Theory of Religious Education* (New York: Charles Scribner's Sons, 1917).

8. Lasch, *Haven in a Heartless World*, xx–xxi. Some of this move toward scientific expertise began in the latter years of the nineteenth century through the publication of

books such as L. Emmett Holt's *The Care and Feeding of Children* (1894). As Paula Fass has suggested, it was indeed Holt's "genius" to market his book as "A *Catechism* for the Use of Mothers and Children's Nurses," thus "bridging the gap between the religiously informed motherhood of the nineteenth century and the scientifically informed motherhood of the twentieth." See Paula S. Fass, *The End of American Childhood: A History of Parenting from Life on the Frontier to the Managed Child* (Princeton: Princeton University Press, 2016), 96. On Holt, see also Hulbert, *Raising America*, 41–49.

9. After World War I, parent-education programs exploded. The PTA itself grew from 60,000 members in 1915 to 1,500,000 in 1930. The Children's Foundation was established in 1921 to bring the findings of scientific knowledge to the people who were on the front lines, including parents, teachers, and Sunday school workers. The Child Study Association of America (CSAA) grew significantly as well, and by 1925 had pulled together many smaller groups into a consolidated National Council of Parent Education. See Steven Schlossman, "Before Home Start: Notes toward a History of Parent Education in America," *Harvard Educational Review* 46, no. 3 (September 1976): 436–67. From the Protestant angle, the International Council of Religious Education (ICRE) set up a 1931 Joint Committee on Family and Parent Education that sponsored, among other things, a 1934 campaign titled "Christ in the Life of the Home." The committee consisted of representatives of not only the Federal Council of Churches but also the National Council of Parent Education, the National Congress of Parents and Teachers, and the Child Study Association of America. See Harry C. Munro, "Christ in the Life of the Home," *International Journal of Religious Education* 10, no. 6 (February 1934): 8, 32. On church programs, see, for example, C. Harry Atkinson, "The Home Beautiful," *International Journal of Religious Education* 11, no. 6 (February 1935): 6–7, 34; Evelyn Tyndall, "Parental Education in New York City Churches," *International Journal of Religious Education* 7, no. 5 (February 1931): 20–21; Blanche Carrier, *Church Education for Family Life* (New York: Harper & Brothers, 1937).

10. Tyndall, "Parental Education," 20–21. See also Percy R. Hayward and Myrtle Harmon Hayward, *The Home and Christian Living* (Philadelphia: Westminster, 1931).

11. George Walter Fiske, *The Christian Family* (New York: Abingdon, 1929), 18.

12. George Walter Fiske, *The Changing Family: Social and Religious Aspects of the Modern Family* (New York: Red Label Reprints, 1928), 58–77. See also Arthur E. Holt, *The Fate of the Family in the Modern World* (Chicago: Willett, Clark, 1936), 62–70.

13. Luther Allan Weigle, *The Training of Children in the Christian Family* (Boston: Pilgrim, 1922), 14–15; David Nasaw, *Children of the City: At Work and at Play* (New York: Oxford University Press, 1985); David Nasaw, *Going Out: The Rise and Fall of Public Amusements* (New York: Basic Books, 1993).

14. Barnett Brickner, "Our Moral Muddle," *Religious Education* 27, no. 7 (September 1932): 617; William Johnston, "What Has Happened to Home?," *Collier's*, August 16, 1924,

8–9; Warren I. Susman, *Culture as History: The Transformation of American Society in the Twentieth Century* (New York: Pantheon Books, 1982).

15. On this shift, see Beth Bailey, *From Front Porch to Back Seat: Courtship in Twentieth-Century America* (Baltimore: Johns Hopkins University Press, 1989); Johnston, "What Has Happened to Home?"; "Dr. Cadman on the Moral Plight of Youth," *Forum* 96 (1928): 28–29; John Modell, *Into One's Own: From Youth to Adulthood in the United States, 1920–1975* (Berkeley: University of California Press, 1989), 85–97.

16. J. T. Larsen, "What Is Becoming of the Christian Home?," *King's Business*, June 1928, 346.

17. R. E. Magill, *Christian Homes: The Bulwark of Civilization* (Richmond, VA: Presbyterian Committee of Publication), 7.

18. Alexis McCrossen, *Holy Day, Holiday: The American Sunday* (Ithaca, NY: Cornell University Press, 2001), 93–110; Gerrit Verkuyl, *Christ in the Home* (New York: Revell, 1932), 133–38.

19. George N. Luccock, *The Home God Meant* (Philadelphia: Westminster, 1936), 123; McCrossen, *Holy Day, Holiday*, 90–92; Mary E. Moxcey, *Parents and Their Children: An Introductory Manual for Parents' Classes* (New York: Methodist Book Concern, 1922), 104, 121.

20. Margaret E. Sangster, *The Art of Home-Making* (New York: Christian Herald Bible House, 1898), 165.

21. Fiske, *Changing Family*, 111.

22. James H. Smylie, "Of Secret and Family Worship: Historical Meditations, 1875–1975," *Journal of Presbyterian History* 58, no. 2 (Summer 1980): 99.

23. Fiske, *Changing Family*, 106, 111. See also Ella Broadus Robertson, *Worship in the Home* (New York: Abingdon, 1922), 6–8.

24. Weigle, *Training of Children*, 14. For a contemporary take on this reality, see Andy Crouch, *The Tech-Wise Family: Everyday Steps for Putting Technology in Its Proper Place* (Grand Rapids: Baker Books, 2017).

25. Colleen McDannell, *Material Christianity: Religion and Popular Culture in America* (New Haven: Yale University Press, 1995), 100; Colleen McDannell, "Parlor Piety: The Home as Sacred Space in Protestant America," in *American Home Life, 1880–1930: A Social History of Spaces and Services*, ed. Jessica H. Foy and Thomas J. Schlereth (Knoxville: University of Tennessee Press, 1992), 162–89.

26. Fiske, *Changing Family*, 61.

27. P. H. Lotz, *Current Week-Day Religious Education* (New York: Abingdon, 1925).

28. Fiske, *Changing Family*, 7.

29. Henry Frederick Cope, *Religious Education in the Family* (Chicago: University of Chicago Press, 1915), 17.

30. Thomas Bender, *Community and Social Change in America* (Baltimore: Johns Hopkins University Press, 2000), 114; Sidonie Matsner Gruenberg, "The Home and Social Attitudes," *International Journal of Religious Education* 11, no. 5 (January 1935): 6, 39.

31. Fiske, *Changing Family*, 47–53.

32. Fiske, *Changing Family*, 54–55.

33. Ernest R. Groves, *Social Problems of the Family* (Philadelphia: J. B. Lippincott, 1927), 89–105.

34. Luccock, *Home God Meant*, 42. See also Groves, *Social Problems of the Family*, 100; Regina Westcott Wieman, *The Modern Family and the Church* (New York: Harper & Brothers, 1937), 16. The eugenics movement demonstrated further fears that birthrate declines were taking place disproportionately among the "best" (white, middle-class, native-born Protestant) sorts of people. See Amy Laura Hall, *Conceiving Parenthood: American Protestantism and the Spirit of Reproduction* (Grand Rapids: Eerdmans, 2008), 213–90; Clyde W. Votaw, "The Progress of Moral and Religious Education in the American Home," *Religious Education* 6, no. 1 (April 1911): 1–29; G. Stanley Hall, "Eugenics: Its Ideals and What It Is Going to Do," *Religious Education* 6, no. 2 (June 1911): 152–59; Edwin T. Dahlberg, *Youth and the Homes of Tomorrow* (Philadelphia: Judson, 1934), 92.

35. Fiske, *Changing Family*, 51.

36. Harold L. Lundquist, "The Decay of the Home," *Moody Monthly* 29, no. 12 (August 1929): 582–83.

37. Groves, *Social Problems of the Family*, 165.

38. Shailer Mathews, "The Call to American Parents," *Religious Education* 6, no. 1 (April 1911): 50.

39. See "The Religious Press on Youthful Morals," *Literary Digest*, May 21, 1921, 28–38.

40. Paula S. Fass, *The Damned and the Beautiful: American Youth in the 1920s* (New York: Oxford University Press, 1977), 25.

41. Ernest R. Groves, "Social Influences Affecting Home Life," *American Journal of Sociology* 31, no. 2 (September 1925): 235.

42. E. Anthony Rotundo, *American Manhood: Transformations in Masculinity from the Revolution to the Modern Era* (New York: Basic Books, 1993), 223–46; Michael S. Kimmel, *Manhood in America: A Cultural History*, 2nd ed. (New York: Oxford University Press, 2006), 120–24; David I. Macleod, *Building Character in the American Boy* (Madison: University of Wisconsin Press, 1983), 47–48; Clifford Putney, *Muscular Christianity: Manhood and Sports in Protestant America, 1880–1920* (Cambridge, MA: Harvard University Press, 2001). For just a few of the resources written about the "boy problem" in this era, see William Byron Forbush, *The Boy Problem: A Study in Social Pedagogy* (Boston: Pilgrim, 1900); Forbush, *The Boy Problem in the Home* (Boston: Pilgrim, 1915); George Walter Fiske, *Boy Life and Self-Government* (New York: Young Men's Christian Association Press, 1910); Eugene Foster, *The Boy and the Church*, 4th ed. (Philadelphia: Sunday School Times, 1909); Hanford M. Burr, *Studies in Adolescent*

Boyhood (Springfield, MA: Seminar, 1910); A. H. McKinney, *Guiding Boys over Fool Hill: Studies in Adolescence* (New York: Revell, 1918); Lilburn Merrill, *Winning the Boy* (New York: Revell, 1908); Henry W. Gibson, *Boyology; or, Boy Analysis* (New York: Association Press, 1916); William McCormick, *Fishers of Boys* (New York: George H. Doran, 1915). See also David P. Setran, "Developing the 'Christian Gentleman': The Medieval Impulse in Protestant Ministry to Adolescent Boys, 1890–1920," *Religion and American Culture* 20, no. 2 (Summer 2010): 165–204.

43. Ralph Larossa, *The Modernization of Fatherhood: A Social and Political History* (Chicago: University of Chicago Press, 1996), 139–43. Despite fathers' status as companions and "chums," studies between 1900 and 1930 indicated that children preferred their mothers "by a large margin." See Robert L. Griswold, *Fatherhood in America: A History* (New York: Basic Books, 1993), 132–34.

44. McDannell, "Parlor Piety"; J. H. Montgomery, *Christian Parenthood in a Changing World* (New York: Methodist Book Concern, 1933), 7; Fass, *The Damned and the Beautiful*.

45. McDannell, "Parlor Piety," 163.

46. See Frank Hayes, "The Family Altar League," *New York Observer*, September 8, 1910, 302. For an example of the continued importance of such father-led devotions among fundamentalists, see R. K. Johnson, *Builder of Bridges: The Biography of Dr. Bob Jones, Sr.* (Murfreesboro, TN: Sword of the Lord, 1982), 10–11.

47. Clarence Benson, "How Parents Can Help the Sunday School," *Moody Monthly* 32, no. 1 (September 1931): 6.

48. See, for example, Billy Sunday, *Mother's Sermon* (Sturgis, MI: Journal, 1909), 12, 14; "Wanted—More Mothers," *King's Business*, February 1921, 107–8; "The Education of Women," *King's Business*, April 1916, 293–94; William Parker, "True Womanhood," *Christian Worker's Magazine*, November 1915, 184.

49. Margaret Bendroth, "Fundamentalism and the Family: Gender, Culture, and the American Pro-Family Movement," *Journal of Women's History* 10 (Winter 1999): 35–54; Betty A. DeBerg, *Ungodly Women: Gender and the First Wave of American Fundamentalism* (Macon, GA: Mercer University Press, 2000).

50. George R. Stuart, "The American Home," in *Winona Echoes: Notable Addresses Delivered at the Twenty-Fifth Annual Bible Conference* (Winona Lake, IN: Winona Publishing Society, 1919), 240–41.

51. McDannell, "Parlor Piety," 180–84. See also Bendroth, "Fundamentalism and the Family," 35–54.

52. See, for example, "The Parental Frown," *King's Business*, July 1927, 414; John R. Rice, "The Bible on Correction and Discipline," *Sword of the Lord*, March 1940, 1–4.

53. Margaret Bendroth, *Growing Up Protestant: Parents, Children, and Mainline Churches* (New Brunswick, NJ: Rutgers University Press, 2002), 61–80.

54. Fred L. Brownlee, "Religious Education in the Home," *Religious Education* 14, no. 6 (February 1919): 387.

55. Brownlee, "Religious Education in the Home," 387. See also Henry Frederick Cope, *The Home as the School for Social Living* (Philadelphia: American Baptist Publication Society, 1910).

56. Cope, *Religious Education in the Family*, 90.

57. See, for example, Leland Foster Wood, *Growing Together in the Family* (New York: Abingdon, 1935), 97–100; Christopher Lasch, "Social Pathologists and the Socialization of Reproduction," in *The American Family in Social-Historical Perspective*, ed. Michael Gordon, 3rd ed. (New York: St. Martin's Press, 1983), 84–85.

58. Henry Frederick Cope, *The Parent and the Child: Case Studies in the Problems of Parenthood* (New York: George H. Doran, 1921), 30–37.

59. Fiske, *Christian Family*, 55. See also Wood, *Growing Together in the Family*, 119–29.

60. Bendroth, *Growing Up Protestant*, 76.

61. Dahlberg, *Youth and the Homes of Tomorrow*, 110–11.

62. Cope, *Religious Education in the Family*, 155–56.

63. Dahlberg, *Youth and the Homes of Tomorrow*, 110–11.

64. Bendroth, *Growing Up Protestant*, 117.

65. Bendroth, *Growing Up Protestant*, 119–34.

66. See, for example, James Dobson, *Dare to Discipline* (Waco, TX: Word, 1970); Dobson, *The Strong-Willed Child* (Wheaton, IL: Tyndale House, 1978); Bill Gothard, *Institute in Basic Youth Conflicts: Research in Principles of Life* (Chicago: Institute in Basic Youth Conflicts, 1974); John R. Rice, *God in Your Family* (Murfreesboro, TN: Sword of the Lord, 1971); Rice, *The Home: Courtship, Marriage, and Children* (Murfreesboro, TN: Sword of the Lord, 1946).

67. Bendroth, *Growing Up Protestant*, 134–43. On this rising movement for family values, see Hilde L. Stephens, *Family Matters: James Dobson and Focus on the Family's Crusade for the Christian Home* (Tuscaloosa: University of Alabama Press, 2019); Seth Dowland, *Family Values and the Rise of the Christian Right* (Philadelphia: University of Pennsylvania Press, 2015); Emily Hunter McGowin, *Quivering Families: The Quiverfull Movement and Evangelical Theology of the Family* (Minneapolis: Fortress, 2018); Sally K. Gallagher, *Evangelical Identity and Gendered Family Life* (New Brunswick, NJ: Rutgers University Press, 2003).

68. Bendroth, *Growing Up Protestant*, 143.

69. Christian Smith, Bridget Ritz, and Michael Rotolo, *Religious Parenting: Transmitting Faith and Values in Contemporary America* (Princeton: Princeton University Press, 2020), 8.

70. Smith, Ritz, and Rotolo, *Religious Parenting*, 197.

71. Smith, Ritz, and Rotolo, *Religious Parenting*, 179.

72. Smith, Ritz, and Rotolo, *Religious Parenting*, 65–67.

73. Smith, Ritz, and Rotolo, *Religious Parenting*, 263–64.

74. James K. A. Smith, *You Are What You Love: The Spiritual Power of Habit* (Grand Rapids: Brazos, 2016), 127.

75. Smith, *You Are What You Love*, 128.

76. Diana Baumrind, "Child Care Practices Anteceding Three Patterns of Preschool Behavior," *Genetic Psychology Monographs* 75, no. 1 (1967): 43–88.

77. Smith and Adamczyk, *Handing Down the Faith*, 47–50.

78. Smith and Adamczyk, *Handing Down the Faith*, 69–92.

79. Rodney Clapp, *Families at the Crossroads: Beyond Traditional and Modern Options* (Downers Grove, IL: InterVarsity Press, 1993), 67–88.

Selected Bibliography

Sources on American Protestant parenting are documented throughout the notes in each chapter. The following represent just a sampling of the key primary and secondary texts from each of the three time periods mentioned in the book for those who want to begin exploring these issues in greater depth.

Colonial New England Protestantism (Roughly 1620–1770)

KEY PRIMARY SOURCES

Barnard, John. *A Call to Parents, and Children*. Boston: T. Fleet, 1737.

Colman, Benjamin. *An Argument for and Persuasive unto the Great and Important Duty of Family Worship: With Rules and Directions for the Due Performance of it.* Boston: Gamaliel Rogers, 1728.

Lawson, Deodat. *The Duty and Property of a Religious Householder*. Boston: B. Green, 1693.

Mather, Cotton. *A Family Well-Ordered*. Boston: B. Green & J. Allen, 1699.

Mather, Increase. *The Duty of Parents to Pray for their Children*. Boston: B. Green and J. Allen, 1703.

Sewall, Joseph. *Desires that Joshua's Resolution May Be Revived, or Excitations to the Constant and Diligent Exercise of Family Religion*. Boston: B. Green, 1716.

Wadsworth, Benjamin. *The Well-Ordered Family*. Boston: B. Green, 1712.

Williams, William. *The Duty of Parents to Transmit Religion to their Children*. Boston: B. Green, 1721.

KEY SECONDARY SOURCES

Axtell, James. *The School upon a Hill: Education and Society in Colonial New England*. New York: Norton, 1976.

Brekus, Catherine A. *Sarah Osborn's World: The Rise of Evangelical Christianity in Early America*. New Haven: Yale University Press, 2013.

Cremin, Lawrence A. *American Education: The Colonial Experience, 1607–1783*. New York: Harper & Row, 1970.

Demos, John. *A Little Commonwealth: Family Life in Plymouth Colony*. New York: Oxford University Press, 1970.

Graham, Judith S. *Puritan Family Life: The Diary of Samuel Sewall*. Boston: Northeastern University Press, 2000.

Greven, Philip. *The Protestant Temperament: Patterns of Child-Rearing, Religious Experience, and the Self in Early America*. Chicago: University of Chicago Press, 1977.

Hambrick-Stowe, Charles. *The Practice of Piety: Puritan Devotional Disciplines in Seventeenth-Century New England*. Chapel Hill: University of North Carolina Press, 1982.

Mintz, Steven. *Huck's Raft: A History of American Childhood*. Cambridge, MA: Belknap, 2004.

Moran, Gerald F., and Maris A. Vinovskis. *Religion, Family, and the Life Course: Explorations in the Social History of Early America*. Ann Arbor: University of Michigan Press, 1992.

Morgan, Edmund S. *The Puritan Family: Religion and Domestic Relations in Seventeenth-Century New England*. New York: Harper & Row, 1966.

Slater, Peter Gregg. *Children in the New England Mind: In Death and in Life*. Hamden, CT: Archon Books, 1977.

Nineteenth-Century Northern Protestantism (Roughly 1830–1890)

KEY PRIMARY SOURCES

Abbott, John S. C. *The Mother at Home; or The Principles of Maternal Duty*. Boston: Crocker & Brewster, 1833.

Alexander, James. *Thoughts on Family-Worship*. Philadelphia: Presbyterian Board of Publication, 1847.

Beecher, Catherine. *Religious Training of Children in the School, the Family, and the Church*. New York: Harper & Brothers, 1864.

Bushnell, Horace. *Christian Nurture*. New York: Charles Scribner, 1861.

Hopkins, Erastus. *The Family a Religious Institution; or Heaven Its Model.* Troy, NY: Elias Gates, 1840.

Humphrey, Heman. *Domestic Education.* Amherst, MA: J. S. & C. Adams, 1840.

Muzzey, A. B. *The Fireside: An Aid to Parents.* Boston: Crosby, Nichols, 1854.

Phillips, Samuel. *The Christian Home, as it is in the Sphere of Nature and the Church.* Springfield, MA: Gurdon Bill, 1865.

Power, John H. *Discourse on Domestic Piety and Family Government in Four Parts.* Cincinnati: Swormstedt & A. Poe, 1854.

Thayer, William H. *Life at the Fireside.* Boston: Congregational Board of Publication, 1857.

KEY SECONDARY SOURCES

Bendroth, Margaret. *Growing Up Protestant: Parents, Children, and Mainline Churches.* New Brunswick, NJ: Rutgers University Press, 2002.

Calvert, Karin. *Children in the House: The Material Culture of Early Childhood, 1600–1900.* Boston: Northeastern University Press, 1992.

Frank, Stephen M. *Life with Father: Parenthood and Masculinity in the Nineteenth-Century American North.* Baltimore: Johns Hopkins University Press, 1998.

Gillis, John R. *A World of Their Own Making: Myth, Ritual, and the Quest for Family Values.* Cambridge, MA: Harvard University Press, 1996.

McDannell, Colleen. *The Christian Home in Victorian America, 1840–1900.* Bloomington: Indiana University Press, 1986.

Mintz, Steven. *A Prison of Expectations: The Family in Victorian Culture.* New York: New York University Press, 1985.

Ryan, Mary P. *The Empire of the Mother: American Writing about Domesticity, 1830–1860.* New York: Harrington Park, 1985.

Schneider, A. Gregory. *The Way of the Cross Leads Home: The Domestication of American Methodism.* Bloomington: Indiana University Press, 1993.

Van Die, Marguerite. "The Rise of the Domestic Ideal in the United States and Canada." In *Turning Points in the History of American Evangelicalism,* edited by Heath W. Carter and Laura Rominger Porter, 84–106. Grand Rapids: Eerdmans, 2017.

Wishy, Bernard. *The Child and the Republic: The Dawn of Modern American Child Nurture.* Philadelphia: University of Pennsylvania Press, 1968.

Early Twentieth-Century Northern Protestantism (Roughly 1900–1940)

KEY PRIMARY SOURCES

Carrier, Blanche. *Church Education for Family Life.* New York: Harper & Brothers, 1937.

Cope, Henry Frederick. *Religious Education in the Family.* Chicago: University of Chicago Press, 1915.

Fiske, George Walter. *The Changing Family: Social and Religious Aspects of the Modern Family*. New York: Red Label Reprints, 1928.

———. *The Christian Family*. New York: Abingdon, 1929.

Luccock, George N. *The Home God Meant*. Philadelphia: Westminster, 1936.

Montgomery, J. H. *Christian Parenthood in a Changing World*. New York: Methodist Book Concern, 1933.

Verkuyl, Gerrit. *Christ in the Home*. New York: Revell, 1932.

Votaw, Clyde W. "The Progress of Moral and Religious Education in the American Home." *Religious Education* 6, no. 1 (April 1911): 1–29.

Weigle, Luther Allan. *The Training of Children in the Christian Family*. Boston: Pilgrim, 1922.

Wieman, Regina Westcott. *The Modern Family and the Church*. New York: Harper & Brothers, 1937.

Wood, Leland Foster. *Growing Together in the Family*. New York: Abingdon, 1935.

KEY SECONDARY SOURCES

Bendroth, Margaret. *Growing Up Protestant: Parents, Children, and Mainline Churches*. New Brunswick, NJ: Rutgers University Press, 2002.

Fass, Paula S. *The End of American Childhood: A History of Parenting from Life on the Frontier to the Managed Child*. Princeton: Princeton University Press, 2016.

Hulbert, Ann. *Raising America: Experts, Parents, and a Century of Advice about Children*. New York: Vintage Books, 2003.

MacLeod, David I. *The Age of the Child: Children in America, 1890–1920*. New York: Twayne, 1998.

McDannell, Colleen. "Parlor Piety: The Home as Sacred Space in Protestant America." In *American Home Life, 1880–1930: A Social History of Spaces and Services*, edited by Jessica H. Foy and Thomas J. Schlereth, 162–89. Knoxville: University of Tennessee Press, 1992.

Stearns, Peter N. *Anxious Parents: A History of Modern Childrearing in America*. New York: New York University Press, 2002.

Index

Abbott, Jacob, 134, 156, 173, 180

Abbott, John S. C., 128, 133, 144, 160, 184, 190, 193, 277n116

Adamczyk, Amy, 2–3, 85–86, 197, 202, 227

"affective individualism," 170–71

"Age of Homespun, The" (Bushnell), 151

Alcott, Bronson, 120

Alexander, Cecil Frances, 132

Alexander, James, 160–61, 181

Ambrose, Isaac, 18, 52, 77, 97, 102, 226

American Sunday School Association, 174

American Sunday School Union, 183

American Tract Society, 120–21, 135, 174, 182, 183

Anglicans, 17, 21, 233n16, 254n41

Apostles' Creed, 66

apprenticeship arrangements, colonial, 20, 235n39

Ariès, Philippe, 75

associationism, theory of, 185–86

associations, Christian: maternal associations devoted to equipping mothers, 145–46, 279n16; nineteenth-century, 145–46, 157–58, 279n16, 287n3; voluntary, 17; women's social reform organizations, 157–58; youth organizations of the 1920s, 190, 211–12, 214

"attachment" parenting, 3

"authoritative" parenting, 227

authority. *See* discipline and parental authority, colonial; discipline and parental authority, nineteenth-century

Axtell, James, 247n77

Bailey, Rufus, 134

baptism: colonial, 33, 40–42; and the "half-way covenant," 33, 240n114; infant, 272

Barna Group, 164–65, 197

Barnard, John, 18, 43, 72–73, 80, 97, 101, 104–6

Bartlett, Phebe, 27, 74, 256n69

Baxter, Richard, 22–23, 64, 67, 84, 126

Bay Psalm Book, 45